ENCYCLOPAEDIC DICTIONARY OF COMPUTER SCIENCE

Volume 2

G-Q

Edited by

Dr. Akshaya Kumar Nayak

Dr. Avinash Chiranjeev

Er. Haojam Rocky S.

JNANADA PRAKASHAN (P&D)

in association with

THE GLOBAL OPEN UNIVERSITY

NAGALAND (INDIA)

Published by :
JNANADA PRAKASHAN (P&D)
4837/2, 24, Ansari Road, Daryaganj
New Delhi-110 002, India
Phone : +91-11-23272047
Mobile : +91-9212137080

Assisted by :
Text Book Promotion Society of India
4837/2, 24, Ansari Road, Daryaganj
New Delhi-110 002, India
Phone : +91-11-23272047
Mobile : +91-9212137080

Edition : 2016

Encyclopaedic Dictionary of Computer Science

ISBN: 978-81-7139-362-6 (Set)

Typesetting by :
Vardhman Computers
New Delhi-110 017, India

Published by Mrs. S. Chowdhary for M/s. Jnanada Prakashan (P&D) Daryaganj, Ansari Road, New Delhi-110002, India and printed at Balaji Offset, Navin Shahdara, Delhi-110032, India.

PREFACE

As we enter the 21st century, technology involving computer science proliferates in most areas of our lives. How we work, how we study, how we run errands, how we spend our leisure time, and how we communicate all entail the use of computers. The past decade has seen an explosion of new growth on the internet and the introduction of personal computers into millions of homes. Along with this growth has come the proliferation of specialised terminology—related not just to the internet, but to software, multimedia systems, information processing, and more. The Dictionary of Computer Science includes the newest terminology and makes it accessible to anyone who works with a computer at home, school, or work. This dictionary contains over 6,000 entries in the first edition—as well as a comprehensive cross-referencing system, providing clear and concise definitions for the newest terms in computing.

The wide range of topics covered include computer applications in industry, the office, science, education, and the home; the means of achieving these applications—the hardware, software, computer organisation, telecommunications, and user interaction; security, safety, and legal issues; underlying concepts and theories in computing and associated fields; and major computer manufacturers and organisations. Special emphasis is placed on terms widely used in relation to the latest advances in personal computing, computer graphics, networking, artificial intelligence, and computer security. Full coverage is also given to the Internet, World Wide Web, and multimedia programmes.

From browser and sniffer programme to millennium bug and spam, the Dictionary of Computer Science, First Edition will prove invaluable to students and teachers of computing, and everyone who uses computers in the home, lab, or business.

— **Editors**

G

Gain *n.* The increase in the amplitude of a signal, as of voltage, current, or power, that is produced by a circuit. Gain can be expressed as a factor or in decibels. See also decibel.

Gallium arsenide *n.* A semiconductor compound used in place of silicon to make devices that perform faster, require less power, and are more tolerant of temperature changes and radiation than those made with silicon. Also called: GaAs.

Game *n.* See computer game.

Game Boy *n.* Nintendo Corporation's popular battery-powered, portable handheld gaming system first introduced in 1990 and updated frequently. Games are supplied on cartridges. The latest Game Boy, Game Boy Advance, features a 32-bit ARM CPU with embedded memory and a 2.9-inch TFT reflective screen with 240x160 resolution. See also computer game, TFT.

Game card *n.* See ROM card.

Game cartridge *n.* See ROM cartridge.

Game console *n.* See console game.

Game Control Adapter *n.* In IBM personal computers and compatibles, a circuit that processes input signals at a game port. Devices such as joysticks and game paddles use potentiometers to represent their positions as varying voltage levels; the Game Control Adapter converts these levels to numbers using an analog-to-digital converter (ADC). See also analog-to-digital converter, game port, potentiometer.

GameCube *n.* Nintendo Corporation's console gaming system. It features a developer-friendly format and introduces 1T-RAM technology, which reduces delays to the main memory and the graphics LSI mixed memory. The microprocessor is a custom IBM Power PC "Gekko" featuring a secondary cache (Level One: Instruction 32 KB, Data 32 KB (8-way); Level Two: 256 KB (2-way)). Games are supplied on a GameCube game disc. See also computer game, console game.

Game pad *n.* An action-control input device used with arcade-type games played on PCs and game consoles such as Microsoft's Xbox, Nintendo's GameCube, Sega's Dreamcast, and Sony's PlayStation. A game pad, unlike a joystick, is meant to be held in a player's hands. Buttons on the game pad allow a player to control direction, speed, and other screen actions. Also called: joypad.

Game port *n.* In IBM personal computers and compatibles, an I/O port for devices such as joysticks and game paddles. The game port is often included with other I/O ports on a single expansion card. See the illustration. See also Game Control Adapter.

Gamer *n.* Refers to a person who plays games, sometimes role-playing games or trading card games; often a person who plays computer, console, arcade, or online games as a primary hobby or avocation.

Game theory *n.* A mathematical theory, ascribed to John von Neumann, that considers strategy and probability in terms of competitive games in which all players have partial control and each seeks the most advantageous moves in relation to the others.

Game tree *n.* A tree structure representing contingencies in a game and used by game developers for design purposes. Each node in a game tree represents a possible position (for example, the configuration of pieces on a chessboard) in the game, and each branching represents a possible move. See also computer game.

Gamut *n.* The complete range of colours a display or printer is capable of producing. If a colour falls outside the gamut of a device, it cannot be accurately displayed or printed from that device.

Gamut alarm *n.* A feature in graphics programmes that alerts the user if a chosen colour will fall outside the currently selected gamut. See also gamut.

Gantt chart *n.* A bar chart that shows individual parts of a project as bars against a horizontal time scale. Gantt charts are used as a project-planning tool for developing schedules. Most project-planning software can produce Gantt charts.

Gap *n.* See inter-record gap.

Garbage *n.* 1. Incorrect or corrupted data. 2. Gibberish displayed on screen, either due to faulty hardware or software or because a programme is unable to display a file's content. For example, an executable file is not meant to be displayed by a text editor and so is indecipherable on screen.

Garbage collection *n.* A process for automatic recovery of heap memory. Blocks of memory that had been allocated but are no longer in use are freed, and blocks of memory still in use may be moved to consolidate the free memory into larger blocks. Some programming languages require the programmer to handle garbage collection. Others, such as Java, perform this task for the programmer. See also heap (definition 1).

Garbage in, garbage out *n.* A computing axiom meaning that if the data put into a process is incorrect, the data output by the process will also be incorrect. Acronym: GIGO.

Gas-discharge display *n.* A type of flat-panel display, used on some portable computers, containing neon between a horizontal and a vertical set of electrodes. When one electrode in each set is charged, the neon glows (as in a neon lamp) where the two electrodes intersect, representing a pixel. Also called: gas-plasma display. See also flat-panel display, pixel.

Gas-plasma display *n.* See gas-discharge display.

Gate *n.* 1. An electronic switch that is the elementary component of a digital circuit. It produces an electrical output signal that represents a binary 1 or 0 and is related to the states of one or more input signals by an operation of Boolean logic, such as AND, OR, or NOT. Also called: logic gate. See also gate array. 2. The input terminal of a field-effect transistor (FET). Also called: gate electrode. See also drain (definition 1), FET, MOSFET, source (definition 2). 3. A data structure used by 80386 and higher microprocessors to control access to privileged functions, to change data segments, or to switch tasks.

Gate array *n.* A special type of chip that starts out as a nonspecific collection of logic gates. Late in the manufacturing process, a layer is added to connect the gates for a specific function. By changing the pattern of connections, the manufacturer can make the chip suitable for many needs. This process is very popular because it saves both design and manufacturing time. The drawback is that much of the chip goes unused. Also called: application-specific integrated circuit, logic array.

Gated *adj.* 1. Transmitted through a gate to a subsequent electronic logic element. 2. Transmitted through a gateway to a subsequent network or service. For example, a mailing list on BITNET may be gated to a newsgroup on the Internet.

Gate electrode *n.* See gate (definition 2).

Gateway *n.* A device that connects networks using different communications protocols so that information can be passed from one to the other. A gateway both transfers information and converts it to a form compatible with the protocols used by the receiving network.

Gateway page *n.* See doorway page.

Gating circuit *n.* An electronic switch whose output is either on or off, depending on the state of two or more inputs. For example, a gating circuit may be used to pass or not pass an input signal, depending on the states of one or more control signals. A gating circuit can be constructed from one or more logic gates. See also gate (definition 1).

Gatored *vb.* To have been the victim of a hijackware programme that seized control of an Internet shopping or surfing experience and caused the victim's browser to display ads and Web sites chosen by the programme. Users may be gatored when they have unknowingly installed a programme or plug-in with a hidden marketing agenda, which intrudes on the user's Web shopping to display ads or Web sites promoting competing products. The term gatored comes from the name of a plug-in that was one of the first hijackware products to be used by Web marketers. See also hijackware.

GDI *n.* Acronym for Graphical Device Interface. In Windows, a graphics display system used by applications to display or print bitmapped text (TrueType fonts), images, and other graphical elements. The GDI is responsible for drawing dialog boxes, buttons, and other elements in a consistent style on screen by calling the appropriate screen drivers and passing them the information on the item to be drawn. The GDI also works with GDI printers, which have limited ability to prepare a page for printing. Instead, the GDI handles that task by calling the appropriate printer drivers and moving the image or document directly to the printer, rather than reformatting the image or document in PostScript or another printer language. See also bitmapped font, dialog box, driver, PostScript.

Gecko *n.* A cross-platform Web browsing engine introduced by Netscape in 1998, distributed and developed as open-source software through Mozilla.org. Designed to be small, fast, and modular, the Gecko engine supports Internet standards including HTML, cascading style sheets (CSS), XML, and the Document Object Model (DOM). Gecko is the layout engine in Netscape's Communicator software.

Geek *n.* 1. Generally, a person who enjoys cerebral activities (such as wordplay or computer programming) more than the mainstream population does. Geeks in this sense increasingly claim the word with pride, but it may give offense when used by others, suggesting inadequacy in normal social relationships. 2. A computer expert or specialist. For issues of etiquette, see definition 1.

GENA *n.* Acronym for General Event Notification Architecture. An extension to HTTP defined by an Internet Engineering Task Force (IETF) Internet-Draft and used to communicate events over the Internet between HTTP resources. Universal Plug and Play (UPnP) services use GENA to send XML event messages to control points.

Gender bender *n.* See gender changer.

Gender changer *n.* A device for joining two connectors that are either both male (having pins) or both female (having sockets). See the illustration. Also called: gender bender.

General Event Notification Architecture *n.* See GENA.

General Inter-ORB Protocol *n.* See IIOP.

General Packet Radio Service *n.* See GPRS.

General Protection Fault *n.* The error condition that occurs in an 80386 or higher processor running in protected mode (such as Windows 3.1) when an application attempts to access memory outside of its authorised memory space or when an invalid instruction is issued. Acronym: GPF. See also protected mode.

General Public License *n.* The agreement under which software, such as the GNU (GNU's Not UNIX) utilities, is distributed by the Free Software Foundation. Anyone who has a copy of such a programme may redistribute it to another party and may charge for distribution and support services, but may not restrict the other party from doing the same. A user may modify the programme, but if the modified version is distributed, it must be clearly identified as such and is also covered under the General Public License. A distributor must also either provide source code or indicate where source code can be obtained. Acronym: GPL. Also called: copyleft. See also free software, Free Software Foundation, GNU.

General-purpose computer *n.* A computer that can perform any computational task for which software is available. A PC is a general-purpose computer.

General-purpose controller *n.* A controller that is designed for multiple uses. See also controller.

General-Purpose Interface Bus *n.* A bus developed for the exchange of information between computers and industrial automation equipment. The electrical definition of this bus has been incorporated into an IEEE standard. Acronym: GPIB. See also IEEE 488.

General-purpose language *n.* A programming language, such as Ada, Basic, C, or Pascal, designed for a variety of applications and uses. By contrast, SQL is a language designed to be used only with databases.

General-purpose register *n.* 1. A register within a microprocessor that is available for any use rather than being reserved, like a segment selector or stack pointer, for a specific use by the processor design or operating system. 2. Any digital circuit capable of storing binary data.

Generation *n.* 1. A concept used to distinguish stored versions of a set of files. The oldest is called the grandfather, the next oldest is the father, and the newest is the son. 2. A concept used to distinguish among a process, another process that it initiates (its child), and the process that initiated it (its parent or the child's grandparent). See also process. 3. A category that distinguishes products, such as computers or programming languages, according to the technological advances they represent. See also computer.

Generic icon *n.* An icon on a Macintosh screen that identifies a file only as a document or an application. Ordinarily the icon for an application will be specific to that application, and the icon for a document will be specific to the application that opens it. If a generic icon appears instead, the information that the Macintosh Finder uses to identify the application has been damaged. See also Finder, icon, Macintosh.

Genetic algorithm *n.* A computational method for adapting problem solutions based on genetic aspects of evolution. Implementations typically use fixed-length text strings to represent information, together with a population of individuals that undergo crossover and mutation in order to find promising results. Genetic algorithms typically have three distinct stages: 1) Encoding of the potential solutions into bit strings that support the necessary variation, 2) mating and mutation algorithms that produce a new generation of individuals that recombine features of the parents, and 3) a fitness function that judges the results based on what is most appropriate for a potential solution to the problem. See also algorithm, genetic programming.

Genetic programming *n.* A paradigm in which the principle of natural selection (whereby a biological entity whose structure is more fit for its environment than its peers produces descendants better able to survive) is applied to the creation of computer programmes. Thus, genetic programming seeks to find and develop, from the set of all possible programmes, code that is highly fit to solve problems, but not necessarily explicitly designed for a specific task. This inductive discovery method aims to mimic the natural selection process by developing computer code based on its adaptability and suitability. See also artificial intelligence.

Genie *n.* An online information service originally developed by General Electric (GE) Information Services as GEnie (General Electric network for information exchange); currently owned and provided by IDT Corporation as Genie (lowercase e). Genie provides business information, forums, home shopping, and news and can exchange e-mail with the Internet.

GEO *n.* See geostationary orbit satellite.

Geographic information system *n.* An application or suite of applications for viewing and creating maps. Generally, geographic information systems contain a viewing system (sometimes allowing users to view maps with a Web browser), an environment for creating maps, and a server for managing maps and data for real-time online viewing. Acronym: GIS.

Geometry *n.* The branch of mathematics that deals with the construction, properties, and relationships of points, lines, angles, curves, and shapes. Geometry is an essential part of computer-aided design and graphics programmes.

GeoPort *n.* A fast serial input/output port on a range of Macintosh computers, including Macintosh Centris 660AV, Quadra 660AV, Quadra 840AV, or PowerMac. Any Macintosh-compatible serial device can be connected to a GeoPort, but with GeoPort-specific hardware and software the GeoPort can transmit data at up to 2 Mbps (megabits per second) and can handle voice, fax, data, and video transmission.

GEOS *n.* An operating system developed by Geoworks Corporation, used in some handheld devices. GEOS is designed to provide broad functionality in resource-constrained environments that have limited storage or memory capability, such as enhanced phones, some Internet access devices, and PDAs and other handheld computers.

Geostationary *adj.* See geosynchronous.

Geostationary orbit satellite *n.* A communications satellite that rotates with the earth and thus appears to remain fixed, or stationary, over a particular location. This travels in orbit 22,282 miles above the equator, where its period of rotation matches the earth's rotation. The service area, or footprint, of the satellite is approximately one-third of the earth's surface, so global satellite coverage can be achieved with three satellites in orbit. In a voice communication system, a round-trip to and from this satellite takes approximately 250 milliseconds. Satellite-based data communications are necessary for delivering high bandwidth options to rural areas. Acronym: GEO.

Geosynchronous *adj.* Completing one revolution in the same time that the earth completes one rotation, as a communications satellite. Also called: geostationary.

Germanium *n.* A semiconductor element (atomic number 32) that is used in some transistors, diodes, and solar cells but has been replaced by silicon in most applications. Germanium has a lower bias voltage than silicon but is more sensitive to heat (as in soldering).

Get *n.* An FTP command that instructs the server to transfer a specified file to the client. See also FTP client, FTP commands, FTP server.

GFLOP *n.* See gigaflops.

GGA *n.* Acronym for Good Game All. GGA is often used in online and chat games at the conclusion of play. See also role-playing game.

Ghost 1 *n.* 1. A dim, secondary image that is displaced slightly from the primary image on a video display (due to signal reflection in transmission) or on a printout (due to unstable printing elements). 2. An abandoned or no-longer-maintained Web site that remains accessible to visitors.

Ghost 2 *vb.* 1. To produce a duplicate, such as duplicating an application in memory. See also screen saver. 2. To display an option on a menu or on a submenu in faint type to show that it cannot be selected at the present time.

Ghosting *n.* See burn in (definition 2).

Giant magnetoresistive head *n.* A type of hard-disk head developed by IBM and based on a physical property known as the giant magnetoresistive effect. Discovered by European scientists in the late 1980s, the giant magnetoresistive effect, or GMR, produces large resistance changes in magnetic fields when various metallic materials are "sandwiched" together in thin, alternating layers. When incorporated into disk heads, GMR technology allows for very dense data storage—currently, as much as 11.6 billion bits per square inch, or the equivalent of more than 700,000 typewritten pages. Acronym: GMR. See also head.

.gif *n.* The file extension that identifies GIF bit map images. See also GIF.

GIF *n.* 1. Acronym for Graphics Interchange Format. A graphics file format developed by CompuServe and used for transmitting raster images on the Internet. An image may contain up to 256 colours, including a transparent colour. The size of the file depends on the number of colours actually used. The LZW compression method is used to reduce the file size still further. See also LZW compression, raster graphics. 2. A graphic stored as a file in the GIF format.

GIF animation *n.* A file containing a series of graphics that are displayed in rapid sequence in a Web browser to appear as though they are a moving picture.

Giga- prefix 1. One billion (1000 million, 109). 2. In data storage, 1024 ¥ 1,048,576 (230) or 1000 ¥ 1,048,576. See also gigabyte, gigaflops, gigahertz, kilo-, mega-.

Gigabit Ethernet *n.* The IEEE standard dubbed 802.3z, which includes support for transmission rates of 1 Gbps (gigabit per second)—1000 Mbps (megabits per second)—over an Ethernet network. The usual Ethernet standard (802.3) supports only up to 100 Mbps.

Gigabit over copper *n.* See Cat 5 cable.

Gigabits per second *n.* A measurement of data transfer speed, as on a network, in multiples of 1,073,741,824 (230) bits. Acronym: Gbps.

Gigabyte *n.* 1. 1024 megabytes (1024 x 1,048,576 [230] bytes). 2. One thousand megabytes (1000 x 1,048,576 bytes). Acronym: GB.

Gigaflops *n.* A measure of computing performance: one billion (1000 million) floating-point operations per second. Acronym: GFLOP. See also floating-point operation.

Gigahertz *n.* A measure of frequency: one billion (1000 million) cycles per second.Abbreviation: GHz.

GigaPoP *n.* Short for gigabit Point of Presence.. A point of access for Internet2 (and possibly other high-speed networks) that supports data transfer speeds of at least 1 Gbps. Approximately 30 gigaPoPs are located at various points across the United States.

GIGO *n.* See garbage in, garbage out.

GIMP *n.* Acronym for GNU Image Manipulation Programme. A free and expandable graphics programme for image creation and photo manipulation. GIMP is available for various UNIX-related platforms, including Linux and Mac OS X.

GIOP *n.* See IIOP. Short for General Inter-ORB Protocol.

GIS *n.* See geographic information system.

GKS *n.* See Graphical Kernel System.

Glare filter *n.* A transparent mask placed over the screen of a video monitor to reduce or eliminate light reflected from its glass surface.

Glitch *n.* 1. A problem, usually minor. 2. A brief surge in electrical power.

Global *adj.* Pertaining to an entire document, file, or programme rather than to a restricted segment of it.

Global assembly cache *n.* A machine-wide code cache, introduced with Microsoft's .NET systems, that stores assemblies specifically installed to be shared by many applications on the computer. Applications deployed in the global assembly cache must have a strong name. Acronym: GAC. See also assembly cache, strong name.

Global catalog *n.* A directory Windows database that applications and clients can query to locate any object in a forest. The global catalog is hosted on one or more domain controllers in the forest. It contains a partial replica of every domain directory partition in the forest. These partial replicas include replicas of every object in the forest, as follows: the attributes most frequently used in search operations and the attributes required to locate a full replica of the object. See also Active Directory, attribute, domain controller, forest, replication.

Globally unique identifier *n.* In the Component Object Model (COM), a 16-byte code that identifies an interface to an object across all computers and networks. Such an identifier is unique because it contains a time stamp and a code based on the network address hardwired on the host computer's LAN interface card. These identifiers are generated by a utility programme. Acronym: GUID.

Global operation *n.* An operation, such as a search and replace, that affects an entire document, programme, or other object such as a disk.

Global Positioning System *n.* See GPS.

Global search and replace *n.* A search-and-replace operation that finds and changes all instances of the selected string throughout a document. See also search and replace.

Global System for Mobile Communications *n.* See GSM.

Global universal identification *n.* An identification scheme in which only one name is associated with a particular object; this name is accepted across platforms and applications. Acronym: GUID. See also globally unique identifier.

Global variable *n.* A variable whose value can be accessed and modified by any statement in a programme, not merely within a single routine in which it is defined. See also global.

GMR *n.* See giant magnetoresistive head.

GNOME *n.* Acronym for GNU Network Object Model Environment. A popular open-source desktop environment for UNIX and UNIX-based operating systems such as Linux. GNOME provides a GUI desktop interface and basic applications that correspond to those found with Microsoft Windows or the Macintosh operating system. By providing a mainstream environment and familiar desktop appearance GNOME is intended to make UNIX easier for users. Development of GNOME is overseen by the GNOME Foundation, an association of computer industry companies and organisations with interests in the UNIX operating system. GNOME and KDE are leading contenders for consideration as a Linux desktop standard. See also KDE.

Gnomon *n.* In computer graphics, a representation of the three-dimensional (x-y-z) axis system.

GNU *n.* Acronym for GNU's Not UNIX. A collection of software based on the UNIX operating system maintained by the Free Software Foundation. GNU is distributed under the GNU General Public License, which requires that anyone who distributes GNU or a programme based on GNU may charge only for distribution and support and must allow the user to modify and redistribute the code on the same terms. See also Free Software Foundation, General Public License.

GNU Image Manipulation Programme *n.* See GIMP.

Gnutella *n.* A file-sharing protocol that forms the basis of a number of peer-to-peer networking products. Gnutella forms a loose decentralised network with each user able to see and access all shared files of other Gnutella users. Unlike Napster, Gnutella does not require a central server, and any file type can be exchanged. Gnutella was originally developed by researchers at America Online's Nullsoft group but the original implementation of the protocol was never publicly released. An open-source Gnutella preview appeared that resulted in a number of variations becoming available. See also Napster.

Godwin's Law *n.* As originally proposed by Internet activist Michael Godwin, the theory that as an online discussion grows longer, a comparison involving Nazis or Hitler will inevitably be made. When a participant in an online discussion resorts to invoking such a comparison, other participants might cite Godwin's Law to indicate both that the person has lost the argument and that the discussion has continued too long.

Good Times virus *n.* A purported e-mail virus alluded to in a warning that has been propagated widely across the Internet, as well as by fax and standard mail. The letter claims that reading an e-mail message with the subject "Good Times" will cause damage to the user's system. In fact, it is currently impossible to harm a system by reading an e-mail message, although it is possible to include a virus in a file that is attached to an e-mail message. Some consider the chain letter itself to be the "virus" that wastes Internet bandwidth and the reader's time. Information on such hoaxes and on real viruses can be obtained from CERT (http://www.cert.org/). See also urban legend, virus.

Gopher or gopher *n.* An Internet utility for finding textual information and presenting it to the user in the form of hierarchical menus, from which the user selects submenus or files that can be downloaded and displayed. One Gopher client may access all available Gopher servers, so the user accesses a common "Gopherspace." The name of the programme is a three-way pun: it is designed to go for desired information; it tunnels through the Internet and digs the information up; and it was developed at the University of Minnesota, whose athletic teams are named the Golden Gophers. Gopher is being subsumed by the World Wide Web.

Gopher server *n.* The software that provides menus and files to a Gopher user. See also Gopher.

Gopher site *n.* A computer on the Internet on which a Gopher server runs. See also Gopher, Gopher server.

Gopherspace *n.* The total set of information on the Internet that is accessible as menus and documents through Gopher. See also Gopher.

GOSIP *n.* Acronym for Government Open Systems Interconnection Profile. A U.S. government requirement that all of its new network purchases comply with the ISO/OSI standards. GOSIP went into effect on August 15, 1990, but was never fully implemented and was replaced by POSIT.

GOTO statement *n.* A control statement used in programmes to transfer execution to some other statement; the high-level equivalent of a branch or jump instruction. Use of GOTO statements is generally discouraged because they make it difficult not only for a programmer to trace the logic of a programme but also for a compiler to generate optimised code. See also branch instruction, jump instruction, spaghetti code.

.gov *n.* In the Internet's Domain Name System, the top-level domain that identifies addresses operated by government agencies. The domain name .gov appears as a suffix at the end of the address. In the United States, only nonmilitary federal government agencies may use the .gov domain. State governments in the United States use the top-level domain of .state.us, with .us preceded by the two-letter abbreviation for the state, or just .us; other regional governments in the United States are registered under the .us domain. See also DNS (definition 1), domain (definition 3), .state.us, .us.

Government Open Systems Interconnection Profile *n.* See GOSIP.

GPF *n.* See General Protection Fault.

GPIB *n.* See General-Purpose Interface Bus.

GPL *n.* See General Public License.

GPRS *n.* Acronym for General Packet Radio Service. A third-generation enhancement to the Global System for Mobile Communications (GSM), which supports non-voice applications such as Web browsing and other servicing requiring transfer of data packets without limits in message size. Systems using the service can be immediately connected when needed and therefore seem to the users to be always on. See also GSM, TDMA.

GPS *n.* Acronym for Global Positioning System. A radio navigation system developed by the U.S. Department of

Defense that uses a constellation of 24 earth satellites, which are monitored by ground-based control stations, to provide precise, continuous worldwide positioning and timing information. GPS offers two services: a public Standard Positioning Service that provides positioning data accurate to within 100 meters horizontally and 156 meters vertically and time accurate to within 340 nanoseconds; and a Precise Positioning Service, principally for government and military use, with positioning data accurate to within 22 meters horizontally and 27.7 meters vertically and time accurate to within 100 nanoseconds. See also GPS receiver.

GPS receiver *n.* A device that includes an antenna, a radio receiver, and a processor for use with the worldwide GPS (Global Positioning System). A GPS receiver uses position and time information from four GPS satellites to calculate precise information about its current location, its speed of travel, and the current time. A portable GPS receiver may be a stand-alone device or a plug-in unit for use with a portable computer. GPS receivers are used for scientific work, such as surveying, mapping, and studies of volcanoes, as well as for land, sea, and air navigation. On the consumer front, they are used in outdoor activities such as hiking and sailing and in cars to provide location, destination, and traffic information. See also GPS.

Grabber *n.* 1. A device for capturing graphical image data from a video camera or another full-motion video source and putting it into memory. Also called: frame grabber, video digitizer. 2. Any device for capturing data. 3. Software that takes a snapshot of the currently displayed screen image by transferring a portion of video memory to a file on disk. 4. In some graphics-based applications, a special type of mouse pointer.

Graceful exit *n.* The methodical termination of a process, even under error conditions, that allows the operating system or parent process to regain normal control, leaving the system in a state of equilibrium. This is expected behaviour. See also fail-soft system.

Grade *n.* In communications, the range of frequencies available for transmission on a single channel. For example, voice-grade telephone frequencies range from about 300 hertz (Hz) through 3400 Hz.

Grade of service *n.* The probability that a user of a shared communications network, such as a public telephone system, will receive an "all channels busy" signal. The grade of service is used as a measure of the traffic-handling ability of the network and is usually applied to a specific period, such as the peak traffic hour. A grade of service of 0.002, for example, assumes that a user has a 99.8 per cent chance that a call made during the specified period will reach its intended destination.

Gradient *n.* A smooth progression of colours and shades, usually from one colour to another colour, or from one shade to another shade of the same colour.

Graffiti *n.* A software application developed by Palm to allow handwriting recognition on personal digital assistants (PDAs). Graffiti contains preprogrammed shapes for each letter, which users of the application must match as closely as possible when writing. Text is written directly onto the PDA's display screen using a stylus. The Graffiti application then passes the translated letter to the PDA's application.

GrafPort *n.* A structure used on the Apple Macintosh to define a graphics environment with its own pen size, font, fill patterns, and so on. Each window has a grafPort, and grafPorts can be used to send graphics to off-screen windows or files.

Graftal *n.* One of a family of geometric forms, similar to fractals but easier to compute. Graftals are often used in the special-effects industry to create synthetic images of structures such as trees and plants. See also fractal.

Grammar checker *n.* A software accessory that checks text for errors in grammatical construction.

Granularity *n.* A description, from "coarse" to "fine," of a computer activity or feature (such as screen resolution, searching and sorting, or time slice allocation) in terms of the size of the units it handles (pixels, sets of data, or time slices). The larger the pieces, the coarser the granularity.

Graph *n.* 1. In programming, a data structure consisting of zero or more nodes and zero or more edges, which connect pairs of nodes. If any two nodes in a graph can be connected by a path along edges, the graph is said to be connected. A subgraph is a subset of the nodes and edges within a graph. A graph is directed (a digraph) if each edge links two nodes together only in one direction. A graph is weighted if each edge has some value associated with it. See also node (definition 3), tree. 2. See chart.

Graphical Device Interface *n.* See GDI.

Graphical interface *n.* See graphical user interface.

Graphical Kernel System *n.* A computer graphics standard, recognised by ANSI and ISO, that specifies methods of describing, manipulating, storing, and transferring graphical images. It functions at the application level rather than the hardware level and deals with logical workstations (combinations of input and output devices such as keyboard, mouse, and monitor) rather than with individual devices. Graphical Kernel System was developed in 1978 to handle two-dimensional graphics; the later modification, GKS-3D, extended the standard to three-dimensional graphics. Acronym: GKS. See also ANSI, ISO.

Graphical user interface *n.* A visual computer environment that represents programmes, files, and options with graphical images, such as icons, menus, and dialog boxes, on the screen. The user can select and activate these options by pointing and clicking with a mouse or, often, with the keyboard. A particular item (such as a scroll bar) works the same way for the user in all applications, because the graphical user interface provides standard software routines to handle these elements and report the user's actions (such as a mouse click on a particular icon or at a particular location in text, or a key press); applications call these routines with specific parameters rather than attempting to reproduce them from scratch. Acronym: GUI.

Graphic character *n.* Any character that is represented by a visible symbol, such as an ASCII character. A graphic character is not the same as a graphics character.

Graphic limits *n.* On a computer screen, the boundary of a graphical image in a graphics software programme, including all the area enclosed within the graphic. In some graphics environments the limits of a graphic consist of the smallest rectangle that can completely enclose it, called its bounding rectangle or bounding box.

Graphics accelerator *n.* A video adapter that contains a graphics coprocessor. A graphics accelerator can update the video display much more quickly than the CPU can, and it frees the CPU for other tasks. A graphics accelerator is a necessity for modern software such as graphical user interfaces and multimedia applications. See also graphics coprocessor, video adapter.

Graphics adapter *n.* A video adapter capable of displaying graphics as well as alphanumeric characters. Almost all video adapters in common use today are graphics adapters.

Graphics card *n.* See video adapter.

Graphics character *n.* A character that can be combined with others to create simple graphics, such as lines, boxes, and shaded or solid blocks. See the illustration.

Graphics controller *n.* The part of the EGA and VGA video adapters that allows the computer to access the video buffer. See also EGA, VGA.

Graphics coprocessor *n.* A specialised microprocessor, included in some video adapters, that can generate graphical images such as lines and filled areas in response to instructions from the CPU, freeing the CPU for other work.

Graphics data structure *n.* A data structure that is designed specifically for representing one or more elements of a graphical image.

Graphics engine *n.* 1. A display adapter that handles high-speed graphics-related processing, freeing the CPU for other tasks. Also called: graphics accelerator, video accelerator. 2. Software that, based on commands from an application, sends instructions for creating graphic images to the hardware that actually creates the images. Examples are Macintosh QuickDraw and Windows Graphics Device Interface (GDI).

Graphics export component *n.* A technology developed by Apple for creating, editing, publishing, and viewing multimedia content. The graphics export component provides an application programming interface that enables a QuickTime player to export still images into a variety of file formats.

Graphics import component *n.* A technology developed by Apple for creating, editing, publishing, and viewing multimedia content. The graphics import component provides an application programming interface that enables a QuickTime player to import still images from a variety of file formats.

Graphics Interchange Format *n.* See GIF.

Graphics interface *n.* See graphical user interface.

Graphics mode *n.* 1. On computers such as the IBM PC, the display mode in which lines and characters on the screen are drawn pixel by pixel. Because graphics mode creates images from individual dots on the screen, programmes have more flexibility in creating images than they do in text (or character) mode. Thus, the computer is able to display a mouse pointer as an arrowhead or other shape rather than as a blinking square or rectangle, and it can display character attributes, such as boldface and italics, as they will appear in print rather than using conventions such as highlighting, underlining, or alternate colours. 2. A particular set of colour and resolution values, often related to a particular video adapter, such as VGA colour with 16 colours and 640 x 480 pixels on the screen. See also high resolution, low resolution, resolution (definition 1).

Graphics port *n.* See grafPort.

Graphics primitive *n.* A drawing element, such as a text character, an arc, or a polygon, that is drawn and manipulated as a single unit and is combined with other primitives to create an image.

Graphics printer *n.* A printer, such as a laser, ink-jet, or dot-matrix impact printer, that can produce graphics formed pixel by pixel and not merely text characters. Nearly all printers presently used with personal computers are graphics printers; daisy-wheel printers are the exception.

Graphics processor *n.* See graphics coprocessor.

Graphics tablet *n.* A device used to input graphics position information in engineering, design, and illustration applications. A flat rectangular plastic board is equipped with a puck or a pen (also called a stylus) and sensing electronics that report the position of the puck or stylus to the computer, which translates that data into a cursor position on the screen. Also called: digitizing tablet. See also puck, stylus.

Graphics terminal *n.* A terminal capable of displaying graphics as well as text. Such terminals usually interpret graphics control commands rather than receiving streams of already-processed pixels.

Graphite *n.* An alternate appearance option in Mac OS X that features a gray interface with more subtle highlights than the colourful standard Aqua appearance. See also Aqua.

Gray code *n.* See cyclic binary code.

Gray market *n.* Resellers and other sources for hardware and software that obtain their inventory from distributors other than those authorised by the manufacturer. Gray market transactions may involve items that wholesalers purchase at discount and resell at higher prices, or they may refer to purchases made when sudden spikes in demand cannot be satisfied through normal distribution channels. On a more unsavory front, gray market transactions can also illegally involve stolen or counterfeit hardware, such as CPU chips and software packages.

Gray scale *n.* A sequence of shades ranging from black through white, used in computer graphics to add detail to images or to represent a colour image on a monochrome output device. Like the number of colours in a colour image, the number of shades of gray depends on the number of bits stored per pixel. Grays may be represented by actual gray shades, by halftone dots, or by dithering. See also dithering, halftone.

Greater than *adj.* See relational operator.

Greater than or equal to *adj.* See relational operator.

Great Plains *n.* Microsoft Corporation's suite of business solution applications for finance, accounting, and management. Microsoft acquired the Great Plains applications in December 2000, when it purchased Great Plains Software, which had originally developed the suite of business accounting and management solutions. Great Plains Business Solutions include applications for accounting and finance, customer relations management, e-commerce, human resources, manufacturing, project accounting, and supply-chain management.

Great Renaming *n.* The changeover to the current system of Usenet hierarchies throughout the Internet. Before the Great Renaming, which took place in 1985, nonlocal newsgroup names had the form net.*; for example, a group that carried source code, formerly named net.sources, was renamed comp.sources.misc. See also local newsgroups, newsgroup, traditional newsgroup hierarchy, Usenet.

Greeking *n.* 1. The use of gray bars or other graphics to represent lines of characters too small to be drawn legibly on a screen at the chosen resolution, such as when viewing the layout of a whole page or pair of facing pages. 2. The use of nonsense words to represent the text of a document in design samples. A garbled Latin text beginning "Lorem ipsum dolor sit amet" is traditionally used for this purpose. Greeking does not involve substituting the Greek alphabet for the Roman one.

Greek text *n.* See greeking.

Green Book *n.* A specifications book written by the Sony and Philips Corporations, covering the CD-I (compact disc-interactive) technology. See also CD-I.

Green PC *n.* A computer system designed to conserve energy For example, some computers shut off power to nonessential systems when no input has been detected for a certain amount of time, a condition known as sleep mode. Green PCs may also be distinguished by the use of minimal packaging materials and replaceable components, such as toner cartridges, that are recyclable.

Grep 1 *n.* Acronym for global regular expression print. A UNIX command used to search a file or files by keyword.

Grep 2 *vb.* To search text, especially with the UNIX grep utility.

Grid *n.* 1. Two sets of lines or linear elements at right angles to each other. 2. A spreadsheet is a grid of rows and columns; a graphics screen is a grid of horizontal and vertical lines of pixels. 3. In optical character recognition, a grid is used for measuring or specifying characters. See also Cartesian coordinates.

Gridlines *n.* 1. Lines across a page in a graphics programme that correspond to intervals on a ruler. 2. In many word-processing and spreadsheet programmes, thin lines that indicate the cell boundaries in a table. 3. Lines you can add to a chart that make it easier to view and evaluate data. Gridlines extend from the tick marks on an axis across the plot area. Gridlines do not print when you print a document.

Grok *vb.* To understand deeply and appreciatively. The term comes from Robert A. Heinlein's novel Stranger in a Strange Land, where it is also a Martian word for "to drink" and implies the kind of devoted interest that a Martian—native of a dry planet—would have in water. Hackers often use it (for example, in Internet discussions) in reference to computer expertise. See also cyberpunk.

Ground *n.* A conducting path from an electric circuit to earth or to a conducting body serving in place of earth, usually used as a safety device. See also grounding.

Grounding *n.* The connection of sections of an electrical circuit to a common conductor, called the ground, which serves as the reference for the other voltages in the circuit. The ground conductor on installed circuit boards is usually connected to the chassis, or metal frame, holding the electronic parts; the chassis is in turn usually connected to the third (round) prong on the power plug, which connects to a ground circuit that is, in fact, connected to the earth. This is important to avoid creating a shock hazard.

Group 1 *n.* A collection of elements that can be treated as a whole, such as a collection of records in a database report, or a collection of objects that can be moved and transformed as a single object in a drawing programme. In various multiuser operating systems, a group is a set of user accounts, sometimes called members; privileges can be specified for the group, and each member will then have those privileges. See also built-in groups.

Group 2 *vb.* In a drawing programme, to transform a number of objects into a group. See also drawing programme.

Group Policy Object *n.* A collection of Group Policy settings that are essentially the documents created by the Group Policy snap-in, a utility in Microsoft Windows 2000. These settings are stored at the domain level and affect users and computers contained in sites, domains, and organisational units. Acronym: GPO.

Groupware *n.* Software intended to enable a group of users on a network to collaborate on a particular project. Groupware may provide services for communication (such as e-mail), collaborative document development, scheduling, and tracking. Documents may include text, images, or other forms of information.

Grovel *vb.* 1. To search or do other work at great length without apparent progress. Some programmes grovel over a whole input file before they begin to produce output. A programmer may have to grovel through manuals in search of documentation on a particular command, or through code in search of a bug. 2. To post a plea for some favour to a newsgroup.

Grunge *n.* See dead code.

GSL *n.* Acronym for Grammar Specification Language. A grammar description format used by VoiceXML applications and other speech recognition systems. GSL was developed by Nuance and supports a number of XML-based speech editing and voice-browsing applications.

GSM *n.* Acronym for Global System for Mobile Communications. A digital cellular phone technology first deployed in 1992. In 2000, GSM was the predominant phone technology in Europe, and was used by 250 million subscribers worldwide. GSM phones offer a removable smart card containing subscriber account information. This card can be transferred from phone to phone quickly and easily, allowing the user to access his account from any phone in the system. Various enhancements to the GSM system allow increased Web browsing and data transfer options. See also GPRS, TDMA.

Guest *n.* A common name for a login account that can be accessed without a password. BBSs and service providers often maintain such an account so that prospective subscribers can sample the services offered.

Guest account *n.* An account used to log onto a system or domain where the user does not have access. Generally, resources and access are severely limited. On Windows NT technology, this account is built in to all domains. See also domain.

GUI *n.* See graphical user interface.

GUID *n.* See globally unique identifier, global universal identification.

GUID partition table *n.* A disk-partitioning scheme that is used by the eXtensible Firmware Interface (EFI) in Itanium-based computers. A GUID partition table offers more advantages than master boot record (MBR) partitioning because it allows up to 128 partitions per disk, provides support for volumes up to 18 exabytes in size, allows primary and backup partition tables for redundancy, and supports unique disk and partition IDs (GUIDs). Acronym: GPT. See also eXtensible Firmware Interface, Itanium, master boot record.

Gunzip *n.* A GNU utility for decompressing files compressed with gzip. See also GNU, uncompress.

Guru *n.* A technical expert who is available to help solve problems and to answer questions in an intelligible way. See also techie, wizard (definition 1).

Gutter *n.* The blank area between two or more columns of text or between two facing pages in a publication.

Gzip *n.* A GNU utility for compressing files. See also compress2, GNU.

H

H *n.* See henry.

H.320 *n.* An International Telecommunications Union (ITU) standard that enables interoperability among video-conferencing equipment from different manufacturers over circuit-switched services such as ISDN, thus making desktop video conferencing viable. H.320 establishes the common formats necessary to make audio and video inputs and outputs compatible and defines a protocol that makes it possible for a multimedia terminal to use audio/visual communications links and synchronisation. See also International Telecommunications Union, ISDN, video conferencing.

H.323 *n.* An International Telecommunications Union (ITU) interoperability protocol enabling cross-communication of multimedia products and applications over packet-based networks. Under H.323, multimedia products offered by one vendor can work with those of another, regardless of hardware compatibility. For example, a PC can share audio and video streams over either an intranet or the Internet. Applications are thus network-, platform-, and application-independent. See also International Telecommunications Union, packet switching.

H.324 *n.* An International Telecommunications Union (ITU) standard for simultaneously transmitting video, data, and voice over POTS (Plain Old Telephone Service) modem connections. See also POTS.

Hack 1 *n.* 1. A modification to the code in a programme, often made without taking the time to find an elegant solution. 2. A sloppy job. See also kludge (definition 2), patch1.

Hack 2 *vb.* 1. To apply creative ingenuity to a programming problem or project. 2. To alter the behaviour of an application or an operating system by modifying its code rather than by running the programme and selecting options.

Hacker *n.* 1. A computerphile; a person who is totally engrossed in computer technology and computer programming or who likes to examine the code of operating systems and other programmes to see how they work. 2. A person, more commonly considered a cracker, who uses computer expertise for illicit ends, such as by gaining access to computer systems without permission and tampering with programmes and data. Also called: cracker. See also hacktivist.

Hacktivist *n.* An individual who furthers political or social agendas through hacking activity. Hacktivists may break into computer systems to disrupt traffic or cause confusion, and may alter Web pages or e-mail to display content sympathetic to a specific cause. See also hacker.

HAGO *n.* Acronym for have a good one. An expression used to conclude e-mail messages or in signing off from IRC.

HailStorm *n.* See .NET My Services.

Hairline *n.* The smallest amount of visible space or the narrowest line that is displayable on a printed page. The size of a hairline depends on the materials, hardware, and software used or on the organisations involved. The United States Postal Service defines a hairline as 1/2 point (roughly 0.007 inch), whereas the Graphic Arts Technical Foundation (GATF) defines a hairline as 0.003 inch. See also point 1(definition 1), rule (definition 1).

HAL *n.* 1. See hardware abstraction layer. 2. In the 1968 book and movie "2001: A Space Odyssey" by novelist Arthur C. Clarke, the intelligent but eventually psychotic computer, HAL 9000, that takes over a spaceship bound for Jupiter. The name HAL is an acronym for Heuristic/ALgorithmic computer, but the letters H-A-L are also one letter removed from I-B-M in the alphabet.

Half adder *n.* A logic circuit that can add two input data bits and produce a sum bit and a carry bit as output. A half adder cannot accept a carry bit from a previous addition; to add two input bits and a carry bit, a full adder is required. To add two multibit binary numbers, a computer uses a half adder and one or more full adders. See also carry bit, full adder.

Half-card *n.* See short card.

Half-duplex 1 *adj.* Of or pertaining to two-way communication that takes place in only one direction at a time. For example, transmission between half-duplex modems occurs when one modem waits to transmit until the other has finished sending.

Half-duplex 2 *n.* Two-way electronic communication that takes place in only one direction at a time. Also called: half-duplex transmission.

Half-duplex transmission *n.* See half-duplex2.

Half-height drive *n.* Any of a generation of disk drives that are roughly one-half the height of the previous generation of drives.

Half router *n.* A device that connects a local area network (LAN) to a communications line (such as one to the Internet) using a modem and that controls the routing of data to individual stations on the LAN.

Halftone *n.* A printed reproduction of a photograph or other illustration, using evenly spaced spots of varying diameter to produce apparent shades of gray. The darker the shade at a particular point in the image, the larger the corresponding spot in the halftone. In traditional publishing, halftones are created by photographing an image through a screen. In desktop publishing, each halftone spot is represented by an area containing a number of dots printed by a laser printer or digital imagesetter. In both cases, the frequency of the halftone dots is measured in lines per inch. Higher printer resolution enables effective use of higher frequencies of halftone dots, enhancing image quality. See also dithering, gray scale, imagesetter, spot function.

Half-word *n.* Half the number of bits considered to be a word in a particular computer; if a word is 32 bits, a half-word will be 16 bits or 2 bytes. See also word.

Hammer *n.* The part of an impact printer that strikes or causes another component to strike the ribbon to print a character on the paper. In a dot-matrix printer, the pins or wires are the hammers; in a daisy-wheel printer, the hammer strikes the daisy wheel.

Hamming code *n.* A family of error-correction codes named for R. W. Hamming of Bell Labs. In one of the simplest Hamming codes, every 4 data bits are followed by 3 check bits, each computed from the 4 data bits. If any one of the 7 bits becomes altered, a simple computation can detect the error and determine which bit is altered. See also error-correction coding, forward error correction.

Handheld computer *n.* A computer small enough to be held in one hand while being operated with the other hand. Handheld computers are commonly used in transportation and other field service industries. They are usually built to perform specific tasks. They often have restricted specialised keyboards rather than the standard QWERTY layout, smaller displays, input devices such as bar code readers, and communications devices for sending their data to a central computer; they rarely have disk drives. Their software is usually proprietary and stored in ROM. See also QWERTY keyboard, ROM.

Handheld PC *n.* A computer that is small enough to fit in a jacket pocket and can run, for example, Windows CE (an operating system for handheld PCs and embedded systems) and applications made for that operating system. See the illustration. Acronym: HPC.

Handheld scanner *n.* A type of scanner used as follows: the user passes the scan head, contained within a handheld unit, over the medium being scanned, such as a piece of paper. See also scan head, scanner.

Handle *n.* 1. A pointer to a pointer; that is, a variable that contains the address of another variable, which in turn contains the address of the desired object. In certain operating systems, the handle points to a pointer stored in a fixed location in memory, whereas that pointer points to a movable block. If programmes start from the handle whenever they access the block, the operating system can perform-memory-management tasks such as garbage collection without affecting the programmes. See also pointer. 2. Any token that a programme can use to identify and access an object such as a device, a file, a window, or a dialog box. 3. One of several small squares displayed around a graphical object in a drawing programme. The user can move or reshape the object by clicking on a handle and dragging. See the illustration. 4. In online communication, such as chats and bulletin boards, the name a person uses to identify himself or herself. A handle is comparable to an alias or a nickname and is like those used with CB radio. 5. A

Handler *n.* 1. A routine that manages a common and relatively simple condition or operation, such as error recovery or data movement. 2. In some object-oriented programming languages that support messages, a subroutine that processes a particular message for a particular class of objects. See also message, object-oriented programming.

Handoff *n.* The process of transferring a wireless telephone signal between cell towers as a caller travels from one cell to another. A caller will not notice a smooth handoff, but an abrupt handoff can interfere with reception, with results ranging from momentary static to a disconnected call. Also called: handover. See also cell.

Hands-free kit *n.* Wireless phone accessory that allows users to make calls without holding the phone. A basic kit includes a headset or an earpiece with a microphone. More elaborate sets for use in automobiles may include a power amplifier, dashboard microphone, phone cradle, and speakers.

Handshake *n.* A series of signals acknowledging that communication or the transfer of information can take place between computers or other devices. A hardware handshake is an exchange of signals over specific wires (other than the data wires) in which each device indicates its readiness to send or receive data. A software handshake consists of signals transmitted over the same wires used to transfer data, as in modem-to-modem communications over telephone lines.

Hands-on *adj.* Involving interactive work with a computer or a computer programme. A hands-on tutorial, for example, would teach a skill (such as the use of a programme) by means of practice sessions and question-and-answer dialogues.

Handwriting input device *n.* A tool, such as a digital pen and tablet, used to enter text by writing instead of typing. Along with writing tablets, additional devices include 3-D drawing or computer-aided design (CAD) tablets, a tablet PC, or moving a mouse on the mouse pad.

Handwriting recognition *n.* 1. The ability of a computer to identify a user by recognising features of handwriting, especially a signature. 2. The ability of a computer to translate handwritten text into character data for input. This technology is still under considerable development, and most handwriting recognition programmes require users to form letters and words in a very consistent and clear manner to work adequately. The development of handwriting recognition programmes has been spurred by PDAs, which frequently have keyboards that are too small for data entry, and software designed for Asian markets that have languages with numerous characters, which makes keyboards a cumbersome method for entering text. See also PDA.

Hang *vb.* To stop responding. A hung programme or computer system does not respond to user input, but the screen looks as if everything is running normally. The programme or system might be waiting for something—for example, information from a network—or it might have terminated abnormally. It might resume running normally on its own, or the user might need to terminate and restart the programme or reboot the computer. A hung computer system is said to be locked up. See also crash2 (definition 1).

Hanging indent *n.* Placement of the beginning of the first line of a paragraph farther to the left than the subsequent lines. Also called: outdent.

Haptics *n.* The study of the sense of touch. This study has extended to the study of human interaction with computer technology through tactile means. Haptics technology is central to virtual reality gaming settings, in which computers could sense and respond to finger, hand, body, or head movements. The computer could also re-create the sense of touch by altering texture, increasing resistance, or other simulations appropriate to the user's virtual reality experience. See also force feedback.

Hard *adj.* 1. Permanent, fixed, or physically defined; unchangeable by the ordinary operation of a computer system. See also hard copy, hard error, hard return, hard-sectored disk. 2. Retaining magnetisation even in the absence of an external magnetic field.

Hard card *n.* A circuit board, carrying a hard disk and containing its controller, that plugs into an expansion slot and uses the expansion bus for power as well as for data and control signals. By contrast, a hard disk in a drive bay communicates with a separate controller card by a ribbon cable and has a direct cable to the computer's main power supply. See also controller, drive bay, expansion slot, ribbon cable.

Hard-coded *adj.* 1. Designed to handle a specific situation only. 2. Depending on values embedded in the programme code rather than on values that can be input and changed by the user.

Hard copy *n.* Printed output on paper, film, or other permanent medium.

Hard disk *n.* A device containing one or more inflexible platters coated with material in which data can be recorded magnetically, together with their read/write heads, the head-positioning mechanism, and the spindle motor in a sealed case that protects against outside contaminants. The protected environment allows the head to fly 10 to 25 millionths of an inch above the surface of a platter rotating typically at 3600 to 7200 rpm; therefore, much more data can be stored and accessed much more quickly than on a floppy disk. Most hard disks contain from two to eight platters. See the illustration. Also called: hard disk drive.

Hard disk drive *n.* See hard disk.

Hard disk type *n.* One or more numbers that inform a computer about the characteristics of a hard disk, such as the number of read/write heads and the number of cylinders the hard disk contains. The hard disk type numbers are usually marked on a label attached to the disk and must be input to the computer when the hard disk is installed, often by means of the computer's CMOS setup programme. See also CMOS setup.

Hard error *n.* 1. An error caused by a hardware failure or by accessing incompatible hardware. See also hard failure. 2. An error that prevents a programme from returning to normal operation. See also fatal error.

Hard failure *n.* A cessation of function from which no recovery is possible, usually requiring a call to a repair service to correct. Also called: hardware failure.

Hard hyphen *n.* See hyphen.

Hard return *n.* A character input by the user to indicate that the current line of text is to end and a new line is to begin. In word-processing programmes that automatically break lines within the margins of a page, a hard return indicates the end of a paragraph. In text-entry programmes that lack wordwrap, on the other hand, a hard return is required to end each line, and often two or more hard returns are needed to end a paragraph. See also wordwrap.

Hard-sectored disk *n.* A floppy disk whose data sectors have been physically marked with punched holes that are detected by sensors in the drive to locate the beginning of each sector.

Hard space *n.* See nonbreaking space.

Hardware *n.* The physical components of a computer system, including any peripheral equipment such as printers, modems, and mouse devices.

Hardware abstraction layer *n.* In advanced operating systems such as Windows NT, Windows 2000, and Windows XP a layer in which assembly language code is isolated. A hardware abstraction layer functions similarly to an application programming interface (API) and is used by programmers to write device-independent applications. Acronym: HAL. See also application programming interface, device independence.

Hardware address *n.* See physical address.

Hardware check *n.* 1. An automatic check performed by hardware to detect internal errors or problems. 2. On a PC, a check of system hardware performed by a PC's BIOS (Basic Input/ Output System) during the POST (Power On Self Test) portion of the startup process.

Hardware conversion *n.* Changing all or part of a computer system to work with new or different devices.

Hardware cryptographic module *n.* Hardware designed to handle the cryptographic functions necessary for data security. For example, a hardware cryptographic module, or HCM, can be used in an SSL-enabled Web server to reduce CPU processing time and improve overall performance by working to secure data during online transactions. Using an HCM allows the Web server to continue processing customer requests. Acronym: HCM. See also SSL.

Hardware-dependent *adj.* Of or pertaining to programmes, languages, or computer components and devices that are tied to a particular computer system or configuration. Assembly language, for example, is hardware-dependent because it is created for and works only with a particular make or model of microprocessor.

Hardware emulation layer *n.* In advanced operating systems such as Windows NT, Windows 2000, and Windows XP a layer in which software drivers duplicate hardware functionality. This allows software programmes to use hardware features even if the hardware is not present. Acronym: HEL.

Hardware failure *n.* A malfunction of a physical component in a computer system, such as a disk head crash or memory error. See also hard failure.

Hardware handshake *n.* See handshake.

Hardware interrupt *n.* A request for service from the central processing unit, generated either externally by a hardware device such as a disk drive or an input/output port, or internally by the CPU itself. External hardware interrupts are used for such situations as a character received from a port and needing to be processed, a disk drive ready to transfer a block of data, or a tick of the system timer. Internal hardware interrupts occur when a programme attempts an impossible action such as accessing an unavailable address or dividing by zero. Hardware interrupts are assigned levels of importance or priority. The highest priority is given to a type of interrupt called a nonmaskable interrupt—one that indicates a serious error, such as a memory failure, that must be serviced immediately. See also external interrupt, interrupt.

Hardware key *n.* 1. A security device connected to an input/output port to permit the use of a particular software package on that computer. The use of the hardware key permits backup copying of software but prevents its unlicensed use on additional computers. Also called: dongle. 2. Any physical device used to secure a computer system from unauthorised access, such as the lock on the front of the cabinet of some personal computers.

Hardware monitor *n.* A separate board-level circuit used to oversee the performance of a hardware/software system. A hardware monitor can detect the cause of a fatal error such as a system crash, whereas a software monitor or debugger cannot.

Hardware profile *n.* A set of data that describes the configuration and characteristics of a given piece of computer equipment. Such data is typically used to configure computers for use with peripheral devices.

Hardware tree *n.* In Windows 9x, a data structure containing information about the configuration and requirements of a system's hardware devices. Consisting of nodes that point to active devices, the hardware tree is dynamic and is reconstructed every time the operating system is started or refreshed. The hardware tree facilitates the Plug and Play capability of Windows 9x.

Hardwired *adj.* 1. Built into a system using hardware such as logic circuits, rather than accomplished through programming. 2. Physically connected to a system or a network, as by means of a network connector board and cable.

Harvard architecture *n.* A processor architecture that uses separate address buses for code and for data. This increases throughput by allowing the system to fetch instructions at the same time that it reads and writes data. This architecture also allows optimisation of memory system design because instructions tend to be fetched sequentially, whereas data reads and writes are more random.

Harvard Mark I *n.* See Mark I.

Harvest research project *n.* See ICP.

Hash 1 *n.* In many FTP client programmes, a command that instructs the FTP client to display a pound sign (#) each time it sends or receives a block of data. See also FTP client.

Hash 2 *vb.* To be mapped to a numerical value by a transformation known as a hashing function. Hashing is used to convert an identifier or key, meaningful to a user, into a value for the location of the corresponding data in a structure, such as a table. For example, given the key MOUSE and a hashing function that added up the ASCII values of the characters, divided the total by 127, and took the remainder, MOUSE would hash to 12 and the data identified by MOUSE would be found among the items in entry 12 in the table.

Hash coding *n.* See hash2.

Hashing algorithm *n.* A formula used to generate hash values and digital signatures. Also called: hash function.

Hash search *n.* A search algorithm that uses hashing to find an element of a list. Hash searches are highly efficient because the hashing enables direct or almost direct access to the target element. See also binary search, hash, linear search, search algorithm.

Hash total *n.* An error-checking value derived from the addition of a set of numbers taken from data (not necessarily numeric data) that is to be processed or manipulated in some way. After processing, the hash total is recalculated and compared with the original total. If the two do not match, the original data has been changed in some way.

Hash value *n.* A value used in creating digital signatures. This value is generated by imposing a hashing algorithm onto a message. This value is then transformed, or signed, by a private key to produce a digital signature. Also called: message digest.

Haskell *n.* A functional programming language based on lambda calculus and suitable for the creation of applications that need to be highly modifiable.

Hayes-compatible *adj.* Responding to the same set of commands as the modems manufactured by Hayes Microcomputer Products. This command set has become the de facto standard for microcomputer modems.

HCM *n.* See hardware cryptographic module.

HDBMS *n.* See hierarchical database management system.

HDCP *n.* Acronym for High-bandwidth Digital Content Protection. An encryption and authentication specification created by Intel for Digital Video Interface (DVI) devices such as digital cameras, high-definition televisions, and video disk players. HDCP is designed to protect transmissions between DVI devices from being copied.

HDF *n.* See Hierarchical Data Format.

HDLC *n.* Acronym for High-level Data Link Control. A protocol for information transfer adopted by the ISO. HDLC is a bit-oriented, synchronous protocol that applies to the data-link (message-packaging) layer (layer 2 of the ISO/OSI reference model) for computer-to-microcomputer communications. Messages are transmitted in units called frames, which can contain differing amounts of data but which must be organised in a particular way. See also frame (definition 1), ISO/OSI reference model.

HDML *n.* Acronym for Handheld Device Markup Language. A simple, first-generation markup language used to define hypertext-like content and applications for wireless and other handheld devices with small displays. This language is used primarily to create Web sites viewed via wireless phones and personal digital assistants (PDAs). HDML provides content consisting mainly of text with limited graphics. See also WML.

HDSL *n.* Acronym for High-bit-rate Digital Subscriber Line. A form of DSL, HDSL is a protocol for digital transmission of data over standard copper telecommunications lines (as opposed to fiber-optic lines) at rates of 1.544 Mbps in both directions. Also called: High-data-rate Digital Subscriber Line. See also DSL.

HDTP *n.* Acronym for Handheld Device Transport Protocol. Protocol that enables a handheld device, such as a wireless phone or personal digital assistant (PDA), to access the Internet. HDTP regulates the input and output of data interpreted by the device's microbrowser. See also WAP.

HDTV *n.* Acronym for High-Definition TeleVision. A new television display standard that doubles the existing screen resolution and increases the screen aspect ratio from 4:3 to 16:9. This aspect ratio creates a television screen that is shaped like a movie screen.

HDTV-over-IP *n.* An Internet-based delivery option for High Definition Television (HDTV). HDTV-over-IP provides options for new and expanded services to ISPs, cable companies, telecommunications carriers, and business intranets, with its most extensive use in education. Universities use high-speed networks such as Internet2 to provide the intensive bandwidth demanded by HDTV-over-IP. Because HDTV-over-IP offers extreme image fidelity and sharpness, it is seen as ideal for delivery of distance education courses requiring precise visuals for which conventional video cannot provide sufficient resolution. Also called: iHDTV.

Head *n.* 1. The read/write mechanism in a disk or tape drive. It converts changes in the magnetic field of the material on the disk or tape surface to changing electrical signals and vice versa. Disk drives usually contain one head for each surface that can be read from and written to. 2. In relation to software or documents, the top or beginning of something. 3. In HTML, a section of coding that precedes the body of a document and is used to describe the document itself (title, author, and so on) rather than the elements within the document.

Head arm *n.* See access arm.

Head-cleaning device *n.* An apparatus for applying a small amount of cleaning fluid to a magnetic head to remove accumulated debris.

Head crash *n.* A hard disk failure in which a read/write head, normally supported on a cushion of air only millionths of an inch thick, comes into contact with the platter, damaging the magnetic coating in which data is recorded. Still more damage occurs when the head picks up material gouged out of the surface and pushes it. A head crash can be caused by mechanical failure or by heavy shaking of the disk drive. If the crash occurs on a directory track, the whole disk may become instantly unreadable.

Header *n.* 1. In word processing or printing, text that is to appear at the top of pages. A header might be specified for the first page, all pages after the first, even pages, or odd pages. It usually includes the page number and may also show the date, the title, or other information about a document. Also called: heading, running head. 2. An information structure that precedes and identifies the information that follows, such as a block of bytes in communications, a file on a disk, a set of records in a database, or an executable programme. 3. One or more lines in a programme that identify and describe for human readers the programme, function, or procedure that follows.

Header file *n.* A file that is identified to be included at the beginning of a programme in a language such as C and that contains the definitions of data types and declarations of variables used by the functions in the programme.

Header label *n.* An initial structure, such as an opening record, in the linear organisation of a file or communication that describes the length, type, and structure of the data that follows.

Header record *n.* The first record in a sequence of records.

Heading *n.* See header (definition 1).

Headless computer *n.* A computer system that does not have a keyboard, mouse, or video monitor during normal operation.

Head-mounted device *n.* A headset or helmet used with virtual reality systems ranging from gaming to military, medical, educational, and industrial applications. A head-mounted device contains small screens that display images in such a way that the headset allows the wearer to view and move about in a three-dimensional, virtual world. The simulated environment is generated by a controlling computer, which adjusts the images in accordance with the wearer's head and body movements. A head-mounted device can include audio capability and is often used with an interactive input device, such as a joystick or glove. Acronym: HMD. See also virtual reality, wearable computer.

Head-per-track disk drive *n.* A disk drive that has one read/write head for every data track. Such a disk drive has a very low seek time because the heads do not have to move across the disk surface to the required track for reading and writing. Because read/write heads are expensive, this type of drive is uncommon.

Head positioning *n.* The process of moving the read/write head of a disk drive to the proper track for reading and writing.

Head slot *n.* The oblong opening in the jacket of a floppy disk that provides access to the magnetic surface of the disk for the read/write head. See the illustration.

Head switching *n.* The process of electrically switching among multiple read/write heads in a disk drive.

Heap *n.* 1. A portion of memory reserved for a programme to use for the temporary storage of data structures whose existence or size cannot be determined until the programme is running. To build and use such elements, programming languages such as C and Pascal include functions and procedures for requesting free memory from the heap, accessing it, and freeing it when it is no longer needed. In contrast to stack memory, heap memory blocks are not freed in reverse of the order in which they were allocated, so free blocks may be interspersed with blocks that are in use. As the programme continues running, the blocks may have to be moved around so that small free blocks can be merged together into larger ones to meet the program's needs. See also garbage collection. 2. A complete binary tree in which the value of any node is not exceeded by the value of either of its children. See also binary tree.

Heap sort or heapsort *n.* A space-efficient sorting method that fi: ' arranges the key fields into a heap structure; then repeatedly removes the root of the heap, which must, by definition, have the largest key; and re-forms the heap. See also heap (definition 1).

Heat pipe *n.* A cooling device consisting of a sealed metal tube containing a liquid and a wick. The liquid evaporates at the hot end; the vapor spreads along the tube to the cold end, where it condenses onto the wick; the liquid flows back along the wick to the hot end by capillary action. Heat pipes have been used in Pentium-based laptop computers, which have high cooling requirements and little room for conventional heat sinks.

Heat sink *n.* A device that absorbs and dissipates heat produced by an electrical component, such as an integrated circuit, to prevent overheating. Heat sinks are usually made of metal and often have fins that assist in transferring heat to the atmosphere. See the illustration.

hecto- prefix Metric prefix meaning 102 (one hundred).

HEL *n.* See hardware emulation layer.

Hello, world *n.* The output of the first programme in Brian Kernighan and Dennis Ritchie's The C Programming Language. The programme is traditionally the first test a C programmer makes in a new environment.

Help *n.* 1. The capability of many programmes and operating systems to display advice or instructions for using their features when so requested by the user, as by a screen button or a menu item or a function key. The user can access help without interrupting work in progress or leafing through a manual. Some help facilities are context-sensitive, meaning that the user receives information specific to the task or command being attempted. Also called: online help. 2. In many applications, a command that displays an explanation of another command that follows it. For instance, in many FTP programmes, the command help can be followed by other commands, such as cd (change directory) or ls (list files and directories), to discover the purpose of these other commands.

3. In versions 5 and 6 of MS-DOS, the command used to request information about MS-DOS commands, command parameters, and switches.

Help *n.* An item on a menu bar in a graphical user interface that enables the user to access the help feature of the present application. See also graphical user interface, help (definition 1), menu bar.

Help desk *n.* 1. Technical support staff who help solve users' problems with hardware or software systems or refer such problems to those who can solve them. Help desks are typically run by larger organisations, such as corporations, universities, or vendors to corporations, to assist users in the organisation. 2. A software application for tracking problems with hardware and software and their solutions.

Helper *n.* See helper application.

Helper application *n.* An application intended to be launched by a Web browser when the browser downloads a file that it is not able to process itself. Examples of helper applications are sound and movie players. Helper applications generally must be obtained and installed by users; they usually are not included in the browser itself. Many current Web browsers no longer require helper applications for common multimedia file formats. Also called: helper programme.

Helper programme *n.* See helper application.

Help key *n.* A key on the keyboard that the user can press to request help. See also function key, help (definition 1).

Help screen *n.* A screen of information that is displayed when the user requests help. See also help (definition 1).

Henry *n.* The unit of inductance. A current changing at a rate of one ampere per second will generate one volt across an inductance of one henry. In practice, a henry is a very large unit; inductances measured in millihenries (mH = 10–3 H), microhenries (<MU>H = 10–6 H), or nanohenries (nH = 10–9 H) are more commonly encountered. Abbreviated H. See also inductance.

Hercules Graphics Card *n.* See HGC.

Hertz *n.* The unit of frequency measurement; one cycle (of a periodic event such as a waveform) per second. Frequencies of interest in computers and electronic devices are often measured in kilohertz (kHz = 1000 Hz = 103 Hz), megahertz (MHz = 1000 kHz = 106 Hz), gigahertz (GHz = 1000 MHz = 109 Hz), or terahertz (THz = 1000 GHz = 1012 Hz). Abbreviated Hz.

Hertz time *n.* See clock rate.

Heterogeneous environment *n.* A computing milieu, usually within an organisation, in which hardware and software from two or more manufacturers are used.

Heuristic *n.* An approach or algorithm that leads to a correct solution of a programming task by nonrigorous or self-learning means. One approach to programming is first to develop a heuristic and then to improve on it. The term comes from Greek heuriskein ("to discover, find out") and is related to "eureka" ("I have found it").

Hewlett-Packard Graphics Language *n.* See HPGL.

Hewlett-Packard Printer Control Language *n.* See Printer Control Language.

Hex *n.* See hexadecimal.

Hexadecimal *adj.* Using 16 rather than 10 as the base for representing numbers. The hexadecimal system uses the digits 0 through 9 and the letters A through F (uppercase or lowercase) to represent the decimal numbers 0 through 15. One hexadecimal digit is equivalent to 4 bits, and 1 byte can be expressed by two hexadecimal digits. For example, binary 0101 0011 corresponds to hexadecimal 53. To prevent confusion with decimal numbers, hexadecimal numbers in programmes or documentation are usually followed by H or preceded by &, $, or 0x. Thus, 10H = decimal 16; 100H = decimal 162 = decimal 256. Equivalents and conversion tables for binary, decimal, hexadecimal, and octal numbers are given in Appendix E. Also called: hex.

Hexadecimal conversion *n.* Conversion of a number to or from the hexadecimal system. See Appendix E.

HFS *n.* See Hierarchical File System.

HFS+ *n.* Acronym for Hierarchal File System Plus. The primary file system .format available on the Macintosh operating system. With Mac OS 8.1, HFS+ replaced the earlier HFS format, adding support for names longer than 31 characters and Unicode representation of file and directory names. Also called: Mac OS Extended format.

HGA *n.* Acronym for Hercules Graphics Adapter. See HGC.

HGC *n.* Acronym for Hercules Graphics Card. A video adapter introduced in 1982 by Hercules Computer Technology for IBM personal computers and compatibles and now superseded by VGA and its successors. It offered a monochrome graphics mode with 720 x 348 pixels. See also VGA.

HGC Plus *n.* A video adapter, introduced in 1986 by Hercules Computer Technology, that offered additional video buffer space to store 12 fonts of 256 characters each, which could be used for graphics characters.

HHOK *n.* Acronym for ha, ha, only kidding. An indication of humour or facetiousness often used in e-mail and online communications.

Hibernation *n.* A state in which a computer shuts down after saving everything in memory to the hard disk. When the computer is powered on, programmes and documents that were open are restored to the desktop. See also standby.

Hidden file *n.* A file that, in order to protect it from deletion or modification, is not shown in the normal listing of the files contained in a directory. Such a file is often used to store code or data critical to the operating system.

Hidden line *n.* In any application, such as a CAD programme, that represents solid three-dimensional objects, a line in a drawing that would (or should) be hidden if the object were perceived as a solid construction. The process of removing such lines in an application is called hidden-line removal. See also CAD, hidden surface.

Hidden surface *n.* A surface of a solid three-dimensional object, such as one represented in a CAD programme, that would not be visible when the object is viewed from a particular angle—for example, the underside of the wing of an airplane when viewed from above. See also CAD, hidden line.

Hide *vb.* To temporarily remove the onscreen display of an application's active window while leaving the application running. Windows that have been hidden are returned to active display by issuing the appropriate command to the operating system.

Hierarchical *adj.* Of, relating to, or organised as a hierarchy. See also hierarchy.

Hierarchical computer network *n.* 1. A network in which one host computer controls a number of smaller computers, which may in turn act as hosts to a group of PC workstations. 2. A network in which control functions are organised according to a hierarchy and in which data processing tasks may be distributed.

Hierarchical database *n.* A database in which records are grouped in such a way that their relationships form a branching, treelike structure. This type of database structure, most commonly used with databases for large computers, is well suited for organising information that breaks down logically into successively greater levels of detail. The organisation of records in a hierarchical database should reflect the most common or the most time-critical types of access expected.

Hierarchical database management system *n.* A database management system that supports a hierarchical model. Acronym: HDBMS. See also hierarchical model.

Hierarchical Data Format *n.* A file format for storing multiple types of graphical and numerical data and transferring them between different types of machines, together with a library of functions for handling such files in a uniform way. NCSA developed and supports the file function and library and has placed them in the public domain. Hierarchical Data Format files are supported on most common types of computers. The format can easily be extended to accommodate additional data models. The library functions have both FORTRAN and C interfaces. Acronym: HDF. See also NCSA (definition 1).

Hierarchical file system *n.* A system for organising files on a disk in which files are contained in directories or folders, each of which can contain other directories as well as files. The main directory for the disk is called the root; the chain of directories from the root to a particular file is called the path. See also hierarchy, path (definition 2), root.

Hierarchical File System *n.* A tree-structured file system used on the Apple Macintosh in which folders can be nested within other folders. Acronym: HFS. See also hierarchy, path (definition 2), root.

Hierarchical menu *n.* A menu that has one or more submenus. Such a menu/submenu arrangement is hierarchical because each level subsumes the next.

Hierarchical model *n.* A model used in database management in which each record may be the "parent" of one or more child records, which may or may not have the same structure as the parent; a record can have no more than one parent. Conceptually, therefore, a hierarchical model can be, and usually is, regarded as a tree. The individual records are not necessarily contained in the same file. See also tree.

Hierarchical Storage Management *n.* See HSM.

Hierarchy *n.* A type of organisation that, like a tree, branches into more specific units, each of which is "owned" by the higher-level unit immediately above. Hierarchies are characteristic of several aspects of computing because they provide organisational frameworks that can reflect logical links, or relationships, between separate records, files, or pieces of equipment. For example, hierarchies are used in organising related files on a disk, related records in a database, and related (interconnected) devices on a network. In applications such as spreadsheets, hierarchies of a sort are used to establish the order of precedence in which arithmetic operations are to be performed by the computer. See also hierarchical file system.

High availability *n.* The ability of a system or device to be usable when it is needed. When expressed as a percentage, high availability is the actual service time divided by the required service time. Although high availability does not guarantee that a system will have no downtime, a network often is considered highly available if it achieves 99.999 per cent network uptime. Also called: RAS (reliability/availability/serviceability), fault resilience. See also five-nines availability, four-nines availability, three-nines availability, two-nines availability.

High-bit-rate Digital Subscriber Line *n.* See HDSL.

High byte *n.* The byte containing the most significant bits (bits 8 through 15) in a 2-byte grouping representing a 16-bit (bits 0 through 15) value. See the illustration. See also hexadecimal.

High Contrast *n.* An accessibility display feature in Microsoft Windows that instructs programmes to use the colour scheme specified in the Settings dialog box and to increase legibility whenever possible.

High-data-rate Digital Subscriber Line *n.* See HDSL.

High-Definition Television *n.* See HDTV.

High-density disk *n.* 1. A 3.5-inch floppy disk that can hold 1.44 MB. 2. A 5.25-inch floppy disk that can hold 1.2 MB.

High DOS memory *n.* See high memory.

High-end *adj.* A descriptive term for something that uses the latest technology to maximise performance. There is usually a direct correlation between high-end technology and higher prices.

High-level Data Link Control *n.* See HDLC.

High-level language *n.* A computer language that provides a level of abstraction from the underlying machine language. Statements in a high-level language generally use keywords similar to English and translate into more than one machine-language instruction. In practice, every computer language above assembly language is a high-level language. Acronym: HLL. Also called: high-order language.

Highlight *vb.* To alter the appearance of displayed characters as a means of calling attention to them, as by displaying them in reverse video (light on dark rather than dark on light, and vice versa) or with greater intensity. Highlighting is used to indicate an item, such as an option on a menu or text in a word processor, that is to be acted on in some way.

High memory *n.* 1. Memory locations addressed by the largest numbers. 2. In IBM PCs and compatibles, the range of addresses between 640 kilobytes and 1 megabyte, used primarily for the ROM BIOS and control hardware such as the video adapter and input/output ports.

High memory area *n.* In IBM PCs and compatibles, the 64-kilobyte range of addresses immediately above 1 megabyte. By means of the file HIMEM.SYS, MS-DOS (versions 5 and later) can move portions of itself into the high memory area, thereby increasing the amount of conventional memory available for applications. Acronym: HMA. See also conventional memory, expanded memory.

High-order *adj.* Having the most weight or significance. The high-order term usually appears first or leftmost in writing systems based on the Roman alphabet or Arabic numerals. For example, in the 2-byte hex value 6CA2, the high-order byte 6C has a value by itself of decimal 108 but counts for 108 x 256 = 27,648 in the group, whereas the low-order byte A2 counts only for decimal 162.

High-order language *n.* See high-level language.

Highpass filter *n.* An electronic circuit that passes all frequencies in a signal that are above a specified frequency.

High-Performance File System *n.* See HPFS.

High-Performance Parallel Interface *n.* See HIPPI.

High-Performance Serial Bus *n.* See IEEE 1394.

High-persistence phosphor *n.* A phosphor that glows for a relatively long time after being struck by electrons. High-persistence phosphors are used in direct view storage tubes, but most CRTs (cathode-ray tubes) use phosphors of relatively low persistence so that their images can be changed quickly without "ghosts" of earlier images remaining on the screen. See also CRT, direct view storage tube.

High resolution *n.* The capability for reproducing text and graphics with relative clarity and fineness of detail. High resolution is achieved by using a large number of pixels (dots) to create an image in a given area. For screen displays, the resolution is stated in terms of the total number of pixels in the horizontal and vertical dimensions. For example, the VGA video adapter has a resolution of 640 by 480 pixels. In printing, resolution refers to the number of dots per inch (dpi) produced by the printer, such as 300 to 600 dpi for a desktop laser or ink-jet printer or 1000 to 2000 dpi for a production-quality imagesetter. Also called: hi-res.

High Sierra specification *n.* An industry-wide format specification for the logical structure, file structure, and record structures on a CD-ROM. The specification is named after a meeting on CD-ROM held near Lake Tahoe in November 1985. It served as the basis for the international standard, ISO 9660.

High tech *n.* 1. Cutting-edge applied science and engineering, usually involving computers and electronics. 2. Sophisticated, often complex, specialised technical innovation.

Hijackware *n.* Software that appears to be a useful plug-in or utility, but which will take over a user's Internet surfing or shopping activity by creating pop-up advertisements for competing products or redirecting the user to competitor's Web sites. Typically users will download and install a hijackware product believing it to be free browser enhancement software. Businesses pay the makers of hijackware products to push their shopping sites and product advertising onto Internet users, sometimes to the point of denying the user access to competing Web sites. See also gatored.

Hijiri calendar *n.* The lunar calendar used in Islamic countries. See Julian calendar.

HIPPI *n.* Acronym for High-Performance Parallel Interface. An ANSI communications standard used with supercomputers.

Hi-res *n.* See high resolution.

Histogram *n.* A chart consisting of horizontal or vertical bars, the widths or heights of which represent the values of certain data.

History *n.* A list of the user's actions within a programme, such as commands entered in an operating system shell, menus passed through using Gopher, or links followed using a Web browser.

Hit *n.* 1. A successful retrieval of data from a cache rather than from the slower hard disk or RAM. See also cache, hard disk, RAM. 2. A successful retrieval of a record matching a query in a database. See also query (definition 1), record. 3. Retrieval of a file from a Web site. Each separate file accessed on a Web page, including HTML documents and graphics, counts as a hit. 4. In computer war and other games, when a character is successfully fired on, attacked, or otherwise taken out.

Hit points *n.* Used in most computer and console war games to refer to the amount of times a player can be damaged before his or her character passes out or dies.

Hive *n.* One of the top-level sets of keys, subkeys, and values in Windows 9x, Windows NT, Windows 2000, and -Windows CE Registries. The term was created by a Microsoft programmer who thought the structure of the Registry resembled a beehive. Each hive is a permanent part of the Registry and is associated with a set of files containing information related to the configuration (applications, user preferences, devices, and so on) of the computer on which the operating system is installed. Registry hives include HKEY_LOCAL_MACHINE, HKEY_CURRENT_USER, and HKEY_CURRENT_CONFIG. See also Registry.

HKEY *n.* Short for hkey handle. In Windows 9x, -Windows NT, and Windows 2000, a handle to a Registry key in which configuration information is stored. Each key leads to subkeys containing configuration information that, in earlier versions of Windows, was stored in .ini files. For example, the handle key HKEY_CURRENT_USERControl Panel leads to the subkey for the Windows Desktop. See also handle (definition 1).

HLL *n.* See high-level language.

HLS *n.* Acronym for hue-lightness-saturation. See HSB.

HMA *n.* See high memory area.

HMD *n.* See head-mounted device.

Hollerith tabulating/recording machine *n.* An electromechanical machine invented by Herman Hollerith in the late 1800s for processing data supplied in the form of holes punched at predetermined locations in cards. Contacts made through the holes completed electrical circuits, allowing signals to be passed to counting and tabulating devices. This machine is considered to have reduced the time required to finish the 1890 U.S. census by two-thirds. Such machines were manufactured in the early 1900s by Hollerith's Tabulating Machine Company, which eventually became the International Business Machines Corporation (IBM).

Hologram *n.* A three-dimensional image record created by holography. The hologram consists of a light interference pattern preserved in a medium such as photographic film. When suitably illuminated, it produces an image that changes its appearance as the viewer changes viewing angle. See also holography.

Holography *n.* A method of reproducing three-dimensional visual images by recording light interference patterns on a medium such as photographic film, creating a hologram. See also hologram.

Holy war *n.* 1. A widespread and acrimonious debate among computer professionals over some aspect of the computer field, such as the debate over use of the GOTO statement in programming or that over big-endian versus little-endian data storage. 2. An argument in a mailing list, newsgroup, or other forum over some emotional and controversial topic, such as abortion or Northern Ireland. Introducing a holy war that is off the purported topic of the forum is considered a violation of netiquette.

Home *n.* A beginning position, such as the upper left corner of a character-based display, the left end of a line of text, cell A1 of a spreadsheet, or the top of a document.

Home automation *n.* The process of programmatically controlling appliances, lighting, heating and cooling systems, and other devices in a home network. See also home network.

Homebrew *n.* Hardware or software developed by an individual at home or by a company for its own use rather than as a commercial product, such as hardware developed by electronics hobbyists when microcomputers first appeared in the 1970s.

Home computer *n.* A personal computer designed and priced for use in the home.

Home controller *n.* A software or hardware interface used to control the systems in a home network for home automation.

Home directory *n.* A directory associated with a user account under UNIX. The home directory is the current directory when the user first logs in, and the user can return to it by entering the command cd (change directory) without a pathname. The user's files will ordinarily be stored in the home directory and its descendants.

Homegrown software *n.* Software developed by an individual at home rather than in a professional environment. Most public-domain and shareware programmes are created this way.

Home key *n.* A key, found on most keyboards, whose function usually involves sending the cursor to some type of home position in an application. See also home.

Home network *n.* 1. A communications network in a home or building used for home automation. Home networks can use wiring (existing or new) or wireless connections. See also home automation, home controller. 2. Two or more computers in a home that are interconnected to form a local area network (LAN).

Home office *n.* 1. An office set up within a residence. 2. The main headquarters of a company.

Home page *n.* 1. A document intended to serve as a starting point in a hypertext system, especially the World Wide Web. A home page is called a start page in Microsoft Internet Explorer. 2. An entry page for a set of Web pages and other files in a Web site. 3. A personal Web page, usually for an individual.

Home Phoneline Networking Alliance *n.* See -HomePNA.

HomePNA *n.* Short for Home Phoneline Networking Alliance. An association of more than 100 companies working toward the adoption of a unified technology for setting up home networks over existing telephone wiring. Phoneline networking allows multiple PCs, printers, and peripheral devices to be connected for such purposes as multiplayer gaming, sharing printers and other peripherals, and rapid downloads over the Internet. The alliance was founded by a number of companies including IBM, Intel, AT&T, and Lucent Technologies.

Home Radio Frequency *n.* See HomeRF.

home record *n.* See header record.

HomeRF *n.* Acronym for Home Radio Frequency. A wireless home-networking specification that uses the 2.4-GHz frequency band to communicate between computers, peripherals, cordless phones, and other devices. HomeRF is supported by Siemens, Compaq, Motorola, National Semiconductor, Proxim, and other companies.

Homogeneous environment *n.* A computing milieu, usually within an organisation, in which only one manufacturer's hardware and one manufacturer's software are used.

Homogeneous network *n.* A network on which all the hosts are similar and only one protocol is used.

Honeynet Project *n.* A nonprofit security research group created to collect and analyse data on hacking tools and methods by maintaining a decoy network of computers that is potentially attractive to hackers. The Honeynet Project sets up entire networks of computers in different combinations of operating systems and security to realistically simulate those used in businesses and organisations. Hackers are lured to the network where all inbound and outbound data is captured and contained to help researchers learn about hacker tactics and motives.

Honeypot *n.* A security programme designed to lure and distract a network attacker with decoy data. The honeypot appears to be a system that the intruder would like to crack but which, in reality, is safely separated from the actual network. This allows network administrators to observe attackers and study their activities without the intruders knowing they are being monitored. Honeypot programmes get their name from the "like a bear to honey" metaphor.

Honker *n.* A slang term for a hacker, the term originated in China. The Honker Union of China is an active group of Chinese hackers with nationalistic or hacktivist aims. The Honker Union of China has claimed patriotic motivation for defacing Japanese and U.S. Web sites, hacking U.S. networks, and releasing the Lion worm and other malicious programmes. See also hacktivist, Lion worm.

Hook *n.* A location in a routine or programme in which the programmer can connect or insert other routines for the purpose of debugging or enhancing functionality.

Hop *n.* In data communications, one segment of the path between routers on a geographically dispersed network. A hop is comparable to one "leg" of a journey that includes intervening stops between the starting point and the destination. The distance between each of those stops (routers) would be a communications hop.

Horizontal market *n.* A broad category of business activity, such as accounting or inventory control, that carries across many types of business.

Horizontal market software *n.* Application programmes, such as word processors, that can be used in all types of business, as opposed to those geared for a certain industry.

Horizontal retrace *n.* The movement of the electron beam in a raster-scan video display from the right end of one scan line to the left end (the beginning) of the next. During horizontal retrace, the electron beam is turned off, so the time required for the beam to move is called the horizontal blanking interval. See also blanking.

Horizontal scrolling *n.* A feature of programmes such as word processors and spreadsheets that enables the user to scroll left and right to display information beyond the horizontal limits of the screen (or window, in a graphical user interface).

Horizontal synchronisation *n.* On raster displays, the timing produced by a signal that controls the sweep of the display's electron beam as it moves from left to right and back again to form an image line by line. The horizontal synchronisation signal is usually controlled by a circuit known as a phase-locked loop, which maintains a constant precise frequency so that a clear image is formed.

Host 1 *n.* 1. The main computer in a mainframe or minicomputer environment—that is, the computer to which terminals are connected. 2. In PC-based networks, a computer that provides access to other computers. 3. On the Internet or other large networks, a server computer that has access to other computers on the network. A host computer provides services, such as news, mail, or data, to computers that connect to it.

Host 2 *vb.* To provide services to client computers that connect from remote locations—for example, to offer Internet access or to be the source for a news or mail service.

Host adapter *n.* A device for connecting a peripheral to the main computer, typically in the form of an expansion card. Also called: controller, host bus adapter.

Hosting *n.* The practice of providing computer and communication facilities to businesses or individuals, especially for use in creating Web and electronic commerce sites. A hosting service can provide high-speed access to the Internet, redundant power and data storage, and 24-hour maintenance at lower cost than implementing the same services independently. See also host, virtual hosting.

Host Integration Server *n.* A software application from Microsoft Corporation to allow businesses to integrate existing application, data, and network assets with new business applications and technologies. Host Integration Server preserves a company's existing legacy infrastructure and investments, while providing out-of-the-box development tools that enable integration with client/server and Web networks.

Host language *n.* 1. The machine language of a CPU. 2. A high-level language that is specifically supported by an operating system with its toolbox routines and native development systems.

Host name *n.* The name of a specific server on a specific network within the Internet, leftmost in the complete host specification. For example, www.microsoft.com indicates the server called "www" within the network at Microsoft Corporation.

Host not responding *n.* An error message issued by an Internet client indicating that the computer to which a request has been sent is refusing the connection or is otherwise unavailable to respond to the request.

Host replacement *n.* See rehosting.

Host timed out *n.* An error condition that occurs when a remote system fails to respond within a reasonable amount of time (a few minutes) during an exchange of data over a TCP connection. This condition may mean that the remote system has crashed or been disconnected from the network. The error message the user sees may or may not be phrased in this manner. See also TCP.

Host unreachable *n.* An error condition that occurs when the particular computer to which the user wishes to connect over a TCP/IP network cannot be accessed on its LAN because it is either down or disconnected from the network. The error message the user sees may or may not be phrased in this manner. See also TCP/IP.

Hot *adj.* Of special or urgent interest, or deemed popular.

HotBot *n.* An Internet search engine developed by Inktomi Corporation and HotWired, Inc. Using Slurp, a Web robot, this tool maintains a database of documents that can be matched to key words entered by the user, in a fashion similar to other search engines. HotBot incorporates many workstations in parallel to search and index Web pages. See also spider.

Hot carrier diode *n.* See Schottky diode.

Hot docking *n.* The process of attaching a laptop computer to a docking station while the computer is running, and automatically activating the docking station's video display and other functions. See also docking station, laptop.

Hot insertion *n.* The insertion of a device or card while there is power to the system. Many newer laptops allow for hot insertion of PCMCIA cards. High-end servers may also allow hot insertion to reduce downtimes.

HotJava *n.* A Web browser developed by Sun Microsystems, Inc., that is optimised to run Java applications and applets embedded in Web pages. See also applet, Java, Java applet.

Hot key1 *n.* A keystroke or combination of keystrokes that switches the user to a different programme, often a terminate-and-stay-resident (TSR) programme or the operating system user interface. See also TSR.

Hot key2 *vb.* To transfer to a different programme by pressing a hot key.

Hot link *n.* A connection between two programmes that instructs the second programme to make changes to data when changes occur in the first programme. For example, a word processor or desktop publishing programme could update a document based on information obtained from a database through a hot link. See hyperlink.

Hotlist *n.* A list of frequently accessed items, such as Web pages in a Web browser, from which the user can select one. The hotlist of Web pages is called the bookmark list in Netscape Navigator and Lynx and is called the Favourites folder in Microsoft Internet Explorer.

Hotmail *n.* A Web-based e-mail service launched in 1996 and owned and operated by Microsoft since December 1997. Hotmail provides free e-mail accounts and can be used by anyone with Internet access and Web browsing software.

Hot plugging *n.* A feature that allows equipment to be connected to an active device, such as a computer, while the device is powered on.

Hot-potato routing *n.* A packet routing scheme that relies on keeping data moving, even if it may temporarily move away from its final destination. Also called: deflection routing.

Hot spare *n.* In RAID (redundant array of independent disks) systems, a spare drive in the array that is configured as a backup on which data can be rebuilt in the event that another drive fails. Hot spares are kept on line and do not require operator intervention to be activated. See also RAID.

Hot spot *n.* The position in a mouse pointer, such as the position at the tip of an arrow or the intersection of the lines in a cross, that marks the exact location that will be affected by a mouse action, such as a button press.

Hot swapping *n.* See hot plugging.

HotSync *n.* Software application from Palm that permits data synchronisation between a Palm handheld computing device and another computing device, such as a laptop or personal computer. The synchronisation occurs via a cable connection or wirelessly (for example, via infrared signals).

HotWired *n.* A Web site affiliated with Wired magazine that contains news, gossip, and other information about the culture of the Internet.

Housekeeping *n.* Any of various routines, such as updating the clock or performing garbage collection, designed to keep the system, the environment within which a programme runs, or the data structures within a programme in good working order.

Hover button *n.* Text or an image on a Web page, usually in the form of a button, that changes appearance when a cursor passes over it. The hover button may change colour, blink, display a pop-up with additional information, or produce other similar effects. Hover buttons are usually implemented through ActiveX objects and scripting, although hover behaviour can also be set through HTML attributes.

HPC *n.* See handheld PC.

HPFS *n.* Acronym for High Performance File System. A file system available with OS/2 versions 1.2 and later. See also FAT file system, NTFS.

HPGL *n.* Acronym for Hewlett-Packard Graphics Language. A language originally developed for images destined for plotters. An HPGL file consists of instructions that a programme can use to reconstruct a graphical image.

HPIB *n.* Acronym for Hewlett-Packard Interface Bus. See general-purpose interface bus.

HPPCL *n.* Acronym for Hewlett-Packard Printer Control Language. See Printer Control Language.

HP/UX or HP-UX *n.* Acronym for Hewlett-Packard UNIX. A version of the UNIX operating system specifically designed to be run on Hewlett-Packard's workstations. See also UNIX.

.hqx *n.* A file extension for a file encoded with BinHex. See also BinHex.

HREF *n.* Short for hypertext reference. An attribute in an HTML document that defines a link to another document on the Web. See also HTML.

HSB *n.* Acronym for hue-saturation-brightness. A colour model in which hue is the colour itself as placed on a colour wheel, where 0° is red, 60° is yellow, 120° is green, 180° is cyan, 240° is blue, and 300° is magenta; saturation is the percentage of the specified hue in the colour; and brightness is the percentage of white in the colour. Also called: HLS, HSV, hue. See also colour model.

HSM *n.* Short for Hierarchical Storage Management.. A technology for managing online data and data storage in which the medium on which the information resides is linked to the frequency with which the information is accessed. By migrating data to and from primary (rapidly accessed but expensive) and secondary (slower but less expensive) storage, HSM maintains often-used information on primary storage media and less frequently used data on secondary storage such as tape or an optical jukebox. Although information resides on different storage media, all of it appears to be on line and remains accessible to the user. When users request data residing on secondary storage, HSM moves the information back to the primary storage medium.

HSV *n.* Acronym for hue-saturation-value. See HSB.

H-sync *n.* See horizontal synchronisation.

HTCPCP *n.* Acronym for Hyper Text Coffee Pot Con-trol Protocol. A protocol defined in jest as an April Fools' Day spoof of open Internet standards. HTCPCP/1.0 was proposed in RFC 2324 on April 1, 1998 by Larry Masinter of Xerox PARC. In this RFC, Masinter described a protocol for controlling, monitoring, and diagnosing coffee pots.

.htm *n.* The MS-DOS/Windows 3.x file extension that identifies Hypertext Markup Language (HTML) files, most commonly used as Web pages. Because MS-DOS and Windows 3.x cannot recognise file extensions longer than three letters, the .html extension is truncated to three letters in those environments. See also HTML.

.html *n.* The file extension that identifies Hypertext Markup Language (HTML) files, most commonly used as Web pages. See also HTML.

HTML *n.* Acronym for Hypertext Markup Language. The markup language used for documents on the World Wide Web. A tag-based notation language used to format documents that can then be interpreted and rendered by an Internet browser. HTML is an application of SGML (Standard Generalised Markup Language) that uses tags to mark elements, such as text and graphics, in a document to indicate how Web browsers should display these elements to the user and should respond to user actions such as activation of a link by means of a key press or mouse click. HTML 2, defined by the Internet Engineering Task Force (IETF), included features of HTML common to all Web browsers as of 1994 and was the first version of HTML widely used on the World Wide Web. HTML+ was proposed for extending HTML 2 in 1994, but it was never implemented. HTML 3, which also was never standardised or fully implemented by a major browser developer, introduced tables. HTML 3.2 incorporated features widely implemented as of early 1996, including tables, applets

HTML attribute *n.* A value within an HTML tag that assigns additional properties to the object being defined. Some HTML editing software assigns some attributes automatically when you create an object such as a paragraph or table.

HTML code fragment *n.* HTML code that you add to a Web page to create features such as a script, a counter, or a scrolling marquee. Often used in the context of webrings to add a link and standard graphics or automation to an individual page to indicate membership.

HTML document *n.* A hypertext document that has been coded with HTML. See Web page.

HTML editor *n.* A software programme used to create and modify HTML documents (Web pages). Most HTML editors include a method for inserting HTML tags without actually having to type out each tag. A number of HTML editors will also automatically reformat a document with HTML tags, based on formatting codes used by the word processing programme in which the document was created. See also tag (definition 3), Web page.

HTML extensions *n.* A feature or setting that is an extension to the formal HTML specification. Extensions may not be supported by all Web browsers, but they may be used widely by Web authors. An example of an extension is marquee scrolling text.

HTML page *n.* See Web page.

HTML server control *n.* An ASP.NET server control that belongs to the System.Web.UI.HtmlControls namespace. An HTML server control maps directly to an HTML element and is declared on an ASP.NET page as an HTML element marked by a runat=server attribute. In contrast to Web server controls, HTML server controls do not have an <asp:ControlName> tag prefix. See also Web server control.

HTML source *n.* See source (definition 2).

HTML source file *n.* See source (definition 2).

HTML tag *n.* See tag (definition 3).

HTML validation service *n.* A service used to confirm that a Web page uses valid HTML according to the latest standard and/or that its hyperlinks are valid. An HTML validation service can catch small syntactical errors in HTML coding as well as deviations from the HTML standards. See also HTML.

HTTP *n.* Acronym for Hypertext Transfer Protocol. The protocol used to carry requests from a browser to a Web server and to transport pages from Web servers back to the requesting browser. Although HTTP is almost universally used on the Web, it is not an especially secure protocol.

HTTPd *n.* Acronym for Hypertext Transfer Protocol Daemon. A small, fast HTTP server that was available free from NCSA. HTTPd was the predecessor for Apache. Also called: HTTP Daemon. See also Apache, HTTP server, NCSA (definition 1).

HTTP Daemon *n.* See HTTPd.

HTTP Next Generation *n.* See HTTP-NG.

HTTP-NG *n.* Acronym for Hypertext Transfer Protocol Next Generation. A standard under development by the World Wide Web Consortium (W3C) for improving performance and enabling the addition of features such as security. Whereas the current version of HTTP establishes a connection each time a request is made, HTTP-NG will set up one connection (which consists of separate channels for control information and data) for an entire session between a particular client and a particular server.

HTTPS *n.* 1. Acronym for Hypertext Transfer Protocol Secure. A variation of HTTP that provides for encryption and transmission through a secure port. HTTPS was devised by Netscape and allows HTTP to run over a security mechanism known as SSL (Secure Sockets Layer). See also HTTP, SSL. 2. Web server software for Windows NT. Developed by the European Microsoft Windows NT Academic Centre (EMWAC) at the University of Edinburgh, Scotland, it offers such features as WAIS search capability. See also HTTP server, WAIS.

HTTP server *n.* 1. Server software that uses HTTP to serve up HTML documents and any associated files and scripts when requested by a client, such as a Web browser. The connection between client and server is usually broken after the requested document or file has been served. HTTP servers are used on Web and Intranet sites. Also called: Web server. See also HTML, HTTP, server (definition 2). 2. Any machine on which an HTTP server programme is running.

HTTP status codes *n.* Three-digit codes sent by an HTTP server that indicate the results of a request for data. Codes beginning with 1 respond to requests that the client may not have finished sending; with 2, successful requests; with 3, further action that the client must take; with 4, requests that failed because of client error; and with 5, requests that failed because of server error. See also 400, 401, 402, 403, 404, HTTP.

HTTP streaming *n.* The process of downloading streaming digital media using an HTTP server (a standard Internet server) rather than a server designed specifically to transmit streaming media. HTTP streaming downloads the media file onto a computer, which plays the downloaded file as it becomes available. See also real-time streaming.

Hub *n.* In a network, a device joining communication lines at a central location, providing a common connection to all devices on the network. The term is an analogy to the hub of a wheel. See also active hub, switching hub.

Hue *n.* In the HSB colour model, one of the three characteristics used to describe a colour. Hue is the attribute that most readily distinguishes one colour from other colours. It depends on the frequency of a light wave in the visible spectrum. See also colour model, HSB.

Huffman coding *n.* A method of compressing a given set of data based on the relative frequency of the individual elements. The more often a given element, such as a letter, occurs, the shorter, in bits, is its corresponding code. It was one of the earliest data compression codes and, with modifications, remains one of the most widely used codes for a large variety of message types.

Human engineering *n.* The designing of machines and associated products to suit the needs of humans. See also ergonomics.

Human-machine interface *n.* The boundary at which people make contact with and use machines; when applied to programmes and operating systems, it is more widely known as the user interface.

Hung *adj.* See hang.

Hybrid circuit *n.* A circuit in which fundamentally different types of components are used to perform similar functions, such as a stereo amplifier that uses both tubes and transistors.

Hybrid computer *n.* A computer that contains both digital and analog circuits.

Hybrid microcircuit *n.* A microelectronic circuit that combines individual microminiaturised components and integrated components.

Hybrid network *n.* A network constructed of different topologies, such as ring and star. See also bus network, ring network, star network, Token-Ring network, topology.

Hybris virus *n.* A slow-spreading but persistent self-updating Internet worm first detected in late 2000. The Hybris virus is activated whenever an infected computer is connected to the Internet. It attaches itself to all outgoing e-mail messages, maintains a list of all e-mail addresses in the headers of incoming e-mail messages, and sends copies of itself to all e-mail addresses on the list. Hybris is difficult to eradicate because it updates itself regularly, accessing and downloading updates and plug-ins from anonymous postings to the alt.comp.virus newsgroup. Hybris incorporates downloaded extensions into its code, and it e-mails its modified form to additional potential victims. Hybris often includes a spiral plug-in which produces a spinning disk on top of any active windows on a user's screen.

HyperCard *n.* An information-management software tool, designed for the Apple Macintosh, that implements many hypertext concepts. A HyperCard document consists of a series of cards, collected into a stack. Each card can contain text, graphical images, sound, buttons that enable travel from card to card, and other controls. Programmes and routines can be coded as scripts in an object-oriented language called HyperTalk or developed as external code resources (XCMDs and XFCNs). See also hypertext, object-oriented programming, XCMD, XFCN.

Hyperlink *n.* A connection between an element in a hypertext document, such as a word, a phrase, a symbol, or an image, and a different element in the document, another document, a file, or a script. The user activates the link by clicking on the linked element, which is usually underlined or in a colour different from the rest of the document to indicate that the element is linked. Hyperlinks are indicated in a hypertext document through tags in markup languages such as SGML and HTML. These tags are generally not visible to the user. Also called: hot link, hypertext link, link. See also anchor (definition 2), HTML, hypermedia, hypertext, URL.

Hypermedia *n.* The combination of text, video, graphic images, sound, hyperlinks, and other elements in the form typical of Web documents. Essentially, hypermedia is the modern extension of hypertext, the hyperlinked, text-based documents of the original Internet. Hypermedia attempts to offer a working and learning environment that parallels human thinking—that is, one in which the user can make associations between topics, rather than move sequentially from one to the next, as in an alphabetic list. For example, a hypermedia presentation on navigation might include links to astronomy, bird migration, geography, satellites, and radar. See also hypertext.

Hyperspace *n.* The set of all documents that can be accessed by following hyperlinks in the World Wide Web.

HyperTalk *n.* A programming language used to manipulate HyperCard stacks developed by Apple Computer, Inc. See also HyperCard.

Hypertext *n.* Text linked together in a complex, nonsequential web of associations in which the user can browse through related topics. For example, in an article with the word iron, traveling among the links to iron might lead the user to the periodic table of the elements or a map of the migration of metallurgy in Iron Age Europe. The term hypertext was coined in 1965 to describe documents presented by a computer that express the nonlinear structure of ideas as opposed to the linear format of books, film, and speech. The term hypermedia, more recently introduced, is nearly synonymous but emphasizes the nontextual element, such as animation, recorded sound, and video. See also HyperCard, hypermedia.

Hypertext Transfer Protocol Next Generation *n.* See HTTP-NG.

HyperWave *n.* A World Wide Web server that specialises in database manipulation and multimedia.

Hyphen *n.* A punctuation mark (-) used to break a word between syllables at the end of a line or to separate the parts of a compound word. Word processing programmes with sophisticated hyphenation capabilities recognise three types of hyphens: normal, optional, and nonbreaking. Normal hyphens, also called required or hard hyphens, are part of a word's spelling and are always -visible, as in long-term. Optional hyphens, also called discretionary or soft hyphens, appear only when a word is broken between syllables at the end of a line; they are usually supplied by the word processing programme itself. Nonbreaking hyphens are always visible, like normal hyphens, but they do not allow a line break. See also hyphenation programme.

Hyphenation programme *n.* A programme (often included as part of a word processing application) that introduces optional hyphens at line breaks. A good hyphenation programme will avoid ending more than three lines in a row with hyphens and will prompt the user for confirmation or tag ambiguous breaks, as in the word desert (did the army de-sert in the des-ert?). See also hyphen.

Hysteresis *n.* The tendency of a system, a device, or a circuit to behave differently depending on the direction of change of an input parameter. For example, a household thermostat might turn on at 68 degrees when the house is cooling down, but turn off at 72 degrees when the house is warming up. Hysteresis is important in many devices, especially those employing magnetic fields, such as transformers and read/ write heads.

HYTELNET *n.* A menu-driven index of Internet resources that are accessible via telnet, including library catalogs, databases and bibliographies, bulletin boards, and network information services. HYTELNET can operate through a client programme on a computer connected to the Internet, or through the World Wide Web.

HyTime *n.* Acronym for Hypermedia/Time-based Structuring Language. A markup language standard that describes links within and between documents and hypermedia objects. The standard defines structures and some semantic features, enabling description of traversal and presentation information of objects.

Hz *n.* See hertz.

I

I2L *n.* See integrated injection logic.

I2O *n.* Short for Intelligent Input/Output. A specification for I/O device driver architecture that is independent of both the device being controlled and the host operating system. See also driver, input/output device.

i386 *n.* A family of 32-bit microprocessors developed by Intel. The i386 was introduced in 1985. See also 80386DX.

i486 *n.* A family of 32-bit microprocessors developed by Intel that extended and built upon the capabilities of the i386. The i486 was introduced in 1989. See also i486DX.

i486DX *n.* An Intel microprocessor introduced in 1989. In addition to the features of the 80386 (32-bit registers, 32-bit data bus, and 32-bit addressing), the i486DX has a built-in cache controller, a built-in floating-point coprocessor, provisions for multiprocessing, and a pipelined execution scheme. Also called: 486, 80486. See also pipelining (definition 1).

i486DX2 *n.* An Intel microprocessor introduced in 1992 as an upgrade to certain i486DX processors. The i486DX2 processes data and instructions at twice the system clock frequency. The increased operating speed leads to the generation of much more heat than in an i486DX, so a heat sink is often installed on the chip. Also called: 486DX, 80486. See also heat sink, i486DX, microprocessor.

i486SL *n.* A low-power-consumption version of Intel's i486DX microprocessor designed primarily for laptop computers. The i486SL operates at a voltage of 3.3 volts rather than 5 volts, can shadow memory, and has a System Management Mode

(SMM) in which the microprocessor can slow or halt some system components when the system is not performing CPU-intensive tasks, thus prolonging battery life. See also i486DX, shadow memory.

i486SX *n.* An Intel microprocessor introduced in 1991 as a lower-cost alternative to the i486DX. It runs at slower clock speeds and has no floating-point processor. Also called: 486, 80486. See also 80386DX, 80386SX.

IA-64 *n.* Short for Intel Architecture 64. Intel's 64-bit microprocessor architecture based on EPIC (Explicitly Parallel Instruction Computing) technology. IA-64 is the foundation for the 64-bit Merced chip, as well as future chips to be based on the same architecture. Unlike architectures based on the sequential execution of instructions, IA-64 is designed to implement the parallel execution defined by EPIC technology. It also provides for numerous registers (128 general registers for integer and multimedia operations and 128 floating-point registers) and for grouping instructions in threes as 128-bit bundles. IA-64 architecture also features inherent scalability and compatibility with 32-bit software. See also EPIC, Merced.

IAB *n.* See Internet Architecture Board.

IAC *n.* Acronym for Information Analysis Center. One of several organisations chartered by the U.S. Department of Defense to facilitate the use of existing scientific and technical information. IACs establish and maintain comprehensive knowledge bases, including historical, technical, and scientific data, and also develop and maintain analytical tools and techniques for their use.

IANA *n.* Acronym for Internet Assigned Numbers Authority. The organisation historically responsible for assigning IP (Internet Protocol) addresses and overseeing technical parameters, such as protocol numbers and port numbers, related to the Internet protocol suite. Under the direction of the late Dr. Jon Postel, IANA operated as an arm of the Internet Architecture Board (IAB) of the Internet Society (ISOC) under contract with the U.S. government. However, given the international nature of the Internet, IANA's functions, along with the domain name administration handled by U.S.-based Network Solutions, Inc. (NSI), were privatised in 1998 and turned over to a new, nonprofit organisation known as ICANN (Internet Corporation for Assigned Names and Numbers). See also ICANN, NSI.

I-beam *n.* A mouse cursor used by many applications, such as word processors, when in text-editing mode. The I-beam cursor indicates sections of the document where text can be inserted, deleted, changed, or moved. The cursor is named for its I shape. Also called: I-beam pointer. See also cursor (definition 3), mouse.

I-beam pointer *n.* See I-beam.

IBG *n.* Acronym for inter block gap. See inter-record gap.

IBM AT *n.* A class of personal computers introduced in 1984 and conforming to IBM's PC/AT (Advanced Technology) specification. The first AT was based on the Intel 80286 processor and dramatically outperformed its predecessor, the XT, in speed. See also 80286.

IBM PC *n.* Short for IBM Personal Computer. A class of personal computers introduced in 1981 and conforming to IBM's PC specification. The first PC was based on the Intel 8088 processor. For a number of years, the IBM PC was the de facto standard in the computing industry for PCs, and clones, or PCs that conformed to the IBM specification, have been called PC-compatible. See also PC-compatible, Wintel.

IBM PC/XT *n.* A class of personal computers released by IBM in 1983. XT, Short for eXtended Technology. enabled users to add a wider range of peripherals to their machines than was possible with the original IBM PC. Equipped with a 10-megabyte hard disk drive and one or two 51/4-inch floppy drives, the PC/XT was expandable to 256K of RAM on the motherboard and was loaded with MS-DOS v2.1, which supported directories and subdirectories. The popularity of this machine contributed to the production of what came to be known in the industry as "clones," copies of its design by many manufacturers. See also IBM AT, IBM PC, XT.

IBM PC-compatible *adj.* See PC-compatible.

iBook *n.* A notebook computer introduced by Apple in July 1999. The iBook was intended as a portable version of the iMac and is easily distinguished by its rounded shape and the bright colours of its case. Initial iBook models were powered by a 300-MHz G3 (PowerPC 750) processor and had the capability for wireless networking. See also iMac, PowerPC 750.

IC1 *adj.* Acronym for In Character. Used to refer to events going on within a role-playing game, such as MUD, as opposed to events in real life. It is also used in the context of online chat, e-mail, and newsgroup postings. See also MUD, role-playing game.

IC2 *n.* See integrated circuit.

ICANN *n.* Acronym for Internet Corporation for Assigned Names and Numbers. The private, nonprofit corporation to which the U.S. government in 1998 delegated authority for administering IP (Internet Protocol) addresses, domain names, root servers, and Internet-related technical matters, such as management of protocol parameters (port numbers, protocol numbers, and so on). The successor to IANA (IP address administration) and NSI (domain name registration), ICANN was created to internationalise and privatise Internet management and administration. See also IANA, NSI.

I-CASE *n.* Acronym for Integrated Computer-Aided Software Engineering. Software that performs a wide variety of software engineering functions, such as programme design, coding, and testing parts or all of the completed programme.

ICE *n.* 1. Acronym for Information and Content Exchange. A protocol based on XML (Extensible Markup Language) designed to automate the distribution of syndicated content over the World Wide Web. Based on the concept of content syndicators (distributors) and subscribers (receivers), ICE defines the responsibilities of the parties involved, as well as the format and means of exchanging content so that data can easily be transferred and reused. The protocol has been submitted to the World Wide Web Consortium by Adobe Systems, Inc., CNET, Microsoft, Sun Microsystems, and

Vignette Corporation. It is intended to help in both publishing and inter-business exchanges of content. 2. Acronym for in circuit emulator. A chip used as a stand-in for a microprocessor or a microcontroller. An in-circuit emulator is used to test and debug logic circuits. 3. Acronym for Intrusion Countermeasure Electronics. A fictional type of security software, popularised by science fiction novelist William Gibson, that responds to intruders by at

ICM *n.* See image colour matching.

ICMP *n.* Acronym for Internet Control Message Protocol. A network-layer (ISO/OSI level 3) Internet protocol that provides error correction and other information relevant to IP packet processing. For example, it can let the IP software on one machine inform another machine about an unreachable destination. See also communications protocol, IP, ISO/OSI reference model, packet (definition 1).

Icon *n.* 1. A small image displayed on the screen to represent an object that can be manipulated by the user. By serving as visual mnemonics and allowing the user to control certain computer actions without having to remember commands or type them at the keyboard, icons contribute significantly to the user-friendliness of graphical user interfaces and to PCs in general. See also graphical user interface. 2. A high-level programming language designed to process non-numerical data structures and character strings using a Pascal-like syntax.

Iconic interface *n.* A user interface that is based on icons rather than on typed commands. See also graphical user interface, icon.

Icon parade *n.* The sequence of icons that appears during the boot-up of a Macintosh computer.

ICP *n.* Acronym for Internet Cache Protocol. A networking protocol used by cache servers to locate specific Web objects in neighboring caches. Typically implemented over UDP, ICP also can be used for cache selection. ICP was developed for the Harvest research project at the University of Southern California. It has been implemented in SQUID and other Web proxy caches.

ICQ *n.* A downloadable software programme developed by Mirabilis, and now owned by AOL Time-Warner Inc., that notifies Internet users when friends, family, or other selected users are also on line and allows them to communicate with one another in real time. Through ICQ, users can chat, send e-mail, exchange messages on message boards, and transfer URLs and files, as well as launch third-party programmes, such as games, in which multiple people can participate. Users compile a list of other users with whom they want to communicate. All users must register with the ICQ server and have ICQ software on their computer. The name is a reference to the phrase "I seek you." See also instant messaging.

ICSA *n.* Acronym for International Computer Security Association. An education and information organisation concerned with Internet security issues. Known as the NCSA (National Computer Security Association) until 1997, the ICSA provides security assurance systems and product certification; disseminates computer security information in white papers, books, pamphlets, videos, and other publications; organises consortiums devoted to various security issues; and maintains a Web site that provides updated information on viruses and other computer security topics. Founded in 1987, the ICSA is currently located in Reston, VA.

ID *n.* Acronym for intrusion detection. See IDS.

IDE *n.* 1. Acronym for Integrated Device Electronics. A type of disk-drive interface in which the controller electronics reside on the drive itself, eliminating the need for a separate adapter card. The IDE interface is compatible with the controller used by IBM in the PC/AT computer but offers advantages such as look-ahead caching. 2. See integrated development environment.

Identifier *n.* Any text string used as a label, such as the name of a procedure or a variable in a programme or the name attached to a hard disk or floppy disk.

IDL *n.* Acronym for Interface Definition Language. In object-oriented programming, a language that lets a programme or object written in one language communicate with another programme written in an unknown language. An IDL is used to define interfaces between client and server programmes. For example, an IDL can provide interfaces to remote CORBA objects. See also CORBA, MIDL, object-oriented programming.

Idle *adj.* 1. Operational but not in use. 2. Waiting for a command.

Idle character *n.* In communications, a control character transmitted when no other information is available or ready to be sent. See also SYN.

Idle interrupt *n.* An interrupt that occurs when a device or process becomes idle.

Idle state *n.* The condition in which a device is operating but is not being used.

IDS *n.* Acronym for intrusion-detection system. A type of security management system for computers and networks that gathers and analyses information from various areas within a computer or a network to identify possible security breaches, both inside and outside the organisation. An IDS can detect a wide range of hostile attack signatures, generate alarms, and, in some cases, cause routers to terminate communications from hostile sources. Also called: intrusion detection.

IDSL *n.* Acronym for Internet digital subscriber line. A high-speed digital communications service that provides Internet access as fast as 1.1 Mbps (megabits per second) over standard telephone lines. IDSL uses a hybrid of ISDN and digital subscriber line technology. See also digital subscriber line, ISDN.

IE *n.* Acronym for information engineering. A methodology for developing and maintaining information-processing systems, including computer systems and networks, within an organisation.

IEEE *n.* Acronym for Institute of Electrical and Electronics Engineers. A society of engineering and electronics professionals based in the United States but boasting membership from numerous other countries. The IEEE (pronounced "eye triple ee") focuses on electrical, electronics, computer engineering, and science-related matters.

IEEE 1284 *n.* The IEEE standard for high-speed signaling through a bidirectional parallel computer interface. A computer that is compliant with the IEEE 1284 standard can communicate through its parallel port in five modes: outbound data transfer to a printer or similar device ("Centronics" mode), inbound transfer 4 (nibble mode) or 8 (byte mode) bits at a time, bidirectional Enhanced Parallel Ports (EPP) used by storage devices and other nonprinter peripherals, and Enhanced Capabilities Ports (ECP) used for bidirectional communication with a printer. See also Centronics parallel interface, ECP, enhanced parallel port.

IEEE 1394 *n.* A nonproprietary, high-speed, serial bus input/output standard. IEEE 1394 provides a means of connecting digital devices, including personal computers and consumer electronics hardware. It is platform-independent, scalable (expandable), and flexible in supporting peer-to-peer (roughly, device-to-device) connections. IEEE 1394 preserves data integrity by eliminating the need to convert digital signals into analog signals. Created for desktop networks by Apple Computer and later developed by the IEEE 1394 working group, it is considered a low-cost interface for devices such as digital cameras, camcorders, and multimedia devices and is seen as a means of integrating personal computers and home electronics equipment. FireWire is the proprietary implementation of the standard by Apple Computer. See also analog data, IEEE.

IEEE 1394 connector *n.* A type of connector that enables you to connect and disconnect high-speed serial devices. An IEEE 1394 connector is usually on the back of your computer near the serial port or the parallel port. The IEEE 1394 bus is used primarily to connect high-end digital video and audio devices to your computer; however, some hard disks, printers, scanners, and DVD drives can also be connected to your computer using the IEEE 1394 connector.

IEEE 1394 port *n.* A 4- or 6-pin port that supports the IEEE 1394 standard and can provide direct connections between digital consumer electronics and computers. See also IEEE 1394.

IEEE 488 *n.* The electrical definition of the General-Purpose Interface Bus (GPIB), specifying the data and control lines and the voltage and current levels for the bus. See also General-Purpose Interface Bus.

IEEE 696/S-100 *n.* The electrical definition of the S-100 bus, used in early personal computer systems that used microprocessors such as the 8080, Z-80, and 6800. The S 100 bus, based on the architecture of the Altair 8800, was extremely popular with early computer enthusiasts because it permitted installation of a wide range of expansion boards. See also Altair 8800, S-100 bus.

IEEE 802.x *n.* A series of networking specifications developed by the IEEE. The x following 802 is a placeholder for individual specifications. The IEEE 802.x specifications correspond to the physical and data-link layers of the ISO/OSI reference model, but they divide the data-link layer into two sublayers. The logical link control (LLC) sublayer applies to all IEEE 802.x specifications and covers station-to-station connections, generation of message frames, and error control. The media access control (MAC) sublayer, dealing with network access and collision detection, differs from one IEEE 802 standard to another. IEEE 802.3 is used for bus networks that use CSMA/CD, both broadband and baseband, and the baseband version is based on the Ethernet standard. IEEE 802.4 is used for bus networks that use token passing, and IEEE 802.5 is used for ring networks that use token passing (token ring networks).

IEEE 802.11 *n.* The Institute of Electrical and Electronics Engineers' (IEEE) specifications for wireless networking. These specifications, which include 802.11, 802.11a, 802.11b, and 802.11g, allow computers, printers, and other devices to communicate over a wireless local area network (LAN).

IEEE printer cable *n.* A cable used to connect a printer to a PC's parallel port that adheres to the IEEE 1284. See also IEEE 1284.

IEPG *n.* Acronym for Internet Engineering and Planning Group. A collaborative group of Internet service providers whose goal is to promote the Internet and coordinate technical efforts on it.

IESG *n.* See Internet Engineering Steering Group.

IETF *n.* Acronym for Internet Engineering Task Force. A worldwide organisation of individuals interested in networking and the Internet. Managed by the IESG (Internet Engineering Steering Group), the IETF is charged with studying technical problems facing the Internet and proposing solutions to the Internet Architecture Board (IAB). The work of the IETF is carried out by various Working Groups that concentrate on specific topics, such as routing and security. The IETF is the publisher of the specifications that led to the TCP/IP protocol standard. See also Internet Engineering Steering Group.

IFC *n.* See Internet Foundation Classes.

.iff *n.* The file extension that identifies files in the IFF (Interchange File Format) format. IFF was most commonly used on the Amiga platform, where it constituted almost any kind of data. On other platforms, IFF is mostly used to store image and sound files.

IFF *n.* Acronym for Interchange File Format. See .iff.

IFIP *n.* Acronym for International Federation of Information Processing. An organisation of societies, representing over 40 member nations, that serves information-processing professionals. The United States is represented by the Federation on Computing in the United States (FOCUS). See also AFIPS, FOCUS.

IFS *n.* See Installable File System Manager.

IF statement *n.* A control statement that executes a block of code if a Boolean expression evaluates to true. Most programming languages also support an ELSE clause, which specifies code that is to be executed only if the Boolean expression evaluates to false. See also conditional.

IGRP *n.* Acronym for Interior Gateway Routing Protocol. A protocol developed by Cisco Systems that allows coordination between the routing of a number of gateways. Goals of IGRP include stable routing in large networks, fast response to changes in network topology, and low overhead. See also communications protocol, gateway, topology.

IIA *n.* See SIIA.

IIL *n.* See integrated injection logic.

IIOP *n.* Acronym for Internet Inter-ORB Protocol. A networking protocol that enables distributed programmes written in different programming languages to communicate over the Internet. IIOP, a specialised mapping in the General Inter-ORB Protocol (GIOP) based on a client/server model, is a critical part of CORBA. See also CORBA.

IIS *n.* See Internet Information Server.

ILEC *n.* Acronym for Incumbent Local Exchange Carrier. A telephone company that provides local service to its customers.

Illegal *adj.* Not allowed, or leading to invalid results. For example, an illegal character in a word processing programme would be one that the programme cannot recognize; an illegal operation might be impossible for a programme or system because of built-in constraints.

Illuminance *n.* 1. The amount of light falling on, or illuminating, a surface area. 2. A measure of illumination (such as watts per square meter) used in reference to devices such as televisions and computer displays.

IM *n.* See instant messaging.

iMac *n.* A family of Apple Macintosh computers introduced in 1998. Designed for nontechnical users, the iMac has a case that contains both the CPU and the monitor and is available in several bright colours. The "i" in iMac stands for Internet; the iMac was designed to make setting up an Internet connection extremely simple. The first version of the iMac included a 266-MHz PowerPC processor, a 66-MHz system bus, a hard drive, a CD-ROM drive, and a 15-inch monitor, with a translucent blue case. Later iMacs came with faster processors and a choice of case colours. See the illustration. See also Macintosh.

.image *n.* A file extension for a Macintosh Disk Image, a storage type often used on Apple's FTP software download sites.

Image *n.* 1. A stored description of a graphic picture, either as a set of brightness and colour values of pixels or as a set of instructions for reproducing the picture. See also bit map, pixel map. 2. A duplicate, copy, or representation of all or part of a hard or floppy disk, a section of memory or hard drive, a file, a programme, or data. For example, a RAM disk can hold an image of all or part of a disk in main memory; a virtual RAM programme can create an image of some portion of the computer's main memory on disk. See also RAM disk.

Image-based rendering *n.* See immersive imaging.

Image colour matching *n.* The process of image output correction to match the same colours that were scanned or input.

Image compression *n.* The use of a data compression technique on a graphical image. Uncompressed graphics files tend to use up large amounts of storage, so image compression is useful to conserve space. See also compressed file, data compression, video compression.

Image compression dialog component *n.* An application programming interface that sets parameters for compressing images and image sequences in QuickTime, a technology from Apple for creating, editing, publishing, and viewing multimedia content. The component displays a dialog box as a user interface, validates and stores the settings selected in the dialog box, and oversees the compression of the image or images based on the selected criteria.

Image Compression Manager *n.* A major software component used in QuickTime, a technology from Apple for creating, editing, publishing, and viewing multimedia content. The Image Compression Manager is an interface that provides image-compression and image-decompression services to applications and other managers. Because the Image Compression Manager is independent of specific compression algorithms and drivers, it can present a common application interface for software-based compressors and hardware-based compressors and offer compression options so that it or its application can use the appropriate tool for a particular situation. See also QuickTime.

Image compressor component *n.* A software component used by the Image Compression Manager to compress image data in

QuickTime, a technology from Apple for creating, editing, publishing, and viewing multimedia content. See also Image Compression Manager, QuickTime.

Image decompressor component *n.* A software component used by the Image Compression Manager to decompress image data in QuickTime, a technology from Apple for creating, editing, publishing, and viewing multimedia content. See also Image Compression Manager, QuickTime.

Image editing *n.* The process of changing or modifying a bitmapped image, usually with an image editor.

Image editor *n.* An application programme that allows users to modify the appearance of a bitmapped image, such as a scanned photo, by using filters and other functions. Creation of new images is generally accomplished in a paint or drawing programme. See also bitmapped graphics, filter (definition 4), paint programme.

Image enhancement *n.* The process of improving the quality of a graphic image, either automatically by software or manually by a user through a paint or drawing programme. See also anti-aliasing, image processing.

Image map *n.* An image that contains more than one hyperlink on a Web page. Clicking different parts of the image links the user to other resources on another part of the Web page or a different Web page or in a file. Often an image map, which can be a photograph, drawing, or a composite of several different drawings or photographs, is used as a map to the resources found on a particular Web site. Older Web browsers support only server-side image maps, which are executed on a Web server through CGI script. However, most newer Web browsers (Netscape Navigator 2.0 and higher and Internet Explorer 3.0 and higher) support client-side image maps, which are executed in a user's Web browser. Also called: clickable maps. See also CGI script, hyperlink, Web page.

Image processing *n.* The analysis, manipulation, storage, and display of graphical images from sources such as photographs, drawings, and video. Image processing spans a sequence of three steps. The input step (image capture and digitizing) converts the differences in colouring and shading in the picture into binary values that a computer can process. The processing step can include image enhancement and data compression. The output step consists of the display or printing of the processed image. Image processing is used in such applications as television and film, medicine, satellite weather mapping, machine vision, and computer-based pattern recognition. See also image enhancement, video digitizer.

Image sensor *n.* A light-sensitive integrated circuit or group of integrated circuits used in scanners, digital cameras, and video cameras.

Imagesetter *n.* A typesetting device that can transfer camera-ready text and artwork from computer files directly onto paper or film. Imagesetters print at high resolution (commonly above 1000 dpi) and are usually PostScript-compatible.

Image transcoder component *n.* A component that transfers compressed images from one file format to another in QuickTime, a technology developed by Apple for creating, editing, publishing, and viewing multimedia content.

Imaginary number *n.* A number that must be expressed as the product of a real number and i, where i 2 = –1. The sum of an imaginary number and a real number is a complex number. Although imaginary numbers are not directly encountered in the universe (as in "1.544 i megabits per second"), some pairs of quantities, especially in electrical engineering, behave mathematically like the real and imaginary parts of complex numbers.

Iimaging *n.* The processes involved in the capture, storage, display, and printing of graphical images.

IMAP4 *n.* Acronym for Internet Message Access Protocol 4. The latest version of IMAP, a method for an e-mail programme to gain access to e-mail and bulletin board messages stored on a mail server. Unlike POP3, a similar protocol, IMAP allows a user to retrieve messages efficiently from more than one computer.

IMC *n.* See Internet Mail Consortium.

IMHO *n.* Acronym for in my humble opinion. IMHO, used in e-mail and in online forums, flags a statement that the writer wants to present as a personal opinion rather than as a statement of fact. See also IMO.

Imitation Game *n.* See Turing test.

Immediate access *n.* See direct access, random access.

Immediate operand *n.* A data value, used in the execution of an assembly language instruction, that is contained in the instruction itself rather than pointed to by an address in the instruction.

Immediate printing *n.* A process in which text and printing commands are sent directly to the printer without being stored as a printing file and without the use of an intermediate page-composition procedure or a file containing printer setup commands.

Immersive imaging *n.* A method of presenting photographic images on a computer by using virtual reality techniques. A common immersive image technique puts the user in the center of the view. The user can pan 360 degrees within the image and can zoom in and out. Another technique puts an object in the center of the view and allows the user to rotate around the object to examine it from any perspective. Immersive imaging techniques can be used to provide virtual reality experiences without equipment such as a headpiece and goggles. Also called: image-based rendering. See also imaging, virtual reality.

IMO *n.* Acronym for in my opinion. A shorthand phrase used often in e-mail and Internet news and discussion groups to indicate an author's admission that a statement he or she has just made is a matter of judgment rather than fact. See also IMHO.

Impact printer *n.* A printer, such as a wire-pin dot-matrix printer or a daisy-wheel printer, that drives an inked ribbon mechanically against the paper to form marks. See also daisy-wheel printer, dot-matrix printer.

Impedance *n.* Opposition to the flow of alternating current. Impedance has two aspects: resistance, which impedes both direct and alternating current and is always greater than zero; and reactance, which impedes alternating current only, varies with frequency, and can be positive or negative. See also resistance.

Implementor *n.* In role-playing games, the administrator, coder, or developer of the game. Also called: Imp. See also role-playing game.

Import *vb.* To bring information from one system or programme into another. The system or programme receiving the data must somehow support the internal format or structure of the data. Conventions such as the TIFF (Tagged Image File Format) and PICT formats (for graphics files) make importing easier. See also PICT, TIFF.

IMT-2000 *n.* See International Mobile Telecommunications for the Year 2000.

Inactive window *n.* In an environment capable of displaying multiple onscreen windows, any window other than the one currently being used for work. An inactive window can be partially or entirely hidden behind another window, and it remains inactive until the user selects it.

In-band signaling *n.* Transmission within the voice or data-handling frequencies of a communication channel.

In-betweening *n.* See tween.

Inbox *n.* In many e-mail applications, the default mailbox where the programme stores incoming messages. See also e-mail, mailbox.

Incident light *n.* The light that strikes a surface in computer graphics. See also illuminance.

In-circuit emulator *n.* See ICE (definition 2).

INCLUDE directive *n.* A statement within a source-code file that causes another source-code file to be read in at that spot, either during compilation or during execution. It enables a programmer to break up a programme into smaller files and enables multiple programmes to use the same files.

Inclusive OR *n.* See OR.

Increment 1 *n.* A scalar or unit amount by which the value of an object such as a number, a pointer within an array, or a screen position designation is increased.

Increment 2 *vb.* To increase a number by a given amount. For example, if a variable has the value 10 and is incremented successively by 2, it takes the values 12, 14, 16, 18, and so on.

Indent 1 *n.* 1. Displacement of the left or right edge of a block of text in relation to the margin or to other blocks of text. 2. Displacement of the beginning of the first line of a paragraph relative to the other lines in the paragraph.

Indent 2 *vb.* To displace the left or right edge of a text item, such as a block or a line, relative to the margin or to another text item.

Indeo *n.* A codec technology developed by Intel for compressing digital video files. See also codec.

Independent content provider *n.* A business or organisation that supplies information to an online information service, such as America Online, for resale to the information service's customers. See also online information service.

Independent software vendor *n.* A third-party software developer; an individual or an organisation that independently creates computer software. Acronym: ISV.

Index 1 *n.* 1. A listing of keywords and associated data that point to the location of more comprehensive information, such as files and records on a disk or record keys in a database. 2. In programming, a scalar value that allows direct access into a multi-element data structure such as an array without the need for a sequential search through the collection of elements. See also array, element (definition 1), hash, list.

Index 2 *vb.* 1. In data storage and retrieval, to create and use a list or table that contains reference information pointing to stored data. 2. In a database, to find data by using keys such as words or field names to locate records. 3. In indexed file storage, to find files stored on disk by using an index of file locations (addresses). 4. In programming and information processing, to locate information stored in a table by adding an offset amount, called the index, to the base address of the table.

Indexed address *n.* The location in memory of a particular item of data within a collection of items, such as an entry in a table. An indexed address is calculated by starting with a base address and adding to it a value stored in a register called an index register.

Indexed search *n.* A search for an item of data that uses an index to reduce the amount of time required.

Indexed sequential access method *n.* A scheme for decreasing the time necessary to locate a data record within a large database, given a key value that identifies the record. A smaller index file is used to store the keys along with pointers that locate the corresponding records in the large main database file. Given a key, first the index file is searched for the key and then the associated pointer is used to access the remaining data of the record in the main file. Acronym: ISAM.

Index hole *n.* The small, round hole near the large, round spindle opening at the center of a 5.25-inch floppy disk. The index hole marks the location of the first data sector, enabling a computer to synchronise its read/write operations with the disk's rotation.

Indexing Service Query Language *n.* A query language available in addition to SQL for the Indexing Service in Windows 2000. Formerly known as Index Server, its original function was to index the content of Internet Information Services (IIS) Web servers. Indexing Service now creates indexed catalogs for the contents and properties of both file systems and virtual Webs.

Index mark *n.* 1. A magnetic indicator signal placed on a soft-sectored disk during formatting to mark the logical start of each track. 2. A visual information locator, such as a line, on a microfiche.

Indicator *n.* A dial or light that displays information about the status of a device, such as a light connected to a disk drive that glows when the disk is being accessed.

Indirect address *n.* See relative address.

Inductance *n.* The ability to store energy in the form of a magnetic field. Any length of wire has some inductance, and coiling the wire, especially around a ferromagnetic core, increases the inductance. The unit of inductance is the henry.

Induction *n.* The creation of a voltage or current in a material by means of electric or magnetic fields, as in the secondary winding of a transformer when exposed to the changing magnetic field caused by an alternating current in the primary winding. See also impedance.

Inductor *n.* A component designed to have a specific amount of inductance. An inductor passes direct current but impedes alternating current to a degree dependent on its frequency. An inductor usually consists of a length of wire coiled in a cylindrical or toroidal (doughnut-shaped) form, sometimes with a ferromagnetic core. See the illustration. Also called: choke.

Industry Standard Architecture *n.* See ISA.

INET *n.* 1. Short for Internet. 2. An annual conference held by the Internet Society.

.inf *n.* The file extension for device information files, those files containing scripts used to control hardware operations.

Infection *n.* The presence of a virus or Trojan horse in a computer system. See also Trojan horse, virus, worm.

Infer *vb.* To formulate a conclusion based on specific information, either by applying the rules of formal logic or by generalising from a set of observations. For example, from the facts that canaries are birds and birds have feathers, one can infer (draw the inference) that canaries have feathers.

Inference engine *n.* The processing portion of an expert system. It matches input propositions with facts and rules contained in a knowledge base and then derives a conclusion, on which the expert system then acts.

Inference programming *n.* A method of programming (as in Prolog) in which programmes yield results based on logical inference from a set of facts and rules. See also Prolog.

Infinite loop *n.* 1. A loop that, because of semantic or logic errors, can never terminate through normal means. 2. A loop that is intentionally written with no explicit termination condition but will terminate as a result of side effects or direct intervention. See also loop1 (definition 1), side effect.

Infix notation *n.* A notation, used for writing expressions, in which binary operators appear between their arguments, as in 2 + 4. Unary operators usually appear before their arguments, as in –1. See also operator precedence, postfix notation, prefix notation, unary operator.

.info *n.* One of seven new top-level domain names approved in 2001 by the Internet Corporation for Assigned Names and Numbers (ICANN). Unlike the other new domain names, which focus on specific types of Web sites, .info is meant for unrestricted use.

Infobahn *n.* The Internet. Infobahn is a mixture of the terms information and Autobahn, a German highway known for the high speeds at which drivers can legally travel. Also called: Information Highway, Information Superhighway, the Net.

Infomediary *n.* A term created from the phrase information intermediary. A service provider that positions itself between buyers and sellers, collecting, organising, and distributing focused information that improves the interaction of consumer and online business.

Information *n.* The meaning of data as it is intended to be interpreted by people. Data consists of facts, which become information when they are seen in context and convey meaning to people. Computers process data without any understanding of what the data represents.

Information Analysis Center *n.* See IAC.

Information and Content Exchange *n.* See ICE (definition 1).

Information appliance *n.* A specialised computer designed to perform a limited number of functions and, especially, to provide access to the Internet. Although devices such as electronic address books or appointment calendars might be considered information appliances, the term is more typically used for devices that are less expensive and less capable than a fully functional personal computer. Set-top boxes are a current example; other devices, envisioned for the future, would include network-aware microwaves, refrigerators, watches, and the like. Also called: appliance.

Information center *n.* 1. A large computer center and its associated offices; the hub of an information management and dispersal facility in an organisation. 2. A specialised type of computer system dedicated to information retrieval and decision-support functions. The information in such a system is usually read-only and consists of data extracted or downloaded from other production systems.

Information engineering *n.* See IE (definition 1).

Information explosion *n.* 1. The current period in human history, in which the possession and dissemination of information has supplanted mechanisation or industrialisation as a driving force in society. 2. The rapid growth in the amount of information available today. Also called: information revolution.

Information hiding *n.* A design practice in which implementation details for both data structures and algorithms within a module or subroutine are hidden from routines using that module or subroutine, so as to ensure that those routines do not depend on some particular detail of the implementation. In theory, information hiding allows the module or subroutine to be changed without breaking the routines that use it. See also break, module, routine, subroutine.

Information Highway or information highway *n.* See Information Superhighway.

Information Industry Association *n.* See SIIA.

Information kiosk *n.* See kiosk.

Information management *n.* The process of defining, evaluating, safeguarding, and distributing data within an organisation or a system.

Information packet *n.* See packet (definition 1).

Information processing *n.* The acquisition, storage, manipulation, and presentation of data, particularly by electronic means.

Information resource management *n.* The process of managing the resources for the collection, storage, and manipulation of data within an organisation or system.

Information retrieval *n.* The process of finding, organising, and displaying information, particularly by electronic means.

Information revolution *n.* See information explosion.

Information science *n.* The study of how information is collected, organised, handled, and communicated. See also information theory.

Information Services *n.* The formal name for a company's data processing department. Acronym: IS. Also called: Data Processing, Information Processing, Information Systems, Information Technology, Management Information Services, Management Information Systems.

Information Superhighway *n.* The existing Internet and its general infrastructure, including private networks, online services, and so on. See also National Information Infrastructure.

Information Technology Industry Council *n.* Trade organisation of the information technology industry. The council promotes the interests of the information technology industry and compiles information on computers, software, telecommunications, business equipment, and other topics related to information technology. Acronym: ITIC.

Information theory *n.* A mathematical discipline founded in 1948 that deals with the characteristics and the transmission of information. Information theory was originally applied to communications engineering but has proved relevant to other fields, including computing. It focuses on such aspects of communication as amount of data, transmission rate, channel capacity, and accuracy of transmission, whether over cables or within society.

Information warehouse *n.* The total of an organisation's data resources on all computers.

Information warfare *n.* Attacks on the computer operations on which an enemy country's economic life or safety depends. Possible examples of information warfare include crashing air traffic control systems or massively corrupting stock exchange records.

Infoseek *n.* A Web search site that provides full-text results for user searches plus categorised lists of related sites. InfoSeek is powered by the Ultraseek search engine and searches Web pages, Usenet newsgroups, and FTP and Gopher sites.

Infrared *adj.* Having a frequency in the electromagnetic spectrum in the range just below that of red light. Objects radiate infrared in proportion to their temperature. Infrared radiation is traditionally divided into four somewhat arbitrary categories based on its wavelength. See the table. Acronym: IR.

Table I.1 Infrared Radiation Categories.

near infrared	750–1500 nanometers (nm)
middle infrared	1500–6000 nm
far infrared	6000–40,000 nm
far-far infrared	40,000 nm–1 millimeter (mm)

Infrared Data Association *n.* See IrDA.

Infrared device *n.* A computer, or a computer peripheral such as a printer, that can communicate by using infrared light. See also infrared.

Infrared file transfer *n.* Wireless file transfer between a computer and another computer or device using infrared light. See also infrared.

Infrared network connection *n.* A direct or incoming network connection to a remote access server using an infrared port. See also infrared port.

Infrared port *n.* An optical port on a computer for interfacing with an infrared-capable device. Communication is achieved without physical connection through cables. Infrared ports can be found on some laptops, notebooks, and printers. See also cable, infrared, port.

Inherent error *n.* An error in assumptions, design, logic, algorithms, or any combination thereof that causes a programme to work improperly, regardless of how well written it is. For example, a serial communications programme that is written to use a parallel port contains an inherent error. See also logic, semantics (definition 1), syntax.

Inherit *vb.* To acquire the characteristics of another class, in object-oriented programming. The inherited characteristics may be enhanced, restricted, or modified. See also class.

Inheritance *n.* 1. The transfer of the characteristics of a class in object-oriented programming to other classes derived from it. For example, if "vegetable" is a class, the classes "legume" and "root" can be derived from it, and each will inherit the properties of the "vegetable" class: name, growing season, and so on. See also class, object-oriented programming. 2. The transfer of certain properties, such as open files, from a parent programme or process to another programme or process that the parent causes to run. See also child (definition 1).

Inheritance code *n.* A set of structural and procedural attributes belonging to an object that has been passed on to it by the class or object from which it was derived. See also object-oriented programming.

Inhibit *vb.* To prevent an occurrence. For example, to inhibit interrupts from an external device means to prevent the external device from sending any interrupts.

.ini *n.* In MS-DOS and Windows 3.x, the file extension that identifies an initialisation file, which contains user preferences and startup information about an application programme.

Ini file *n.* Short for initialisation file, a text file containing information about the initial configuration of Windows and Windows-based applications, such as default settings for fonts, margins, and line spacing. Two ini files, win.ini and system.ini, are required to run the Windows operating system through version 3.1. In later versions of Windows, ini files are replaced by a database known as the registry. In addition to Windows itself, many older applications create their own ini files. Because they are composed only of text, ini files can be edited in any text editor or word processor to change information about the application or user preferences. All initialisation files bear the extension .ini. See also configuration, configuration file, registry, system.ini, win.ini.

INIT *n.* On older Macintosh computers, a system extension that is loaded into memory at startup time. See also extension (definition 4).

Initial Graphics Exchange Specification *n.* A standard file format for computer graphics, supported by the American National Standards Institute (ANSI), that is particularly suitable for describing models created with computer-aided design (CAD) programmes. It includes a wide variety of basic geometric forms (primitives) and, in keeping with CAD objectives, offers methods for describing and annotating drawings and engineering diagrams. Acronym: IGES. See also ANSI.

Initialisation *n.* The process of assigning initial values to variables and data structures in a programme.

Initialisation file *n.* See ini file.

Initialisation string *n.* A sequence of commands sent to a device, especially a modem, to configure it and prepare it for use. In the case of a modem, the initialisation string consists of a string of characters.

Initialise *vb.* 1. To prepare a storage medium, such as a disk or a tape, for use. This may involve testing the medium's surface, writing startup information, and setting up the file system's index to storage locations. 2. To assign a beginning value to a variable. 3. To start up a computer. See also cold boot, startup.

Initializer *n.* An expression whose value is the first (initial) value of a variable. See also expression.

Initial programme load *n.* The process of copying an operating system into memory when a system is booted. Acronym: IPL. See also boot, startup.

Initiator *n.* The device in a SCSI connection that issues commands. The device that receives the commands is the target. See also SCSI, target.

Ink cartridge *n.* A disposable module that contains ink and is typically used in an ink-jet printer. See also ink-jet printer.

Ink-jet printer or inkjet printer *n.* A nonimpact printer in which liquid ink is vibrated or heated into a mist and sprayed through tiny holes in the print head to form characters or graphics on the paper. Ink-jet printers are competitive with some laser printers in price and print quality if not in speed. However, the ink, which must be highly soluble to avoid clogging the nozzles in the print head, produces fuzzy-looking output on some papers and smears if touched or dampened shortly after printing. See also nonimpact printer, print head.

Inline *adj.* 1. In programming, referring to a function call replaced with an instance of the function's body. Actual arguments are substituted for formal parameters. An inline function is usually done as a compile-time transformation to increase the efficiency of the programme. Also called: unfold, unroll. 2. In HTML code, referring to graphics displayed along with HTML-formatted text. Inline images placed in the line of HTML text use the tag <IMG>. Text within an inline image can be aligned to the top, bottom, or middle of a specific image.

Inline code *n.* Assembly language or machine language instructions embedded within high-level source code. The form it takes varies considerably from compiler to compiler, if it is supported at all.

Inline discussion *n.* Discussion comments that are associated with a document as a whole or with a particular paragraph, image, or table of a document. In Web browsers, inline discussions are displayed in the body of the document; in word-processing programmes, they are usually displayed in a separate discussion or comments pane.

Inline graphics *n.* Graphics files that are embedded in an HTML document or Web page and viewable by a Web browser or other programme that recognises HTML. By avoiding the need for separate file opening operations, inline graphics can speed the access and loading of an HTML document. Also called: inline image.

Inline image *n.* An image that is embedded within the text of a document. Inline images are common on Web pages. See also inline graphics.

Inline processing *n.* Operation on a segment of low-level programme code, called inline code, to optimise execution speed or storage requirements. See also inline code.

Inline stylesheet *n.* A stylesheet included within an HTML document. Because an inline stylesheet is directly associated with an individual document, any changes made to that document's appearance will not affect the appearance of other Web site documents.

Inline subroutine *n.* A subroutine whose code is copied at each place in a programme at which it is called, rather than kept in one place to which execution is transferred. Inline subroutines improve execution speed, but they also increase code size. Inline subroutines obey the same syntactical and semantic rules as ordinary subroutines.

Inmarsat *n.* Acronym for International Maritime Satellite. Organisation based in London, England, that operates satellites for international mobile telecommunications services in more than 80 nations. Inmarsat provides services for maritime, aviation, and land use.

Inner join *n.* An operator in relational algebra, often implemented in database management. The inner join produces a relation (table) that contains all possible ordered concatenations (joinings) of records from two existing tables that meet certain specified criteria on the data values. It is thus equivalent to a product followed by a select applied to the resulting table.

Inoculate *vb.* To protect a programme against virus infection by recording characteristic information about it. For example, checksums on the code can be recomputed and compared with the stored original checksums each time the programme is run; if any have changed, the programme file is corrupt and may be infected. See also checksum, virus.

Input 1 *n.* Information entered into a computer or programme for processing, as from a keyboard or from a file stored on a disk drive.

Input 2 *vb.* To enter information into a computer for processing.

Input area *n.* See input buffer.

Input-bound *adj.* See input/output-bound.

Input buffer *n.* A portion of computer memory set aside for temporary storage of information arriving for processing. See also buffer1.

Input channel *n.* See input/output channel.

Input device *n.* A peripheral device whose purpose is to allow the user to provide input to a computer system. Examples of input devices are keyboards, mice, joysticks, and styluses. See also peripheral.

Input driver *n.* See device driver.

Input language *n.* 1. A language to be inputted into the system through the keyboard, a speech-to-text converter, or an Input Method Editor (IME). 2. In Microsoft Windows XP, a Regional and Language Options setting that specifies the combination of the language being entered and the keyboard layout, IME, speech-to-text converter, or other device being used to enter it. This setting was formerly known as input locale.

Input Method Editor *n.* Programmes used to enter the thousands of different characters in written Asian languages with a standard 101-key keyboard. An IME consists of both an engine that converts keystrokes into phonetic and ideograph characters and a dictionary of commonly used ideographic words. As the user enters keystrokes, the IME engine attempts to identify which character or characters the keystrokes should be converted into. Acronym: IME.

Input/output *n.* The complementary tasks of gathering data for a computer or a programme to work with, and of making the results of the computer's activities available to the user or to other computer processes. Gathering data is usually done with input devices such as the keyboard and the mouse, while the output is usually made available to the user via the display and the printer. Other data resources, such as disk files and communications ports for the computer, can serve as either input or output devices. Acronym: I/O.

Input/output area *n.* See input/output buffer.

Input/output-bound *adj.* Characterised by the need to spend lengthy amounts of time waiting for input and output of data that is processed much more rapidly. For example, if the processor is capable of making rapid changes to a large database stored on a disk faster than the drive mechanism can perform the read and write operations, the computer is input/output-bound. A computer may be just input-bound or just output-bound if only input or only output limits the speed at which the processor accepts and processes data. Also called: I/O-bound.

Input/output buffer *n.* A portion of computer memory reserved for temporary storage of incoming and outgoing data. Because input/output devices can often write to a buffer without intervention from the CPU, a programme can continue execution while the buffer fills, thus speeding programme execution. See also buffer1.

Input/output bus *n.* A hardware path used inside a computer for transferring information to and from the processor and various input and output devices. See also bus.

Input/output channel *n.* A hardware path from the CPU to the input/output bus. See also bus.

Input/output controller *n.* Circuitry that monitors operations and performs tasks related to receiving input and transferring output at an input or output device or port, thus providing the processor with a consistent means of communication (input/output interface) with the device and also freeing the processor's time for other work. For example, when a read or write operation is performed on a disk, the drive's controller carries out the high-speed, electronically sophisticated tasks involved in positioning the read-write heads, locating specific storage areas on the spinning disk, reading from and writing to the disk surface, and even checking for errors. Most controllers require software that enables the computer to receive and process the data the controller makes available. Also called: device controller, I/O controller.

Input/output device *n.* A piece of hardware that can be used both for providing data to a computer and for receiving data from it, depending on the current situation. A disk drive is an example of an input/output device. Some devices, such as a keyboard or a mouse, can be used only for input and are thus called input (input-only) devices. Other devices, such as printers, can be used only for output and are thus called output (output-only) devices. Most devices require installation of software routines called device drivers to enable the computer to transmit and receive data to and from them.

Input/output interface *n.* See input/output controller.

Input/output port *n.* See port.

Input/output processor *n.* Hardware designed to handle input and output operations to relieve the burden on the main processing unit. For example, a digital signal processor can perform time-intensive, complicated analysis and synthesis of sound patterns without CPU overhead. See also digital signal processor, front-end processor (definition 1).

Input/output statement *n.* A programme instruction that causes data to be transferred between memory and an input or output device.

Input port *n.* See port.

Input stream *n.* A flow of information used in a programme as a sequence of bytes that are associated with a particular task or destination. Input streams include series of characters read from the keyboard to memory and blocks of data read from disk files.

Inquiry *n.* A request for information. See also query.

INS *n.* See WINS.

Insertion point *n.* A blinking vertical bar on the screen, such as in graphical user interfaces, that marks the location at which inserted text will appear. See also cursor (definition 1).

Insertion sort *n.* A list-sorting algorithm that starts with a list that contains one item and builds an ever-larger sorted list by inserting the items to be sorted one at a time into their correct positions on that list. Insertion sorts are inefficient when used with arrays, because of constant shuffling of items, but are ideally suited for sorting linked lists. See also linked list, sort algorithm.

Insert key *n.* A key on the keyboard, labeled "Insert" or "Ins," whose usual function is to toggle a program's editing setting between an insert mode and an overwrite mode, although it may perform different functions in different applications. Also called: Ins key.

Insert mode *n.* A mode of operation in which a character typed into a document or at a command line pushes subsequent existing characters farther to the right on the screen rather than overwriting them. Insert mode is the opposite of overwrite mode, in which new characters replace subsequent existing characters. The key or key combination used to change from one mode to the other varies among programmes, but the Insert key is most often used.

Insider attack *n.* An attack on a network or system carried out by an individual associated with the hacked system. Insider attacks are typically the work of current or former employees of a company or organisation who have knowledge of passwords and network vulnerabilities.

Ins key *n.* See Insert key.

Install *vb.* To set in place and prepare for operation. Operating systems and application programmes commonly include a disk-based installation, or setup, programme that does most of the work of preparing the programme to work with the computer, printer, and other devices. Often such a programme can check for devices attached to the system, request the user to choose from sets of options, create a place for the programme on the hard disk, and modify system startup files as necessary.

Installable device driver *n.* A device driver that can be embedded within an operating system, usually in order to override an existing, less-functional service.

Installable File System Manager *n.* In Windows 9x and Windows 2000, the part of the file system architecture responsible for arbitrating access to the different file system components. Acronym: IFS.

Installation programme *n.* A programme whose function is to install another programme, either on a storage medium or in memory. An installation programme, also called a setup programme, might be used to guide a user through the often complex process of setting up an application for a particular combination of machine, printer, and monitor.

Installer *n.* A programme, provided with the Apple Macintosh operating system, that allows the user to install system upgrades and make bootable (system) disks.

Instance *n.* An object, in object-oriented programming, in relation to the class to which it belongs. For example, an object myList that belongs to a class List is an instance of the class List. See also class, instance variable, instantiate, object (definition 2).

Instance variable *n.* A variable associated with an instance of a class (an object). If a class defines a certain variable, each instance of the class has its own copy of that variable. See also class, instance, object (definition 2), object-oriented programming.

Instantiate *vb.* To create an instance of a class. See also class, instance, object (definition 2).

Instant messaging *n.* A service that alerts users when friends or colleagues are on line and allows them to communicate with each other in real time through private online chat areas. With instant messaging, a user creates a list of other users with whom he or she wishes to communicate; when a user from his or her list is on line, the service alerts the user and enables immediate contact with the other user. While instant messaging has primarily been a proprietary service offered by Internet service providers such as AOL and MSN, businesses are starting to employ instant messaging to increase employee efficiency and make expertise more readily available to employees.

Institute of Electrical and Electronics Engineers *n.* See IEEE.

Instruction *n.* An action statement in any computer language, most often in machine or assembly language. Most programmes consist of two types of statements: declarations and instructions. See also declaration, statement.

Instruction code *n.* See operation code.

Instruction counter *n.* See instruction register.

Instruction cycle *n.* The cycle in which a processor retrieves an instruction from memory, decodes it, and carries it out. The time required for an instruction cycle is the sum of the instruction (fetch) time and the execution (translate and execute) time and is measured by the number of clock ticks (pulses of a processor's internal timer) consumed.

Instruction mix *n.* The assortment of types of instructions contained in a programme, such as assignment instructions, mathematical instructions (floating-point or integer), control instructions, and indexing instructions. Knowledge of instruction mixes is important to designers of CPUs because it tells them which instructions should be shortened to yield the greatest speed, and to designers of benchmarks because it enables them to make the benchmarks relevant to real tasks.

Instruction pointer *n.* See programme counter.

Instruction register *n.* A register in a central processing unit that holds the address of the next instruction to be executed.

Instruction set *n.* The set of machine instructions that a processor recognises and can execute. See also assembler, microcode.

Instruction time *n.* The number of clock ticks (pulses of a computer's internal timer) required to retrieve an instruction from memory. Instruction time is the first part of an instruction cycle; the second part is the execution (translate and execute) time. Also called: I-time.

Instruction word *n.* 1. The length of a machine language instruction. 2. A machine language instruction containing an operation code identifying the type of instruction, possibly one or more operands specifying data to be affected or its address, and possibly bits used for indexing or other purposes. See also assembler, machine code.

Insulator *n.* 1. Any material that is a very poor conductor of electricity, such as rubber, glass, or ceramic. Also called:

nonconductor. 2. A device used to separate elements of electrical circuits and prevent current from taking unwanted paths, such as the stacks of ceramic disks that suspend high-voltage power lines from transmission towers.

Integer *n.* 1. A positive or negative "whole" number, such as 37, –50, or 764. 2. A data type representing whole numbers. Calculations involving only integers are much faster than calculations involving floating-point numbers, so integers are widely used in programming for counting and numbering purposes. Integers can be signed (positive or negative) or unsigned (positive). They can also be described as long or short, depending on the number of bytes needed to store them. Short integers, stored in 2 bytes, cover a smaller range of numbers (for example, –32,768 through 32,767) than do long integers (for example, –2,147,483,648 through 2,147,483,647), which are stored in 4 bytes. Also called: integral number. See also floating-point notation.

Integral modem *n.* A modem that is built into a computer, as opposed to an internal modem, which is a modem on an expansion card that can be removed. See also external modem, internal modem, modem.

Integral number *n.* See integer (definition 2).

Integrated circuit *n.* A device consisting of a number of connected circuit elements, such as transistors and resistors, fabricated on a single chip of silicon crystal or other semiconductor material. Integrated circuits are categorised by the number of elements they contain. See the table. Acronym: IC. Also called: chip. See also central processing unit.

Table I.2 Types of Integrated Circuits.

Category	Elements
small-scale integration (SSI)	in the 10s
medium-scale integration (MSI)	in the 100s
large-scale integration (LSI)	in the 1000s
very-large-scale integration (VLSI)	in the 100,000s
ultra-large-scale integration (ULSI)	1,000,000 or more

Integrated development environment *n.* A set of integrated tools for developing software. The tools are generally run from one user interface and consist of a compiler, an editor, and a debugger, among others. Acronym: IDE.

Integrated Device Electronics *n.* See IDE (definition 1).

Integrated injection logic *n.* A type of circuit design that uses both NPN and PNP transistors and does not require other components, such as resistors. Such circuits are moderately fast, consume little power, and can be manufactured in very small sizes. Acronym: I2L, IIL. Also called: merged transistor logic. See also NPN transistor, PNP transistor.

Integrated Services Digital Network *n.* See ISDN.

Integrated Services LAN *n.* See isochronous network.

Integrated software *n.* A programme that combines several applications, such as word processing, database management, and spreadsheets, in a single package. Such software is "integrated" in two ways: it can transfer data from one of its applications to another, helping users coordinate tasks and merge information created with the different software tools; and it provides the user with a consistent interface for choosing commands, managing files, and otherwise interacting with the programmes so that the user will not have to master several, often very different, programmes. The applications in an integrated software package are often not, however, designed to offer as much capability as single applications, nor does integrated software necessarily include all the applications needed in a particular environment.

Integration *n.* 1. In computing, the combining of different activities, programmes, or hardware components into a functional unit. See also integral modem, integrated software, ISDN. 2. In electronics, the process of packing multiple electronic circuit elements on a single chip. See also integrated circuit. 3. In mathematics, specifically calculus, a procedure performed on an equation and related to finding the area under a given curve or the volume within a given shape.

Integrator *n.* A circuit whose output represents the integral, with respect to time, of the input signal—that is, its total accumulated value over time. See the illustration.

Integrity *n.* The completeness and accuracy of data stored in a computer, especially after it has been manipulated in some way. See also data integrity.

Intel Architecture 64 *n.* See IA-64.

Intellectual property *n.* Content of the human intellect deemed to be unique and original and to have marketplace value—and thus to warrant protection under the law. Intellectual property includes but is not limited to ideas; inventions; literary works; chemical, business, or computer processes; and company or product names and logos. Intellectual property protections fall into four categories: copyright (for literary works, art, and music), trademarks (for company and product names and logos), patents (for inventions and processes), and trade secrets (for recipes, code, and processes). Concern over defining and protecting intellectual property in cyberspace has brought this area of the law under intense scrutiny.

Intelligence *n.* 1. The ability of hardware to process information. A device without intelligence is said to be dumb; for example, a dumb terminal connected to a computer can receive input and display output but cannot process information independently. 2. The ability of a programme to monitor its environment and initiate appropriate actions to achieve a desired state. For example, a programme waiting for data to be read from disk might switch to another task in the meantime. 3. The ability of a programme to simulate human thought. See also artificial intelligence. 4. The ability of a machine such as a robot to respond appropriately to changing stimuli (input).

Intelligent *adj.* Of, pertaining to, or characteristic of a device partially or totally controlled by one or more processors integral to the device.

Intelligent agent *n.* See agent (definition 2).

Intelligent cable *n.* A cable that incorporates circuitry to do more than simply pass signals from one end of the cable to the other, such as to determine the characteristics of the connector into which it is plugged. Also called: smart cable.

Intelligent Concept Extraction *n.* A technology owned by Excite, Inc., for searching indexed databases to retrieve documents from the World Wide Web. Intelligent Concept Extraction is like other search technologies in being able to locate indexed Web documents related to one or more key words entered by the user. Based on proprietary search technology, however, it also matches documents conceptually by finding relevant information even if the document found does not contain the key word or words specified by the user. Thus, the list of documents found by Intelligent Concept Extraction can include both documents containing the specified search term and those containing alternative words related to the search term. Acronym: ICE.

Intelligent database *n.* A database that manipulates stored information in a way that people find logical, natural, and easy to use. An intelligent database conducts searches relying not only on traditional data-finding routines but also on predetermined rules governing associations, relationships, and even inferences regarding the data. See also database.

Intelligent hub *n.* A type of hub that, in addition to transmitting signals, has built-in capability for other network chores, such as monitoring or reporting on network status. Intelligent hubs are used in different types of networks, including ARCnet and 10Base-T Ethernet. See also hub.

Intelligent Input/Output *n.* See I2O.

Intelligent terminal *n.* A terminal with its own memory, processor, and firmware that can perform certain functions independently of its host computer, most often the rerouting of incoming data to a printer or video screen.

Intelligent Transportation Infrastructure *n.* A system of automated urban and suburban highway and mass transit control and management services proposed in 1996 by U.S. Secretary of Transportation Federico Peña. Acronym: ITI.

IntelliSense *n.* A Microsoft technology used in various Microsoft products, including Internet Explorer, Visual Basic, Visual

Basic C++, and Office that is designed to help users perform routine tasks. In Visual Basic, for example, information such as the properties and methods of an object is displayed as the developer types the name of the object in the Visual Basic code window.

Intensity Red Green Blue *n.* See IRGB.

Interactive *adj.* Characterised by conversational exchange of input and output, as when a user enters a question or command and the system immediately responds. The interactivity of microcomputers is one of the features that makes them approachable and easy to use.

Interactive fiction *n.* A type of computer game in which the user participates in a story by giving commands to the system. The commands given by the user determine, to some extent, the events that occur during the story. Typically the story involves a goal that must be achieved, and the puzzle is to determine the correct sequence of actions that will lead to the accomplishment of that goal. See also adventure game.

Interactive graphics *n.* A form of user interface in which the user can change and control graphic displays, often with the help of a pointing device such as a mouse or a joystick. Interactive graphics interfaces occur in a range of computer products, from games to computer-aided design (CAD) systems.

Interactive processing *n.* Processing that involves the more or less continuous participation of the user. Such a command/response mode is characteristic of microcomputers.

Interactive programme *n.* A programme that exchanges output and input with the user, who typically views a display of some sort and uses an input device, such as a keyboard, mouse, or joystick, to provide responses to the programme. A computer game is an interactive programme.

Interactive services *n.* See BISDN.

Interactive session *n.* A processing session in which the user can more or less continuously intervene and control the activities of the computer.

Interactive television *n.* A video technology in which a viewer interacts with the television programming. Typical uses of interactive television include Internet access, video on demand, and video conferencing. See also video conferencing.

Interactive TV *n.* See iTV.

Interactive video *n.* The use of computer-controlled video, in the form of a CD-ROM or videodisc, for interactive education or entertainment. See also CD-ROM, interactive, interactive television, videodisc.

Interactive voice response *n.* A computer that operates through the telephone system, in which input commands and data are transmitted to the computer as spoken words and numbers or tones and dial pulses generated by a telephone instrument; and output instructions and data are received from the computer as prerecorded or synthesized speech. For example, a dial-in service that provides airline flight schedules when you press certain key codes on your telephone is an interactive voice response system. Also called: IVR.

Interactive voice system *n.* See interactive voice response.

Interapplication communication *n.* The process of one programme sending messages to another programme. For example, some e-mail programmes allow users to click on a URL within the message. After the user clicks on the URL, browser software will automatically launch and access the URL.

Interblock gap *n.* See inter-record gap.

Interchange File Format *n.* See .iff.

Interchange Format *n.* See Rich Text Format.

Interconnect *n.* 1. See System Area Network. 2. An electrical or mechanical connection. Interconnect is the physical connection and communication between two components in a computer system.

Interface *n.* 1. The point at which a connection is made between two elements so that they can work with each other or exchange information. 2. Software that enables a programme to work with the user (the user interface, which can be a command-line interface, menu-driven interface, or a graphical user interface), with another programme such as the operating system, or with the computer's hardware. See also application programming interface, graphical user interface. 3. A card, plug, or other device that connects pieces of hardware with the computer so that information can be moved from place to place. For example, standardised interfaces such as RS-232-C standard and SCSI enable communications between computers and printers or disks. See also RS-232-C standard, SCSI.

Interface adapter *n.* See network adapter.

Interface card *n.* See adapter.

Interface Definition Language *n.* See IDL.

Interference *n.* 1. Noise or other external signals that affect the performance of a communications channel. 2. Electromagnetic signals that can disturb radio or television reception. The signals can be generated naturally, as in lightning, or by electronic devices, such as computers.

Interior Gateway Protocol *n.* A protocol used for distributing routing information among routers (gateways) in an autonomous network—that is, a network under the control of one administrative body. The two most often used interior gateway protocols are RIP (Routing Information Protocol) and OSPF (Open Shortest Path First). Acronym: IGP. See also autonomous system, OSPF, RIP.

Interior Gateway Routing Protocol *n.* See IGRP.

Interix *n.* A software application from Microsoft that allows businesses to run existing UNIX-based legacy applications while adding applications based on the Microsoft Windows operating system. Interix serves as a single enterprise platform from which to run UNIX-based, Internet-based, and Windows-based applications.

Interlaced *adj.* Pertaining to a display method on raster-scan monitors in which the electron beam refreshes or updates all odd-numbered scan lines in one vertical sweep of the screen and all even-numbered scan lines in the next sweep.

Interlaced GIF *n.* A picture in GIF format that is gradually displayed in a Web browser, showing increasingly detailed versions of the picture until the entire file has finished downloading. Users of slower modems have a perceived shorter wait time for the image to appear, and they can sometimes get enough information about the image to decide whether to proceed with the download or move on. Users with faster connections will notice little difference in effect between an interlaced GIF and a noninterlaced GIF.

Interlace scanning *n.* A display technique designed to reduce flicker and distortions in television transmissions; also used with some raster-scan monitors. In interlace scanning the electron beam in the television or monitor refreshes alternate sets of scan lines in successive top-to-bottom sweeps, refreshing all even lines on one pass, and all odd lines on the other. Because of the screen phosphor's ability to maintain an image for a short time before fading and the tendency of the human eye to average or blend subtle differences in light intensity, the human viewer sees a complete display, but the amount of information carried by the display signal and the number of lines that must be displayed per sweep are halved. Interlaced images are not as clear as those produced by the progressive scanning typical of newer computer monitors. Interlace scanning is, however, the standard method of displaying analog broadcast television images. Also called: interlacing.

Interlacing *n.* See interlace scanning.

Interleave *vb.* To arrange the sectors on a hard disk in such a way that after one sector is read, the next sector in numeric sequence will arrive at the head when the computer is ready to accept it rather than before, which would make the computer wait a whole revolution of the platter for the sector to come back. Interleaving is set by the format utility that initialises a disk for use with a given computer.

Interleaved memory *n.* A method of organising the addresses in RAM memory in order to reduce wait states. In interleaved memory, adjacent locations are stored in different rows of chips so that after accessing a byte, the processor does not have to wait an entire memory cycle before accessing the next byte. See also access time (definition 1), wait state.

Interlock *vb.* To prevent a device from acting while the current operation is in progress.

Intermediate language *n.* 1. A computer language used as an intermediate step between the original source language, usually a high-level language, and the target language, usually machine code. Some high-level compilers use assembly language as an intermediate language. See also compiler (definition 2), object code. 2. See Microsoft intermediate language.

Intermittent *adj.* Pertaining to something, such as a signal or connection, that is not unbroken but occurs at periodic or occasional intervals.

Intermittent error *n.* An error that recurs at unpredictable times.

Internal clock *n.* See clock/calendar.

Internal command *n.* A routine that is loaded into memory along with the operating system and resides there for as long as the computer is on.

Internal font *n.* A font that is already loaded in a printer's memory (ROM) when the printer is shipped.

Internal interrupt *n.* An interrupt generated by the processor itself in response to certain predefined situations, such as an attempt to divide by zero or an arithmetic value exceeding the number of bits allowed for it. See also interrupt.

Internal memory *n.* See primary storage.

Internal modem *n.* A modem constructed on an expansion card to be installed in one of the expansion slots inside a computer.

Internal schema *n.* A view of information about the physical files composing a database, including file names, file locations, accessing methodology, and actual or potential data derivations, in a database model such as that described by ANSI/X3/SPARC, that supports a three-schema architecture. The internal schema corresponds to the schema in systems based on CODASYL/DBTG. In a distributed database, there may be a different internal schema at each location. See also conceptual schema, schema.

Internal sort *n.* 1. A sorting operation that takes place on files completely or largely held in memory rather than on disk during the process. 2. A sorting procedure that produces sorted subgroups of records that will be subsequently merged into one list.

International Computer Security Association *n.* See ICSA.

International Federation of Information Processing *n.* See IFIP.

International Maritime Satellite *n.* See Inmarsat.

International Mobile Telecommunications for the Year 2000 *n.* Specifications set forth by the International Telecommunications Union (ITU) to establish third-generation wireless telecommunication network architecture. The specifications include faster data transmission speeds and improved voice quality. Acronym: IMT-2000.

International Organisation for Standardisation *n.* See ISO.

International Telecommunication Union *n.* See ITU.

International Telecommunication Union-Telecommunication Standardisation Sector *n.* See ITU-T.

International Telegraph and Telephone Consultative Committee *n.* English-language form of the name for the Comité Consultatif International Télégraphique et Téléphonique, a standards organisation that became part of the International Telecommunication Union in 1992. See ITU-T. See also CCITT.

Internaut *n.* See cybernaut.

Internet *n.* Short for internetwork. A set of computer networks that may be dissimilar and are joined together by means of gateways that handle data transfer and conversion of messages from the sending networks' protocols to those of the receiving network.

Internet *n.* The worldwide collection of networks and gateways that use the TCP/IP suite of protocols to communicate with one another. At the heart of the Internet is a backbone of high-speed data communication lines between major nodes or host computers, consisting of thousands of commercial, government, educational, and other computer systems, that route data and messages. One or more Internet nodes can go off line without endangering the Internet as a whole or causing communications on the Internet to stop, because no single computer or network controls it. The genesis of the Internet was a decentralised network called ARPANET created by the U.S. Department of Defense in 1969 to facilitate communications in the event of a nuclear attack. Eventually other networks, including BITNET, Usenet, UUCP, and NSFnet, were connected to ARPANET. Currently the Internet offers a range of services to users, such as FTP, e-mail, the World Wide Web, Usenet news, Gopher, IRC, telnet, and others. Also called: the Net. See also BITNET,

Internet 2 *n.* A computer-network development project launched in 1996 by a collaborative group of 120 universities under the auspices of the University Corporation for Advanced Internet Development (UCAID). The consortium is now being led by over 190 universities working with industry and government. The goal of Internet2, whose high-speed, fiberoptic backbone was brought on line in early 1999, is the development of advanced Internet technologies and applications for use in research and education at the university level. Though not open for public use, Internet2 and the technologies and applications developed by its members are intended to eventually benefit users of the commercial Internet as well. Some of the new technologies Internet2 and its members are developing and testing include IPv6, multicasting, and quality of service (QoS). Internet2 and the Next Generation Internet (NGI) are complementary initiatives.

Internet access *n.* 1. The capability of a user to connect to the Internet. This is generally accomplished through one of two ways. The first is through a dialing up of an Internet service provider or an online information services provider via a modem connected to the user's computer. This method is the one used by the majority of home computer users. The second way is through a dedicated line, such as a T1 carrier, that is connected to a local area network, to which, in turn, the user's computer is connected. The dedicated line solution is used by larger organisations, such as corporations, which either have their own node on the Internet or connect to an Internet service provider that is a node. A third way that is emerging is for users to use set-top boxes with their TVs. Generally, however, this will give a user access only to documents on the World Wide Web. See also dedicated line (definition 1), ISP, LAN, modem, node (definition 2), set-top box. 2. The capability of an online information service to exchange data with

Internet access device *n.* A communications and signal-routing mechanism, possibly incorporating usage tracking and billing features, for use in connecting multiple remote users to the Internet.

Internet access provider *n.* See ISP.

Internet account *n.* A generic term for a registered username at an Internet Service Provider (ISP). An Internet account is accessed via username and password. Services such as dial-in PPP Internet access and e-mail are provided by ISPs to Internet account owners.

Internet address *n.* See domain name address, e-mail address, IP address.

Internet appliance *n.* 1. See set-top box. 2. See server appliance.

Internet Architecture Board *n.* The body of the Internet Society (ISOC) responsible for overall architectural considerations regarding the Internet. The IAB also serves to adjudicate disputes in the standards process. Acronym: IAB. See also Internet Society.

Internet Assigned Numbers Authority *n.* See IANA, ICANN.

Internet backbone *n.* One of several high-speed networks connecting many local and regional networks, with at least one connection point where it exchanges packets with other Internet backbones. Historically, the NSFnet (predecessor to the modern Internet) was the backbone to the entire Internet in the United States. This backbone linked the supercomputing centers that the National Science Foundation (NSF) runs.

Today, different providers have their own backbones so that the backbone for the supercomputing centers is independent of backbones for commercial Internet providers such as MCI and Sprint. See also backbone.

Internet broadcasting *n.* Broadcasting of audio, or audio plus video, signals across the Internet. Internet broadcasting includes conventional over-the-air broadcast stations that transmit their signals into the Internet as well as Internet-only stations. Listeners use audio Internet software, such as RealAudio. One method of Internet broadcasting is MBONE. See also MBONE, RealAudio.

Internet Cache Protocol *n.* See ICP.

Internet Control Message Protocol *n.* See ICMP.

Internet Corporation for Assigned Names and Numbers *n.* See ICANN.

Internet cramming *n.* See Web cramming.

Internet Directory *n.* 1. Online database of sites organised by category where you can search for files and information by subject, keyword, or other criteria. 2. Storage place for information such as names, Web addresses, organisations, departments, countries, and locations. Typically, Internet Directories are used to look up e-mail addresses that are not in a local address book or a corporate-wide directory.

Internet Draft *n.* A document produced by the Internet Engineering Task Force (IETF) for purposes of discussing a possible change in standards that govern the Internet. An Internet Draft is subject to revision or replacement at any time; if not replaced or revised, the Internet Draft is valid for no more than six months. An Internet Draft, if accepted, may be developed into an RFC. See also IETF, RFC.

Internet Engineering and Planning Group *n.* See IEPG.

Internet Engineering Steering Group *n.* The group within the Internet Society (ISOC) that, along with the Internet Architecture Board (IAB), reviews the standards proposed by the Internet Engineering Task Force (IETF). Acronym: IESG.

Internet Engineering Task Force *n.* See IETF.

Internet Explorer *n.* Microsoft's Web browsing software. Introduced in October 1995, the latest versions of Internet Explorer include many features that allow you to customise your experience on the Web. Internet Explorer is also available for the Macintosh and UNIX platforms. See also ActiveX control, Java applet, Web browser.

Internet Foundation Classes *n.* A Java class library developed by Netscape to facilitate the creation of full-feature, mission-critical Java applications. Internet Foundation Classes (IFC) comprises user-interface objects and frameworks intended to extend Java's Abstract Window Toolkit (AWT) and includes a multifont text editor; essential application controls; and drag-and-drop, drawing/event, windowing, animation, object persistence, single-thread, and localisation frameworks. See also Abstract Window Toolkit, Application Foundation Classes, Java Foundation Classes, Microsoft Foundation Classes.

Internet gateway *n.* A device that provides the connection between the Internet backbone and another network, such as a LAN (local area network). Usually the device is a computer dedicated to the task or a router. The gateway generally performs protocol conversion between the Internet backbone and the network, data translation or conversion, and message handling. A gateway is considered a node on the Internet. See also gateway, Internet backbone, node (definition 2), router.

Internet Group Membership Protocol *n.* A protocol used by IP hosts to report their host group memberships to any immediately neighboring multicast routers. Acronym: IGMP.

Internet home *n.* See smart home.

Internet Information Server *n.* Microsoft's brand of Web server software, utilising HTTP (Hypertext Transfer Protocol) to deliver World Wide Web documents. It incorporates various functions for security, allows for CGI programmes, and also provides for Gopher and FTP services.

Internet Inter-ORB Protocol *n.* See IIOP.

Internet Mail Consortium *n.* An international membership organisation of businesses and vendors involved in activities related to e-mail transmission over the Internet. The goals of the Internet Mail Consortium are related to the promotion and expansion of Internet mail. The group's interests range from making Internet mail easier for new users to advancing new mail technologies and expanding the role played by Internet mail into areas such as electronic commerce and entertainment. For example, the Internet Mail Consortium supports two companion specifications, vCalendar and vCard, designed to facilitate electronic exchange of scheduling and personal information. Acronym: IMC.

Internet Naming Service *n.* See WINS.

Internet Printing Protocol *n.* A specification for transmission of documents to printers through the Internet. Development of the Internet Printing Protocol (IPP) was proposed in 1997 by members of the Internet Engineering Task Force (IETF). Intended to provide a standard protocol for Internet-based printing, IPP covers both printing and printer management (printer status, job cancellation, and so on). It is applicable to print servers and to network-capable printers.

Internet reference model *n.* See TCP/IP reference model.

Internet Relay Chat *n.* See IRC.

Internet Research Steering Group *n.* The governing body of the Internet Research Task Force (IRTF). Acronym: IRSG.

Internet Research Task Force *n.* A volunteer organisation that is an arm of the Internet Society (ISOC) focused on making long-term recommendations concerning the Internet to the Internet Architecture Board (IAB). Acronym: IRTF. See also Internet Society.

Internet robot *n.* See spider.

Internet security *n.* A broad topic dealing with all aspects of data authentication, privacy, integrity, and verification for transactions over the Internet. For example, credit card purchases made via a World Wide Web browser require attention to Internet security issues to ensure that the credit card number is not intercepted by an intruder or copied from the server where the number is stored, and to verify that the credit card number is actually sent by the person who claims to be sending it.

Internet Security and Acceleration Server *n.* A software application from Microsoft Corporation to increase the security and performance of Internet access for businesses. Internet Security and Acceleration Server provides an enterprise firewall and high-performance Web cache server to securely manage the flow of information from the Internet through the enterprise's internal network. Acronym: ISA Server.

Internet Server Application Programming Interface *n.* See ISAPI.

Internet service provider *n.* See ISP.

Internet Society *n.* An international, nonprofit organisation based in Reston, Virginia, comprising individuals, companies, foundations, and government agencies, that promotes the use, maintenance, and development of the Internet. The Internet Architecture Board (IAB) is a body within the Internet Society. In addition, the Internet Society publishes the Internet Society News and produces the annual INET conference. Acronym: ISOC. See also INET, Internet Architecture Board.

Internet Software Consortium *n.* A nonprofit organisation that develops software that is available for free, via the World Wide Web or FTP, and engages in development of Internet standards such as the Dynamic Host Configuration Protocol (DHCP). Acronym: ISC. See also DHCP.

Internet SSE *n.* See SSE.

Internet Streaming Media Alliance *n.* See ISMA.

Internet synchronisation *n.* 1. The process of synchronising data between computing and communication devices that are connected to the Internet. 2. A feature in Microsoft Jet and Microsoft Access that allows replicated information to be synchronised in an environment in which an Internet server is configured with Microsoft Replication Manager, a tool included with Microsoft Office 2000 Developer.

Internet Talk Radio *n.* Audio programmes similar to radio broadcasts but distributed over the Internet in the form of files that can be downloaded via FTP. Internet Talk Radio programmes, prepared at the National Press Building in Washington, D.C., are 30 minutes to 1 hour in length; a 30-minute programme requires about 15 MB of disk space. Acronym: ITR.

Internet telephone *n.* Point-to-point voice communication that uses the Internet instead of the public-switched telecommunications network to connect the calling and called parties. Both the sending and the receiving party need a computer, a modem, an Internet connection, and an Internet telephone software package to make and receive calls.

Internet Telephony Service Provider *n.* See ITSP.

Internet telephony *n.* See VoIP.

Internet television *n.* The transmission of television audio and video signals over the Internet.

Internetwork1 *adj.* Of or pertaining to communications between connected networks. It is often used to refer to communication between one LAN (local area network) and another over the Internet or another WAN (wide-area network). See also LAN, WAN.

Internetwork2 *n.* A network made up of smaller, interconnected networks.

Internetwork Packet Exchange *n.* See IPX.

Internetwork Packet Exchange/Sequenced Packet Exchange *n.* See IPX/SPX.

Internet World *n.* Series of international conferences and exhibitions on e-commerce and Internet technology sponsored by Internet World magazine. Major conferences include the world's largest Internet conferences, Internet World Spring and Internet World Fall.

Internet Worm *n.* A string of self-replicating computer code that was distributed through the Internet in November 1988. In a single night, it overloaded and shut down a large portion of the computers connected to the Internet at that time by replicating itself over and over on each computer it accessed, exploiting a bug in UNIX systems. Intended as a prank, the Internet Worm was written by a student at Cornell University. See also back door, worm.

InterNIC *n.* Short for NSFnet (Internet) Network Information Center. The organisation that has traditionally registered domain names and IP addresses as well as distributed information about the Internet. InterNIC was formed in 1993 as a consortium involving the U.S. National Science Foundation, AT&T, General Atomics, and Network Solutions, Inc. (Herndon, Va.). The latter partner administers InterNIC Registration Services, which assigns Internet names and addresses.

Interoperability *n.* Referring to components of computer systems that are able to function in different environments. For example, Microsoft's NT operating system is interoperable on Intel, DEC Alpha, and other CPUs. Another example is the SCSI standard for disk drives and other peripheral devices that allows them to interoperate with different operating systems. With software, interoperability occurs when programmes are able to share data and resources. Microsoft Word, for example, is able to read files created by Microsoft Excel.

Interpolate *vb.* To estimate intermediate values between two known values in a sequence.

Interpret *vb.* 1. To translate a statement or instruction into executable form and then execute it. 2. To execute a programme by translating one statement at a time into executable form and executing it before translating the next statement, rather than by translating the programme completely into executable code (compiling it) before executing it separately. See also interpreter.

Interpreted language *n.* A language in which programmes are translated into executable form and executed one statement at a time rather than being translated completely (compiled) before execution. Basic, LISP, and APL are generally interpreted languages, although Basic can also be compiled. See also compiler.

Interpreter *n.* A programme that translates and then executes each statement in a programme written in an interpreted language. See also compiler, interpreted language, language processor.

Interprocess communication *n.* The ability of one task or process to communicate with another in a multitasking operating system. Common methods include pipes, semaphores, shared memory, queues, signals, and mailboxes. Acronym: IPC.

Inter-record gap *n.* An unused space between data blocks stored on a disk or tape. Because the speed of disks and tapes fluctuates slightly during operation of the drives, a new data block may not occupy the exact space occupied by the old block it overwrites. The inter-record gap prevents the new block from overwriting part of adjacent blocks in such a case. Acronym: IRG. Also called: gap, interblock gap.

Interrogate *vb.* To query with the expectation of an immediate response. For example, a computer may interrogate an attached terminal to determine the terminal's status (readiness to transmit or receive).

Interrupt *n.* A signal from a device to a computer's processor requesting attention from the processor. When the processor receives an interrupt, it suspends its current operations, saves the status of its work, and transfers control to a special routine known as an interrupt handler, which contains the instructions for dealing with the particular situation that caused the interrupt. Interrupts can be generated by various hardware devices to request service or report problems, or by the processor itself in response to programme errors or requests for operating-system services. Interrupts are the processor's way of communicating with the other elements that make up a computer system. A hierarchy of interrupt priorities determines which interrupt request will be handled first if more than one request is made. A programme can temporarily disable some interrupts if it needs the full attention of the processor to complete a particular task. See also exception, external interrupt, hardware interrupt, internal interrupt, software

Interrupt-driven processing *n.* Processing that takes place only when requested by means of an interrupt. After the required task has been completed, the CPU is free to perform other tasks until the next interrupt occurs. Interrupt-driven processing is usually employed for responding to events such as a key pressed by the user or a floppy disk drive that has become ready to transfer data. See also interrupt.

Interrupt handler *n.* A special routine that is executed when a specific interrupt occurs. Interrupts from different causes have different handlers to carry out the corresponding tasks, such as updating the system clock or reading the keyboard. A table stored in low memory contains pointers, sometimes called vectors, that direct the processor to the various interrupt handlers. Programmers can create interrupt handlers to replace or supplement existing handlers, such as by making a clicking sound each time the keyboard is pressed.

Interrupt priority *n.* See interrupt.

Interrupt request line *n.* A hardware line over which a device such as an input/output port, the keyboard, or a disk drive can send interrupts (requests for service) to the CPU. Interrupt request lines are built into the computer's internal hardware and are assigned different levels of priority so that the CPU can determine the sources and relative importance of incoming service requests. They are of concern mainly to programmers dealing with low-level operations close to the hardware. Acronym: IRQ.

Interrupt vector *n.* A memory location that contains the address of the interrupt handler routine that is to be called when a specific interrupt occurs. See also interrupt.

Interrupt vector table *n.* See dispatch table.

Intersect *n.* An operator in relational algebra, used in database management. Given two relations (tables), A and B, that have corresponding fields (columns) containing the same types of values (that is, they are union-compatible), then INTERSECT

A, B builds a third relation containing only those tuples (rows) that appear in both A and B. See also tuple.

Interstitial *n.* An Internet ad format that appears in a pop-up window between Web pages. Interstitial ads download completely before appearing, usually while a Web page the user has chosen is loading. Because interstitial pop-up windows don't appear until the entire ad has downloaded, they often use animated graphics, audio, and other attention-getting multimedia technology that require longer download time.

In the wild *adj.* Currently affecting the computing public, particularly in regard to computer viruses. A virus that is not yet contained or controlled by antivirus software or that keeps reappearing despite virus detection measures is considered to be in the wild. See also virus.

Intranet *n.* A private network based on Internet protocols such as TCP/IP but designed for information management within a company or organisation. Its uses include such services as document distribution, software distribution, access to databases, and training. An intranet is so called because it looks like a World Wide Web site and is based on the same technologies, yet is strictly internal to the organisation and is not connected to the Internet proper. Some intranets also offer access to the Internet, but such connections are directed through a firewall that protects the internal network from the external Web.

Intrinsic font *n.* A font (type size and design) for which a bit image (an exact pattern) exists that can be used as is, without such modification as scaling.

Intruder *n.* An unauthorised user or unauthorised programme, generally considered to have malicious intent, on a computer or computer network. See also bacterium, cracker, Trojan horse, virus.

Intruder attack *n.* A form of hacker attack in which the hacker enters the system without prior knowledge or access to the system. The intruder will typically use a combination of probing tools and techniques to learn about the network to be hacked.

Intrusion Countermeasure Electronics *n.* See ICE (definition 3).

Intrusion detection *n.* See IDS.

Intrusion-detection system *n.* See IDS.

Invalid *adj.* Erroneous or unrecognizable because of a flaw in reasoning or an error in input. Invalid results, for example, might occur if the logic in a programme is faulty.

Inverse video *n.* See reverse video.

Invert *vb.* 1. To reverse something or change it to its opposite. For example, to invert the colours on a monochrome display means to change light to dark and dark to light. See the illustration. 2. In a digital electrical signal, to replace a high level by a low level and vice versa. This type of operation is the electronic equivalent of a Boolean NOT operation.

Inverted file *n.* See inverted list.

Inverted list *n.* A method for creating alternative locators for sets of information. For example, in a file containing data about cars, records 3, 7, 19, 24, and 32 might contain the value "Red" in the field COLOUR. An inverted list (or index) on the field COLOUR would contain a record for "Red" followed by the locator numbers 3, 7, 19, 24, and 32. See also field, record.

Inverted-list database *n.* A database similar to a relational database but with several differences that make it much more difficult for the database management system to ensure data consistency, integrity, and security than with a relational system. The rows (records or tuples) of an inverted-list table are ordered in a specific physical sequence, independent of any orderings that may be imposed by means of indexes. The total database can also be ordered, with specified logical merge criteria being imposed between tables. Any number of search keys, either simple or composite, can be defined. Unlike the keys of a relational system, these search keys are arbitrary fields or combinations of fields. No integrity or uniqueness constraints are enforced; neither the indexes nor the tables are transparent to the user.

Inverted structure *n.* A file structure in which record keys are stored and manipulated separately from the records themselves.

Inverter *n.* 1. A logic circuit that inverts (reverses) the signal input to it—for example, inverting a high input to a low output. 2. A device that converts direct current (DC) to alternating current (AC).

Invoke *vb.* To call or activate; used in reference to commands and subroutines.

I/O *n.* See input/output.

I/O-bound *adj.* See input/output-bound.

I/O controller *n.* See input/output controller.

I/O device *n.* See input/output device.

Ion-deposition printer *n.* A page printer in which the image is formed in electrostatic charges on a drum that picks up toner and transfers it to the paper, as in a laser, LED, or LCD printer, but the drum is charged using a beam of ions rather than light. These printers, used mainly in high-volume data-processing environments, typically operate at speeds from 30 to 90 pages per minute. In ion-deposition printers, toner is typically fused to paper by a method that is fast and does not require heat but leaves the paper a little glossy, making it unsuitable for business correspondence. In addition, ion-deposition printers tend to produce thick, slightly fuzzy characters; the technology is also more expensive than that of a laser printer. See also electrophotographic printers, nonimpact printer, page printer.

I/O port *n.* See port1 (definition 1).

I/O processor *n.* See input/output processor.

IO.SYS *n.* One of two hidden system files installed on an MS-DOS startup disk. IO.SYS in IBM releases of MS-DOS (called IBMBIO.COM) contains device drivers for peripherals such as the display, keyboard, floppy disk drive, hard disk drive, serial port, and real-time clock. See also MSDOS.SYS.

IP *n.* Acronym for Internet Protocol. The protocol within TCP/IP that governs the breakup of data messages into packets, the routing of the packets from sender to destination network and station, and the reassembly of the packets into the original data messages at the destination. IP runs at the internetwork layer in the TCP/IP model—equivalent to the network layer in the ISO/OSI reference model. See also ISO/OSI reference model, TCP/IP.

IP address *n.* Short for Internet Protocol address. A 32-bit (4-byte) binary number that uniquely identifies a host (computer) connected to the Internet to other Internet hosts, for the purposes of communication through the transfer of packets. An IP address is expressed in "dotted quad" format, consisting of the decimal values of its 4 bytes, separated with periods; for example, 127.0.0.1. The first 1, 2, or 3 bytes of the IP address identify the network the host is connected to; the remaining bits identify the host itself. The 32 bits of all 4 bytes together can signify almost 232, or roughly 4 billion, hosts. (A few small ranges within that set of numbers are not used.) Also called: Internet Protocol number, IP number. See also host, IANA, ICANN, InterNIC, IP, IP address classes, packet.

IP address classes *n.* Short for Internet Protocol address classes. The classes into which IP addresses were divided to accommodate different network sizes. Each class is associated with a range of possible IP addresses and is limited to a specific number of networks per class and hosts per network. See the table. See also Class A IP address, Class B IP address, Class C IP address, IP address.

Address Class	**Range of IP Addresses**	**Networks per Class**	**Hosts per Network (maximum number)**
Class A (/8)	1.x.x.x to 126.x.x.x	126	16,777,214
Class B (/16)	128.0.x.x to 191.255.x.x	16,384	65,534
Class C (/24)	192.0.0.x to 223.255.255.x	2,097,152	254

IP address classes. Each x represents the host-number field assigned by the network administrator.

IP aliasing *n.* See NAT.

IPC *n.* See interprocess communication.

Ipchains *n.* See iptables.

IP Filter *n.* Short for Internet Protocol Filter. A TCP/IP packet filter for UNIX, particularly BSD. Similar in functionality to netfilter and iptables in Linux, IP Filter can be used to provide network address translation (NAT) or firewall services. See also firewall.

IPL *n.* See initial programme load.

IP masquerading *n.* See NAT.

IP multicasting *n.* Short for Internet Protocol multicasting. The extension of local area network multicasting technology to a TCP/IP network. Hosts send and receive multicast datagrams, the destination fields of which specify IP host group addresses rather than individual IP addresses. A host indicates that it is a member of a group by means of the Internet Group Management Protocol. See also datagram, Internet Group Membership Protocol, IP, MBONE, multicasting.

IPng *n.* Acronym for Internet Protocol next generation. A revised version of the Internet Protocol (IP) designed primarily to address growth on the Internet. IPng is compatible with, but an evolutionary successor to, the current version of IP, IPv4 (IP version 4), and was approved as a draft standard in 1998 by the IETF (Internet Engineering Task Force). It offers several improvements over IPv4 including a quadrupled IP address size (from 32 bits to 128 bits), expanded routing capabilities, simplified header formats, improved support for options, and support for quality of service, authentication, and privacy. Also called: IPv6. See also IETF, IP, IP address.

IP number *n.* See IP address.

IPP *n.* See Internet Printing Protocol.

IPSec *n.* Short for Internet Protocol Security. A security mechanism under development by the IETF (Internet

Engineering Task Force) designed to ensure secure packet exchanges at the IP (Internet Protocol) layer. IPSec is based on two levels of security: AH (Authentication Header), which authenticates the sender and assures the recipient that the information has not been altered during transmission, and ESP (Encapsulating Security Protocol), which provides data encryption in addition to authentication and integrity assurance. IPSec protects all protocols in the TCP/IP protocol suite and Internet communications by using Layer Two Tunneling Protocol (L2TP) and is expected to ensure secure transmissions over virtual private networks (VPNs). See also anti-replay, communications protocol, Diffie-Hellman, ESP, IETF, IP, IPv6, Layer L2TP, TCP/IP, packet, virtual private network.

IP Security *n.* See IPSec.

IP/SoC Conference and Exhibition *n.* Acronym for Intellectual Property/System on a Chip Conference and Exhibition. Leading conference and exhibition for executives, architects, and engineers using intellectual property in the design and production of system-on-a-chip semiconductors. The event features product exhibits and forums for the exchange of information.

IP splicing *n.* See IP spoofing.

IP spoofing *n.* The act of inserting a false sender IP address into an Internet transmission in order to gain unauthorised access to a computer system. Also called: IP splicing. See also IP address, spoofing.

IP switching *n.* A technology developed by Ipsilon Networks (Sunnyvale, Calif.) that enables a sequence of IP packets with a common destination to be transmitted over a high-speed, high-bandwidth Asynchronous Transfer Mode (ATM) connection.

Iptables *n.* A utility used to configure firewall settings and rules in Linux. Part of the netfilter framework in the Linux kernel, iptables replaces ipchains, a previous implementation. See also netfilter.

IP telephony *n.* Telephone service including voice and fax, provided through an Internet or network connection. IP telephony requires two steps: conversion of analog voice to digital format by a coding/uncoding device (codec) and conversion of the digitised information to packets for IP transmission. Also called: Internet telephony, Voice over IP (VoIP). See also H.323, VoIP.

IP tunneling *n.* A technique used to encapsulate data inside a TCP/IP packet for transmission between IP addresses. IP tunneling provides a secure means for data from different networks to be shared over the Internet.

IPv4 *n.* Short for Internet Protocol version 4. The current version of the Internet Protocol (IP), as compared with the next-generation IP, which is known familiarly as IPng and more formally as IPv6 (IP version 6). See also IP.

IPv6 *n.* Short for Internet Protocol version 6. The next-generation Internet Protocol from the Internet Engineering Task Force (IETF), IPv6 is now included as part of IP support in many products and in the major operating systems. IPv6 offers several improvements from IPv4, most significantly an increase of available address space from 32 to 128 bits, which makes the number of available addresses effectively unlimited. Usually called IPng (next generation), IPv6 also includes support for multicast and anycast addressing. See also anycasting, IP, IPng.

Ipvs *n.* Acronym for IP Virtual Server. See LVS.

IPX *n.* Acronym for Internetwork Packet Exchange. The protocol in Novell NetWare that governs addressing and routing of packets within and between LANs. IPX packets can be encapsulated in Ethernet packets or Token Ring frames. IPX operates at ISO/OSI levels 3 and 4 but does not perform all the functions at those levels. In particular, IPX does not guarantee that a message will be complete (no lost packets); SPX has that job. See also Ethernet (definition 1), packet, Token Ring network.

IPX/SPX *n.* Acronym for Internetwork Packet Exchange/Sequenced Packet Exchange. The network and transport level protocols used by Novell NetWare, which together correspond to the combination of TCP and IP in the TCP/IP protocol suite. IPX is a connectionless protocol that handles addressing and routing of packets. SPX, which runs above IPX, ensures correct delivery. See also IPX, SPX (definition 1).

IR *n.* See infrared.

IRC *n.* Acronym for Internet Relay Chat. A service that enables an Internet user to participate in a conversation on line in real time with other users. An IRC channel, maintained by an IRC server, transmits the text typed by each user who has joined the channel to all other users who have joined the channel. Generally, a channel is dedicated to a particular topic, which may be reflected in the channel's name. An IRC client shows the names of currently active channels, enables the user to join a channel, and then displays the other participants' words on individual lines so that the user can respond. IRC was invented in 1988 by Jarkko Oikarinen of Finland. See also channel (definition 2), server (definition 2).

IrDA *n.* Acronym for Infrared Data Association. The industry organisation of computer, component, and telecommunications vendors who have established the standards for infrared communication between computers and peripheral devices such as printers.

IRE scale *n.* Short for Institute of Radio Engineers scale. Scale to determine video signal amplitudes as devised by the Institute of Radio Engineers, which is now part of the Institute of Electrical and Electronic Engineers (IEEE). The IRE scale includes a total of 140 units, with 100 up and 40 down from zero.

IRG *n.* See inter-record gap.

IRGB *n.* Acronym for Intensity Red Green Blue. A type of colour encoding originally used in IBM's Colour/Graphics Adapter (CGA) and continued in the EGA (Enhanced Graphics Adapter) and VGA (Video Graphics Array). The standard 3-bit RGB colour encoding (specifying eight colours) is supplemented by a fourth bit (called Intensity) that uniformly increases the intensity of the red, green, and blue signals, resulting in a total of 16 colours. See also RGB.

IRL *n.* Acronym for in real life. An expression used by many online users to denote life outside the computer realm, especially in conjunction with virtual worlds such as online talkers, IRC, MUDs, and virtual reality. See also IRC, MUD, talker, virtual reality.

IRQ *n.* Acronym for interrupt request. One of a set of possible hardware interrupts, identified by a number, on a Wintel computer. The number of the IRQ determines which interrupt handler will be used. In the AT bus, ISA, and EISA, 15 IRQs are available; in Micro Channel Architecture, 255 IRQs are available. Each device's IRQ is hardwired or set by a jumper or DIP switch. The VL bus and the PCI local bus have their own interrupt systems, which they translate to IRQ numbers. See also AT bus, DIP switch, EISA, interrupt, IRQ conflict, ISA, jumper, Micro Channel Architecture, PCI local bus, VL bus.

IRQ conflict *n.* The condition on a Wintel computer in which two different peripheral devices use the same IRQ to request service from the central processing unit (CPU). An IRQ conflict will prevent the system from working correctly; for example, the CPU may respond to an interrupt from a serial mouse by executing an interrupt handler for interrupts generated by a modem. IRQ conflicts can be prevented by the use of Plug and Play hardware and software. See also interrupt handler, IRQ, Plug and Play.

Irrational number *n.* A real number that cannot be expressed as the ratio of two integers. Examples of irrational numbers are the square root of 3, pi, and e. See also integer, real number.

ISA *n.* Acronym for Industry Standard Architecture. A bus design specification that allows components to be added as cards plugged into standard expansion slots in IBM Personal Computers and compatibles. Originally introduced in the IBM PC/XT with an 8-bit data path, ISA was expanded in 1984, when IBM introduced the PC/AT, to permit a 16-bit data path. A 16-bit ISA slot actually consists of two separate 8-bit slots mounted end-to-end so that a single 16-bit card plugs into both slots. An 8-bit expansion card can be inserted and used in a 16-bit slot (it occupies only one of the two slots), but a 16-bit expansion card cannot be used in an 8-bit slot. See also EISA, Micro Channel Architecture.

ISAM *n.* See indexed sequential access method.

ISAPI *n.* Acronym for Internet Server Application Programming Interface. An easy-to-use, high-performance interface for back-end applications for Microsoft's Internet Information Server (IIS). ISAPI has its own dynamic-link library, which offers significant performance advantages over the CGI (Common Gateway Interface) specification. See also API, dynamic-link library, Internet Information Server.

ISAPI filter *n.* A DLL file used by Microsoft Internet Information Server (IIS) to verify and authenticate ISAPI requests received by the IIS.

ISA Server *n.* See Internet Security and Acceleration Server.

ISA slot *n.* A connection socket for a peripheral designed according to the ISA (Industry Standard Architecture) standard, which applies to the bus developed for use in the 80286 (IBM PC/AT) motherboard. See also ISA.

ISC *n.* See Internet Software Consortium.

ISDN *n.* Acronym for Integrated Services Digital Network. A high-speed digital communications network evolving from existing telephone services. The goal in developing ISDN was to replace the current telephone network, which requires digital-to-analog conversions, with facilities totally devoted to digital switching and transmission, yet advanced enough to replace traditionally analog forms of data, ranging from voice to computer transmissions, music, and video. ISDN is available in two forms, known as BRI (Basic Rate Interface) and PRI (Primary Rate Interface). BRI consists of two B (bearer) channels that carry data at 64 Kbps and one D (data) channel that carries control and signal information at 16 Kbps. In North America and Japan, PRI consists of 23 B channels and 1 D channel, all operating at 64 Kbps; elsewhere in the world, PRI consists of 30 B channels and 1 D channel. Computers and other devices connect to ISDN lines through simple, standardised interfaces. See also BRI, channel (definition 2), PRI.

ISDN terminal adapter *n.* The hardware interface between a computer and an ISDN line. See also ISDN.

I seek you *n.* See ICQ.

ISIS or IS-IS *n.* Acronym for Intelligent Scheduling and Information System. A toolkit designed to help prevent and eliminate faults in manufacturing systems. Developed in 1980 at Cornell University, ISIS is now available commercially.

ISLAN *n.* See isochronous network.

ISMA *n.* Acronym for Internet Streaming Media Alliance. A nonprofit organisation promoting the adoption of open standards for the streaming of rich media over Internet Protocol (IP) networks. ISMA membership consists of a number of technology companies and groups including Apple Computer, Cisco Systems, IBM, Kasenna, Philips, and Sun Microsystems. See also Windows Metafile Format.

ISO *n.* Short for International Organisation for Standardisation (often incorrectly identified as an acronym for International Standards Organisation), an international association of 130 countries, each of which is represented by its leading standard-setting organisation—for example, ANSI (American National Standards Institute) for the United States. The ISO works to establish global standards for communications and information exchange. Primary among its accomplishments is the widely accepted ISO/OSI reference model, which defines standards for the interaction of computers connected by communications networks. ISO is not an acronym; rather, it is derived from the Greek word isos, which means "equal" and is the root of the prefix "iso-."

ISO 8601:1988 *n.* A standard entitled "Data elements and interchange formats" from the International Organisation for Standardisation (ISO) that covers a number of date formats.

ISO 9660 *n.* An international format standard for CD-ROM adopted by the International Organisation for Standardisation (ISO) that follows the recommendations embodied in the High Sierra specification, with some modifications. See also High Sierra specification.

ISOC *n.* See Internet Society.

Isochronous network *n.* A type of network defined in the IEEE 802.9 specification that combines ISDN and LAN technologies to enable networks to carry multimedia. Also called: Integrated Services LAN, ISLAN.

Isometric view *n.* A display method for three-dimensional objects in which every edge has the correct length for the scale of the drawing and in which all parallel lines appear parallel. An isometric view of a cube, for example, shows the faces in symmetrical relation to one another and the height and width of each face evenly proportioned; the faces do not appear to taper with distance as they do when the cube is drawn in perspective.

ISO/OSI reference model *n.* Short for International Organisation for Standardisation Open Systems Interconnection reference model. A layered architecture (plan) that standardises levels of service and types of interaction for computers exchanging information through a communications network. The ISO/OSI reference model separates computer-to-computer communications into seven protocol layers, or levels, each building—and relying—upon the standards contained in the levels below it. The lowest of the seven layers deals solely with hardware links; the highest deals with software interactions at the application-programme level. It is a fundamental blueprint designed to help guide the creation of networking hardware and software. See the illustration. Also called: OSI reference model.

ISP *n.* Acronym for Internet service provider. A business that supplies Internet connectivity services to individuals, businesses, and other organisations. Some ISPs are large national or multinational corporations that offer access in many locations, while others are limited to a single city or region. Also called: access provider, service provider.

ISSE *n.* See SSE.

ISV *n.* See independent software vendor.

IT *n.* Acronym for Information Technology. See Information Services.

Italic *n.* A type style in which the characters are evenly slanted toward the right. *This sentence is in italics.* Italics are commonly used for emphasis, foreign-language words and phrases, titles of literary and other works, technical terms, and citations. See also font family.

Itanium *n.* An Intel microprocessor that uses explicitly parallel instruction set computing and 64-bit memory addressing.

Iterate *vb.* To execute one or more statements or instructions repeatedly. Statements or instructions so executed are said to be in a loop. See also iterative statement, loop.

Iterative statement *n.* A statement in a programme that causes the programme to repeat one or more statements. Examples of iterative statements in Basic are FOR, DO, REPEAT..UNTIL, and DO..WHILE. See also control statement.

ITI *n.* See Intelligent Transportation Infrastructure.

I-time *n.* See instruction time.

ITM *n.* Short for Internet traffic management. The analysis and control of Internet traffic to improve efficiency and optimise for high availability. With ITM, Web traffic is distributed among multiple servers using load balancers and other devices. See also load balancing.

ITR *n.* See Internet Talk Radio.

ITSP *n.* Acronym for Internet Telephony Service Provider. A business that supplies PC-to-telephone calling capabilities to individuals, businesses, and organisations. Through an ITSP, calls initiated on a PC travel over the Internet to a gateway that, in turn, sends the call to the standard public switched phone network and, eventually, to the receiving telephone. See also ISP, telephony.

ITU *n.* Acronym for International Telecommunication Union. An international organisation based in Geneva, Switzerland, that is responsible for making recommendations and establishing standards governing telephone and data communications systems for public and private telecommunications organisations. Founded in 1865 under the name International Telegraph Union, it was renamed the International Telecommunication Union in 1934 to signify the full scope of its responsibilities. ITU became an agency of the United Nations in 1947. A reorganisation in 1992 aligned the ITU into three governing bodies: the Radiocommunication Sector, the Telecommunication Standardisation Sector (ITU-TSS, ITU-T, for short; formerly the CCITT), and the Telecommunication Development Sector. See also ITU-T.

ITU-T *n.* The standardisation division of the International Telecommunication Union, formerly called Comité Consultatif International Télégraphique et Téléphonique (CCITT). The ITU-T develops communications recommendations for all analog and digital communications. Also called: ITU-TSS. See also CCITT Groups 1-4, ITU.

ITU-TSS *n.* See ITU-T.

ITU-T V series *n.* See V series.

ITU-T X series *n.* See X series.

iTV *n.* Acronym for Interactive television. A communications medium combining television with interactive services. iTV offers two-way communications between users and communications providers. From their televisions, users can order special programming, respond to programming options, and access the Internet and additional services such as instant messaging and telephone functions.

IVR *n.* See interactive voice response.

IVUE *n.* A proprietary image format (from Live Pictures) that allows files to be adjusted to screen resolution at any zoom level.

i-way *n.* See Information Superhighway.

J

J2EE *n.* Acronym for Java 2 Platform Enterprise Edition. An application server framework from Sun Microsystems, Inc., for the development of distributed applications. It includes all the previous Java APIs targeted for multi-tiered distributed enterprise information systems. The J2EE platform consists of a set of services, application programming interfaces (APIs), and protocols that provide the functionality for developing multitiered, Web-based applications. See also application programming interface, Enterprise Java Beans, IDL, Java, JDBC, Jini, JMS, JNDI, JSP, JTA, JTS, RMI-IIOP.

J *n.* A high-level programming language created by Kenneth Iverson, developer of APL, and Roger Hui. J is a successor language to APL that may be run on many platforms, including Windows 95, Windows NT, Macintosh, Linux, RS/6000, and Sun Sparc. Like APL, J is used primarily by mathematicians. See also APL.

Jabber *n.* A continuous stream of random data transmitted over a network as the result of some malfunction.

Jabber *n.* An XML-based instant messaging system. Jabber software is available for most operating systems and allows user access to other instant messaging services. Jabber is an open source application overseen by Jabber.org.

Jack *n.* A connector designed to receive a plug. A jack is commonly used in making audio and video connections.

Jacket *n.* See disk jacket.

Jack in *vb.* 1. To log on to a computer. 2. To connect to a network or BBS, especially for purposes of entering an IRC or a virtual reality simulation, such as a MUD. (To leave is to jack out.) See also IRC, MUD.

Jack out *vb.* 1. To log off a computer. 2. To disconnect from a network or online bulletin board system. See also jack in, log on.

Jacquard loom *n.* The first machine that used punched cards to control its operation. In this loom, developed in 1801 by French inventor Joseph-Marie Jacquard, up to 24,000 cards were placed on a rolling drum. Where a hole was punched on a card, one of a set of rods could pass through and select a particular thread to be woven into the pattern. Jacquard was awarded a medal by the Emperor Napoleon for his invention. Later in the nineteenth century, punched cards were used in Charles Babbage's computerlike Analytical Engine and in Herman Hollerith's statistical tabulating machine. See also Analytical Engine, Hollerith tabulating/recording machine.

Jaggies *n.* The "stairsteps" that appear in diagonal lines and curves drawn at low resolutions in computer graphics. Also called: aliasing.

Janet *n.* Short for the Joint Academic Network. A wide area network in the United Kingdom that serves as the principal backbone for the Internet in that country. See also backbone (definition 1).

.jar *n.* A file name extension that identifies a compressed JAR (Java Archive) file.

Note: By changing the .jar extension to .zip, you can use popular extraction tools such as PKZIP or WINZIP to look at a .jar file's contents. See also compressed file, JAR, PKZIP, .zip.

JAR *n.* Acronym for Java Archive file. JAR files allow Java developers to efficiently deploy Java classes and their associated resources. The elements in a JAR file are compressed just as in a standard zip file. JAR files include a security mechanism and a special META-INF directory that contains administrative information about the contents of the files. Using a combination of a digital signature and the META-

INF data, JAR files can be signed to ensure authenticity and security. See also .jar.

Java *n.* An object-oriented programming language developed by Sun Microsystems, Inc. Similar to C++, Java is smaller, more portable, and easier to use than C++ because it is more robust and it manages memory on its own. Java was also designed to be secure and platform-neutral (meaning that it can be run on any platform) through the fact that Java programmes are compiled into bytecode, which is not refined to the point of relying on platform-specific instructions and runs on a computer in a special software environment known as a virtual machine. This characteristic of Java makes it a useful language for programming Web applications, since users access the Web from many types of computers. Java is used in programming small applications, or applets, for the World Wide Web, as well as in creating distributed network applications. See also bytecode, Java applet, Jini, object-oriented programming.

Java applet *n.* A Java class that is loaded and run by an already-running Java application such as a Web browser or an applet viewer. Java applets can be downloaded and run by any Web browser capable of interpreting Java, such as Internet Explorer, Netscape Navigator, and HotJava. Java applets are frequently used to add multimedia effects and interactivity to Web pages, such as background music, real-time video displays, animations, calculators, and interactive games. Applets can be activated automatically when a user views a page, or they may require some action on the part of the user, such as clicking on an icon in the Web page. See also applet, Java.

JavaBean *n.* A Java component architecture defined in the JavaBeans specification developed by Sun Microsystems. A JavaBean, or Bean, is a reusable application component—an independent code segment—that can be combined with other JavaBean components to create a Java applet or application. The JavaBean concept emphasizes the platform-independence of the Java language, in which ideally a programme, once written, can run on any computing platform. JavaBeans are similar to Microsoft's ActiveX controls. ActiveX controls, however, can be developed in different programming languages but executed only on a Windows platform. JavaBeans can be developed only in the Java programming language but ideally can run on any platform. See also ActiveX, Java.

Java Card *n.* An application programming interface (API) from Sun Microsystems, Inc., that allows Java applets and programmes to run on smart cards and other devices with limited memory. Java Card uses a Java Card Virtual Machine designed for severely memory-constrained devices. See also applets, Java Card Virtual Machine, smart card (definition 2).

Java Card Virtual Machine *n.* An ultra-small-footprint, highly optimised foundation of a runtime environment within the Java 2 Platform Micro Edition. Derived from the Java Virtual Machine (JVM), it is targeted at smart cards and other severely memory-constrained devices. The Java Card Virtual Machine can run in devices with memory as small as 24 KB of ROM, 16 KB of EEPROM, and 512 bytes of RAM. See also EEPROM, Java Card, RAM, ROM.

Java chip *n.* An implementation on a single integrated circuit of the virtual machine specified for execution of the Java programming language. Such chips, which are being developed by Sun Microsystems, Inc., could be used in very small devices and as controllers for appliances. See also integrated circuit, Java, virtual machine.

Java-compliant browser *n.* A Web browser with support for the Java programming language built into it. Most current Web browsers are Java-compliant. See also Java, Web browser.

Java Developer's Kit *n.* A set of software tools developed by Sun Microsystems, Inc., for writing Java applets or applications. The kit, which is distributed free, includes a Java compiler, interpreter, debugger, viewer for applets, and documentation. Acronym: JDK. See also applet, Java, Java applet.

Java Foundation Classes *n.* A Java-based set of class libraries developed by Sun Microsystems, Inc. Encompassing fundamentals of the Internet Foundation Classes created by

Netscape Communications Corp., the Java Foundation Classes extend the Java Abstract Window Toolkit (AWT) by providing graphical user interface components for use in developing commercial and Internet-related Java applications. See also Abstract Window Toolkit, Application Foundation Classes, Internet Foundation Classes, Java, JavaBean, Microsoft Foundation Classes.

Java HotSpot *n.* A Java performance engine introduced by Sun Microsystems, Inc., in 1999 that is designed to run Java applications faster than just-in-time (JIT) compilers. The core of Java HotSpot, and the feature for which it is named, is its ability to perform adaptive optimisation—the identification and optimisation of "hot spots," or sections of performance-critical code. Improved garbage collection (freeing of memory occupied by objects no longer in use) and better multithreading are additional features designed to contribute to increased performance. See also Java.

Java IDL *n.* Short for Java Interface Definition Language. A Java technology that provides CORBA interoperability and connectivity capabilities for the Java platform. These capabilities enable Java applications to invoke operations on remote network services using the Object Management Group Interface Definition Language and Internet Inter-ORB Protocol. See also CORBA, IDL, J2EE, RMI-IIOP.

JavaMail *n.* An API in the Sun Microsystems, Inc., Java platform for sending and receiving mail. A set of abstract APIs that model a mail system, JavaMail provides a platform-independent and protocol-independent framework to build Java-based e-mail client applications. See also application programming interface, e-mail, J2EE.

Java Management Application Programming Interface *n.* A set of application programming interface specifications, proposed by Sun Microsystems, Inc., to enable the Java language to be used for network management. Acronym: JMAPI. See also application programming interface, Java.

JavaOS *n.* An operating system designed to run applications written in the Java programming language. JavaOS was created by JavaSoft, an operating company of Sun Microsystems, Inc., to run the Java Virtual Machine (JVM) directly on microprocessors, and thus eliminate the need for a resident operating system. JavaOS is small and designed for network computers, as well as devices ranging from game machines to pagers and cellular telephones. See also Java.

JavaScript *n.* A scripting language developed by Netscape Communications and Sun Microsystems that is loosely related to Java. JavaScript, however, is not a true object-oriented language, and it is limited in performance compared with Java because it is not compiled. Basic online applications and functions can be added to Web pages with JavaScript, but the number and complexity of available application programming interface functions are fewer than those available with Java. JavaScript code, which is included in a Web page along with the HTML code, is generally considered easier to write than Java, especially for novice programmers. A JavaScript-compliant Web browser, such as Netscape Navigator or Internet Explorer, is necessary to run JavaScript code. See also application programming interface, HTML, scripting language.

JavaServer Pages *n.* See JSP.

Java Speech Grammar Format *n.* A platform-independent grammar description format developed for use with speech recognition systems. Java Speech Grammar Format is used extensively with Voice XML and can be used with most speech recognition systems and related applications. Acronym: JSGF.

Java Virtual Machine *n.* The environment in which Java programmes run. The Java Virtual Machine gives Java programmes a software-based "computer" they can interact with. (Programmes, even the most seemingly unchallenging ones designed for children or entertainment, must run within an environment from which they can use memory, display information, gather input, and so on.) Because the Java Virtual Machine is not a real computer but exists in software, a Java programme can run on any physical computing platform, such as a Windows 9x computer or a Macintosh, equipped with an interpreter—usually an Internet browser—that can carry out the program's instructions and a Java Virtual Machine that provides the "hardware" on which the programme can run. Acronym: JVM.

JCL *n.* Acronym for Job Control Language. A command language used in IBM OS/360 mainframe systems. JCL is used to launch applications and specifies information on running time, programme size, and the programme files used for each application. See also command language.

JDBC *n.* A Java API designed to provide access to relational databases and other tabular material, such as spreadsheets and flat files. Using JDBC, a developer can create a cross-platform Java application that can connect with, and send SQL statements to, a number of different relational databases. Although it is commonly thought to stand for Java Database Connectivity, JDBC is the name of the technology; it is not an acronym.

JDK *n.* See Java Developer's Kit.

jDoc *n.* A cross-platform, interactive format for display, distribution, and interaction with live Web pages. jDoc documents are small in size and can be embedded in HTML documents to offer client-side interactivity. jDoc was created by EarthStones and is an extension to Sun's Java platform.

JetSend Protocol *n.* A platform-independent communications protocol developed by Hewlett-Packard to enable direct device-to-device communication. The JetSend protocol is designed to provide JetSend-enabled devices with the ability to exchange information and data without the need for device drivers or reliance on servers or user intervention. The protocol is intended for use with printers, scanners, fax machines, and other such information "appliances" and was developed to simplify and improve interoperability between and among a wide range of devices.

Jet SQL *n.* A query language. Jet SQL is a dialect used by the Microsoft Access application, specifically by the Microsoft Jet database engine, to extract, manipulate, and structure data that resides in a relational database management system

(RDBMS). Jet SQL is based largely on the ANSI SQL-92 standard, with additional extensions.

Jewel box *n.* A clear plastic container used to package and store a compact disc. Also called: jewel case.

JFC *n.* See Java Foundation Classes.

JFIF *n.* Acronym for JPEG File Interchange Format. A means of saving photographic images stored according to the Joint Photographic Experts Group image compression technique. JFIF represents a "common language" file format in that it is designed specifically to allow users to transfer JPEG images easily between different computers and applications. See also JPEG, TIFF JPEG.

Jini *n.* A technical specification developed by Sun Microsystems that uses a small piece (48 KB) of Java code to allow any network device with a Java Virtual Machine (JVM) to announce its availability and provide its services to any other device connected to the same network. Jini is based on the concept of creating a "federation" of self-configuring devices capable of transparently exchanging code when necessary to simplify interactions between network devices. See also Java.

JIT *adj.* See just-in-time.

Jitter *n.* 1. Small vibrations or fluctuations in a displayed video image caused by irregularities in the display signal. Jitter is often visible in the form of horizontal lines that are of the same thickness as scan lines. 2. A rough appearance in a fax caused by dots that are incorrectly recorded during the scanning process and thus wrongly positioned in the output. 3. In digital communication, distortion caused by lack of synchronisation of signals.

JMAPI *n.* See Java Management Application Programming Interface.

JMS *n.* Acronym for Java Messaging Service. In the J2EE network platform, JMS is an API for using enterprise messaging systems such as IBM MQ Series, TIBCO Rendezvous, and others. See also application programming interface, J2EE.

JNDI *n.* Acronym for Java Naming and Directory Interface. A set of APIs in the J2EE platform from Sun Microsystems, Inc., that assists with the interfacing to multiple naming and directory services. See also application programming interface, J2EE.

Job *n.* A specified amount of processing performed as a unit by a computer. On early mainframe computers, data was submitted in batches, often on punched cards, for processing by different programmes; work was therefore scheduled and carried out in separate jobs, or operations.

Job Control Language *n.* See JCL.

Job processing *n.* A computing method in which a series of jobs, each consisting of one or more tasks grouped together as a computationally coherent whole, is processed sequentially. See also batch processing (definition 2).

Job queue *n.* A list of programmes or tasks waiting for execution by a computer. Jobs in the queue are often ordered according to some basis of priority. See also queue.

Join *n.* 1. A database table operation that creates a resultant entry in another table for each entry in the one table whose key field matches that of an entry in the other. See also inner join. 2. A multiprocessing command that causes a child process to return control to its parent. See also child (definition 1), multiprocessing.

Join line *n.* In a database query, a line that connects fields between two tables and shows how the data is related. Generally, a join line starts with an arrow just beyond the boundary of the table window pointing at the field in one table and ends just beyond the boundary of another table with an arrow pointing at the related field. The type of join indicates which records are selected for the query's result set.

Joint Photographic Experts Group *n.* See JPEG (definition 1).

Joliet *n.* An extension to the ISO 9660 (1988) standard developed to include long filenames or filenames outside the 8.3 convention. This format is used in some new CD-ROMs for operating systems, such as Windows 9x, that can handle such filenames. See also 8.3, ISO 9660, long filenames.

Josephson junction *n.* A cryoelectronic device that can attain extremely high circuit-switching speeds. In the Josephson effect, when two superconducting materials are in close proximity but are separated by an insulator, electric current can jump or tunnel through the gap.

Journal *n.* A computer-based log or record of transactions that takes place in a computer or across a network. A journal could be used, for example, to record message transfers on a communications network, to keep track of system activities that alter the contents of a database, or to maintain a record of files that have been archived for storage or deleted from the system. A journal is often kept as a means of reconstructing events or sets of data should they become lost or damaged. See also audit trail.

Journaled file system *n.* A fault-resilient file system that includes backup and recovery capabilities. When file server indexes are updated, all changes and related information are recorded and stored in a separate log. If a system failure or other abnormal interruption occurs, the system will use stored backup files to repair files corrupted in the crash. Journaled file systems are widely used for business and intranet file servers. In 2001, IBM contributed journaled file system technology to the open source community to allow development of similar file systems for Linux servers.

Joystick *n.* A pointing device used mainly but not exclusively for computer games. A joystick has a base, on which control buttons can be mounted, and a vertical stem, which the user can move in any direction to control the movement of an object on the screen; the stem may also have control buttons. The buttons activate various software features, generally producing onscreen events. A joystick is usually used as a relative pointing device, moving an object on the screen when the stem is moved and stopping the movement when the stem is released. In industrial control applications, the joystick can also be used as an absolute pointing device, with each position of the stem mapped to a specific location on the screen. See the illustration. See also absolute pointing device, relative pointing device.

.jpeg *n.* The file extension that identifies graphic image files in the JPEG format. See also JPEG.

JPEG *n.* 1. Acronym for Joint Photographic Experts Group. An ISO/ITU standard for storing images in compressed form using a discrete cosine transform. JPEG trades off compression against loss; it can achieve a compression ratio of 100:1 with significant loss and possibly 20:1 with little noticeable loss. 2. A graphic stored as a file in the JPEG format.

JPEG File Interchange Format *n.* See JFIF.

.jpg *n.* The file extension that identifies graphic images encoded in the JPEG File Interchange Format, as originally specified by the Joint Photographic Experts Group (JPEG). Inline graphics on World Wide Web pages are often .jpg files, such as coolgraphic.jpg. See also JPEG (definition 2).

JScript *n.* An interpreted, object-based scripting language that borrows from C, C++, and Java. It is Microsoft's implementation of the ECMA 262 language specification (ECMAScript Edition 3). The latest versions of JavaScript and JScript are compliant with the European Computer Manufacturing Association's ECMAScript Language Specification (ECMA 262 standard, for short).

JSGF *n.* See Java Speech Grammar Format.

JSP *n.* Short for Java Server Pages. A technology created by Sun Microsystems to enable development of platform-independent Web-based applications. Using HTML and XML tags and Java scriptlets, JSP helps Web site developers create cross-platform programmes. JSP scriptlets run on the server, not in a Web browser, and generate dynamic content on Web pages, with the ability to integrate content from a variety of data sources, such as databases, files, and JavaBean components. Web site developers can concentrate on design and display of a Web site without the need for application development expertise. See also Java, JavaBean.

JSP container *n.* Short for Java Server Pages container. In the J2EE platform, a JSP container provides the same services as a servlet container, such as providing network services over which requests and responses are sent, decoding requests, and formatting responses. All servlet containers must support HTTP as a protocol for requests and responses, but they may also support additional request-response protocols such as HTTPS. The JSP container is also an engine that interprets and processes JSP pages into a servlet. See also container, HTTP, HTTPS, J2EE, servlet, servlet container.

JTA *n.* Acronym for Java Transaction API. In the J2EE platform, JTA specifies transactions, comments, and rollbacks used by EJBs (Enterprise JavaBeans). It is a high-level, implementation-independent protocol API that allows applications and application servers to access transactions. See also application programming interface, J2EE, JTS, rollback.

JTS *n.* Acronym for Java Transaction Services. In the J2EE platform, JTS specifies the implementation of a transaction manager that supports JTA and implements the Java mapping of the OMG Object Transaction Service specification at a level below the API. JTS propagates transactions using the Internet Inter-ORB Protocol (IIOP). See also application programming interface, J2EE, JTA, rollback.

JUG *n.* Acronym for Java User Group. A user group that meets to discuss the Java programming language and the Java platform. See also user group.

Jughead *n.* Acronym for Jonzy's Universal Gopher Hierarchy Excavation and Display. An Internet service that enables a user to locate directories in Gopherspace through a keyword search. A Jughead server indexes keywords appearing in directory titles in top-level Gopher menus but does not index the files within the directories. To access Jughead, users must point their Gopher clients to a Jughead server. See also Gopher, Gopherspace.

Jukebox *n.* Software that is designed to play a list of sound files in a user-specified order reminiscent of jukeboxes used to play vinyl records. See also CD-ROM jukebox.

Jumper *n.* A small plug or wire that can be connected between different points in an electronic circuit in order to alter an aspect of a hardware configuration.

Jump instruction *n.* An instruction that transfers the flow of execution from one statement or instruction to another. See also GOTO statement, transfer statement.

Jump page *n.* See doorway page.

Jump table *n.* See dispatch table.

Jump to .NET *n.* Acronym for Java User Migration Path to Microsoft .NET. A set of Microsoft technologies and services that enable Java programmers to preserve, enhance, and migrate Java language projects onto the Microsoft .NET platform. It includes tools for interoperability of existing code, Java language syntax support, and automated conversion of Java source code to C#. JUMP to .NET enables programmers using the Java language to move existing code to the Microsoft .NET platform. See also C#, .NET.

Junction *n.* 1. Any point at which two or more electrical components are connected. 2. The contact between two types of semiconductors, such as N-type and P-type semiconductors. See also N-type semiconductor, P-type semiconductor, semiconductor.

Justify *vb.* 1. To align vertically. 2. To align lines of text evenly along both the left and right margins of a column by inserting extra space between the words in each line. If the spacing is excessive, it can be reduced by rewriting or by hyphenating words at the ends of lines. See also align (definition 1).

Just-in-time *adj.* 1. Describing a system of inventory control and industrial production management based on the Japanese kanban system. Under a just-in-time system, workers receive materials from suppliers "just in time" for scheduled manufacturing to take place. Line workers generally signal that they require materials by means of a card or a computerised request system. 2. Describing an action that is taken only when it becomes necessary, such as just-in-time compilation or just-in-time object activation. 3. Describing a compiler that compiles Java on the fly. Acronym: JIT. See also Java, on the fly.

JVM *n.* See Java Virtual Machine.

K

K 1 *n.* Short for kilobyte.

K 2 prefix See kilo-.

K&R C *n.* Short for (Brian W.) Kernighan and (Dennis M.) Ritchie C. The version of the C programming language, defined by those two authors, that was the informal C standard until a more formal standard was developed by an ANSI committee. See also C.

Kalman filter *n.* An adaptive filter used to estimate the state of a system from measurements that contain random errors. This recursive adaptive filter determines the correct parameters of a process model. Each new measurement allows the parameters of a model to be predicted and adjusted, thus providing an estimate of error at each update. The Kalman filter's computational structure and its ability to incorporate the effects of noise (from both measurement and modeling) recommends itself for use in computer vision tracking applications. See also active vision, distortion, modeling, noise.

Kamikaze packet *n.* See Chernobyl packet.

Kashidas *n.* Special characters that are used to extend the joiner between two Arabic characters. Kashidas are used to improve the appearance of justified text by visually lengthening words rather than increasing the spacing between words. See the illustration.

Kashidas.

Kb *n.* See kilobit.

KB *n.* 1. See kilobyte. 2. Short for Knowledge Base. Primary source of product information for Microsoft support engineers and customers. This comprehensive collection of articles, updated daily, contains detailed how-to information, answers to technical-support questions, and known issues. Also called: Microsoft Knowledge Base.

KDE *n.* Acronym for K Desktop Environment. A popular open-source desktop environment originally intended for UNIX workstations and now developed for the Linux operating system. KDE provides a graphical user interface (GUI) and basic applications that correspond to those found with Microsoft Windows or the Macintosh operating system. By providing a mainstream environment and familiar desktop appearance, KDE is intended to make Linux easier for users. KDE and GNOME are leading contenders for consideration as a Linux desktop standard. See also GNOME, GUI.

Kerberos *n.* A network authentication protocol developed by MIT. Kerberos authenticates the identity of users attempting to log on to a network and encrypts their communications through secret-key cryptography. A free implementation of Kerberos is available from MIT, although it is also available in many commercial products. Also called: Kerberos v5 authentication protocol. See also authentication, cryptography, IPSec.

Kermit *n.* A file transfer protocol used in asynchronous communications between computers. Kermit is a very flexible protocol used in many software packages designed for communications over telephone lines.

Kern *vb.* To alter selectively the distance between pairs of letters for readability and to make the type spacing more balanced and proportional. See the illustration. The first three letters of the second example are kerned.

Kernel *n.* The core of an operating system—the portion of the system that manages memory, files, and peripheral devices; maintains the time and date; launches applications; and allocates system resources.

Kernel Extension *n.* See KEXT.

Kernel panic *n.* In Mac OS X and UNIX-based systems, a type of error that occurs when the core level of the operating system is unable to properly handle an instruction. A kernel panic appears to the user as a text screen containing information about the nature of the error, which often can be corrected with a system reboot.

KEXT *n.* Acronym for Kernel Extension. In Mac OS X, an extension mechanism created to expand the functionality of the operating system kernel. KEXTs are modular and dynamic loading, and they may be created for any service that requires access to kernel internal interfaces. Creation of a KEXT allows the loading of pieces of code into the kernel without the need to recompile.

Key *n.* 1. On a keyboard, the combination of a plastic keycap, a tension mechanism that suspends the keycap but allows it to be pressed down, and an electronic mechanism that records the key press and key release. 2. In database management, an identifier for a record or group of records in a datafile. See also B-tree, hash, index(definition 1), inverted list, key field. 3. In encryption and digital signatures, a string of bits used for encrypting and decrypting information to be transmitted. Encryption commonly relies on two different types of keys, a public key known to more than one person (say, both the sender and the receiver) and a private key known only to one person (typically, the sender). 4. A metal object used with a physical lock to disable a computer system.

Key binary large object *n.* A key binary large object (BLOB) provides a way to store keys outside of the cryptographic service provider (CSP) and is used to transfer keys securely from one CSP to another. A key BLOB consists of a standard header followed by data representing the key. Acronym: key BLOB.

Key BLOB *n.* See key binary large object.

Keyboard *n.* A hardware unit with a set of switches that resembles a typewriter keyboard and that conveys information from a user to a computer or data communications circuit. See also Alt key, Apple key, arrow key, Backspace key, Break key, Caps Lock key, character code, Clear key, Command key, control character, Control key, Delete key, Dvorak keyboard, End key, enhanced keyboard, Enter key, ergonomic keyboard, Escape key, function key, Help key, Home key, Insert key, keyboard buffer, keyboard controller, keyboard enhancer, keycap, key code, numeric keypad, Num Lock key, Option key, original Macintosh keyboard, Page Down key, Page Up key, Pause key, PC/XT keyboard, Power-on key, Print Screen key, QWERTY keyboard, Return key, scan code, Scroll Lock key, Shift key, Sys Req key, Tab key.

Keyboard buffer *n.* A small amount of system memory that stores the most recently typed characters. This buffer is used to store typed characters that have not yet been processed. Also called: type-ahead buffer.

Keyboard controller *n.* A microprocessor installed in a keyboard whose primary function is to wait for and report on keystrokes.

Keyboard enhancer *n.* A programme that monitors keystrokes as they are typed and that can be used to redefine the meaning of certain keys or key combinations. Keyboard enhancers are used to create and store macros—sets of keystrokes, mouse actions, menu selections, or other instructions—that are then assigned to keys. Also called: macro programme.

Keyboard layout *n.* The key arrangement used for a particular keyboard, including such factors as the number of keys (101 is the current standard) and the configuration of the keys (QWERTY is the United States standard). Some proprietary systems use different layouts, and many allow you to map the keys to characters according to your preferences.

Keyboard port *n.* The connector on a computer that receives data from the keyboard. See also port1 (definition 1).

Keyboard processor *n.* See keyboard controller.

Keyboard repeat *n.* See typematic.

Keyboard shortcut *n.* See application shortcut key.

Keyboard template *n.* A piece of plastic or heavy paper that fits over or around part of the keyboard, such as the function keys, and has information printed on it about the meanings of the keys.

Keycap *n.* The plastic piece identifying a key on a keyboard.

Key code *n.* A unique code number assigned to a particular key on a computer keyboard, used to tell the computer which key has been pressed or released. A key code is a special identifier for the key itself and is always the same for a particular key, regardless of the letter, number, or symbol on the key or the character generated by the key.

Key escrow *n.* An approach to key recovery in which an encryption key is provided to a third party approved by a government agency so that any encrypted message can, if necessary, be decrypted and read by the government. See also encryption, key recovery.

Key field *n.* A field in a record structure or an attribute of a relational table that has been designated to be part of a key. Any field can be keyed, or indexed, to improve or simplify the performance of retrieval and/or update operations. See also attribute (definition 1), field (definition 1), primary key.

Key-frame *adj.* Describing animation in which starting and ending positions of an object are given, and all frames in between are interpolated by a computer to produce smooth automated animation. Most ray-traced computer animation is created using this technique. See also ray tracing.

Key in *vb.* To enter information into a computer by typing it on the computer's keyboard.

Keymaster *n.* A common host name assigned by network administrators to a gateway or router. Popularised in part by the Keymaster character in the 1984 movie "Ghostbusters." See also gatekeeper.

Keypad *n.* See numeric keypad.

Key pair *n.* A widely used encryption scheme that allows secure use of digital certificate identification. A key pair consists of a public key and a private key. The public key is shared with other individuals; the private key is known only to its owner. The public and private key form an asymmetric pair, meaning the keys on either end of a transmission are different. A message encrypted with the public key can be decrypted only with the private key, and a message encrypted with the private key can be decrypted only with the public key.

Keypunch *n.* An archaic keyboard-activated device used to punch holes in predetermined locations on paper cards roughly the size of a business envelope. It was used to provide programmes and data to early computing systems.

Key recovery *n.* General term referring to the ability to retrieve a cryptographic key in order to decode encrypted information. Key recovery can be used to regain a lost key or, as has been publicised in recent years, can be used as a means of enabling government agencies to decode encrypted information. One method of providing for key recovery is known as key escrow. See also encryption, key escrow, private key.

Key sort *n.* See tag sort.

Keystroke *n.* The act of pressing a key on a keyboard to enter a character or initiate a command in a programme. The efficiency and ease of use of certain applications is often measured in terms of how many keystrokes it takes to perform common operations. See also command, key (definition 1), keyboard.

Keyword *n.* 1. A characteristic word, phrase, or code that is stored in a key field and is used to conduct sorting or searching operations on records in a database. See also key field. 2. Any of the set of words that composes a given programming language or set of operating-system routines. See also reserved word.

Keyword density *n.* A measurement of the keywords on a Web page as a percentage of total text. High keyword density can increase a Web site's probability of being found by search engines, some of which use keyword density to rank a Web page's relevance to an Internet search. See also keyword (definition 1).

Keyword-in-context *n.* An automatic search methodology that creates indexes of document text or titles. Each keyword is stored in the resulting index along with some surrounding text, usually the word or phrase that precedes or follows the keyword in the text or title. Acronym: KWIC.

Keyword stuffing *vb.* See spamdexter.

Khornerstone *n.* A benchmark of floating-point calculation performance used to test UNIX workstations. See also benchmark1, Dhrystone, floating-point operation, Whetstone.

kHz *n.* See kilohertz.

Kiddie script *n.* A simple and easy-to-use executable script used to hack into a computer or network. Unlike the traditional hacker's techniques, which require detailed networking and programming knowledge, a kiddie script does not require any specialised skills or knowledge. See also script, script kiddie.

Kill *vb.* 1. To stop or abort a process in a programme or operating system. 2. In file management, to erase a file, often without hope of reversing the action.

Killer app *n.* 1. An application of such popularity and widespread standardisation that it fuels sales of the hardware platform or operating system for which it was written. See also application. 2. An application that supplants its competition. See also application.

Kill file *n.* See bozo filter.

kilo- prefix 1. Metric prefix meaning 103 (one thousand). 2. In computer-related terms, a prefix meaning 210 (1024).

Kilobaud *n.* A unit of measure of the transmission capacity of a communications channel, equal to 210 (1024) baud. See also baud.

Kilobit *n.* A data unit equal to 1024 bits. Abbreviated Kb or Kbit.

Kilobits per second *n.* Data transfer speed, as through a modem or on a network, measured in multiples of 1024 bits per second. Abbreviated Kbps.

Kilobyte *n.* A data unit of 1024 bytes. Abbreviated K, KB, or Kbyte. See also kilo-.

Kilocycle *n.* A unit of measurement representing 1000 cycles, generally meaning 1000 cycles per second. Abbreviated kc. See also kilohertz.

Kilohertz *n.* A measure of frequency equivalent to 1000 hertz, or 1000 cycles per second. Abbreviated kHz. See also hertz.

Kinesis ergonomic keyboard *n.* A keyboard designed ergonomically to eliminate repetitive strain injuries. See also ergonomic keyboard, repetitive strain injury.

Kiosk *n.* A freestanding computer or terminal that provides information to the public, usually through a multimedia display.

Kludge *n.* 1. A short-term or makeshift hardware construction. 2. A programme characterised by a lack of design or forethought, as if written in a hurry to satisfy an immediate need. A kludge basically operates properly, but its construction or design is severely lacking in elegance or logical efficiency. See also braindamaged, hack1 (definition 1), spaghetti code.

Knockout *n.* 1. In multicolour printing, the process of removing from one image the overlapping parts of a graphic or text that are to be printed in a different colour so that ink colours will not mix. See the illustration. See also spot colour. 2. In hardware, a section of a panel that can be removed to make space for a switch or other component.

Knowbot *n.* Short for knowledge robot. An artificial-intelligence programme that follows a set of predetermined rules to perform work, such as searching for files or looking for documents that contain specific pieces of information on a network, such as the Internet. See also bot (definition 2).

Knowledge acquisition *n.* The process of translating knowledge from one or more human experts into a form of representation usable by a computer, for the purpose of developing an expert system. See also expert system.

Knowledge base *n.* A form of database used in expert systems that contains the accumulated body of knowledge of human specialists in a particular field. The reasoning ability or problem-solving approach that a specialist would use is contained in the inference engine, which forms another crucial part of an expert system. See also expert system, inference engine.

Knowledge-based system *n.* See expert system.

Knowledge domain *n.* The specific area of expertise to which an expert system is devoted. See also expert system.

Knowledge engineer *n.* A computer scientist who builds an expert system by acquiring the needed knowledge and translating it into a programme. See also expert system.

Knowledge representation *n.* The methodology that forms the basis for the decision-making structure in an expert system, usually taking the form of if-then rules. See also expert system.

Knowledge worker *n.* Term invented by a management consultant, Peter Drucker, for an individual whose job centers on the collection, processing, and application of information, especially when meaningful value is added to purely factual information. A knowledge worker is someone with both formal education and the ability to apply that education—knowledge—in a work situation. See also information explosion.

Korn shell *n.* A command-line interface, available under UNIX, that combines features of the Bourne and C shells. The Korn shell is fully compatible with the Bourne shell but also offers the history and command-line editing capabilities of the C shell. See also command-line interface, shell1, UNIX.

KSR terminal *n.* Short for keyboard send/receive terminal. A type of terminal that accepts input from a keyboard only and uses an internal printer rather than a screen to display the keyboard input and the output received from the sending terminal. See also TTY.

KWIC *n.* See keyword-in-context.

L

L1 cache *n.* A memory cache built into i486 and higher-level processors to help improve processing speed. The L1 cache, typically containing 8 KB, can be read in a single clock cycle, so it is tried first. The i486 contains one L1 cache; the Pentium contains two, one for code and one for data. Also called: level 1 cache, on-chip cache. See also cache, i486DX, Pentium.

L2 cache *n.* A memory cache consisting of static RAM on a motherboard that uses an i486 or higher-level processor. The L2 cache, which typically contains 128 KB to 1 MB, is faster than the system DRAM but slower than the L1 cache built into the CPU chip. Also called: level 2 cache. See also cache, dynamic RAM, i486DX, static RAM.

L2TP *n.* See Layer Two Tunneling Protocol.

L8R *adv.* Abbreviation for later, as in "See you later," an expression often used in e-mail or Usenet groups as a closing remark.

Label *n.* An identifier. A label can be a physical item, such as a stick-on tag used to identify disks and other computer equipment, or an electronic label added to floppy disks or hard disks. It can also be a word, symbol, or other group of characters used to identify a file, a storage medium, an element defined in a computer programme, or a specific item in a document such as a spreadsheet or a chart. See also identifier.

Label edge router *n.* See MPLS.

Label prefix *n.* In a spreadsheet, a character at the beginning of a cell entry that identifies the entry to the programme as a label.

Label switching *n.* See MPLS.

Label switch path *n.* See MPLS.

Label switch router *n.* See MPLS.

LACP *n.* Acronym for Link Aggregation Control Protocol. See link aggregation.

Lag *n.* The time difference between two events. In electronics, a lag is a delay between a change in input and a change in output. On computer displays, a lag is a fading brightness left on the phosphor coating of the screen after an image changes. See also persistence.

LAN *n.* Acronym for local area network. A group of computers and other devices dispersed over a relatively limited area and connected by a communications link that enables any device to interact with any other on the network. LANs commonly include PCs and shared resources such as laser printers and large hard disks. The devices on a LAN are known as nodes, and the nodes are connected by cables through which messages are transmitted. See also baseband network, broadband network, bus network, client/server architecture, collision detection, communications protocol, contention, CSMA/CD, network, peer-to-peer architecture, ring network, star network.

Landscape mode *n.* A horizontal print orientation in which text or images are printed "sideways"—that is, the width of the image on the page is greater than the height.

Landscape monitor *n.* A monitor that is wider than it is high. Landscape monitors are usually about 33 per cent wider than they are high—roughly the same proportion as a television screen.

LANE *n.* Acronym for LAN Emulation. See ATM (definition 1), communications protocol, LAN.

LANGID *n.* See language identifier.

Language *n.* See programming language.

Language-description language *n.* See metalanguage.

Language identifier *n.* A standard international numeric abbreviation for a country or geographical region. A language identifier is a 16-bit value that consists of a primary language identifier and a secondary language identifier. Acronym: LANGID. See also locale identifier.

Language processor *n.* A hardware device or a software programme designed to accept instructions written in a particular language and translate them into machine code. See also compiler (definition 2), interpreter.

Language translation programme *n.* A programme that translates statements written in one programming language into another programming language (usually from one high-level language into another). See also high-level language.

LAN Manager *n.* An older LAN (local area network) technology developed by Microsoft and distributed by Microsoft, IBM (as IBM LAN Server), and other original equipment manufacturers. Superseded by TCP/IP networking protocols in Windows 9x, LAN Manager implemented the NetBEUI protocol and was notable for its small stack size. It was used to connect computers running the MS-DOS, OS/2, or UNIX operating systems to allow users to share files and system resources and to run distributed applications using a client/server architecture. See also client/server architecture, LAN, NetBEUI.

LANtastic *n.* A network operating system from Artisoft designed to support both peer-to-peer and client/server networks consisting of PCs running a mix of MS-DOS and Windows operating systems.

Laptop *n.* A small, portable personal computer that runs on either batteries or AC power, designed for use during travel. Laptops have flat LCD or plasma screens and small keyboards. Most can run the same software as their desktop counterparts and can accept similar peripherals, such as sound cards, internal or external modems, floppy disks, and CD-ROM drives. Some laptops are designed to be plugged into a docking station, effectively making them desktop computers. Most have connectors for plugging in external keyboards and full-sized monitors. Older laptops weighed as much as 15 pounds; current laptops can weigh as little as 5 pounds without peripherals. While notebook is the current term for ultralight portable computers, these machines are also commonly referred to as laptops. See also portable computer.

Large model *n.* A memory model of the Intel 80x86 processor family. The large model allows both code and data to exceed 64 kilobytes, but the total of both must generally be less than 1 megabyte. Each data structure must be less than 64 kilobytes in size. See also memory model.

Large-scale integration *n.* A term describing a chip on which circuit elements number in the thousands. Acronym: LSI. See also integrated circuit.

Laser or LASER *n.* Acronym for light amplification by stimulated emission of radiation. A device that uses certain quantum effects to produce coherent light, which travels with greater efficiency than noncoherent light because the beam diverges only slightly as it travels. Lasers are used in computer technology to transmit data through fiberoptic cables, to read and write data on CD-ROMs, and to place an image on a photosensitive drum in laser printers.

Laser engine *n.* See printer engine.

Laser printer *n.* An electrophotographic printer that is based on the technology used by photocopiers. A focused laser beam and a rotating mirror are used to draw an image of the desired page on a photosensitive drum. This image is converted on the drum into an electrostatic charge, which attracts and holds toner. A piece of electrostatically charged paper is rolled against the drum, which pulls the toner away from the drum and onto the paper. Heat is then applied to fuse the toner to the paper. Finally, the electrical charge is removed from the drum, and the excess toner is collected. By omitting the final step and repeating only the toner-application and paper-handling steps, the printer can make multiple copies. The only serious drawback of a laser printer is that it offers less paper-handling flexibility than do dot-matrix printers. Both multipart forms and wide-carriage printing, for example, are better handled by line printers or dot-matrix printers. See also electrophotographic printers, nonimpact printer, page print

Laser storage *n.* The use of optical read/write technology with metallic discs for information storage. See also compact disc.

LaserWriter 35 *n.* The standard set of 35 PostScript fonts for the Apple LaserWriter family of laser printers. See also laser printer, PostScript font.

Last in, first out *n.* A method of processing a queue in which items are removed in inverse order relative to the order in which they were added—that is, the last in is the first out. Acronym: LIFO. See also stack.

Last mile *n.* The connection (which may in fact be more or less than one mile) between an end user's system and that of a service provider, such as a telephone company. The "last mile" connection historically has referred to the twisted-pair copper wires used between a home and the telephone company. While this definition remains accurate, "last mile" is now often used more broadly to refer to the link between an end user's system and the high-speed Internet access technology of a service provider, such as an ISP (Internet service provider). Thus, for modem users accessing the Internet through voice-grade lines, the last mile is still equivalent to the phone company's twisted-pair copper wiring. However, because standard modem transmission over voice-grade lines is sometimes frustratingly slow, other last mile solutions have been designed to provide greater speed and bandwidth. These include coaxial cable (used in cable TV), fiber optics, or a radio link (such as a cellular telephone or a point-to-point link). DSL and I

Latch *n.* A circuit or circuit element used to maintain a particular state, such as on or off, or logical true or false. A latch changes state only in response to a particular input. See also flip-flop.

Late binding *n.* See dynamic binding.

Latency *n.* The time required for a signal to travel from one point on a network to another. See also ping1 (definition 1).

LaTeX1 or LATEX *n.* A document preparation system based on TeX, developed by Leslie Lamport. By using simple, intuitive commands for text elements such as headers, LaTeX lets the user focus more on document content than document appearance. See also header (definition 1), TeX.

LaTeX2 *vb.* To process a LaTeX file. See also LaTeX1.

Launch *vb.* To activate an application programme (especially on the Macintosh) from the operating system's user interface.

Launcher *n.* In Mac OS, a programme that organises frequently used applications and programmes and that allows the user to execute them with a single mouse click.

Layer *n.* 1. The protocol or protocols operating at a particular level within a protocol suite, such as IP within the TCP/IP suite. Each layer is responsible for providing specific services or functions for computers exchanging information over a communications network (such as the layers in the ISO/OSI reference model) and information is passed from one layer to the next. Although different suites have varying numbers of levels, generally the highest layer deals with software interactions at the application level, and the lowest governs hardware-level connections between different computers. 2. In communications and distributed processing, a set of rules and standards that handles a particular class of events.

Layer 4 switching *n.* In Network Address Translation (NAT), a function that handles incoming packets and changes the IP address and destination port to transfer them to the proper server within the private network, and then readdresses return packets leaving the private network. Because layer 4 switching controls the address on packets moving in both directions, the internal network remains transparent to the client. See also LVS, NAT.

Layered architecture *n.* The division of a network model into multiple discrete layers, or levels, through which messages pass as they are prepared for transmission. In a layered architecture, protocols at each layer provide specific services or functions and rely on protocols in the layers above and below them for other needed services. See also protocol.

Layered interface *n.* In programming, one or more levels of routines lying between an application and the computing hardware and separating activities according to the type of task the activities are designed to carry out. Ultimately, such an interface makes it easier to adapt a programme to different types of equipment. See the illustration.

Layering *n.* In computer graphics, the grouping of logically related elements in a drawing. Layering enables a programme user to view, and work on independently, portions of a graphic instead of the entire drawing.

Layer Two Tunneling Protocol *n.* An industry-standard Internet tunneling protocol that provides encapsulation for sending Point-to-Point Protocol (PPP) frames across packet-oriented media. For IP networks, Layer Two Tunneling Protocol traffic is sent as User Datagram Protocol (UDP) messages. In Microsoft operating systems, this protocol is used in conjunction with Internet Protocol security (IPSec) as a virtual private network (VPN) technology to provide remote access or router-to-router VPN connections. Layer Two Tunneling Protocol is described in RFC 2661. Acronym: L2TP. See also IPSec, Point-to-Point Protocol, tunnel, User Datagram Protocol.

Layout *n.* 1. The overall plan or design of a document system. See also page layout. 2. In programming, the order and sequence of input and output. 3. In computer design, the arrangement of circuits and other components of the system.

Lazy evaluation *n.* A programming mechanism that allows an evaluation action to be performed only when needed and only to a certain extent. Lazy evaluation allows a programme to handle data objects such as extremely large tables and lists in a timely and effective manner.

LBA *n.* See logical block addressing.

LCC *n.* See leaded chip carrier, leadless chip carrier.

LCD *n.* In some FTP clients, the command that changes the current directory on the local system. See also FTP client.

LCD *n.* See liquid crystal display.

LCD printer *n.* Short for Liquid Crystal Display printer. An electrophotographic printer similar to a laser printer and often incorrectly labeled as one. LCD printers use a bright light source, typically a halogen lamp. Also called: liquid crystal shutter printer. See also electrophotographic printers, nonimpact printer, page printer.

LCD projector *n.* Short for Liquid Crystal Display projector. A type of data projector that uses electricity to turn the pixels representing a projected image off or on. Unlike the newer DLP projectors, LCD projectors are able to display shades of colour (gray scale) by controlling the amount of electricity used to turn a particular pixel on or off. See also gray scale, liquid crystal display.

LCP *n.* See Point-to-Point Protocol.

LDAP *n.* See Lightweight Directory Access Protocol.

Lead 1 *n.* In electronics, the metallic connector of certain components such as resistors and capacitors.

Lead 2 *n.* In typography, the amount of vertical space between two lines of text.

Leaded chip carrier *n.* A method of mounting chips on boards. A leaded chip carrier has leglike pins for connecting it to the board. The chip makes contact with the board through surface mount technology in which the leads are soldered to the surface rather than into predrilled holes. Somewhat confusingly, a leaded chip carrier goes by the same acronym (LCC) as a leadless chip carrier. Acronym: LCC.

Leader *n.* A row of dots, hyphens, or other such characters used to lead the eye across a printed page to related information. Leaders can be created by many word processors and other programmes.

Leading *n.* The space, expressed in points, between lines of type, measured from the baseline (bottom) of one line to the baseline of the next. The term is derived from the traditional typesetting practice of inserting a thin bar of lead between lines of metal type. See the illustration. See also point.

Leading edge *n.* The initial part of an electronic signal. If a digital signal switches from off to on and then back to off, the transition from off to on is the leading edge of the signal.

Leading zero *n.* A zero that precedes the most significant (leftmost) digit of a number. One or more leading zeros may be used as fill characters in a field containing numeric input. Leading zeros have no significance in the value of a number.

Lead ion battery *n.* An energy storage device that is based on the conversion of chemical to electrical energy as ions flow from one terminal to another through an acid medium in which lead and copper are suspended. This type of battery is used in laptop and notebook computers.

Leadless chip carrier *n.* A method of mounting chips on boards. A leadless chip carrier has contacts, rather than leglike pins, for connecting it to the board. The chip simply rests in a socket that has contacts on its base for completing the connection, and the chip is clamped in place so that the contacts are secure. Acronym: LCC. See also PLCC.

Leaf *n.* Any node (location) in a tree structure that is at the farthest distance from the root (primary node), no matter which path is followed. Thus, in any tree, a leaf is a node at the end of a branch—one that has no descendants. See also root, subtree, tree.

Leapfrog attack *n.* A method used by hackers to make an attack difficult to trace back to the source. In a leapfrog attack the hacker uses a User ID stolen from another source or routes information through a series of hosts to hide their identity and obscure the origin of the attack. Also called: network weaving.

Leapfrog test *n.* A diagnostic routine, used for testing disk or tape storage, that repeatedly copies itself onto the storage medium.

Leap year *n.* A potential problem for some systems that follow an erroneous algorithm for calculating leap years. There are three rules for calculating leap years: (1) A year is a leap year if it is divisible by 4, but (2) not if it is divisible by 100, unless (3) it is also divisible by 400. Thus, 1900 was not a leap year, but 2000 was.

Leased line *n.* See dedicated line (definition 1).

Least significant bit *n.* In a sequence of one or more bytes, the low-order (usually rightmost) bit of a binary number. Acronym: LSB. See also low-order.

Least significant character *n.* The low-order, or rightmost, character in a string. Acronym: LSC. See also low-order.

Least significant digit *n.* The low-order, or rightmost, digit in the normal representation of a number. Acronym: LSD. See also low-order.

LED *n.* See light-emitting diode.

LED printer *n.* Short for light-emitting diode printer. An electrophotographic printer similar to LCD and laser printers. The significant difference between LED and laser or LCD printers is in the light source; LED printers use an array of light-emitting diodes. See also electrophotographic printers, light-emitting diode, nonimpact printer, page printer.

Left justification *n.* In typesetting, word processing, and desktop publishing, the process of aligning text evenly along the left margin of a column or page. The right edge of the text is ragged. See also justify (definition 1), rag.

Left-justify *vb.* To justify, as text, along the left. See also justify (definition 1), rag.

Legacy *adj.* Of or pertaining to documents, data, or hardware that existed prior to a certain time. The designation refers particularly to a change in process or technique that requires translating old data files to a new system.

Legacy data *n.* Data acquired by an organisation that was compiled by another organisation. The acquiring organisation thus receives the existing information as a "legacy" from the information's prior owner.

Legacy system *n.* A computer, software programme, network, or other computer equipment that remains in use after a business or organisation installs new systems. Compatibility with legacy systems is an important consideration when a new version is installed. For example, will a new spreadsheet software release be able to read the existing business records without expensive and time-consuming conversion to a new format? Legacy systems in many organisations are based on mainframe computers, which may be either augmented or slowly replaced by client/server architectures. See also mainframe computer.

Legend *n.* Text that describes or explains a graphic, usually printed below the graphic. On a graph or map, the legend is the key to the patterns or the symbols used.

Lempel Ziv compression *n.* A data compression method designed by Abraham Lempel and Jakob Ziv in 1977 and 1978. Lempel Ziv compression is based on the substitution of certain values for repeated data. It is implemented in two basic forms: LZ77, which is based on values that point to the positions of repeating data, and LZ78, which builds a dictionary and uses the dictionary index to point to repeating data. An enhanced version of LZ78, known as LZW, is implemented in well-known file formats, such as GIF and TIF. See also .lzh, LZW compression.

Length *n.* The number of linear units of storage space occupied by an object, such as a file on disk or a data structure in a programme, typically measured in bits, bytes, or blocks.

LEO *n.* See low-Earth-orbit satellite.

LER *n.* See MPLS.

Less than *adj.* See relational operator.

Less than or equal to *adj.* See relational operator.

Letterbomb *n.* An e-mail message that is intended to impair the recipient's computer use. Some sequences of control characters can lock up a terminal, files attached to the message may contain viruses or Trojan horses, and a sufficiently large message can overflow a mailbox or crash a system. See also control character, e-mail(definition 1), mailbox, Trojan horse, virus.

Letter quality *adj.* Pertaining to or being a level of print quality on dot-matrix printers that is better than draft quality. As the name implies, letter quality is supposed to be crisp and dark enough for use in business letters. See also print quality.

Letter-quality printer *n.* Any printer that produces output high enough in quality to be acceptable for business letters. See also daisy-wheel printer, laser printer.

Level 1 cache *n.* See L1 cache.

Level 2 cache *n.* See L2 cache.

Lexicographic sort *n.* A sort that arranges items in the order in which they would appear if listed in a dictionary. A lexicographic sort puts numbers, for instance, where they would be if they were spelled out; for example, 567 would fall in the Fs.

Lexicon *n.* 1. The words of a language and their definitions. 2. In programming, the identifiers, keywords, constants, and other elements of a language that make up its "vocabulary." The ways in which these vocabulary elements can be put together is the syntax of the language.

LF *n.* See linefeed.

LHARC *n.* A freeware file-compression utility programme developed by Haruyasu Yoshizaki and introduced in 1988. With LHARC, the contents of one or more files can be compressed into a singular, smaller file, with the extension .lha. A copy of the programme is required to uncompress these files. LHARC can also embed a small programme with the compressed information and save everything in a single file, called a self-extracting archive, with an .exe extension. As a result, the recipient of the compressed file does not need a separate utility programme to uncompress the file. See also freeware, PKZIP, utility programme.

Library *n.* 1. In programming, a collection of routines stored in a file. Each set of instructions in a library has a name, and each performs a different task. 2. A collection of software or data files.

Library routine *n.* In programming, a routine stored in a collection of routines (a library) that can be used by any programme that can link into the library. See also function library, library (definition 1).

License agreement *n.* A legal contract between a software provider and a user specifying the rights of the user regarding the software. Usually the license agreement is in effect with retail software once the user opens the software package. See also End-User License Agreement.

Licensing key *n.* A short character string that serves as a password during the installation of licensed commercial software. The use of licensing keys is a security device aimed at reducing illegal duplication of licensed software.

LIFO *n.* See last in, first out.

Ligature *n.* In typography, a single character created from two joined letters that replaces the two separate letters. Because ligatures are not included with all digital fonts, their use may cause text problems in font substitution situations.

Light-emitting diode *n.* A semiconductor device that converts electrical energy into light, used, for example, for the activity lights on computer disk drives. Light-emitting diodes work on the principle of electroluminescence and are highly efficient, producing little heat for the amount of light output. Acronym: LED.

Light guide *n.* A structure, such as a fiberoptic filament, designed to transmit light over distances with minimal attenuation or loss.

Lightmap *n.* A basic lighting scheme used in 3D computer game rendering and other digital animation applications. A lightmap generates a precalculated 3D grid for lighting all objects in a game but cannot be adjusted for player-initiated changes within the scene.

Light pen *n.* An input device consisting of a stylus that is connected to a computer's monitor. The user points at the screen with the stylus and selects items or chooses commands either by pressing a clip on the side of the light pen or by pressing the light pen against the surface of the screen (the equivalent of performing a mouse click). See also absolute pointing device.

Light source *n.* 1. The device that provides the luminescence (for example, a bulb or laser) in any technology based on the use and interpretation of light, such as a scanner or CRT. 2. In computer graphics, the imaginary location of a source of light, which determines the shading in an image.

Lightwave system *n.* A system that transmits information by means of light.

Lightweight Directory Access Protocol *n.* A network protocol designed to work on TCP/IP stacks to extract information from a hierarchical directory such as X.500. This gives users a single tool to comb through data to find a particular piece of information, such as a user name, an e-mail address, a security certificate, or other contact information. Acronym: LDAP. See also CCITT X series.

Lightweight Internet Person Schema *n.* In Lightweight Directory Access Protocol directories, a specification for the retrieval of such information as names and -e-mail addresses. Acronym: LIPS. See also Lightweight Directory Access Protocol.

LIM EMS *n.* Acronym for Lotus/Intel/Microsoft Expanded Memory Specification. See EMS.

Limit check *n.* In programming, a test that checks specified information to verify that it is within acceptable limits. See also array.

Limiting operation *n.* Any routine or operation that constrains the performance of a larger process in which it is included; a bottleneck.

Line *n.* 1. Any wire or wires, such as power lines and telephone lines, used to transmit electrical power or signals. 2. In communications, a connection, usually a physical wire or other cable, between sending and receiving (or calling and called) devices, including telephones, computers, and terminals. 3. In a SONET network, a segment that runs between two multiplexers. See also SONET. 4. In word processing, a string of characters displayed or printed in a single horizontal row. 5. In programming, a statement (instruction) that occupies one line of the programme. In this context, the common reference is to a "programme line" or a "line of code."

Line adapter *n.* A device, such as a modem or network card, that connects a computer to a communications line and converts a signal to an acceptable form for transmission.

Line analyzer *n.* A monitoring device used to verify the integrity of a communications line and to assist in troubleshooting.

Linear *adj.* 1. Having the characteristics of a line. 2. Proceeding sequentially. For example, a linear search is one that moves from A to B to C. 3. In mathematics and electronics, having a direct and proportional relationship among characteristics or variables. For example, the output of a linear amplifier is directly proportional to the input. See also linear programming.

Linear addressing architecture *n.* An architecture that allows a microprocessor to access any individual memory location by means of a single address value. Thus, each memory location within the entire range of addressable memory has a unique, specified address. See also flat address space, segmented address space.

Linear bus *n.* See bus network.

Linear inferences per second *n.* See LIPS (definition 2).

Linear list *n.* A simple ordered list of elements in which each element except the first immediately succeeds one other element, and each except the last immediately precedes one other.

Linear memory *n.* See flat memory.

Linear programming *n.* The process of creating programmes that find optimal solutions for systems of equations (composed of linear functions) in which the terms given are not sufficient tc derive a straightforward solution.

Linear search *n.* A simple, though inefficient, search algorithm that operates by sequentially examining each element in a list until the target element is found or the last item has been completely processed. Linear searches are primarily used for very short lists. Also called: sequential search. See also search algorithm.

Linear structure *n.* A structure in which items are organised according to strict rules of precedence. In a linear structure, two conditions apply: if X precedes Y and Y precedes Z, then X precedes Z; and if X precedes Y and X precedes Z, then either Y precedes Z or Z precedes Y.

Line-based browser *n.* A Web browser whose display is based on text rather than graphics. A popular line-based browser is Lynx. See also Lynx, Web browser.

Line cap *n.* The way in which a line segment is terminated when the segment is printed, especially on a PostScript-compatible printer. See the illustration. See also line join.

Line chart *n.* A business graphic in which values from one or more sets of data are connected by lines. See the illustration.

Line concentration *n.* The funneling of multiple input channels into a smaller number of output channels. See also concentrator.

Line conditioner *n.* A device for filtering electrical power to compensate for brownouts, suppress power surges, and act as a buffer between a power line and the computer (or other piece of equipment). Line conditioners contain transformers, capacitors, and other circuitry that help regulate the quality of power to ensure that electrical flow is constant. See also brownout, UPS.

Line conditioning *n.* See conditioning, line conditioner.

Line drawing *n.* A drawing made up of solid lines without shading or other features that suggest mass or contouring.

Line driver *n.* A device used to increase transmission distance by amplifying a signal before placing it on the line or passing it along the line. See also short-haul.

Line editor *n.* A text-editing programme that numbers each line of text, working with the document on a line-by-line rather than on a word-by-word basis. See also editor.

Linefeed *n.* A control character that tells a computer or printer to advance one line below the current line without moving the position of the cursor or print head. Acronym: LF.

Line join *n.* The way in which two line segments are connected when they are printed, especially on a PostScript-compatible printer. See the illustration. See also line cap.

Line level *n.* The strength of a communications signal at a given point on the line, measured in decibels (a multiple of the base-10 logarithm of the ratio between two values) or nepers (the natural logarithm of the ratio between two values).

Line load *n.* 1. In communications, a measure of the usage of a communications line expressed as a percentage of the maximum capacity of the circuit. 2. In electronics, the amount of current carried by a line.

Line noise *n.* Spurious signals in a communications channel that interfere with the exchange of information. In an analog circuit, line noise may take the form of a pure audio tone, static, or signals leaked from another circuit. In a digital circuit, line noise is any signal that makes it difficult or impossible for the device at the receiving end of the circuit to interpret the transmitted signal accurately. See also channel.

Line number *n.* 1. A number assigned by a line editor to a line of text and used to refer to that line for purposes of viewing, editing, or printing. The line numbers are sequential. See also line editor. 2. In communications, an identifying number assigned to a communications channel.

Line printer *n.* Any printer that prints one line at a time as opposed to one character at a time (as with many dot-matrix printers) or one page at a time (as with some dot-matrix and most laser printers). Line printers typically produce the familiar 11-by-17-inch fanfold "computer" printouts. They are high-speed devices and are often used with mainframes, minicomputers, or networked machines rather than with single-user systems.

Line regulator *n.* See voltage regulator.

Line segment *n.* A portion of a line, defined by its beginning and ending points.

Lines of code *n.* A measure of programme length. Depending on circumstances, a line of code can be each line in the programme (including blank lines and comments), each line containing actual code, or each statement. See also statement.

Line spacing *n.* See leading.

Line speed *n.* See baud rate, data rate.

Lines per minute *n.* A measurement of printer speed, the number of lines of characters printed in one minute. Acronym: LPM.

Line style *n.* In desktop publishing, printing, and high-end word processing, the form and quality of a line, such as a dotted line, a double line, or a hairline. See also hairline.

Line surge *n.* A sudden, transient increase in the voltage or current carried by a line. A nearby lightning strike, for example, can cause a surge in power lines that can damage electrical equipment. Delicate types of equipment such as computers are often protected from line surges by surge suppressors placed in the power lines.

Line voltage *n.* The voltage present in a power line. In North America, line voltage is approximately 115 volts alternating current (VAC).

Line width *n.* The length of a line of type measured from the left margin to the right margin on a piece of paper or on a computer screen. On a typewriter, line width is usually measured in terms of the number of monospace alphanumeric characters that can fit on the line; on a computer monitor or printer, line width is normally measured in inches, centimeters, points, or picas. See also pica (definition 2), point1 (definition 1).

Linguistics *n.* The analytic study of human language. Close ties exist between linguistics and computer science because of the mutual interest in grammar, syntax, semantics, formal language theory, and natural-language processing.

Link 1 *vb.* 1. To produce an executable programme from compiled modules (programmes, routines, or libraries) by merging the object code (assembly language object code, executable machine code, or a variation of machine code) of the programme and resolving interconnecting references (such as a library routine called by a programme). See also linker. 2. To connect two elements in a data structure by using index variables or pointer variables. See also index (definition 1), pointer (definition 1).

Link 2 *n.* See hyperlink.

Linkage editor *n.* See linker.

Link aggregation *n.* A technique for combining two or more Ethernet connections into one logical link, or trunk, between two devices. It is used to increase the bandwidth capacity of connections and to make these connections more resilient. The IEEE 802.3ad specification standardises this process among different vendors using the Link Aggregation Control Protocol (LACP). Also called: bonding, trunking. See also IEEE 802.x.

Link Aggregation Control Protocol *n.* See link aggregation.

Link Control Protocol *n.* See Point-to-Point Protocol.

Link edit *vb.* See link1 (definition 1).

Linked list *n.* In programming, a list of nodes or elements of a data structure connected by pointers. A singly linked list has one pointer in each node pointing to the next node in the list; a doubly linked list has two pointers in each node that point to the next and previous nodes. In a circular list, the first and last nodes of the list are linked together. See also array, key (definition 2), list, node (definition 1), pointer (definition 1).

Linked object *n.* An object that is inserted into a document but still exists in the source file. When information is linked, the new document is updated automatically if the information in the original document changes. If you want to edit the linked information, double-click it and the toolbars and menus from the original programme appear, allowing you to edit it in its native format. If the original document is on your computer, changes that you make to the linked information will also appear in the original document. See also OLE, package, source document.

Linked stylesheet *n.* A stylesheet existing separately from the HTML documents to which it is linked. A linked stylesheet may be used for sets of Web pages or entire Web sites requiring a uniform appearance. Since the style is defined once and linked to associated Web pages, the entire site can be changed by modifying a single stylesheet file.

Linker *n.* A programme that links compiled modules and data files to create an executable programme. A linker can also have other functions, such as creating libraries. See also library, link1 (definition 1), programme creation.

Linkrot *n.* A condition affecting inadequately maintained Web pages that results in outdated, inoperative links to other Web pages.

Link time *n.* 1. The length of time required to link a programme. See also link1 (definition 1). 2. The period during which a programme is being linked. See also compile time (definition 2), link(definition 1), run time (definition 1).

Link-time binding *n.* Assignment of a meaning to an identifier (such as a subroutine label) in a programme at the time that various files of compiled code are linked together to form an executable programme, rather than when the source code is compiled or when the programme is run.

Linotronic *n.* Any in the series of high-quality typesetting devices known as Linotronic laser imagesetters, which can print at resolutions such as 1270 and 2540 dots per inch (dpi). These devices are commonly attached to PostScript raster image processors (RIPs) so that desktop publishing applications can typeset directly from a microcomputer. See also imagesetter, PostScript, raster image processor.

Linpack *n.* A benchmarking routine that solves 100 simultaneous equations in a test of CPU, floating-point processor, and memory access speeds. See also benchmark, central processing unit, floating-point processor.

Linux *n.* A version of the UNIX System V Release 3.0 kernel developed for PCs with 80386 and higher-level microprocessors. Developed by Linus Torvalds (for whom it is named) along with numerous collaborators worldwide, Linux is distributed free, and its source code is open to modification by anyone who chooses to work on it, although some companies distribute it as part of a commercial package with Linux-compatible utilities. The Linux kernel works with the GNU utilities developed by the Free Software Foundation, which did not produce a kernel. It is used by some as an operating system for network servers and in the 1998/1999 timeframe began to gain increased visibility through support from vendors such as IBM and Compaq. See also free software, GNU, kernel, UNIX.

Linux Virtual Server *n.* See LVS.

Linux World Expo *n.* The world's largest trade show for designers, engineers, and businesses using the Linux operating system.

Lion worm *n.* A UNIX shellscript worm first detected in early 2001 that infects Linux servers using Berkeley Internet Name Domain (BIND) tools. After it has used a BIND exploit to infect a machine, Lion steals password files and other critical information and transmits them to the hacker. Lion then installs hacking tools and replaces critical files, hiding itself and opening multiple back doors for further compromise. The Lion worm was apparently launched in early 2001 by a group of Chinese hackers with a specific political agenda. In references to this worm, "Lion" may also be spelled as "1i0n".

LIPS *n.* 1. Acronym for Language Independent Programme Subtitling. A system developed by the GIST group (C-DAC, India) and used by Indian Television for nationwide broadcast of programmes with multilingual subtitles in teletext mode. This system was judged the best design in the VLSI (Very Large Scale Integration) design contest in the VLSI '93 International Conference. Three versions of this application-specific integrated circuit (ASIC) with different features were implemented in Xilinx 3K and 4K series FPLAs (field programmable logic arrays). See also field-programmable logic array, gate array, very-large-scale integration. 2. Acronym for linear inferences per second. A measure of speed for some types of artificial-intelligence machines and expert systems. See also artificial intelligence, expert system. 3. See Lightweight Internet Person Schema.

Liquid crystal display *n.* A type of display that uses a liquid compound having a polar molecular structure, sandwiched between two transparent electrodes. When an electric field is applied, the molecules align with the field, forming a crystalline arrangement that polarises the light passing through it. A polarised filter laminated over the electrodes blocks polarised light. In this way, a grid of electrodes can selectively "turn on" a cell, or a pixel, containing the liquid crystal material, turning it dark. In some types of liquid crystal displays, an electroluminescent panel is placed behind the screen to illuminate it. Other types of liquid crystal displays are capable of reproducing colour. Acronym: LCD. See also supertwist display, twisted nematic display.

Liquid crystal display printer *n.* See LCD printer.

Liquid crystal shutter printer *n.* See LCD printer.

LISP *n.* Short for List Processing. A list-oriented programming language developed in 1959–60 by John McCarthy and used primarily to manipulate lists of data. LISP is heavily used in research and academic circles and is considered the standard language for artificial-intelligence research. See also artificial intelligence.

List *n.* A multielement data structure that has a linear (first, second, third, . . .) organisation but that allows elements to be added or removed in any order. Queues, deques, and stacks are simply lists with restrictions on adding and removing elements. See also deque, element (definition 1), linked list, queue, stack.

List box *n.* A control in Windows that enables the user to choose one option from a list of possibilities. The list box appears as a box, displaying the currently selected option, next to a button marked with a down arrow. When the user clicks the button, the list appears. The list has a scroll bar if there are more options than the list has room to show.

Listing *n.* A printed copy of programme source code. Some compilers and assemblers produce optional assembly listings during compilation or assembly. Such listings of code often have additional information such as line numbers, nested block depth, and cross-reference tables. See also assembly listing.

List processing *n.* The maintenance and manipulation of multielement data structures. This involves adding and deleting elements, writing data into elements, and traversing the list. List processing is the basis of the artificial-intelligence programming language LISP. See also LISP, list, node (definition 1).

LISTSERV *n.* One of the most popular commercial mailing list managers, marketed by L-SOFT International in versions for BITNET, UNIX, and Windows. See also mailing list, mailing list manager.

Literal *n.* A value, used in a programme, that is expressed as itself rather than as a variable's value or the result of an expression. Examples are the numbers 25 and 32.1, the character a, the string Hello, and the Boolean value TRUE. See also constant, variable.

Lithium ion battery *n.* An energy storage device based on the conversion of chemical to electrical energy in "dry" chemical cells. Despite the higher cost, the laptop industry is quickly adopting lithium ion batteries because of their increased storage capacity over both nickel cadmium and nickel metal hydride batteries, in response to the demand for greater power brought on by higher processor speeds and the use of devices such as CD-ROM drives.

Little endian *adj.* Of, pertaining to, or being a method of storing a number so that the least significant byte appears first in the number. For example, given the hexadecimal number A02B, the little endian method would cause the number to be stored as 2BA0. The little endian method is used by Intel microprocessors. Also called: reverse byte ordering.

Live1 *adj.* 1. Of or relating to real-world data or a programme working with it, as opposed to test data. 2. Of or relating to audio or video that is transmitted from one site to another as it is being produced, as opposed to being recorded before broadcast time. See also synchronous transmission. 3. Capable of being manipulated by a user to cause changes in a document or part of a document.

Live2 *n.* Used to identify a Web site that has been published to a Web server and can be browsed by site visitors. Also called: going live.

Live3D *n.* A Netscape proprietary Virtual Reality Modeling Language (VRML) plug-in for Web browsers that allows users to view and interact with a virtual-reality world. See also VRML.

Liveware *n.* A slang term for people, to distinguish them from hardware, software, and firmware. Also called: wetware.

LLC *n.* Acronym for Logical Link Control. In the IEEE 802.x specifications, the higher of two sublayers that make up the ISO/OSI data link layer. The LLC is responsible for managing communications links and handling frame traffic. See also IEEE 802.x, MAC.

Lmhosts file *n.* A local text file that lists the names of network hosts (sometimes called NetBIOS names) to IP addresses for hosts that are not located on the local subnet. See also IP address, systemroot.

Load 1 *n.* 1. The total computing burden a system carries at one time. 2. In electronics, the amount of current drawn by a device. 3. In communications, the amount of traffic on a line.

Load 2 *vb.* To place information from storage into memory for processing, if it is data, or for execution, if it is programme code.

Load-and-go *adj.* In reference to a routine, able to begin execution immediately, once loaded. The term is commonly used in reference to compilers and the machine code they generate.

Load balancing *n.* 1. In distributed processing, the distribution of activity across two or more servers in order to avoid overloading any one with too many requests from users. Load balancing can be either static or dynamic. In the former, the load is balanced ahead of time by assigning different groups of users to different servers. In the latter, software refers incoming requests at runtime to whichever server is most capable of handling them. 2. In client/server network administration, the process of reducing heavy traffic flows either by dividing a busy network segment into multiple smaller segments or by using software to distribute traffic among multiple network interface cards working simultaneously to transfer information to a server. 3. In communications, the process of routing traffic over two or more routes rather than one. Such load balancing results in faster, more reliable transmissions.

Loaded line *n.* A transmission cable fitted with loading coils, usually spaced about a mile apart, that reduce amplitude distortion in a signal by adding inductance (resistance to changes in current flow) to the line. Loaded lines minimise distortion within the range of frequencies affected by the loading coils, but the coils also reduce the bandwidth available for transmission.

Loader *n.* A utility that loads the executable code of a programme into memory for execution. On most microcomputers, the loader is an invisible part of the operating system and is automatically invoked when a programme is run. See also loader routine, load module.

Loader routine *n.* A routine that loads executable code into memory and executes it. A loader routine can be part of an operating system or it can be part of the programme itself. See also loader, overlay1 (definition 1).

Load module *n.* An executable unit of code loaded into memory by the loader. A programme consists of one or more load modules, each of which can be loaded and executed independently. See also loader.

Load point *n.* The beginning of the valid data area on a magnetic tape.

Load sharing *n.* A method of managing one or more tasks, jobs, or processes by scheduling and simultaneously executing portions of them on two or more microprocessors.

Load shedding *n.* In electrical systems, the process of turning off power to some electronic equipment in order to maintain the integrity of the power supply to other connected devices. See also UPS.

Lobby page *n.* A page of information about the broadcast that is displayed in the viewer's browser before the broadcast begins. It can contain a title, subject, host's name, information about the broadcast, and a countdown to the time of the broadcast.

Local *adj.* 1. In general, close at hand or restricted to a particular area. 2. In communications, a device that can be accessed directly rather than by means of a communications line. 3. In information processing, an operation performed by the computer at hand rather than by a remote computer. 4. In programming, a variable that is restricted in scope, that is, used in only one part (subprogram, procedure, or function) of a programme.

Local area network *n.* See LAN.

Local bus *n.* A PC architecture designed to speed up system performance by allowing some expansion boards to communicate directly with the microprocessor, bypassing the normal system bus entirely. See also PCI local bus, VL bus.

Local bypass *n.* A telephone connection used by some businesses that links separate buildings but bypasses the telephone company.

Locale identifier *n.* A 32-bit value that consists of a language identifier and a sort identifier. In code, a locale identifier (LCID) identifies the primary language and any secondary language of a specific locale. Acronym: LCID. See also language identifier.

Localhost *n.* The name that is used to represent the same computer on which a TCP/IP message originates. An IP packet sent to localhost has the IP address 127.0.0.1 and does not actually go out to the Internet. See also IP address, packet (definition 1), TCP/IP.

Localisation *n.* The process of altering a programme so that it is appropriate for the geographic area in which it is to be used. Localisation involves the customisation or translation of the separated data and resources required for a specific region or language. For example, the developers of a word processing programme must localise the sorting tables in the programme for different countries or languages because the correct order of characters in one language might be incorrect in another. L10N is a common abbreviation for Localisation, where the "L" in Localisation is followed by 10 letters and ends with the letter "N."

Localised version *n.* A version of a programme that has been translated into another language. Also called: international version.

Local loop *n.* The (end) portion of a telephone connection that runs from the subscriber to the local telephone exchange. See also last mile.

Local memory *n.* In multiprocessor systems, the memory on the same card or high-speed bus as a particular processor.

Typically, memory that is local to one processor cannot be accessed by another without some form of permission.

Local newsgroups *n.* Newsgroups that are targeted toward a geographically limited area such as a city or educational institution. Posts to these newsgroups contain information that is specific to the area, concerning such topics as events, meetings, and sales. See also newsgroup.

Local reboot *n.* A reboot of the machine that one is directly working on, rather than of a remote host. See also reboot.

LocalTalk *n.* An inexpensive cabling scheme used by AppleTalk networks to connect Apple Macintosh computers, printers, and other peripheral devices. See also AppleTalk.

Local user profile *n.* A user profile that is created automatically on the computer the first time a user logs on to a computer. See also mandatory user profile, roaming user profile, user profile.

Local variable *n.* A programme variable whose scope is limited to a given block of code, usually a subroutine. See also scope (definition 1).

Location *n.* See address1 (definition 1).

Location-based service *n.* A service provided to a wireless mobile device based on the device's location. Location-based services can range from simple services, such as listing nearby restaurants, to more complex features, such as connecting to the Internet to monitor traffic conditions and find the least congested route to a destination.

Lock *n.* 1. A software security feature that requires a key or dongle in order for the application to run correctly. See also dongle. 2. A mechanical device on some removable storage medium (for example, the write-protect notch on a floppy disk) that prevents the contents from being overwritten. See also write-protect notch.

Locked file *n.* 1. A file on which one or more of the usual types of manipulative operation cannot be performed—typically, one that cannot be altered by additions or deletions. 2. A file that cannot be deleted or moved or whose name cannot be changed.

Locked volume *n.* On the Apple Macintosh, a volume (storage device, such as a disk) that cannot be written to. The volume can be locked either physically or through software.

Lockout *n.* The act of denying access to a given resource (file, memory location, I/O port), usually to ensure that only one programme at a time uses that resource.

Lock up *n.* A condition in which processing appears to be completely suspended and in which the programme in control of the system will accept no input. See also crash1.

Log *n.* A record of transactions or activities that take place on a computer system. See logarithm.

Logarithm *n.* Abbreviated log. In mathematics, the power to which a base must be raised to equal a given number. For example, for the base 10, the logarithm of 16 is (approximately) 1.2041 because 101.2041 equals (approximately) 16. Both natural logarithms (to the base e, which is approximately 2.71828) and common logarithms (to the base 10) are used in programming. Languages such as C and Basic include functions for calculating natural logarithms.

Log files *n.* A computer file that records requests received by online applications or the number of hits a Web page receives. Log files are useful in analysing the technical performance of a Web site, redesigning Web site navigation, and revising marketing strategies used by e-businesses.

Logic *n.* In programming, the assertions, assumptions, and operations that define what a given programme does. Defining the logic of a programme is often the first step in developing the program's source code. See also formal logic.

Logical *adj.* 1. Based on true and false alternatives as opposed to arithmetic calculation of numeric values. For example, a logical expression is one that, when evaluated, has a single outcome, either true or false. See also Boolean algebra. 2. Conceptually true to a particular design or idea—for example, network transmissions travel in a circle around a logical ring, even though the ring shape itself is not physically apparent.

Logical block addressing *n.* A technique in which the cylinder, head, and sector locations on a hard disk are converted to 24-

bit addresses for data storage and retrieval. Logical block addressing is used with SCSI drives and is also a feature of Enhanced IDE (EIDE) disk drives, on which it breaks through the earlier 528-MB IDE limit and allows support for drives up to 8.4 GB in capacity if 24-bit logical address space is used. Address conversion is performed by an EIDE drive's disk controller, but also requires support from the BIOS and the computer's operating system. Acronym: LBA. See also EIDE, SCSI.

Logical decision *n.* Any decision that can have one of two outcomes (true/false, yes/no, and so on).

Logical device *n.* A device named by the logic of a software system, regardless of its physical relationship to the system. For example, a single floppy disk drive can simultaneously be, to the MS-DOS operating system, both logical drive A and drive B.

Logical drive *n.* See logical device.

Logical error *n.* See logic error.

Logical expression *n.* See Boolean expression.

Logical file *n.* A file as seen from a conceptual standpoint, without reference to and as distinct from its physical realisation in memory or storage. For example, a logical file might consist of a contiguous series of records, whereas the file might be physically stored in small pieces scattered over the surface of a disk or even on several disks. A logical file might also consist of some subset of columns (fields) and rows (records) extracted from a database. In this case, the logical file (or view) is only that information required by a particular application programme or user.

Logical Link Control *n.* See LLC.

Logical memory *n.* A correlation between physical memory of the computer system and an address range that is accessible to devices. The hardware abstraction layer (HAL) provides this correlation (or mapping). See also map.

Logical network *n.* A way to describe the topology, or layout, of a computer network. Referring to a logical (rather than physical) topology describes the way information moves through the network—for example, in a straight line (bus topology) or in a circle (ring topology). The difference between describing a network as logical or physical is sometimes subtle because the physical network (the actual layout of hardware and cabling) doesn't necessarily resemble the logical network (the path followed by transmissions). A logical ring, for example, might include groups of computers cabled octopus-like to hardware "collection points" which, in turn, are cabled to one another. In such a network, even though the physical layout of computers and connecting hardware might not visually resemble a ring, the logical layout followed by network transmissions would, indeed, be circular. See also bus network, ring network, star network, token ring network, topology.

Logical operator *n.* An operator that manipulates binary values at the bit level. In some programming languages, logical operators are identical to Boolean operators, which manipulate true and false values. See also Boolean operator, mask.

Logical record *n.* Any unit of information that can be handled by an application programme. A logical record can be a collection of distinct fields or columns from a database file or a single line in a text file. See also logical file.

Logical schema *n.* See conceptual schema.

Logic analyzer *n.* A hardware device that facilitates sophisticated low-level debugging of programmes. Typical features include the ability to monitor bus signals during execution, to halt execution when a given memory location is read or written to, and to trace back through some number of instructions when execution is halted for any reason. See also debugger.

Logic array *n.* See gate array.

Logic board *n.* Another name for motherboard or processor board. The term was used in conjunction with older computers to distinguish the video board (analog board) from the motherboard. See also motherboard.

Logic bomb *n.* 1. A logic error in a programme that manifests itself only under certain conditions, usually when least expected or desired. The term bomb implies an error that causes the programme to fail spectacularly. See also logic error. 2. A type of Trojan horse that executes when certain conditions are met, such as when a user performs a specific action. 3. See Year 2000 problem. 4. See fork bomb.

Logic chip *n.* An integrated circuit that processes information, as opposed to simply storing it. A logic chip is made up of logic circuits.

Logic circuit *n.* An electronic circuit that processes information by performing a logical operation on it. A logic circuit is a combination of logic gates. It produces output based on the rules of logic it is designed to follow for the electrical signals it receives as input. See also gate (definition 1).

Logic diagram *n.* A schematic that shows the connections between computer logic circuits and specifies the expected outputs resulting from a specific set of inputs.

Logic error *n.* An error, such as a faulty algorithm, that causes a programme to produce incorrect results but does not prevent the programme from running. Consequently, a logic error is often very difficult to find. See also logic, semantics, syntax.

Logic gate *n.* See gate (definition 1).

Logic operation *n.* 1. An expression that uses logical values and operators. 2. A bit-level manipulation of binary values. See also Boolean operator.

Logic programming *n.* A style of programming, best exemplified by Prolog, in which a programme consists of facts and relationships from which the programming language is expected to draw conclusions. See also Prolog.

Logic-seeking printer *n.* Any printer with built-in intelligence that lets it look ahead of the current print position and move the print head directly to the next area to be printed, thus saving time in printing pages that are filled with spaces.

Logic symbol *n.* A symbol that represents a logical operator such as AND or OR. For example, the symbol + in Boolean algebra represents logical OR, as in A + B (read, "A or B," not "A plus B").

Logic tree *n.* A logic specification method that uses a branching representation. Each of the tree's forks represents a decision point; the ends of the branches denote actions to be taken.

Logo *n.* A programming language with features that are heavily drawn from LISP. Logo is often used to teach programming to children and was developed originally by Seymour Papert at MIT in 1968. Logo is considered an educational language, although some firms have sought to make it more widely accepted in the programming community. See also LISP, turtle, turtle graphics.

Logoff *n.* The process of terminating a session with a computer accessed through a communications line. Also called: logout.

Log off *vb.* To terminate a session with a computer accessed through a communications line—usually a computer that is both distant and open to many users. Also called: log out.

Logon *n.* The process of identifying oneself to a computer after connecting to it over a communications line. Also called: login.

Log on *vb.* To gain access to a specific computer, a programme, or a network by identifying oneself with a username and a password. Also called: log in.

Logon script *n.* A file assigned to certain user accounts on a network system. A logon script runs automatically every time the user logs on. It can be used to configure a user's working environment at every logon, and it allows an administrator to influence a user's environment without managing all aspects of it. A logon script can be assigned to one or more user accounts. Also called: login script. See also user account.

Logout *n.* See logoff.

Log out *vb.* See log off.

LOL *n.* Acronym for laughing out loud. An interjection used in e-mail, online forums, and chat services to express appreciation of a joke or other humourous occurrence. See also ROFL.

Long data type *n.* A fundamental data type that holds large integers. A Long variable is stored as a 32-bit number ranging in value from –2,147,483,648 to 2,147,483,647.

Long filenames *n.* A feature of most current PC operating systems, including the Macintosh, Windows 9x, Windows NT, Windows 2000, and OS/2. Long filenames allow a user to assign a plain-text name to a file, rather than limiting possible names to just a few characters. Names can be over 200 characters long, include uppercase and lowercase letters, and have spaces between characters.

Long-haul *adj.* Of, pertaining to, or being a type of modem that is able to transmit over long distances.

Longitudinal redundancy check *n.* See LRC.

LonWorks *n.* An open standard for network automation created by the Echelon Corporation and supported by the LonMark Interoperability Association. LonWorks, introduced in 1991, can be used in building, transportation, industrial, and home applications to implement a distributed control network.

Lookup *n.* A function, often built into spreadsheet programmes, in which a previously constructed table of values called a lookup table is searched for a desired item of information. A lookup table consists of rows and columns of data. A lookup function examines the table either horizontally or vertically and then retrieves the data that corresponds to the argument specified as part of the lookup function.

Loop 1 *n.* 1. A set of statements in a programme executed repeatedly, either a fixed number of times or until some condition is true or false. See also DO loop, FOR loop, infinite loop, iterative statement. 2. A pair of wires that runs between a telephone central office and customer premises.

Loop 2 *vb.* To execute a group of statements repeatedly.

Loop check *n.* See echo check.

Loop configuration *n.* A communications link in which multiple stations are joined to a communications line that runs in a closed loop. Generally, data sent by one station is received and retransmitted in turn by each station on the loop. The process continues until the data reaches its final destination. See the illustration. See also ring network.

Loophole *n.* In programming, a logical failure to account for all possible situations. See also bug (definition 1), logic error.

Loop invariant *n.* A condition that remains true while a loop iterates.

Loop structure *n.* See iterative statement.

Lo-res *adj.* See low resolution.

Loss balancing *n.* Amplification of a signal or value to compensate for loss during a transmission or translation of a value.

Lossless compression *n.* The process of compressing a file such that, after being compressed and decompressed, it matches its original format bit for bit. Text, code, and numeric data files must be compressed using a lossless method; such methods can typically reduce a file to 40 per cent of its original size.

Lossy compression *n.* The process of compressing a file such that some data is lost after the file is compressed and decompressed. Video and sound files often contain more information than is apparent to the viewer or listener; a lossy compression method, which does not preserve that excess information, can reduce such data to as little as 5 per cent of its original size.

Lost cluster *n.* A cluster (disk storage unit) marked by the operating system as being in use but not representing any part of any chain of stored segments of a file. A lost cluster usually represents debris resulting from incomplete data "housekeeping," as might result from the ungraceful exit (messy or abrupt termination) of an application programme.

Lotus 1-2-3 *n.* An electronic spreadsheet product introduced in 1983 by Lotus Development Corporation. Notable for its inclusion of graphing and data-management (database) capabilities in addition to spreadsheet functionality, Lotus 1-2-3 is important in the history of the personal computer because it was one of the first "killer apps" that convinced businesses to buy and use a PC. Lotus Development was purchased by IBM in 1995. See also killer app.

Lotus cc:Mail *n.* See cc:Mail.

Lotus Domino *n.* A groupware application that transforms Lotus Notes into an application and messaging server. See also Lotus Notes.

Lotus Notes *n.* A groupware application introduced in 1988 by Lotus Development Corporation and now owned by IBM. Lotus Notes combines e-mail, calendar management, group scheduling, contact and task management, newsgroup access, and Web browsing capability (through the integration of Microsoft Internet Explorer) in one client application. Lotus Notes also offers search capabilities across multiple formats and file types on a network or the Web.

Low-Earth-orbit satellite *n.* A communications satellite put into orbit no higher than 500 miles above the earth's surface. A low-Earth-orbit satellite, or LEO, circles the planet in 90 minutes to 2 hours. LEOs allow for use of smaller dishes and handheld devices, so they are well-suited for interactive conferencing. However, because a LEO remains above the local horizon for about only 20 minutes, large numbers of these satellites, in several different orbits, are required to maintain service. Acronym: LEO.

Lowercase *adj.* In reference to letters, not capital—for example, a, b, c.

Low frequency *n.* The portion of the electromagnetic spectrum between 30 kilohertz (kHz) and 300 kHz. This range of frequencies is used for several types of radio communication, including the longwave broadcast band in Europe and Asia.

Low-level language *n.* A language that is machine dependent or that offers few control instructions and data types. Each statement in a programme written in a low-level language usually corresponds to one machine instruction. See also assembly language.

Low memory *n.* On computers running MS-DOS, the first 640 kilobytes of RAM. This RAM is shared by MS-DOS, device drivers, data, and application programmes. Also called: conventional memory.

Low-order *adj.* Carrying the least weight or significance; typically, the rightmost element in a group. For example, the rightmost bit in a group of bits is the low-order bit.

Lowpass filter *n.* An electronic circuit that allows all frequencies below a specified frequency to pass through it.

Low resolution *adj.* Abbreviated lo-res. Appearing in relatively coarse detail, used in reference to text and graphics in raster-oriented computer displays and printing. Low-resolution printing is comparable to draft-quality dot-matrix output printed at 125 dots per inch or less. See also resolution.

LPM *n.* See lines per minute.

LPMUD *n.* A type of multiuser dungeon (MUD), typically combat related, that contains its own object-oriented programming language for the creation of new areas and objects in the virtual world. See also MUD.

LPT *n.* Logical device name for a line printer, a name reserved by the MS-DOS operating system for up to three parallel printer ports designated LPT1, LPT2, and LPT3. The first port, LPT1, is usually the same as the primary MS-DOS hard-copy output device PRN (the logical device name for the printer). The letters LPT were originally used to stand for line print terminal.

LRC *n.* Acronym for longitudinal redundancy check. A procedure used to check the accuracy of data stored on magnetic tape or transmitted over a communications line. See also parity bit.

Ls *n.* A UNIX command that instructs the server to return a list of files and subdirectories in the current directory or the directory specified in the command. Because many FTP sites are built on UNIX systems, this command can also be used on those sites. See also FTP site, UNIX.

LS-120 *n.* Acronym for Laser Storage-120. A floppy disk drive developed by Imation Corporation that uses proprietary laser storage 120-megabyte (MB) media as well as standard 1.44 MB 3.5-inch floppy media. The LS-120 disk drive is capable of storing 120 MB of data on a single 3.5-inch floppy disk and is compatible with other floppy disk formats. LS-120 drives are ATAPI (AT Attachment Packet Interface) compliant so several different drives can use the same EIDE controller. Also called: Super Disk.

LSB *n.* 1. See least significant bit. 2. Acronym for Linux Standard Base. A standard developed to aid in Linux software development by providing a uniform foundation for all versions of the operating system. The Linux model provided by the LSB provides a stable platform for developers to create software that may be used with any version of the operating system, while leaving companies the ability to add other features on top of the base.

LSP *n.* See MPLS.

LSR *n.* See MPLS.

LU *n.* Acronym for logical unit. In an IBM SNA network, a point denoting the beginning or end of a communications session. See also SNA.

LUG *n.* Acronym for Linux Users Group. See user group.

Luggable computer *n.* The first portable computers, produced in the early to mid-1980s. These early units, all of which had built-in CRT-based displays, weighed over 20 pounds and were the size of a medium suitcase—hence their name. See also portable computer.

Luminance *n.* 1. A measure of the amount of light radiated by a given source, such as a computer display screen. 2. The perceived brightness component of a given colour, as opposed to its hue or its saturation. See also HSB.

Luminance decay *n.* See persistence.

Luminosity *n.* The brightness of a colour based on a scale from black to white on your monitor.

Lurk *vb.* To receive and read articles or messages in a newsgroup or other online conference without contributing to the ongoing exchange.

Lurker *n.* A person who lurks in a newsgroup or other online conference. See also lurk.

LVS *n.* Acronym for Linux Virtual Server. A high-performance open source server that handles connections from clients and passes them on to a cluster of real servers. LVS receives incoming packets and forwards them to the proper back-end server. LVS is typically used to build scalable Web, mail, or other network services. Also called: ipvs. See also layer 4 switching.

Lycos *n.* A Web search engine and directory that provides summaries of pages matching search requests. In addition, the Lycos site offers categorised directories of sites, reviews of selected sites, and services for finding names, viewing maps, and so on.

Lynx *n.* A text-only Web browser programme for UNIX platforms.

.lzh *n.* The file extension that identifies archive files compressed with the Lempel Ziv and Haruyasu algorithm. See also compressed file, Lempel Ziv compression, LHARC.

LZW compression *n.* A compression algorithm named after Abraham Lempel and Jakob Ziv (creators of Lempel Ziv compression) and LZW designer Terry Welch that makes use of repeating strings of data in its compression of character streams into code streams. It is also the basis of GIF compression. See also GIF, Lempel Ziv compression.

M

m prefix See milli-.

M prefix See mega-.

Mac- prefix A prefix used to indicate a software product's applicability for the Macintosh computer, as in MacDraw.

Mac *n.* See Macintosh.

MAC *n.* Acronym for Media Access Control. In the IEEE 802.x specifications, the lower of two sublayers that make up the ISO/OSI data link layer. The MAC manages access to the physical network, delimits frames, and handles error control. See also IEEE 802.x, LLC.

MacBinary *n.* A file transfer protocol used to preserve coding for Macintosh-produced files stored in non-Macintosh computers, containing the file's resource fork, data fork, and Finder information block. See also data fork, Finder, resource fork.

Mach *n.* A variant of the UNIX operating system developed at Carnegie-Mellon University. Mach was designed to support advanced features such as multitasking, multiprocessing, and distributed systems. See also UNIX.

Mach 3.0 *n.* The microkernel forming the lowest level of the Mac OS X operating system. Mach 3.0 provides basic services such as memory management, thread-handling, virtual memory, and address space management to the operating system kernel.

Mach 3 kernel *n.* See Mach 3.0.

Machine address *n.* See absolute address.

Machine code *n.* The ultimate result of the compilation of assembly language or any high-level language such as C or

Pascal: sequences of 1s and 0s that are loaded and executed by a microprocessor. Machine code is the only language computers understand; all other programming languages represent ways of structuring human language so that humans can get computers to perform specific tasks. Also called: machine language. See also compiler (definition 2).

Machine cycle *n.* 1. The time required for the fastest operation (usually a NOP, or no-op, which does nothing) a microprocessor can perform. 2. The steps taken for each machine instruction. These steps are, typically, fetch the instruction, decode it, execute it, and perform any necessary storing.

Machine-dependent *adj.* Of, pertaining to, or being a programme or a piece of hardware that is linked to a particular type of computer because it makes use of specific or unique features of the equipment and that cannot easily be used with another computer, if at all.

Machine error *n.* A hardware error. Probably the most common type of machine error involves media, such as an error in reading a hard disk.

Machine identification *n.* A code by which an executing programme can determine the identity and characteristics of the computer and other devices with which it is operating.

Machine-independent *adj.* Of, pertaining to, or being a programme or piece of hardware that can be used on more than one type of computer with little or no modification.

Machine instruction *n.* An instruction (action statement) in machine code that can be directly executed by a processor or microprocessor. See also instruction, statement.

Machine language *n.* See machine code.

Machine-readable *adj.* 1. Presented in a form that a computer can interpret and use as input. For example, bar codes that can be scanned and used directly as computer input contain machine-readable information. 2. Coded in the binary form used by computers and stored on a suitable medium such as magnetic tape. See also optical character recognition.

Machine translation *n.* The use of computer software to translate large amounts of text from one natural language into another. Machine translation is usually used by corporations, publishers, and government agencies that need large amounts of documentation, news stories, or business data translated quickly. See also natural-language processing.

Macintosh *n.* A popular series of personal computers introduced by the Apple Computer Corporation in January 1984. The Macintosh was one of the earliest personal computers to incorporate a graphical user interface and the first to use 3.5-inch floppy disks. It was also the first to use the 32-bit Motorola 68000 microprocessor. Despite its user-friendly features, the Macintosh lost market share to PC-compatible computers during the 1990s, but it still enjoys widespread use in desktop publishing and graphics-related applications. In late 1998, both Apple Computer and Macintosh gained increased visibility with release of the home-oriented iMac computer. See the illustration. Also called: Mac. See also graphical user interface, iMac, PC-compatible.

Macintosh Application Environment *n.* A system shell for open RISC-based systems that provides a Macintosh interface within an X Window System window. The Macintosh Application Environment is compatible with both Mac and UNIX and will support all off-the-shelf products for the Macintosh. Acronym: MAE. See also RISC, X Window System.

Macintosh File System *n.* The early, flat file system used on the Macintosh before the Hierarchical File System was introduced. Acronym: MFS. See also flat file system.

Mac OS *n.* Short for Macintosh operating system. The name given to the Macintosh operating system, beginning with version 7.5 in September 1994, when Apple started licensing the software to other computer manufacturers. See also Macintosh.

Mac OS X *n.* The first complete revision of the Macintosh operating system. Mac OS X is BSD 4.4 UNIX-based, uses the Mach 3.0 microkernel, and is built around Apple's open-source Darwin. Mac OS X adds symmetric multiprocessing, multithreading, preemptive multitasking, advanced memory management, and protected memory to the Macintosh. The UNIX foundation of Mac OS X allows greater options for software development, networking, and update and expansion of the operating system. Mac OS X includes a graphical user interface and a command-line interface.

Macro *n.* 1. In applications, a set of keystrokes and instructions recorded and saved under a short key code or macro name. When the key code is typed or the macro name is used, the programme carries out the instructions of the macro. Users can create a macro to save time by replacing an often-used, sometimes lengthy, series of strokes with a shorter version. 2. In programming languages, such as C or assembly language, a name that defines a set of instructions that are substituted for the macro name wherever the name appears in a programme (a process called macro expansion) when the programme is compiled or assembled. Macros are similar to functions in that they can take arguments and in that they are calls to lengthier sets of instructions. Unlike functions, macros are replaced by the actual instructions they represent when the programme is prepared for execution; function instructions are copied into a programme only once.

Macro assembler *n.* An assembler that can perform macro substitution and expansion. The programmer can define a macro that consists of several statements and then use the macro name later in the programme, thus avoiding having to rewrite the statements. For example, a macro called swap exchanges the values of two variables: After defining swap, the programmer can then insert an instruction such as "swap a, b" in the assembly language programme. While assembling, the assembler replaces the instruction with the statements within the macro that swap the values of the variables a and b.

Macrocontent *n.* The primary text or other content of a Web page.

Macro expansion *n.* The act of replacing a macro with its defined equivalent. Also called: macro substitution. See also macro (definition 2), macro assembler, macro processor.

Macro instruction *n.* An instruction used to manage macro definitions. See also macro language.

Macro language *n.* The collection of macro instructions recognised by a given macro processor. See also macro instruction, macro processor.

Macro processor *n.* A programme that performs macro expansion. All programmes that support macros have some form of macro processor, but macro processors differ from programme to programme and in the macro language they support. See also macro (definition 2), macro expansion, macro instruction.

Macro programme *n.* See keyboard enhancer.

Macro recorder *n.* A programme that records and stores keyboard macros. See also macro (definition 1).

Macro substitution *n.* See macro expansion.

Macro virus *n.* A virus that is written in a macro language associated with an application. The macro virus is carried by a document file used with that application and executes when the document is opened.

MacTCP *n.* A Macintosh extension that allows Macintosh computers to use TCP/IP. See also TCP/IP.

MADCAP *n.* See multicast address dynamic client allocation protocol.

MAE *n.* 1. See Macintosh Application Environment. 2. Acronym for Metropolitan Area Exchange. One of the Internet exchange points operated by MCI WorldCom, through which Internet service providers (ISPs) connect in order to exchange data. The two largest MAEs, MAE East (outside Washington, D.C.) and MAE West (near San Jose, California) are major national and international network interconnect points; more than half of all traffic through the Internet travels through one or both of these points. MCI WorldCom also operates smaller, regional MAEs in Chicago, Dallas, Houston, Los Angeles, New York, Paris, and Frankfurt. See also backbone (definition 1), ISP.

Magellan *n.* A Web directory. Named for the Portuguese explorer, Magellan reviews and rates all Web sites it lists. Published by the McKinley Group, Magellan is now owned by Excite, Inc.

Magic date *n.* A date or dates that in some computer systems resembles a reserved number or flag with a special significance. Examples are the numbers 00 and 99, which have been used in some systems or programmes based on two-digit years. Magic dates indicate some special status—for example, that a system component or resource should never expire or should never be purged. Because 99 in particular has been used in this way in many systems, dates in the year 1999 had the potential to cause problems in those systems.

Magnetic bubble *n.* A movable magnetic domain in a thin-film substrate. In bubble memory, magnetic bubbles representing bits circulate past circuits that can read and write them. High costs and relatively long access times have relegated magnetic bubbles to specialised applications. See also bubble memory, magnetic domain.

Magnetic disk *n.* A computer disk enclosed in a protective case (hard disk) or jacket (floppy disk) and coated with a magnetic material that enables data to be stored in the form of changes in magnetic polarity (with one polarity representing a binary 1 and the other a 0) on many small sections (magnetic domains) of the disk surface. Magnetic disks should be protected from exposure to sources of magnetism, which can damage or destroy the information they hold. See also disk, floppy disk, hard disk.

Magnetic domain *n.* A region of a ferromagnetic material in which the individual atomic or molecular magnetic particles are aligned in the same direction. Also called: ferromagnetic domain.

Magnetic field *n.* The space around a magnetic object in which magnetic force acts. A magnetic field is conceived of as consisting of flux lines that originate at the north magnetic pole and terminate at the south magnetic pole.

Magnetic head *n.* See head.

Magnetic-ink character recognition *n.* A form of character recognition that reads text printed with magnetically charged ink, determining the shapes of characters by sensing the magnetic charge in the ink. Once the shapes have been determined, character recognition methods are used to translate the shapes into computer text. A familiar use of this form of character recognition is to identify bank checks. Acronym: MICR. See also character recognition.

Magnetic oxide *n.* See ferric oxide.

Magnetic storage *n.* A generic term for non-internal-memory computer data storage involving a magnetic medium, such as disk or tape.

Magnetic tape *n.* See tape (definition 1).

Magneto-optical recording *n.* A type of recording technology used with optical discs in which a laser beam heats a small portion of the magnetic material covering the disc. The heating enables a weak magnetic field to change the orientation of the portion, thus recording onto the disc. This technique can also be used to erase the disc, making the disc rewritable.

Magneto-optic disc *n.* An erasable or semi-erasable storage disc, similar to a CD-ROM disc and of very high capacity, in which a laser beam is used to heat the recording surface to a point at which tiny regions on the surface can be magnetically aligned to store bits of data. See also CD-ROM, magneto-optical recording.

Magnitude *n.* The size of a number, regardless of its sign (+ or –). For example, 16 and –16 have the same magnitude. See also absolute value.

Mailbomb1 *n.* An excessively large amount of e-mail data (a very large number of messages or one very large message) sent to a user's e-mail address in an attempt to make the user's mailer programme crash or to prevent the user from receiving further legitimate messages. See also e-mail1 (definition 1).

Mailbomb2 *vb.* To send a mailbomb to a user. One person might mailbomb a user with a single enormous message; a large number of users might mailbomb an unpopular person by simultaneously sending messages of normal size.

Mailbot *n.* A programme that automatically responds to e-mail messages or performs actions based on commands within the messages. A mailing list manager is one example. See also mailing list manager.

Mailbox *n.* A disk storage area assigned to a network user for receipt of e-mail messages. See also e-mail1 (definition 1).

Mail digest *n.* See digest (definition 2).

Mailer-daemon *n.* A programme used to transport e-mail between hosts on a network. See also daemon.

Mail filter *n.* See e-mail filter.

Mail header *n.* A block of text at the top of an e-mail message containing such information as the addresses of the sender and recipients, the date and time sent, the address to which a reply is to be sent, and the subject. The mail header is used by an e-mail client or programme. See also e-mail1 (definition 1).

Mailing list *n.* A list of names and e-mail addresses that are grouped under a single name. When a user places the name of the mailing list in a mail client's To: field, the client sends the message to the machine where the mailing list resides, and that machine automatically sends the message to all the addresses on the list (possibly allowing a moderator to edit it first). See also LISTSERV, mailing list manager, Majordomo, moderator.

Mailing list manager *n.* Software that maintains an Internet or intranet mailing list. The mailing list manager accepts messages posted by subscribers; sends copies of the messages (which may be edited by a moderator) to all the subscribers; and accepts and processes user requests, such as to subscribe or to unsubscribe to the mailing list. The most commonly used mailing list managers are LISTSERV and Majordomo. See also LISTSERV, mailing list, Majordomo, moderator.

Mail merge *n.* A mass-mail facility that takes names, addresses, and sometimes pertinent facts about recipients and merges the information into a form letter or another such basic document.

Mail reflector *n.* A newsgroup that consists simply of the messages posted to a mailing list translated into newsgroup format.

Mailto *n.* A protocol designator used in the HREF of a hyperlink that enables a user to send e-mail to someone. For instance, Anne E. Oldhacker has the e-mail address aeo@baz.foo.com and an HTML document contains the code <A HREF="mailto: aeo@baz.foo.com">E-mail Anne!</A>. If a user clicks on the hyperlink "E-mail Anne!", the user's e-mail application is launched and the user can send e-mail to her without knowing her actual e-mail address. See also e-mail1 (definition 1), HTML, hyperlink.

Mainboard *n.* See motherboard.

Main body *n.* The set of statements in a computer programme at which execution of the programme begins and that invokes the subroutines of the programme.

Mainframe *n.* A type of large computer system (in the past often water-cooled), the primary data processing resource for many large businesses and organisations. Some mainframe operating systems and solutions are over 40 years old and have the capacity to store year values only as two digits.

Mainframe computer *n.* A high-level, typically large and expensive computer designed to handle intensive computational tasks. Mainframe computers are characterised by their ability to simultaneously support many users connected to the computer by terminals. The name is derived from "main frame," the cabinet originally used to house the processing unit of such computers. See also computer, supercomputer.

Main function *n.* The main body of a programme written in a computer language that uses sets of functions to create an entire programme. For example, the C language requires each programme to contain a function called main, which C uses as the starting point of execution. See also main body.

Main loop *n.* A loop in the main body of a programme that performs the principal function of the programme over and over until termination is somehow signaled. In event-driven programmes, this loop checks for events received from the operating system and handles them appropriately. See also event-driven programming, main body.

Main memory *n.* See primary storage.

Main segment *n.* On the Macintosh, the principal code segment of a programme, which must remain loaded throughout the execution of the programme.

Maintenance *n.* The process of taking measures to ensure that a hardware, software, or database system is functioning properly and is up to date.

Majordomo *n.* The name of a popular software programme that manages and supports Internet mailing lists. See also mailing list, mailing list manager.

Major geographic domain *n.* A two-character sequence in an Internet domain name address that indicates the country/region in which a host is located. The major geographic domain is the last part of the domain name address, following the subdomain and domain codes; for example, uiuc.edu.us indicates a host at the University of Illinois in the United States, whereas cam.ac.uk indicates a host at the University of Cambridge in the United Kingdom. The code .us, which indicates a domain in the United States, is usually omitted. Also called: country code. See also DNS (definition 1), domain name address.

Major key *n.* See primary key.

Make Changes *n.* The Macintosh-style permission that gives users the right to make changes to a folder's contents; for example, modifying, renaming, moving, creating, and deleting files. When AppleTalk network integration translates access privileges into permissions, a user who has the Make Changes privilege is given Write and Delete permissions. See also permission.

Make-table query *n.* In Microsoft Office, an action query that moves the resulting data to a new table in either the current database or another database.

Male connector *n.* A type of connector that has pins for insertion into receptacles. Male connector part numbers often include an M (male) or P (plug). For example, a male DB-25 connector might be labeled DB-25M or DB-25P.

Malicious mobile code *n.* A virus or other destructive programme that takes advantage of security weaknesses in wireless transmission systems. Malicious mobile code may affect computers, PDAs, Internet-capable digital phones, and other wireless networking devices.

Malware *n.* Software created and distributed for malicious purposes, such as invading computer systems in the form of viruses, worms, or innocent-seeming plug-ins and extensions that mask other destructive capabilities. Also called: malicious software.

MAME *n.* Acronym for Multiple Arcade Machine Emulator. MAME is software written in C that emulates the hardware and software of original arcade games, allowing them to run on PCs. See also arcade game, C.

MAN *n.* Acronym for metropolitan area network. A high-speed network that can carry voice, data, and images at up to 200 Mbps or faster over distances of up to 75 km. Based on the network architecture, the transmission speed can be higher for shorter distances. A MAN, which can include one or more LANs as well as telecommunications equipment such as microwave and satellite relay stations, is smaller than a wide area network but generally operates at a higher speed.

Managed code *n.* Code that is executed by the common language runtime environment rather than directly by the operating system. Managed code applications gain common language runtime services such as automatic garbage collection, runtime type checking and security support, and so on. These services provide uniform platform- and language-independent behaviour of managed-code applications. See also unmanaged code.

Managed service provider *n.* A business that supplies remote access services to individuals and enterprises. Managed service providers offer remote connections, network management, user support, security, and applications hosting. Acronym: MSP.

Management and Monitoring Tools *n.* Software components that include utilities for network management and monitoring, along with services that support client dialing and the updating of client phone books. Also included is the Simple Network Management Protocol (SNMP). See also SNMP.

Management Information Base *n.* A set of objects that represents various types of information about a device, used by a network management protocol (for example, SNMP) to manage the device. Because different network management services are used for different types of devices and protocols, each service has its own set of objects. Acronym: MIB. See also service, SNMP.

Management Information Services *n.* See Information Services.

Management information system *n.* A computer-based system for processing and organising information so as to provide various levels of management within an organisation with accurate and timely information needed for supervising activities, tracking progress, making decisions, and isolating and solving problems. Acronym: MIS.

Management Information Systems *n.* See Information Services.

Manager *n.* Any programme that is designed to perform a certain set of housekeeping tasks related to computer operation, such as the maintenance of files. On the Macintosh, Manager (with a capital M) is used in the names of various separate portions of the computer's operating system that handle input, output, and internal functions (for example, File Manager and Memory Manager).

Manchester coding *n.* A method of encoding data used in communications, such as on some LANs, that combines both data and timing signals in a stream of transmitted bits. See also phase encoding.

Mandatory user profile *n.* A user profile that is not updated when the user logs off. It is downloaded to the user's desktop each time the user logs on, and it is created by an administrator and assigned to one or more users to create consistent or job-specific user profiles. See also local user profile, roaming user profile, user profile.

Mandelbrot set *n.* See fractal.

Man-in-the-middle attack *n.* A form of attack in which the intruder intercepts messages between parties in a public key exchange. Each party's messages are diverted to the intruder, who may alter them before sending them on. The parties on each end of the exchange remain unaware that their messages are being intercepted and modified. Also called: bucket brigade attack.

Man-machine interface *n.* The set of commands, displays, controls, and hardware devices enabling the human user and the computer system to exchange information. See also user interface.

Man pages *n.* 1. Online documentation for UNIX commands and programmes and the UNIX library routines available for use in C programmes. These documents, also found in the UNIX Programmer's Manual, can be displayed on a user's terminal or printed using the command man. 2. Short for manual pages. A set of help files included with a Linux distribution. Man pages may come with the Linux distribution and be installed along with the operating system or may be available from online sources.

Mantissa *n.* 1. In calculations that have logarithms, the positive decimal fraction of a common (base-10) logarithm. For example, the common logarithm of 16 is 1.2041; the characteristic, or whole-number portion, of the logarithm is 1 (the logarithm of 10); and the mantissa, or fractional portion, is .2041 (the logarithm of 1.6). See also characteristic, logarithm. 2. In floating-point notation, the portion expressing the significant digits of a number. For example, the floating-point representation of 640,000 is 6.4E+05. The mantissa is 6.4; the exponent (E+05) shows the power of 10 to which 6.4 is raised. Also called: significand. See also floating-point notation.

Manual link *n.* A link that requires you to take action to update your data after the data in the source document changes.

Many-to-many relationship *n.* A complex association between two sets of parameters in which many parameters of each set can relate to many others in the second set. A many-to-many relationship is most commonly used to describe an association between two tables in which one record in either table can relate to many records in the other table.

Many-to-one relationship *n.* 1. A server configuration in which several small servers replicate the abilities of one larger, more powerful server. See also key pair. 2. In reference to asymmetric key encryption, the idea that many individuals in possession of the public key can decrypt the digital signature of one individual in possession of the private key.

Map 1 *n.* Any representation of the structure of an object. For example, a memory map describes the layout of objects in an area of memory, and a symbol map lists the associations between symbol names and memory addresses in a programme. See also image map.

map 2 *vb.* To translate one value into another. For example, in computer graphics one might map a three-dimensional image onto a sphere. In reference to virtual memory systems, a computer might translate (map) a virtual address into a physical address. See also virtual memory.

MAPI *n.* Acronym for Messaging Application Programming Interface. The Microsoft interface specification that allows different messaging and workgroup applications (including e-mail, voice mail, and fax) to work through a single client, such as the Exchange client included with Windows 95 and Windows NT. See also application programming interface.

Mapped data field *n.* A field that represents commonly used information, such as "First Name." If a data source contains a "First Name" field or variation, such as "FName," the data source field automatically maps to the corresponding mapped data field.

Mapped drives *n.* 1. In the Windows environment, network drives that have been assigned local drive letters and are locally accessible. 2. Under UNIX, disk drives that have been defined to the system and can be made active.

MapPoint *n.* Business mapping software introduced by Microsoft as an Office-compatible product in 1999. Designed for use by business people, MapPoint consists of a database of United States maps showing detail down to the level of individual streets and demographic data broken out by state, county, zip code, and other regions. See also Office.

Margin *n.* In printing, those portions of a page—top, bottom, and sides—outside the main body of text.

Mark *n.* 1. In applications and data storage, a symbol or other device used to distinguish one item from others like it. 2. In digital transmission, the state of a communications line (positive or negative) corresponding to a binary 1. In asynchronous serial communications, a mark condition is the continuous transmission of binary 1s to indicate when the line is idle (not carrying information). In asynchronous error checking, setting the parity bit to 1 in each group of transmitted bits is known as mark parity. See also parity. 3. In optical sensing, a pencil line, as on a voting form or an IQ test, that can be recognised by an optical reader.

Marker *n.* 1. Part of a data communications signal that enables the communications equipment to recognise the structure of the message. Examples are the start and stop bits that frame a byte in asynchronous serial communications. 2. A symbol that indicates a particular location on a display surface.

Mark I *n.* 1. An electromechanical calculating machine designed in the late 1930s and early 1940s by Howard Aiken of Harvard University and built by IBM. Also called: Automatic Sequence Controlled Calculator, Harvard Mark I. 2. The first fully electronic stored-programme computer, designed and built at Manchester University in England. It successfully executed its first programme in June 1948. 3. The first commercial computer, which was based on the Manchester Mark I and released in 1951.

Markup *n.* Comments and tracked changes such as insertions, deletions, and formatting changes that you can view or print.

Markup language *n.* A set of codes in a text file that instructs a computer how to format the file on a printer or video display or how to index and link its contents. Examples of markup languages are Hypertext Markup Language (HTML) and Extensible Markup Language (XML), which are used in Web pages, and Standard Generalised Markup Language (SGML), which is used for typesetting and desktop publishing purposes and in electronic documents. Markup languages of this sort are designed to enable documents and other files to be platform-independent and highly portable between applications. See also HTML, SGML, XML.

Marquee *n.* A nonstandard HTML extension that causes scrolling text to appear as part of a Web page. Currently, marquees are viewable only with Internet Explorer. See also HTML, Internet Explorer, Web page.

Marquee component *n.* A region on a page that displays a horizontally scrolling text message.

Mask *n.* 1. A binary value used to selectively screen out or let through certain bits in a data value. Masking is performed by using a logical operator (AND, OR, XOR, or NOT) to combine the mask and the data value. For example, the mask 00111111, when used with the AND operator, removes (masks off) the two uppermost bits in a data value but does not affect the rest of the value. See the illustration. See also logical operator, mask bit. 2. In television and display technology, a thin perforated sheet of metal or a close-set series of metal strips on the surface of the screen that helps create a clear, sharp image by ensuring that the electron beam for a particular colour (red, blue, or green) strikes only the phosphor it is intended to illuminate, while the phosphors for the other colours are shadowed by the mask. Three types of masks are in use: a shadow mask, with round perforations; an aperture grill, with vertical stripes; and a slot mask, with elliptical openings. See also aperture mask, shadow mask, slot mask.

Maskable interrupt *n.* A hardware interrupt that can be temporarily disabled (masked) during periods when a programme needs the full attention of the microprocessor. See also external interrupt, hardware interrupt, interrupt.

Mask bit *n.* A given bit within a binary mask whose function is to screen out or let through the corresponding bit in a data value when the mask is used in an expression with a logical operator. See also mask (definition 1).

Masking *n.* The process of using the mask operation to perform operations on bits, bytes, or words of data. See also mask (definition 1).

Mask off *vb.* To use a mask to remove bits from a byte of data. See also mask (definition 1).

Massively parallel processing *n.* A computer architecture in which each of a large number of processors has its own RAM, which contains a copy of the operating system, a copy of the application code, and its own part of the data, on which that processor works independently of the others. Acronym: MPP.

Massively parallel processor *n.* A computer designed to perform massively parallel processing.

Mass storage *n.* A generic term for disk, tape, or optical disc storage of computer data, so called for the large masses of data that can be stored in comparison with computer memory capacity.

Master Boot Record *n.* The first sector of the first hard disk; a physically small but critical element in the startup process on an x86-based computer. When a computer is booted, it processes a series of self-tests and then reads the Master Boot Record, or MBR, into memory. The MBR contains instructions that locate the disk's system (startup) partition, read the contents of the first sector of the system partition into memory, and then carry out the instructions contained in that sector. If the sector represents what is known as a Partition Boot Sector, the instructions found there begin the process of loading and starting the operating system. In other words, the startup process on an x86- based computer is as follows: self-test to Master Boot Record; MBR to system partition and Partition Boot Sector; Partition Boot Sector to operating system; and, finally, a computer ready to go to work. Acronym: MBR. See also Partition Boot Sector.

Master file *n.* In a set of database files, the file containing more or less permanent descriptive information about the principal subjects of the database, summary data, and one or more critical key fields. For example, customers' names, account numbers, addresses, and credit terms might be stored in a master file. See also master record.

Master key *n.* The server-based component of software or data protection. In some systems, data or applications are stored on a server and must be downloaded to the local machine for use. When a client requests the data, it presents a session key. If the session key supplied matches the master key, the key server sends the requested packet. See also client (definition 3), server (definition 2).

Master record *n.* A record in a master file; typically, the descriptive and summary data related to the item that is the subject of the record. See also master file.

Master reseller *n.* A status assigned by computer equipment manufacturers to dealers and distributors who meet certain qualifications, usually related to the number of pieces the reseller expects to sell.

Master/slave arrangement *n.* A system in which one device, called the master, controls another device, called the slave. For example, a computer can control devices connected to it.

Matching *n.* The process of testing whether two data items are identical or of finding a data item that is identical to a key. See also pattern recognition.

Material Requirements Planning *n.* An approach to information management in a manufacturing environment that makes use of software to help monitor and control processes related to manufacturing—for example, managing schedules and determining when and in what quantities to order materials. Acronym: MRP. Also called: Material Resource Planning. See also Enterprise Resource Planning.

Math coprocessor *n.* See floating-point processor.

Mathematical expression *n.* An expression that uses numeric values, such as integers, fixed-point numbers, and floating-point numbers, and operators, such as addition, subtraction, multiplication, and division. See also expression.

Mathematical function *n.* A function in a programme that performs a set of mathematical operations on one or more values or expressions and that returns a numeric value.

Mathematical model *n.* The mathematical assumptions, expressions, and equations that underlie a given programme. Mathematical models are used to model "real-world" physical systems such as planets in orbit around a star or resource production and consumption within a closed system.

MathML *n.* Acronym for Mathematical Markup Language. An XML application for describing mathematical notation and capturing both its structure and content. The goal of MathML is to enable mathematics to be served, received, and processed on the Web, just as HTML has enabled this functionality for text.

Matrix *n.* An arrangement of rows and columns used for organising related items, such as numbers, dots, spreadsheet cells, or circuit elements. Matrices are used in mathematics for manipulating rectangular sets of numbers. In computing and computer applications, matrices are used for the similar purpose of arranging sets of data in table form, as in spreadsheets and lookup tables. In hardware, matrices of dots are used in creating characters on the screen as well as in print (as by dot-matrix printers). In electronics, matrices of diodes or transistors are used to create networks of logic circuits for such purposes as encoding, decoding, or converting information. See also grid.

Matrix line printer *n.* See line printer.

MAU *n.* Acronym for Multistation Access Unit. A hub device in a token-ring network that connects computers in a physical hub-and-spokes arrangement but uses the logical ring required in token ring networks. Also called: MSAU. See also hub, token-ring network.

Maximise *vb.* In a graphical user interface, to cause a window to expand to fill all the space available within a larger window or on the screen. See also enlarge, graphical user interface, Maximise button, window.

Maximise button *n.* In Windows 3.x, Windows 9x, Windows NT, and Windows 2000, a button in the upper right-hand corner of a window that, when clicked, maximises a window to fill all the space available within a larger window or on the screen. See also graphical user interface, window.

Maximum Transmission Unit *n.* See MTU.

Mb *n.* See megabit.

MB *n.* See megabyte.

MBONE or Mbone *n.* Short for multicast backbone. A small set of Internet sites, each of which can transmit real-time audio and video simultaneously to all the others. MBONE sites are equipped with special software to send and receive packets at high speed using the IP one-to-many multicasting protocol. The MBONE has been used for video conferencing and even for a Rolling Stones concert in 1994. See also RealAudio.

Mbps *n.* Short for mega bits per second. One million bits per second.

MBR *n.* See Master Boot Record.

MC *n.* See megacycle.

MC68000 *n.* See 68000.

MC68020 *n.* See 68020.

MC68030 *n.* See 68030.

MC68040 *n.* See 68040.

MC68881 *n.* See 68881.

MCF *n.* See Meta-Content Format.

MCGA *n.* Acronym for Multi-Colour Graphics Array. An older video adapter included in the IBM PS/2 Models 25 and 30. The MCGA was capable of emulating the CGA (Colour/Graphics Adapter) and provided two additional graphics modes: the first mode had 640 horizontal pixels by 480 vertical pixels with 2 colours chosen from a palette of 262,144 colours; the second had 320 horizontal pixels by 200 vertical pixels with 256 colours chosen from a palette of 262,144 colours. See also graphics mode (definition 2).

MCI *n.* 1. Acronym for Media Control Interface. Part of the Windows application programming interface that enables a programme to control multimedia devices. 2. A major long-distance telephone service carrier, originally Microwave Communications, Inc.

M-commerce *n.* Short for mobile commerce. M-commerce involves the use of personal digital assistants (PDAs), digital phones, and other wireless handheld devices equipped with microbrowsers for the online buying and selling of goods. M-commerce is distinguished from other electronic commerce by the level of portability. Wireless Application Protocol (WAP) standards form the foundation of m-commerce technology, which takes advantage of smart phone capabilities with e-mail, fax, Internet, and phone in one mobile unit. See also microbrowser, Wireless Application Protocol.

MCP *n.* Acronym for Microsoft Certified Professional. A basic certification from Microsoft that verifies an individual's ability to successfully implement a Microsoft product or technology as part of a solution for an organisation. The MCP certification is often used as a building block for acquiring additional certifications in specialised skill areas such as databases, programming languages, and Web development.

MCSA *n.* Acronym for Microsoft Certified Systems Administrator. A certification from Microsoft that verifies an individual's ability to implement, manage, and troubleshoot existing Microsoft Windows and Windows .NET network and system environments. See also MCP.

MCSD *n.* Acronym for Microsoft Certified Solution Developer. A certification from Microsoft that verifies an individual's ability to use Microsoft development tools, technologies, and platforms to design and develop business solutions. See also MCP.

MCSE *n.* Acronym for Microsoft Certified System Engineer. A certification from Microsoft that verifies an individual's ability to analyse business requirements and then design and implement business solutions with Microsoft Windows platforms and server software. See also MCP.

MD2 *n.* A hashing algorithm that creates a 128-bit hash value used to verify data integrity. MD2 is an earlier, 8-bit version of the more common MD5. See also hashing algorithm.

MD4 *n.* A hashing algorithm that creates a 128-bit hash value used to verify data integrity. Like the latest version, MD5, MD4 is optimised for 32-bit machines. See also hashing algorithm.

MD5 *n.* An industry-standard, one-way, 128-bit hashing scheme, developed by MIT Laboratory for Computer Science and RSA Data Security, Inc., and used by various Point-to-Point Protocol (PPP) vendors for encrypted authentication. An extension of MD4, MD5 is slightly slower than the earlier version but offers improved data security. See also hashing algorithm.

MDA *n.* Acronym for Monochrome Display Adapter. The video adapter introduced with the earliest model of the IBM PC in 1981. MDA was capable of only one video mode: a character mode with 25 lines of 80 characters each, with underlining, blinking, and high-intensity characters. IBM did not use the name Monochrome Display Adapter or the acronym MDA.

MDI *n.* Acronym for multiple-document interface. A user interface in an application that allows the user to have more than one document open at the same time. See also user interface.

MDIS *n.* See Metadata Interchange Specification.

Mean time between failures *n.* See MTBF.

Mean time to repair *n.* See MTTR.

Mechanical mouse *n.* A type of mouse in which the motion of a ball on the bottom of the mouse is translated into directional signals. As the user moves the mouse, the ball rolls, turning a pair of wheels mounted at right angles inside the mouse that have conductive markings on their surfaces. Because the markings permit an electric current to flow, a set of conductive brushes that ride on the surface of the conductive wheels can detect these conductive markings. The electronics in the mouse translate these electrical movement signals into mouse-movement information that can be used by the computer. See also mouse, trackball.

Mechatronics *n.* A term derived from the words mechanical and electronics to describe a field of engineering that applies mechanical, electrical, and electronic engineering concepts to product design and manufacture. A relatively new discipline, mechatronics is applicable to products in fields as diverse as medicine, robotics, manufacturing, and consumer electronics.

Media *n.* The physical material, such as paper, disk, and tape, used for storing computer-based information. Media is plural; medium is singular.

Media Access Control *n.* See MAC.

Media Control Interface *n.* See MCI (definition 1).

Media conversion *n.* Transferring data from one storage medium to another—for example, from disk to tape.

Media eraser *n.* A device that removes or obliterates data from a storage medium on a wholesale basis, usually by writing meaningless data (such as zeros) over it. See also bulk eraser.

Media filter *n.* 1. A device used with local area networks (LANs) as an adapter between two different types of media. For example, an RJ-45 connector might be used between coaxial cable and unshielded twisted pair (UTP) cables. Media filters are similar in function to transceivers. As with many components to LANs, manufacturers often choose different names for similar products, so a LAN expert is needed to decide which media filters are required for a particular LAN. See also coaxial cable, connector (definition 1), LAN, transceiver, UTP. 2. A device added to data networks to filter out electronic noise from the environment. For example, a media filter might be added to an Ethernet network based on coaxial cabling to prevent data loss from interference by nearby electronic equipment. See also coaxial cable, Ethernet (definition 1).

Media stream *n.* A continuous sequence of audio or audio-and-video through a network.

Medium 1 *adj.* Of or relating to the middle part of a range of possible values.

Medium 2 *n.* A substance in which signals can be transmitted, such as a wire or fiber-optic cable. See media.

Medium model *n.* A memory model of the Intel 80x86 processor family. The medium model allows only 64 kilobytes for data but generally up to 1 megabyte for code. See also memory model.

Medium-scale integration *n.* A concentration of circuit elements in the hundreds on a single chip. Acronym: MSI. See also integrated circuit.

Meg *n.* See megabyte.

Mega- prefix One million (106). In computing, which is based on the binary (base-2) numbering system, mega- has a literal value of 1,048,576, which is the power of 2 (220) closest to one million. Abbreviation: M.

Megabit *n.* Usually 1,048,576 bits (220); sometimes interpreted as 1 million bits. Abbreviation: Mb, Mbit.

Megabyte *n.* Usually 1,048,576 bytes (220); sometimes interpreted as 1 million bytes. Abbreviation: MB.

Megacycle *n.* A term for 1 million cycles—usually used to mean 1 million cycles per second. Abbreviation: MC. See also megahertz.

Megaflops *n.* See MFLOPS.

Megahertz *n.* A measure of frequency equivalent to 1 million cycles per second.

Megapixel *adj.* A reference to image resolution of one million pixels or more. The term is used in reference to devices such as digital cameras, scanners, and computer monitors and display adapters.

Megapixel display *n.* A video display capable of displaying at least 1 million pixels. For example, a video display with a screen size of 1024 horizontal pixels and 1024 vertical pixels is a megapixel display. Also called: megapel display.

Melissa *n.* A macro virus that affects Word files in Microsoft Office 97 and Office 2000 and first appeared in the spring of 1999. Melissa is delivered as an attachment to an e-mail with the subject line "An Important Message From <user name>," a message beginning "Here is that document you asked for...," or both. When the attachment is opened, the virus propagates (if Microsoft Outlook is installed) by sending itself to the first 50 e-mail addresses in the user's Outlook address book. On the infected machine, the virus also changes the registry, infects the Normal.dot Word template (which, in turn, infects new documents), and, in Office 2000, disables the Word macro virus warning. Although the Melissa virus does not destroy data, it can affect e-mail performance through the increased volume of messages. If an infected document is open at a time when the day of the month is the same as the minute value of the current time, the virus inserts the text "Twenty-two points, plus triple-word-score, plus fifty points for using

Meltdown *n.* 1. The complete collapse of a computer network caused by a higher level of traffic than the network can support. The term refers, by analogy, to the accidental melting down of a nuclear reactor core. 2. Colloquially, the breakdown of a person, usually in a job situation, caused by overwork, stress, or failure.

Member *n.* 1. In object-oriented programming, a variable or routine that is part of a class. See also C++, class. 2. A value that is part of a set data structure. See also set2 (definition 1).

Membrane keyboard *n.* A keyboard in which an unbroken plastic or rubber shell (a membrane) covers keys that have little or no travel (movement). Rather than use normal, full-travel keys, membrane keyboards use pressure-sensitive areas that are sometimes, but not always, defined by small bumps under the membrane.

Memo field *n.* A field in a database file that can contain unstructured text.

Memo pad *n.* A note-taking feature offered by many personal digital assistants and other handheld computing devices. Memo pad allows for the entry of short notes via typing or handwriting recognition applications. The notes can be categorised, organised, and edited later.

Memory *n.* A device where information can be stored and retrieved. In the most general sense, memory can refer to external storage such as disk drives or tape drives; in common usage, it refers only to a computer's main memory, the fast semiconductor storage (RAM) directly connected to the processor. See also core, EEPROM, EPROM, flash memory, PROM, RAM, ROM.

Memory bank *n.* The physical location on a motherboard where a memory module can be inserted. See also bank (definition 1).

Memory board *n.* A plug-in printed circuit board that contains one or more memory chips. See also memory chip.

Memory cache *n.* See CPU cache.

Memory card *n.* A memory module that is used to extend RAM storage capacity or in place of a hard disk in a portable computer, such as a laptop, notebook, or handheld PC. The module is usually the size of a credit card and can be plugged into a PCMCIA-compliant portable computer. The module can be composed of EPROM, RAM, or ROM chips or flash memory. Also called: RAM card, ROM card. See also EPROM, flash memory, handheld PC, hard disk, memory cartridge, module (definition 2), PCMCIA, RAM, ROM.

Memory cartridge *n.* A plug-in module containing RAM (random access memory) chips that can be used to store data or programmes. Memory cartridges are used primarily in portable computers as smaller, lighter (but more expensive) substitutes for disk drives. Memory cartridges typically use either a nonvolatile form of RAM, which does not lose its contents when power is turned off, or battery-backed RAM, which maintains its contents by drawing current from a rechargeable battery within the cartridge. Also called: RAM cartridge. See also memory card, RAM.

Memory cell *n.* An electronic circuit that stores one bit of data. See also bit.

Memory chip *n.* An integrated circuit devoted to memory storage. The memory storage can be volatile and hold data temporarily, such as RAM, or nonvolatile and hold data permanently, such as ROM, EPROM, EEPROM, or PROM. See also EEPROM, EPROM, integrated circuit, memory board, nonvolatile memory, PROM, RAM, volatile memory.

Memory management *n.* 1. In operating systems for personal computers, procedures for optimising the use of RAM (random access memory). These procedures include selectively storing data, monitoring it carefully, and freeing memory when the data is no longer needed. Most current operating systems optimise RAM usage on their own; some older operating systems, such as early versions of MS-DOS, required the use of third-party utilities to optimise RAM usage and necessitated that the user be more knowledgeable about how the operating system and applications used memory. See also memory management unit, RAM. 2. In programming, the process of ensuring that a programme releases each chunk of memory when it is no longer needed. In some languages, such as C and C++, the programmer must keep track of memory usage by the programme. Java, a newer language, automatically frees any chunk of memory that is not in use. See also C, C++, garbage collection, Java.

Memory management programme *n.* 1. A programme used to store data and programmes in system memory, monitor their use, and reassign the freed space following their execution. 2. A programme that uses hard disk space as an extension of the random access memory (RAM).

Memory management unit *n.* The hardware that supports the mapping of virtual memory addresses to physical memory addresses. In some systems, such as those based on the 68020, the memory management unit is separate from the processor. In most modern microcomputers, however, the memory management unit is built into the CPU chip. In some systems, the memory management unit provides interfacing between the microprocessor and memory. This type of memory management unit is typically responsible for address multiplexing and, in the case of DRAMs, the refresh cycle. Acronym: MMU. See also physical address, refresh cycle, virtual address.

Memory model *n.* The approach used to address the code and the data that are used in a computer programme. The memory model dictates how much memory can be used in a programme for code and how much for data. Most computers with a flat address space support only a single memory model. Computers with a segmented address space usually support multiple memory models. See also compact model, flat address space, large model, medium model, segmented address space, small model, tiny model.

Memory module *n.* A removable circuit board, cartridge, or other carrier that contains one or more RAM memory chips. See also memory card, memory cartridge, RAM.

Memory-resident *adj.* Permanently located in a computer's memory, rather than swapped in and out of memory as needed. See also memory, TSR.

Memory scrubbing *n.* 1. In mainframe computers, the process of a computer reading its own memory during idle periods in order to find and fix errors. 2. The process of examining and correcting errors as data is transferred from memory to the CPU of a computer.

Memory size *n.* The memory capacity of a computer, usually measured in megabytes. See also megabyte, memory.

Memory typewriter *n.* An electric typewriter with internal memory and typically a one-line liquid crystal display for viewing the contents of that memory. Memory typewriters can usually hold one page of text at a time, to which small modifications can be made. Memory typewriters usually do not retain the contents of memory when power is turned off.

MEMS *n.* Acronym for micro-electromechanical systems. A technology combining computers with extremely tiny mechanical devices. MEMS devices contain microcircuitry on a tiny silicon chip onto which a mechanical device such as a sensor or an actuator is attached. MEMS devices are used in switches, pacemakers, games, GPS tracking, data storage, and for accelerometers in air bags. Because MEMS devices have the potential to be manufactured in large quantities for little cost, many additional MEMS products are being planned or studied.

Menu *n.* A list of options from which a user can make a selection in order to perform a desired action, such as choosing a command or applying a particular format to part of a document. Many application programmes, especially those that offer a graphical interface, use menus as a means of providing the user with an easily learned, easy-to-use alternative to memorising programme commands and their appropriate usage.

Menu bar *n.* A rectangular bar displayed in an application program's onscreen window, often at the top, from which menus can be selected by the user. Names of available menus are displayed in the menu bar; choosing one with the keyboard or with a mouse causes the list of options in that menu to be displayed.

Menu-driven *adj.* Using menus to present choices of commands and available options. Menu-driven programmes are usually considered friendlier and easier to learn than programmes with a command-line interface.

Menu item *n.* A choice on a menu, selectable by either the keyboard or a mouse. In some instances, a menu item that is not available (that is, not appropriate) for a given situation is "grayed" (dimmed in comparison to the valid menu choices).

Merced *n.* Former code name for the next-generation 64-bit microprocessor designed by Intel and Hewlett-Packard and released in 2000. Based on the IA-64 architecture, the 64-bit microprocessor contains upwards of 10 million transistors and is used primarily in servers and high-performance workstations. See also IA-64.

Mercury *n.* A logic/functional programming language that combines the clarity and expressiveness of declarative programming with advanced static analysis and error-detection features.

Merge *vb.* To combine two or more items, such as lists, in an ordered way and without changing the basic structure of either.

Merged transistor logic *n.* See integrated injection logic.

Merge sort *n.* A sorting technique that combines several sorted (input) lists into a single sorted (output) list. See also bubble sort, insertion sort, quicksort, sort algorithm.

Mesa *n.* An area of a germanium or silicon wafer that was protected during the etching process and is therefore higher than the surrounding etched areas. See also photolithography.

Mesh network *n.* A communications network having two or more paths to any node.

Message *n.* 1. In communications, a unit of information transmitted electronically from one device to another. A message can contain one or more blocks of text as well as beginning and ending characters, control characters, a software-generated header (destination address, type of message, and other such information), and error-checking or synchronising information. A message can be routed directly from sender to receiver through a physical link, or it can be passed, either whole or in parts, through a switching system that routes it from one intermediate station to another. See also asynchronous transmission, block (definition 4), control character (definition 1), frame (definition 1), frame (definition 2), header (definition 2), message switching, network, packet (definition 1), packet switching, synchronous transmission. 2. In software, a piece of information passed from the application or operating system to the user to suggest an action, indicate a condition, or inform that an event has occurred.

Message header *n.* A sequence of bits or bytes at the beginning of a message that usually provides a timing sequence and specifies such aspects of the message structure as its length, data format, and block identification number. See also header (definition 2).

Message of the day *n.* A daily bulletin for users of a network, multiuser computer, or other shared system. In most cases, users are shown the message of the day when they log into the system. Acronym: MOTD.

Message Passing Interface *n.* See MPI.

Message queue *n.* An ordered list of messages awaiting transmission, from which they are taken up on a first in, first out (FIFO) basis.

Message Queuing *n.* A message queuing and routing system for Microsoft Windows that enables distributed applications running at different times to communicate across heterogeneous networks and with computers that may be off line. Message Queuing provides guaranteed message delivery, efficient routing, security, and priority-based messaging. Message Queuing was formerly known as MSMQ.

Message reflection *n.* In object-oriented programming environments, such as Visual C++, OLE, and ActiveX, a function that allows a control to handle its own message. See also ActiveX controls, control (definition 2), OCX, VBX.

Message Security Protocol *n.* A protocol for Internet messages that is based on the use of encryption and verification to ensure security. It also allows for permissions at the server level for delivery or rejection of e-mail. Acronym: MSP.

Message switching *n.* A technique used on some communications networks in which a message, with appropriate address information, is routed through one or more intermediate switching stations before being sent to its destination. On a typical message-switching network, a central computer receives messages, stores them (usually briefly), determines their destination addresses, and then delivers them. Message switching enables a network both to regulate traffic and to use communications lines efficiently.

Message transfer agent *n.* See MTA.

Messaging *n.* The use of computers and data communication equipment to convey messages from one person to another, as by e-mail, voice mail, or fax.

Messaging application *n.* An application that enables users to send messages (such as e-mail or fax) to each other.

Messaging Application Programming Interface *n.* See MAPI.

Messaging client *n.* An application programme that enables its user to send or receive messages (such as e-mail or fax) to and from other users with the help of a remote server.

Messaging-oriented middleware *n.* See MOM.

Meta- prefix Literally, a prefix that describes a process or characteristic beyond the normal meaning of the word without the prefix. For example, metaphysics is "beyond physics." In computing, meta- is usually attached to a word to indicate that the "metaterm" describes, defines, or acts upon objects or concepts of the same type as itself. So, for example, metadata is data about data and a metatool is a tool for working on tools.

Metacharacter *n.* A character embedded in a programme source or a data stream that conveys information about other characters, rather than itself representing a character. A simple example is the backslash (\) character, which, when used in strings in the C programming language, indicates that the letter following the backslash is part of an escape sequence that enables C to display a nongraphic character. See also escape character.

Metacompiler *n.* A compiler that produces compilers. The UNIX utility yacc (Yet Another Compiler-Compiler) is a metacompiler. If it is given a language specification, yacc produces a compiler for that language. See also compiler (definition 2).

Meta-Content Format *n.* An open format for describing information about content of a structured body of data such as a Web page, a set of files on a Windows desktop, or a relational database. Meta-Content Format might be used for indexes, data dictionaries, or price lists. Acronym: MCF.

Metadata or meta data *n.* 1. Data about data. For example, the title, subject, author, and size of a file constitute metadata about the file. See also data dictionary, repository. 2. In the Microsoft .NET Framework, information that describes every element managed by the runtime: an assembly, loadable file, type, method, and so on. This can include information required for debugging and garbage collection, as well as security attributes, marshaling data, extended class and member definitions, version binding, and other information required by the runtime.

Metadata Interchange Specification *n.* A set of specifications dealing with the exchanging, sharing, and managing of metadata. Acronym: MDIS. See also metadata.

Metafile *n.* A file that contains or defines other files. Many operating systems use metafiles to contain directory information about other files on a given storage device.

Metaflow *n.* One of the four stages of the data warehousing process, during which metadata (data about data) is tracked and managed; the business modeling stage. During metaflow, the operational environment is mapped to the data warehouse environment. See also data warehouse (definition 2), downflow, inflow, metadata (definition 1), upflow.

Metalanguage *n.* A language used to describe other languages. Backus-Naur form (BNF) is a metalanguage commonly used to define programming languages. Also called: language-description language. See also Backus-Naur form.

Metal-oxide semiconductor *n.* See MOS.

Metal-oxide semiconductor field-effect transistor *n.* See MOSFET.

Metaoperating system *n.* An operating system under which several other operating systems are active. Also called: supervisor.

Metatag or meta tag *n.* A tag in an HTML or XML document that allows a Web-page creator to include such information as the author's name, keywords identifying content, and descriptive details (for example, non-text objects on the page). The information that is marked with metatags does not appear on the Web page when a user views it in a browser, but it can be viewed in the HTML or XML source. Metatags are included in the head of a document and are often used to assist search engines in indexing the page. See also HTML, source, tag, XML.

Method *n.* In object-oriented programming, a process performed by an object when it receives a message. See also object (definition 2), object-oriented programming.

Metropolitan Area Exchange *n.* See MAE (definition 2).

Metropolitan area network *n.* See MAN.

MFC *n.* See Microsoft Foundation Classes.

MFLOPS *n.* Acronym for million floating-point operations per second. A measure of computing speed. Also called: megaflops.

MFM encoding *n.* See modified frequency modulation encoding.

MFP *n.* See multifunction peripheral.

MFS *n.* See Macintosh File System.

mget *n.* Short for multiple get. A command in most FTP clients with which a user can request the transfer of several files at once. See also FTP1 (definition 1).

MHTML *n.* Acronym for Multipurpose Internet Mail Extension Hypertext Markup Language, or MIME HTML. A standard method for sending an HTML document encapsulated with inline graphics, applets, linked documents, and other items referred to in the HTML document. See also HTML, MIME.

MHz *n.* See megahertz.

MI *n.* See multiple inheritance.

MIB *n.* See Management Information Base.

mickey *n.* A unit of measure for mouse movement. One mickey is typically equal to 1/200th of an inch.

MICR *n.* See magnetic-ink character recognition.

Micro- prefix 1. In nonexact measurements, small or compact, as in microprocessor or microcomputer. 2. Metric prefix meaning 10–6 (one millionth).

Microbrowser *n.* An application for mobile phones that allows users to access the Internet to send and receive e-mail and browse the Web. Microbrowsers don't have the full functionality of a Web browser on a PC. For instance, microbrowsers are capable of loading only stripped-down text versions of Web pages. Most microbrowser products are built to utilise the Wireless Application Protocol (WAP) standard. See also Wireless Application Protocol.

Microcapsule *n.* In an electronic paper display, millions of tiny beads filled with dark dye and light pigment that, in response to an electrical charge, change colour to create images and text. See also electronic paper.

Micro Channel Architecture *n.* The design of the bus in IBM PS/2 cosmputers (except Models 25 and 30). The Micro Channel is electrically and physically incompatible with the IBM PC/AT bus. Unlike the PC/AT bus, the Micro Channel functions as either a 16-bit or a 32-bit bus. The Micro Channel also can be driven independently by multiple bus master processors.

Microchip *n.* See integrated circuit.

Microcircuit *n.* A miniaturised electronic circuit etched on a semiconductor chip. A microcircuit is made up of interconnected transistors, resistors, and other components. However, it is fabricated as a unit, rather than as a set of vacuum tubes, discrete transistors, or other elements that have to be wired together. See also integrated circuit.

Microcode *n.* Very low-level code that defines how a processor operates. Microcode is even lower in level than machine code; it specifies what the processor does when it executes a machine-code instruction. See also machine code, microprogramming.

Microcomputer *n.* A computer built around a single-chip microprocessor. Less powerful than minicomputers and mainframes, microcomputers have nevertheless evolved into very powerful machines capable of complex tasks. Technology has progressed so quickly that state-of-the-art microcomputers—essentially, in today's terms, a desktop PC—are as powerful as mainframe computers of only a few years ago, at a fraction of the cost. See also computer.

Microcontent *n.* Short pieces of text on a Web page that help provide an overview of the page's contents. Microcontent introduces, summarises, or enhances the macrocontent of a Web page, and includes headings, page titles, ALT text, links, and subheads.

Microcontroller *n.* A special-purpose, single-chip computer designed and built to handle a particular, narrowly defined task. In addition to the central processing unit (CPU), a microcontroller usually contains its own memory, input/output channels (ports), and timers. When part of a larger piece of equipment, such as a car or a home appliance, a microcontroller is an embedded system. See also embedded system.

Microdisplay *n.* A tiny monitor screen that provides a full-size view when magnified. Microdisplays work by magnifying a screen as small as one-tenth of an inch to fill the user's field of vision. Microdisplays may be used with computers, DVD players, or handheld devices, in headsets and viewfinders, or anywhere a full-size monitor is impractical or undesirable.

Microdrive *n.* A 1-inch disk drive, introduced in 1998 by IBM. The Microdrive is designed for use in handheld computers and special-purpose devices such as digital cameras and cellular telephones.

Micro-electromechanical systems *n.* See MEMS.

Microelectronics *n.* The technology of constructing electronic circuits and devices in very small packages. The most significant advance in microelectronics technology has been the integrated circuit. Circuits that 40 years ago required a roomful of power-hungry vacuum tubes can now be fabricated on a silicon chip smaller than a postage stamp and require only a few milliwatts of power. See also integrated circuit.

Microfiche *n.* A small sheet of film, about 4 by 6 inches, used for recording photographically reduced images, such as document pages, in rows and columns forming a grid pattern. The resulting images are too small to read with the naked eye, and a microfiche reader is required to view the documents.

Microfilm *n.* A thin strip of film stored on a roll and used to record sequential data images. As with microfiche, a special device magnifies the images so that they can be read. See also CIM (definition 2), COM (definition 4).

Microfloppy disk *n.* A 3.5-inch floppy disk of the type used with the Macintosh and with IBM and compatible microcomputers. A microfloppy disk is a round piece of polyester film coated with ferric oxide and encased in a rigid plastic shell equipped with a sliding metal cover. On the Macintosh, a single-sided microfloppy disk can hold 400 kilobytes (KB); a double-sided (standard) disk can hold 800 KB; and a double-sided high-density disk can hold 1.44 megabytes (MB). On IBM and compatible machines, a microfloppy can hold either 720 KB or 1.44 MB of information. See also floppy disk.

Microfluidics *n.* Technology for control and manipulation of fluids on a microscopic scale using microscopic pumps and valves placed on a chip. Microfluidics devices have implications for a number of medical, pharmaceutical, genomics, and other biotechnology applications.

Microform *n.* The medium, such as microfilm or microfiche, on which a photographically reduced image, called a microimage, is stored. A microimage usually represents text, such as archived documents. See also microfiche, microfilm, micrographics.

Micrographics *n.* The techniques and methods for recording data on microfilm. See also microform.

Microimage *n.* A photographically reduced image, usually stored on microfilm or microfiche, that is too small to be read without magnification. See also microform, micrographics.

Microinstruction *n.* An instruction that is part of the microcode. See also microcode.

Microjustification *n.* See microspace justification.

Microkernel *n.* 1. In programming, the strictly hardware-dependent part of an operating system that is intended to be portable from one type of computer to another. The microkernel provides a hardware-independent interface to the rest of the operating system, so only the microkernel needs to be rewritten to port the operating system to a different platform. See also kernel, operating system. 2. A kernel that has been designed with only the basic features and typically in a modular fashion.

Micrologic *n.* A set of instructions, stored in binary form, or a set of electronic logic circuits that defines and governs the operation within a microprocessor.

Microminiature *n.* An extremely small circuit or other electronic component, especially one that is a refinement of an already miniaturised element.

Microphone *n.* 1. A device that converts sound waves into analog electrical signals. Additional hardware can convert the microphone's output into digital data that a computer can process; for example, to record multimedia documents or analyse the sound signal. 2. A communications programme that runs on the Macintosh computer.

Microphotonics *n.* Technology for directing light on a microscopic scale. Microphotonics employs tiny mirrors or photonic crystals to reflect and transmit specific wavelengths of light, which can carry digital signals. Microphotonics technology has implications for optical networks under development for the telecommunications industry. See also MEMS, optical switching.

Microprocessor *n.* A central processing unit (CPU) on a single chip. A modern microprocessor can have several million transistors in an integrated-circuit package that can easily fit into the palm of one's hand. Microprocessors are at the heart of all personal computers. When memory and power are added to a microprocessor, all the pieces, excluding peripherals, required for a computer are present. The most popular lines of microprocessors today are the 680x0 family from Motorola, which powers the Apple Macintosh line, and the 80x86 family from Intel, which is at the core of all IBM PC–compatible computers. See also 6502, 65816, 6800, 68000, 68020, 68030, 68040, 80286, 80386DX, 80386SX, 8080, 8086.

Microprogramming *n.* The writing of microcode for a processor. Some systems, chiefly minicomputers and mainframes, allow modification of microcode for an installed processor. See also microcode.

Microsecond *n.* One millionth (10–6) of a second. Abbreviation: ms.

Microsite *n.* 1. A small Web site targeted to a single message or topic and nested within a larger site. Microsites geared to promotional and sales of specific products and services may be integrated into popular Web sites by advertisers. 2. A small Web site with a single focus. Also called: minisite.

Microsoft Access *n.* See Access.

Microsoft Active Accessibility *n.* See Active Accessibility.

Microsoft DOS *n.* See MS-DOS.

Microsoft Excel *n.* See Excel.

Microsoft Foundation Classes *n.* A C++ class library developed by Microsoft. The Microsoft Foundation Class library, or MFC, provides the framework and classes that make it easier and faster for programmers to build Windows applications. MFC supports ActiveX and is bundled with several C++ compilers, including Microsoft Visual C++, Borland C++, and Symantec C++. Acronym: MFC. See also ActiveX, C++.

Microsoft FrontPage *n.* A programme you can use to create and manage Internet and intranet sites without programming; FrontPage is available as part of one of the Microsoft Office suites or as a stand-alone product.

Microsoft intermediate language *n.* The CPU--independent instruction set into which .NET Framework programmes are compiled. It contains instructions for loading, storing, initialising, and calling methods on objects. Combined with metadata and the common type system, Microsoft intermediate language allows for true cross-language integration. Prior to execution, MSIL is converted to machine code. It is not interpreted. Acronym: MSIL.

Microsoft Internet Explorer *n.* See Internet Explorer.

Microsoft Knowledge Base *n.* See KB (definition 2).

Microsoft Management Console *n.* See MMC.

Microsoft MapPoint *n.* See MapPoint.

Microsoft Money *n.* See Money.

Microsoft MSN Explorer *n.* See MSN Explorer.

Microsoft MSN Messenger Service *n.* See .NET Messenger Service.

Microsoft .NET Messenger Service *n.* See .NET Messenger Service.

Microsoft Network *n.* See MSN.

Microsoft Office *n.* See Office.

Microsoft Operations Manager *n.* A server and application management solution developed by Microsoft Corporation to deliver event and performance management for the Windows 2000–based environment and .NET Enterprise Server applications. Operations management features include enterprise event log reports from across the corporate network, proactive monitoring and alert messaging, and reporting and trend analysis for problem tracking. Microsoft Operations Manager provides flexibility through sophisticated management rules, which can be customised to meet the needs of individual businesses. Microsoft Operations Manager support for management technology standards permits easy integration with other enterprise management systems.

Microsoft Outlook *n.* See Outlook.

Microsoft PowerPoint *n.* See PowerPoint.

Microsoft Project *n.* A software application developed by Microsoft Corporation to simplify the planning and management of projects. Microsoft Project includes features that help you build and manage projects, set schedules and milestones, and communicate and share ideas with team members.

Microsoft Reader *n.* A software application developed by Microsoft for downloading electronic books and other publications onto any personal computer, laptop computer, or Pocket PC handheld device. Additional features allow users to bookmark pages, highlight text, write notes, and look up definitions.

Microsoft Tech•Ed *n.* An annual training conference held by Microsoft Corporation to educate engineers and businesses using Microsoft technology. The conference provides attendees with access to information, experts, and training labs on Microsoft's latest technologies.

Microsoft Visual InterDev *n.* See Visual InterDev.

Microsoft Visual Studio *n.* See Visual Studio.

Microsoft Visual Studio .NET *n.* A complete development environment for building on the Microsoft .NET technology.

Using Visual Studio .NET, developers can create secure, scalable applications and Web services quickly in the language of their choice, leveraging existing systems and skills.

Microsoft Windows *n.* See Windows.

Microsoft Windows 2000 *n.* See Windows 2000.

Microsoft Windows 95 *n.* See Windows 95.

Microsoft Windows 98 *n.* See Windows 98.

Microsoft Windows CE *n.* See Windows CE.

Microsoft Windows Messenger *n.* See .NET Messenger Service.

Microsoft Windows NT *n.* See Windows NT.

Microsoft Word *n.* See Word.

Microsoft XML *n.* See MSXML.

Microspace justification *n.* The addition of thin spaces between characters within words to fill out a line for justification, instead of relying only on adding space between words. Good microspace justification gives justified text a more polished, professional look; excessive microspace justification causes words to lose visual coherence. Also called: microjustification. See also justify (definition 2), microspacing.

Microspacing *n.* In printing, the process of adjusting character placement by very small increments.

Microtransaction *n.* A business transaction that involves a very small amount of money, typically under about $5. See also millicent technology.

Microwave relay *n.* A communications link that uses point-to-point radio transmissions at frequencies higher than approximately 1 gigahertz (1000 megahertz).

Middleware *n.* 1. Software that sits between two or more types of software and translates information between them. Middleware can cover a broad spectrum of software and generally sits between an application and an operating system, a network operating system, or a database management system. Examples of middleware include CORBA and other object broker programmes and network control programmes.

See also CORBA. 2. Software that provides a common application programming interface (API). Applications written using that API will run in the same computer systems as the middleware. An example of this type of middleware is ODBC, which has a common API for many types of databases. See also application programming interface, ODBC. 3. Software development tools that enable users to create simple programmes by selecting existing services and linking them with a scripting language. See also scripting language.

MIDI *n.* Acronym for Musical Instrument Digital Interface. A serial interface standard that allows for the connection of music synthesizers, musical instruments, and computers. The MIDI standard is based partly on hardware and partly on a description of the way in which music and sound are encoded and communicated between MIDI devices. The information transmitted between MIDI devices is in a form called a MIDI message, which encodes aspects of sound such as pitch and volume as 8-bit bytes of digital information. MIDI devices can be used for creating, recording, and playing back music. Using MIDI, computers, synthesizers, and sequencers can communicate with each other, either keeping time or actually controlling the music created by other connected equipment. See also synthesizer.

MIDL *n.* Acronym for Microsoft Interface Definition Language. Microsoft implementation and extension of the Interface Definition Language (IDL). See also IDL.

Midrange computer *n.* A medium-size computer. The term is used interchangeably with minicomputer, except midrange computers do not include single-user workstations. See also minicomputer.

Migration *n.* The process of making existing applications and data work on a different computer or operating system.

.mil *n.* In the Internet's Domain Name System, the top-level domain that identifies addresses operated by U.S. military organisations. The designation .mil appears at the end of the address. See also DNS (definition 1), domain (definition 3).

Military Network *n.* See MILNET.

Millennium bug *n.* See Year 2000 problem.

Millennium-compliant *adj.* See Year 2000-compliant.

Millennium computer bug *n.* See Year 2000 problem.

Millennium transition *n.* See Year 2000 rollover.

Milli- prefix Metric prefix meaning 10–3 (one thousandth). Abbreviation: m.

Millicent technology *n.* A set of protocols for small-scale commercial transactions over the Internet, developed by Digital Equipment Corporation. Millicent technology is intended to handle purchases of items of information at prices less than a cent.

Millions of instructions per second *n.* See MIPS.

Millisecond *n.* One thousandth of a second. Abbreviation: ms or msec.

Millivolt *n.* One thousandth of a volt. Abbreviation: mV.

MILNET *n.* Short for Military Network. A wide area network that represents the military side of the original ARPANET. MILNET carries nonclassified U.S. military traffic. See also ARPANET.

MIMD *n.* Acronym for multiple instruction, multiple data stream processing. A category of computer architecture engaged in parallel processing in which central processing units independently fetch instructions and operate on data. See also architecture (definition 1), central processing unit, instruction, parallel processing.

MIME or mime *n.* Acronym for Multipurpose Internet Mail Extensions. A protocol widely used on the Internet that extends the SMTP (Simple Mail Transfer Protocol) to permit data, such as video, sound, and binary files, to be transmitted by Internet e-mail without having to be translated into ASCII format first. This is accomplished by the use of MIME types, which describe the contents of a document. A MIME-compliant application sending a file, such as some e-mail programmes, assigns a MIME type to the file. The receiving application, which must also be MIME-compliant, refers to a standardised list of documents that are organised into MIME types and subtypes to interpret the content of the file. For instance, one MIME type is text, and it has a number of subtypes, including plain and html. A MIME type of text/html refers to a file that contains text written in HTML. MIME is part of HTTP, and both Web browsers and HTTP servers use MIME to interpret e-mail files they send and receive.

Mindshare *n.* The presence and familiarity of a product, service, or company in the minds of users or consumers. Unlike market share, which is the percentage of the market won by a particular product, service, or company, mindshare is a less quantifiable but still important factor in engaging customer attention and generating sales. The term is used frequently by, but is not limited to, the computer industry.

Miniaturisation *n.* In the development of integrated circuits, the process of reducing the size and increasing the density of transistors and other elements on a semiconductor chip. In addition to providing the benefits of small size, miniaturisation of electronic circuits also lowers power requirements, reduces heat, and shortens delays in the propagation of signals from one circuit element to the next. See also integrated circuit, integration (definition 2).

Minicomputer *n.* A mid-level computer built to perform complex computations while dealing efficiently with a high level of input and output from users connected via terminals. Minicomputers also frequently connect to other minicomputers on a network and distribute processing among all the attached machines. Minicomputers are used heavily in transaction-processing applications and as interfaces between mainframe computer systems and wide area networks. See also computer, mainframe computer, microcomputer, supercomputer, wide area network.

Mini-driver architecture *n.* An architecture in Windows 3.1, Windows 95, Windows 98, Windows NT, and Windows 2000 that uses a relatively small and simple driver, containing any additional instructions needed by a specific hardware device, to interface with the universal driver for that class of devices. See also driver.

Minifloppy *n.* A 5.25-inch floppy disk. See also floppy disk.

Minimise *vb.* In a graphical user interface, to hide a window without shutting down the programme responsible for the window. Usually an icon, a button, or a name for the window is placed on the desktop; when the user clicks on the button, icon, or name, the window is restored to its previous size. See also graphical user interface, Minimise button, taskbar, window.

Minimise button *n.* In Windows 3.x, Windows 9x, Windows NT, and Windows 2000, a button in the upper right-hand corner of a window that when clicked hides the window. In Windows 3.x and Windows NT 3.5 and earlier, an icon appears on the desktop that represents the window; in Windows 95, Windows NT 4, and later versions, the name of the window appears on the taskbar at the bottom of the desktop screen. When the icon or the name is clicked, the window is restored to its previous size. See also graphical user interface, taskbar, window.

Mini-notebook *n.* A portable computer in a case smaller than that of a standard laptop computer. Most mini-notebook computers have small keyboards, LCD screens built into folding cases, Pentium processors, and built-in hard drives. They are designed to run on standard operating systems, such as Windows 98, rather than on the Windows CE operating system used by the even smaller handheld computers.

Miniport driver *n.* A kernel-mode driver that is specific to a device. A miniport driver is linked to a port driver that provides an interface between the port driver and the operating system. This is typically implemented as a dynamic-link library.

Minisite *n.* See microsite.

Minitower *n.* A vertical floor-standing computer cabinet that is about half the height (13 inches) of a tower case (24 inches). See also tower.

Minor key *n.* See alternate key (definition 1).

MIP mapping *n.* Short for multum in parvo (Latin, "much in little") mapping. A form of mapping in which the appearance of a bitmapped image is precalculated from a distance and used in a texture mapper. This allows for smoother texture-mapped images calculated in the distance, since pixel conversion may alter colours relative to human perception.

MIPS *n.* Acronym for millions of instructions per second. A common measure of processor speed. See also central processing unit, MFLOPS.

Mirror image *n.* An image that is an exact duplicate of the original with the exception that one dimension is reversed. For example, a right-pointing arrow and a left-pointing arrow of the same size and shape are mirror images.

Mirroring *n.* 1. In computer graphics, the ability to display a mirror image of a graphic—a duplicate rotated or reflected relative to some reference such as an axis of symmetry. See the illustration. 2. In a network, a means of protecting data on a network by duplicating it, in its entirety, on a second disk. Mirroring is one strategy implemented in RAID security. 3. On the Internet, replicating a Web site or an FTP site on another server. A site is often mirrored if it is frequently visited by multiple users. This eases the network traffic to the site, making it easier for users to gain access to the information or files on it. A site may also be mirrored in different geographic locations to facilitate downloading by users in various areas. See also RAID.

Mirror site *n.* A file server that contains a duplicate set of files to the set on a popular server. Mirror sites exist to spread the distribution burden over more than one server or to eliminate the need to use high-demand international circuits.

MIS *n.* See IS.

Misc. newsgroups *n.* Usenet newsgroups that are part of the misc. hierarchy and have the prefix misc. These newsgroups cover topics that do not fit into the other standard Usenet hierarchies (comp., news., rec., sci., soc., talk.). See also newsgroup, traditional newsgroup hierarchy, Usenet.

Mission critical *adj.* Pertaining to information, equipment, or other assets of a business or project that are essential to the successful operation of the organisation. For example, accounting data and customer records are often considered mission critical information.

Misuse detection *n.* See IDS.

Mixed cell reference *n.* In spreadsheets, a cell reference (the address of a cell needed to solve a formula) in which either the row or the column is relative (automatically changed when the formula is copied or moved to another cell) and the other is absolute (not changed when the formula is copied or moved). See also cell (definition 1).

MMC *n.* Acronym for Microsoft Management Console. A framework for hosting administrative tools called snap-ins. A console might contain tools, folders or other containers, World Wide Web pages, and other administrative items. These items are displayed in the left pane of the console, called a console tree. A console has one or more windows that can provide views of the console tree. The main MMC window provides commands and tools for authoring consoles. The authoring features of MMC and the console tree itself might be hidden when a console is in User Mode. See also snap-in.

MMDS *n.* Short for multichannel multipoint distribution service. A fixed wireless service proposed for use as an alternative when DSL or cable modem options are not practical or desirable. The MMDS spectrum was originally used for distance learning and wireless cable video services before attracting interest for fixed broadband wireless services. See also broadband.

MMU *n.* See memory management unit.

MMX *n.* Short for Multimedia Extensions. An enhancement to the architecture of Intel Pentium processors that improves the performance of multimedia and communications applications.

Mnemonic *n.* A word, rhyme, or other memory aid used to associate a complex or lengthy set of information with something that is simple and easy to remember. Mnemonics are widely used in computing. Programming languages other than machine language, for example, are known as symbolic languages because they use short mnemonics, such as ADD (for addition) and def (for define) to represent instructions and operations. Similarly, operating systems and applications based on typed commands use mnemonics to represent instructions to the programme. MS-DOS, for example, uses dir (for directory) to request a list of files.

MNP10 *n.* Short for Microcom Networking Protocol, Class 10. An industry-standard communication protocol used for modem connections over analog cellular telephone connections. The most recent version of MNP10 is MNP 10EC (EC stands for Enhanced Cellular). See also communications protocol.

Mobile computing *n.* The process of using a computer while traveling. Mobile computing usually requires a portable computer that is battery powered, rather than a desktop system.

Mobile Explorer *n.* A modular wireless applications and services platform designed by Microsoft to power Web-enabled wireless telephones. When connected to a wireless network, Mobile Explorer provides secure mobile access to corporate or personal e-mail, corporate networks, and the Internet. It includes a multimode microbrowser, which can display Web content coded in a variety of markup languages used for small, handheld devices, including cHTML, HTML, WAP 1.1, and WML. See also microbrowser.

Mobile Information Server *n.* A software application developed by Microsoft to allow telecommunications carriers, enterprise customers, and business partners to securely extend Microsoft Exchange Server information, corporate intranet applications, and services to users of wireless handheld computing devices. Microsoft Information Server provides mobile users with access to personal services and data stored on the intranet, such as e-mail, document files, appointment calendars, and contacts.

Mobile IP *n.* Acronym for mobile Internet Protocol. An Internet protocol designed to support host mobility. Mobile IP enables a host to remain connected to the Internet with the same IP address (called the home address) while moving to different locations. Mobile IP tracks a moving host by registering the presence of the host with a foreign agent; the home agent then forwards packets to the remote network. See also IP.

Mobile telephone switching office *n.* Computer that controls wireless phone calls. The mobile telephone switching office controls the operation of wireless cell sites, tracks calls, and transfers signals between wireless networks and traditional wired telephone systems. Acronym: MTSO.

Mode *n.* The operational state of a computer or a programme. For example, edit mode is the state in which a programme accepts changes to a file. See also address mode, compatibility mode, safe mode, video mode, virtual real mode.

Modec *n.* In telecommunications, a device that generates analog modem signals digitally. The term modec is a combination of the terms modem and codec. See also codec (definition 1), modem (definition 2).

Model *n.* A mathematical or graphical representation of a real-world situation or object—for example, a mathematical model of the distribution of matter in the universe, a spreadsheet (numeric) model of business operations, or a graphical model of a molecule. Models can generally be changed or manipulated so that their creators can see how the real version might be affected by modifications or varying conditions. See also modeling, simulation.

Modeling *n.* 1. The use of computers to describe the behaviour of a system. Spreadsheet programmes, for example, can be used to manipulate financial data representing the health and activity of a company, to develop business plans and projections, or to evaluate the impact of proposed changes on the company's operations and financial status. See also simulation, spreadsheet programme. 2. The use of computers to describe physical objects and the spatial relationships among them mathematically. CAD programmes, for example, are used to create onscreen representations of such physical objects as tools, office buildings, complex molecules, and automobiles. These models use equations to create lines, curves, and other shapes and to place those shapes accurately in relation to each other and to the two-dimensional or three-dimensional space in which they are drawn. See also CAD, rendering, solid model, surface modeling, three-dimensional model, two-dimensional model, wire-frame model.

Modem *n.* 1. Short for modulator/demodulator. A communications device that converts between digital data from a computer or terminal and analog audio signals that can pass through a standard telephone line. Because the telephone system was designed to handle voice and other audio signals and a computer processes signals as discrete units of digital information, a modem is necessary at both ends of the telephone line to exchange data between computers. At the transmit end, the modem converts from digital to analog audio; at the receiving end, a second modem converts the analog audio back to its original digital form. In order to move a high volume of data, high-speed modems rely on sophisticated methods for "loading" information onto the audio carrier—for example, they may combine frequency shift keying, phase modulation, and amplitude modulation to enable a single change in the carrier's state to represent multiple bits of data. In addition to the basic modulation and demodulation functions, most modems also include

Modem bank *n.* A collection of modems connected to a server maintained by an ISP or the operator of a BBS or remote-access LAN. Most modem banks are configured to allow a remote user to dial a single phone number that routes calls to an available phone number on the bank. See also BBS (definition 1), ISP, LAN.

Modem eliminator *n.* A device that enables two computers to communicate without modems. See also null modem.

Modem port *n.* A serial port used for connecting an external modem to a personal computer. See also modem (definition 1), serial port.

Modem ready *n.* See MR.

Moderated *adj.* Subjected to review by a moderator, who may remove irrelevant or inflammatory articles or messages before redistributing them through a newsgroup, mailing list, or other messaging system.

Moderated discussion *n.* Communication taking place on a mailing list, newsgroup, or other online forum that is edited by a moderator. When a user submits a message to a moderated discussion, the moderator decides if the message is relevant to the discussion topic. If so, it is forwarded to the discussion group. The content of a moderated discussion is often perceived as more valuable than that of an unmoderated one because the information has been read and approved by a "gatekeeper," who has (presumably) filtered out irrelevant submissions. Some moderators also filter submissions for obscene or pornographic material or material that is potentially offensive. See also mailing list, moderator, newsgroup.

Moderator *n.* In some Internet newsgroups and mailing lists, a person through whom all messages are filtered before they are distributed to the members of the newsgroup or list. The moderator discards or edits any messages that are not considered appropriate. See also mailing list, newsgroup.

Modified frequency modulation encoding *n.* An older method of storing data on disks. Modified frequency modulation encoding is based on an earlier technique called frequency modulation encoding but improves on its efficiency by reducing the need for synchronising information and by basing the magnetic coding of each bit on the status of the previously recorded bit. This method of encoding stores more information on a disk than does -frequency modulation encoding. It is not, however, as -efficient a space saver as the technique known as run-length limited encoding, or RLL. Abbreviation: MFM encoding.

Modifier key *n.* A key on the keyboard that, when held down while another key is pressed, changes the meaning of the keystroke. See also Alt key, Command key, Control key, Shift key.

Modify structure *n.* An operator available in some database management systems that permits fields (columns) to be added or deleted without the need to rebuild the entire database.

MO disk *n.* See magneto-optic disc.

MO disk drive *n.* See magneto-optic disc.

Modula-2 *n.* A modular high-level language designed in 1980 by Niklaus Wirth. Derived from Pascal, Modula-2 is noted for its emphasis on modular programming, its early support for data abstraction, and its lack of standard functions and procedures. See also modular programming.

Modular design *n.* An approach to designing hardware or software in which a project is broken into smaller units, or modules, each of which can be developed, tested, and finished independently before being combined with the others in the final product. Each unit is designed to perform a particular task or function and can thus become part of a library of modules that can often be reused in other products having similar requirements. In programming, for example, one module might consist of instructions for moving the cursor in a window on the screen. Because it is deliberately designed as a stand-alone unit that can work with other sections of the programme, the same module might be able to perform the same task in another programme as well, thus saving time in development and testing.

Modular jack *n.* See phone connector.

Modular programming *n.* An approach to programming in which the programme is broken into several independently compiled modules. Each module exports specified elements (such as constants, data types, variables, functions, and procedures); all other elements remain private to the module. Other modules can use only the exported elements. Modules clarify and regularise the interfaces among the major parts of a programme. Thus, they facilitate group programming efforts and promote reliable programming practices. Modular programming is a precursor of object-oriented programming. See also module (definition 1), object-oriented programming.

Modular software *n.* A programme created from multiple standalone software components. Modular components can work together to perform the work for which the larger programme is designed while still remaining individually usable—and reusable—in other programmes. Modular software is, in effect, made up of recyclable parts. Because each component is functionally autonomous and self-contained, other components can call on its services without having to "know" how it works. Thus, a programmer can change or modify the way one component performs its work without adversely affecting other components in the same programme. See also component software, integrated software, modular design.

Modulate *vb.* To change some aspect of a signal intentionally, usually for the purpose of transmitting information.

Modulation *n.* 1. The process of changing or regulating the characteristics of a carrier wave vibrating at a certain amplitude (height) and frequency (timing) so that the variations represent meaningful information. 2. In computer communications, the means by which a modem converts digital information sent by a computer to the audio form that it sends over a telephone line.

Modulation standards *n.* Protocols that determine how modems convert digital data into analog signals that can be transmitted over telephone lines. Initially, Bell created modulation standards used in the United States, and the CCITT created international recommendations. The ITU-T (formerly called the CCITT) now makes recommendations generally adopted by modem manufacturers both internationally and in the United States. The ITU-TV series recommendations (such as V.34 and V.90) define data communication over the telephone network. The suffixes -bis and -ter (for example, V.32bis) indicate later versions. See also V.34, V.90.

Module *n.* 1. In programming, a collection of routines and data structures that performs a particular task or implements a particular abstract data type. Modules usually consist of two parts: an interface, which lists the constants, data types, variables, and routines that can be accessed by other modules or routines; and an implementation, which is private (accessible only to the module) and which contains the source code that actually implements the routines in the module. See also abstract data type, information hiding, Modula-2, modular programming. 2. In hardware, a self-contained component that can provide a complete function to a system and can be interchanged with other modules that provide similar functions. See also memory card, SIMM.

Modulo *n.* An arithmetic operation whose result is the remainder of a division operation. For example, 17 modulo 3 = 2 because 17 divided by 3 yields a remainder of 2. Modulo operations are used in programming.

Moiré *n.* A visible wavy distortion or flickering in an image that is displayed or printed with an inappropriate resolution. Several parameters affect moiré patterns, including the size and resolution of the image, resolution of the output device, and halftone screen angle.

Molecular beam epitaxy *n.* A process used in the fabrication of semiconductor devices, such as integrated circuits. A device employing molecular beam epitaxy creates thin layers of semiconducting material by vaporising the material and then directing a beam of molecules at the substrate on which the layer is to be formed. This technique allows very precise and very thin layers to be created.

MOM *n.* Acronym for messaging-oriented middleware. A class of programmes that translates data and messages between applications that use one format and communications services (such as NetBIOS and TCP/IP) that expect a different format.

Monadic *adj.* See unary.

Money *n.* Microsoft's Windows-based financial-management software for individuals, families, and small businesses. Money includes tools for managing bank accounts and investments, budgeting, tax estimating and financial planning, and paying bills.

Monitor *n.* The device on which images generated by the computer's video adapter are displayed. The term monitor usually refers to a video display and its housing. The monitor is attached to the video adapter by a cable. See also CRT.

Monitoring software *n.* A programme or set of programmes used to oversee computer-based systems and networks for the purpose of tracking usage or identifying, reporting on, and solving problems at the earliest possible stage. Monitoring software is used in a variety of areas ranging from hardware platforms and their components to operating systems, databases, Internet/intranet access, and business applications. Typically, different tools are used to monitor individual system components, though the individual monitors might feed information to a higher-level monitor in order to encompass an entire computing environment.

Monitor port *n.* See display port.

Monochrome *adj.* Of, pertaining to, or being a monitor that displays images in only one colour—black on white (as on early monochrome Macintosh screens) or amber or green on black (as on early IBM and other monochrome monitors). The term is also applied to a monitor that displays only variable levels of a single colour, such as a gray-scale monitor.

Monochrome adapter *n.* A video adapter capable of generating a video signal for one foreground colour or sometimes for a range of intensities in a single colour, as for a gray-scale monitor.

Monochrome display *n.* 1. A video display capable of rendering only one colour. The colour displayed depends on the phosphor of the display (often green or amber). 2. A display capable of rendering a range of intensities in only one colour, as in a gray-scale monitor.

Monochrome Display Adapter *n.* See MDA.

Monochrome graphics adapter *n.* See HGC.

Monochrome monitor *n.* See monochrome display.

Monographics adapter *n.* Any video adapter that can display only monochrome text and graphics; any video adapter functionally compatible with the Hercules Graphics Card (HGC). See also HGC.

Monospace font *n.* A font (set of characters in a particular style and size), similar to that used on a typewriter, in which each character occupies the same amount of horizontal space regardless of its width—an i, for example, taking as much room as an m. See the illustration. Also called: fixed-width font. See also monospacing.

Monospacing *n.* A form of print and display spacing in which each character occupies the same amount of horizontal space on the line, regardless of whether the character is wide (such as m) or narrow (such as I). Also called: fixed-pitch spacing, fixed spacing, fixed-width spacing. See also monospace font.

Monte Carlo method *n.* A mathematical technique that uses repeated calculations and random numbers to find an approximate solution to a complex problem. The Monte Carlo method, named for its relationship to games of chance played in the casinos at Monte Carlo, Monaco, can be used in situations in which it is possible to calculate the probability of a particular event occurring but not to factor in the complex effects of many other contributing factors.

MOO *n.* Short for MUD, object-oriented. A type of virtual environment on the Internet, similar to a game-oriented MUD but based on an object-oriented language and generally focused more on programming than on games. See also MUD.

Moore's Law *n.* A prediction by Intel cofounder Gordon Moore in the early days of the computer revolution regarding the growth of semiconductor technology. Moore predicted that the number of transistors that could be put on a chip would double every year, and it did. Ten years later, Moore predicted that chip capacity would double every two years, and capacity has actually doubled every 18 months since then. The doubling of capacity every 18 months is popularly referred to as a "law."

.moov *n.* A file extension indicating a QuickTime MooV video file for a Macintosh computer. See also MooV.

MooV *n.* The file format for QuickTime movies that stores synchronised tracks for control, video, audio, and text. See also QuickTime.

Morphing *n.* Short for metamorphosing. A process by which one image is gradually transformed into another, creating the illusion of a metamorphosis occurring in a short time. A common motion picture special-effects technique, morphing is available in many advanced computer animation packages. See also tween.

MOS *n.* Acronym for metal-oxide semiconductor. An integrated-circuit technology in which field-effect transistors (FETs) are made with an insulating layer of silicon dioxide between a metal gate electrode and a semiconductor channel. MOS designs are widely used both in discrete components and in integrated circuits. MOS integrated circuits have the advantages of high component density, high speed, and low power consumption. MOS devices are easily damaged by static electricity, so before they are inserted in a circuit, they should be kept with their connectors embedded in conducting foam to prevent the buildup of static charges. See also FET, MOSFET.

Mosaic *n.* The first popular graphical World Wide Web browser. Released on the Internet in early 1993 by the National Center for Supercomputing Applications (NCSA) at the University of Illinois at Urbana-Champaign, Mosaic is available as freeware and shareware for Windows, Macintosh, and X Window systems. Mosaic is distinguished from other early Web browsers by its ease of use and its addition of inline images to Web documents. Also called: NCSA Mosaic.

MOSFET *n.* Acronym for metal-oxide semiconductor field-effect transistor. A common type of field-effect transistor in which a layer of silicon dioxide insulates the metal gate from the semiconductor current channel. MOSFETs have extremely high input impedance and therefore require almost no driving power. They are used in many audio applications, including high-gain amplifier circuits. Like all metal-oxide semiconductor (MOS) devices, MOSFETs are easily damaged by static electricity. See the illustration. See also FET, MOS.

Most significant bit *n.* In a sequence of one or more bytes, the highest-order bit of a binary number, not including the sign bit. Acronym: MSB. See also high-order.

Most significant character *n.* The high-order, or leftmost, character in a string. Acronym: MSC. See also high-order.

Most significant digit *n.* In a sequence of one or more digits, the highest-order digit, which is the leftmost digit. In 456.78, 4 is the most significant digit. Acronym: MSD.

MOTD *n.* See message of the day.

Motherboard *n.* The main circuit board containing the primary components of a computer system. This board contains the processor, main memory, support circuitry, and bus controller and connector. Other boards, including expansion memory and input/output boards, may attach to the motherboard via the bus connector. See also expansion slot.

Motion JPEG *n.* A standard for storing motion video, proposed by the Joint Photographic Experts Group (JPEG), that uses JPEG image compression for each frame. See also JPEG (definition 1).

Motion path *n.* The path that a specified object or text will follow as part of an animation sequence for a slide.

Mount *vb.* To make a physical disk or tape accessible to a computer's file system. The term is most commonly used to describe accessing disks in Macintosh and UNIX-based computers.

Mount *n.* In NFS, a folder or file retrieved from elsewhere on the network and accessed locally. See also NFS.

MOUS *n.* Acronym for Microsoft Office User Specialist. A certification from Microsoft that verifies an individual's skills with the Microsoft Office desktop programmes. See also MCP.

Mouse *n.* A common pointing device. The basic features of a mouse are a flat-bottomed casing designed to be gripped by one hand, one or more buttons on the top, a multidirectional detection device (usually a ball) on the bottom, and a cable connecting the mouse to the computer. By moving the mouse on a surface (such as a desk top), the user typically controls an onscreen cursor. A mouse is a relative pointing device because there are no defined limits to the mouse's movement and because its placement on a surface does not map directly to a specific screen location. To select items or choose commands on the screen, the user presses one of the mouse's buttons, producing a "mouse click." See the illustration. See also bus mouse, mechanical mouse, optical mouse, optomechanical mouse, relative pointing device, serial mouse.

MouseKeys *n.* A feature in Windows that allows a user to use the numeric keyboard to move the mouse pointer. MouseKeys is primarily intended for people who may have physical limitations that make it difficult to move a conventional mouse. See also mouse.

Mouse pad *n.* A surface on which a mouse can be moved, typically a rectangular rubber pad covered with fabric, providing more traction than a wooden or glass desktop or tabletop. See also mouse.

Mouse pointer *n.* An onscreen element whose location changes as the user moves the mouse. Depending on the location of the mouse pointer and the operation of the programme with which it is working, the area of the screen where the mouse pointer appears serves as the target for an action when the user presses one of the mouse buttons. See also block cursor, cursor (definition 3).

Mouse port *n.* 1. In many PC-compatible computers, a dedicated connector where a mouse or other pointing device plugs into the computer. If a mouse port is not available, a serial port can be used to connect the mouse to the computer. See the illustration. See also connector, mouse, pointing device, serial port. 2. In a Macintosh, the Apple Desktop Bus port. See also Apple Desktop Bus.

Mouse scaling *n.* See mouse sensitivity.

Mouse sensitivity *n.* The relationship of mouse movement to screen cursor movement. A more sensitive mouse signals to the computer more "mouse moves" per inch of physical mouse movement than does a less sensitive mouse. Increasing the sensitivity of the programme or mouse driver can result in smaller cursor moves for a given mouse move, making it easier for the user to position the cursor precisely. High sensitivity is good for exacting work, such as CAD/CAM and graphic art; low sensitivity is good for tasks in which getting around the screen quickly is important and for applications such as Web browsers, word processors, and spreadsheets, in which the cursor is used mostly to select buttons or text. Also called: mouse scaling, mouse tracking.

Mouse tracking *n.* See mouse sensitivity.

Mouse trails *n.* The creation of a shadowlike trail following the mouse pointer on screen in order to make it easier to see. Mouse trails are useful for laptops and notebooks, particularly ones with passive matrix displays or older models with monochrome screens. The relatively low resolution and contrast of these screens made it easy to lose sight of a small mouse pointer. See also mouse pointer, submarining.

Mousetrapping *n.* A practice employed by some Web sites in which the back and exit buttons of a visitor's Web browser are disabled and attempts to leave the site are redirected to other pages on the site or to other sites against the visitor's will. Mousetrapping is most often associated with adult-oriented Web sites.

.mov *n.* A filename extension for a movie file in Apple's QuickTime format. See also QuickTime.

Move *n.* A command or an instruction to transfer information from one location to another. Depending on the operation involved, a move can affect data in a computer's memory or it can affect text or a graphical image in a data file. In programming, for example, a move instruction might transfer a single value from one memory location to another. In applications, on the other hand, a move command might relocate a paragraph of text or all or part of a graphic from one place in a document to another. Unlike a copy procedure, which duplicates information, a move indicates that information either is or can be deleted from its original location.

.movie *n.* See .mov.

Moving Picture Experts Group *n.* See MPEG (definition 1).

Mozilla *n.* 1. A nickname for the Netscape Navigator (later, Netscape Communicator) Web browser, coined by the

Netscape Corporation. See also Mosaic, Netscape Navigator. 2. Since 1998, when the Communicator source code was released for free, for use by any interested parties, the name Mozilla has been extended as a generic reference to any Web browser based on Navigator source code.

Mozilla.org *n.* The name of the group charged by the Netscape Corporation to act as a clearinghouse for Mozilla-related matters, such as questions, changes to code, bug reporting, forums, and so on.

MP3 *n.* Acronym for MPEG Audio Layer-3. A digital audio coding scheme used in distributing recorded music over the Internet. MP3 shrinks the size of an audio file by a factor of 10 to 12 without seriously degrading the quality (CD-recording level) of the sound. MP3 files are given the file extension .mp3. Although MP3 is part of the MPEG family, it is audio-only and is not the same as the now-defunct MPEG-3 standard. See also MPEG-3.

MP3 encoder *n.* See encoder.

MPC *n.* See Multimedia PC.

.mpeg *n.* The file extension that identifies video and sound files compressed in the MPEG format specified by the Moving Pictures Experts Group. See also MPEG.

MPEG *n.* 1. Acronym for Moving Picture Experts Group. A set of standards for audio and video compression established by the Joint ISO/IEC Technical Committee on Information Technology. The MPEG standard has different types that have been designed to work in different situations. 2. A video/audio file in the MPEG format. Such files generally have the extension .mpg. See also JPEG.

MPEG-1 *n.* The original MPEG standard for storing and retrieving video and audio information, designed for CD-ROM technology. MPEG-1 defines a medium bandwidth of up to 1.5 Mbps, two audio channels, and noninterlaced video. See also MPEG (definition 1).

MPEG-2 *n.* An extension of the MPEG-1 standard designed for broadcast television, including HDTV. MPEG-2 defines a higher bandwidth of up to 40 Mbps, five audio channels, a wider range of frame sizes, and interlaced video. See also HDTV, MPEG (definition 1).

MPEG-3 *n.* Initially an MPEG standard designed for HDTV (high-definition television), but it was found that MPEG-2 could be used instead. Therefore, this standard no longer exists. See also HDTV, MPEG (definition 1).

MPEG-4 *n.* A standard currently under development designed for videophones and multimedia applications. MPEG-4 provides a lower bandwidth of up to 64 Kbps. See also MPEG (definition 1).

.mpg *n.* See .mpeg.

MPI *n.* Acronym for Message Passing Interface. A specification for message passing on workstation clusters and massively parallel processing (MPP) architectures. MPI was designed as a proposed standard by the MPI Forum, a committee of vendors and users.

MPLS *n.* Acronym for Multiprotocol Label Switching. A standards-based technique used to manage and optimise traffic flow for large-scale networks. In an MPLS network, incoming packets are assigned a label by a label edge router (LER). Label switch routers (LSRs) use these labels to forward the packets through the network along a label switch path (LSP). Each LSR removes the existing label and assigns a new one. MPLS combines the advantages of bridges (Layer 2 switching, which is used in ATM and frame relay) and routers (Layer 3 switching, which is used in IP). MPLS serves to create faster and more scalable networks to facilitate quality of service, class of service, and the use of VPNs.

MP/M *n.* Acronym for Multitasking Programme for Microcomputers. A multitasking, multiuser version of the CP/M operating system. See also CP/M.

MPOA *n.* Acronym for Multi-Protocol Over ATM. A specification established by the ATM Forum (an industry group of Asynchronous Transfer Mode users and vendors) to integrate ATM into existing Ethernet, token ring, and TCP/IP networks. See also ATM (definition 1).

MPP *n.* See massively parallel processing, massively parallel processor.

MPPP *n.* See Multilink Point-to-Point Protocol.

MPR II *n.* A standard for limiting magnetic and electric field emissions from video monitors, including VLF radiation. MPR II is a voluntary standard developed by the Swedish Board for Measurement and Testing in 1987 and updated in 1990. See also VLF radiation.

Mput *n.* In many FTP clients, the command that instructs the local client to transmit multiple files to the remote server.

MR *n.* Acronym for modem ready. A light on the front panel of a modem indicating that the modem is ready.

MSAA *n.* See Active Accessibility. Short for Microsoft Active Accessibility.

MS Audion. *n.* The code name, or working name, of Windows Media Audio, before the technology was released by Microsoft. See also Windows Media Audio.

MSDN *n.* Acronym for the Microsoft Developer Network. An online, print, and CD-DVD resource for developers that features content and programmes focused on development trends and Microsoft technologies. Some features of MSDN include technical articles and reference material; information on upcoming conferences and events; developer support through peer-to-peer interaction, information sharing, and direct interaction with Microsoft; and software subscription programmes.

MS-DOS *n.* Short for Microsoft Disk Operating System. A single-tasking, single-user operating system with a command-line interface, released in 1981, for IBM PCs and compatibles. MS-DOS, like other operating systems, oversees operations such as disk input and output, video support, keyboard control, and many internal functions related to programme execution and file maintenance.

MS-DOS mode *n.* A shell in which the MS-DOS environment is emulated in 32-bit systems such as Windows 95. See also MS-DOS, shell1.

MS-DOS shell *n.* A shell environment based on a command-line prompt that allows a user to interact with MS-DOS or an MS-DOS-emulating operating system.

MSDOS.SYS *n.* One of two hidden system files installed on an MS-DOS startup disk. MSDOS.SYS, called IBMDOS.SYS in IBM releases of MS-DOS, contains the software that makes up the heart (kernel) of the operating system. See also IO.SYS.

msec *n.* See millisecond.

MSI *n.* See medium-scale integration.

MSIL *n.* See Microsoft intermediate language.

MSN *n.* Acronym for Microsoft Network. An online service and Internet portal, launched with the introduction of Windows 95 in August 1995.

MSN Explorer *n.* Microsoft software that integrates the functionality of Internet Explorer, Windows Media Player, Hotmail, MSN Messenger, MSN Communities, Music Central, and other MSN content and services. See also MSN.

MSN Messenger Service *n.* See .NET Messenger Service.

MSP *n.* See Message Security Protocol, managed service provider.

MS-Windows *n.* See Windows.

MSXML *n.* Acronym for Microsoft XML. A Java-based XML parser from Microsoft that provides support for World Wide Web Consortium (W3C) standards for XML documents and applications.

MTA *n.* Acronym for message transfer agent. An application process, as described in the X.400 message-handling system, responsible for delivering e-mail messages. After receiving a message, an MTA stores it temporarily and either delivers it or forwards it to another MTA. During this process, the MTA can change the message headers. See also X series.

MTBF *n.* Acronym for mean time between failures. The average time interval, usually expressed in thousands or tens of thousands of hours (sometimes called power-on hours or POH), that will elapse before a hardware component fails and requires service.

MTTR *n.* Acronym for mean time to repair. The average time interval, usually expressed in hours, that it takes to repair a failed component.

MTU *n.* Acronym for Maximum Transmission Unit. The largest packet of data that can be transmitted on a network. MTU size varies, depending on the network—576 bytes on X.25 networks, for example, 1500 bytes on Ethernet, and 17,914 bytes on 16 Mbps Token Ring. Responsibility for determining the size of the MTU lies with the link layer of the network. When packets are transmitted across networks, the path MTU, or PMTU, represents the smallest packet size (the one that all networks can transmit without breaking up the packet) among the networks involved.

MUD *n.* Acronym for multiuser dungeon. A virtual environment on the Internet in which multiple users simultaneously participate in a role-playing game—generally a medieval fantasy, hence the "dungeon"—and interact with each other in real time. Also called: multiuser simulation environment.

MUD, object-oriented *n.* See MOO.

Multiband phone *n.* Wireless phone that operates on two or more broadcast frequencies.

Multiboot *n.* 1. Startup capability of some operating systems, such as Windows NT, OS/2, UNIX, and some Power Macs, that allows users to choose which of two or more installed operating systems—for example, Windows NT or UNIX—they want to use for the current session. See also boot. 2. A computer configuration that runs two or more operating systems. See also dual boot, startup.

Multibus *n.* A computer expansion bus designed by Intel Corporation that is used extensively by designers of -high-performance workstations. A high-bandwidth bus (capable of extremely fast data transmission), Multibus also allows multiple bus masters. See also bus.

Multicast address dynamic client allocation protocol *n.* An extension to the DHCP protocol standard used to support dynamic assignment and configuration of IP multicast addresses on TCP/IP-based networks. Acronym: MADCAP.

Multicast backbone *n.* See MBONE.

Multicasting *n.* The process of sending a message simultaneously to more than one destination on a network.

Multichannel multipoint distribution service *n.* See MMDS.

Multi-Colour Graphics Array *n.* See MCGA.

Multi-element *adj.* Consisting of multiple data elements that all have the same format for storing the same kind of information. The data elements may be simple variables, as in an array of integer variables, or they may be more complicated data structures, as in an array of employee records each of which contains fields for an employee's name, Social Security number, pay rate, and so on.

Multifile sorting *n.* The process of sorting a body of data that resides in more than one file.

MultiFinder *n.* A version of the Macintosh Finder that provides support for multitasking. The primary use of MultiFinder is to allow multiple applications to be simultaneously resident in memory. A single mouse-click switches between applications, and information from one application can be copied to another. If the active application allows true multitasking, background tasks can be processed. See also Finder.

Multifunction board *n.* A computer add-in board that provides more than one function. Multifunction boards for personal computers frequently offer additional memory, serial/parallel ports, and a clock/calendar.

Multifunction peripheral *n.* A multipurpose device that combines printing with faxing, scanning (colour or black and white), and copying (colour or black and white) in a single unit. Multifunction peripherals are especially popular with the SOHO (small office, home office) market, where cost-effectiveness and space limitations can be significant considerations. Acronym: MFP. Also called: multifunction printer.

Multifunction printer *n.* See multifunction peripheral.

Multihoming *n.* 1. In Mac OS X, an automatic network selection feature that allows one computer to maintain multiple network addresses. Multihoming may be used with a computer that is used from multiple locations, such as home and office, or to create special connection settings, such as separate systems for communication inside and outside of an intranet. 2. The use of multiple addresses and/or multiple interfaces for a single node. A multihomed host has either multiple network interfaces connected to two or more networks, or a single network interface that has been assigned multiple IP addresses. Multihoming can be used to provide redundancy to achieve quality of service.

Multilayer *adj.* 1. In board design, of or pertaining to a printed circuit board consisting of two or more layers of board material. Each separate layer has its own metallic tracings to provide electrical connections between various electronic components and to provide connections to the other layers. The layers are laminated together to produce a single circuit board to which the components, such as integrated circuits, resistors, and capacitors, are attached. Multilayer design allows many more discrete paths between components than single-layer boards do. 2. In computer-aided design (CAD), of or pertaining to drawings, such as electronic circuits, that are built up using multiple layers, each with a different level of detail or a different object, so that distinct parts of the drawing can easily be manipulated, overlaid, or peeled off.

Multilayer switch *n.* A network switch that uses information from more than one ISO/OSI layer (Layer 2, Layer 3, Layer 4, and/or Layer 7) to forward traffic. See also ISO/OSI reference model, switch (definition 4).

Multilink Point-to-Point Protocol *n.* An Internet protocol that allows computers to establish multiple physical links to combine their bandwidths. This technology creates a virtual link with more capacity than a single physical link. Acronym: MPPP. See also PPP.

Multimedia *n.* The combination of sound, graphics, animation, and video. In the world of computers, multimedia is a subset of hypermedia, which combines the aforementioned elements with hypertext. See also hypermedia, hypertext.

Multimedia PC *n.* Software and hardware standards set forth by the Multimedia PC Marketing Council, which sets minimum standards for a PC's sound, video, and CD-ROM playing capabilities. Acronym: MPC.

Multimode phone *n.* Wireless phone that operates on both analog and digital networks. A multimode phone may be dual-mode (analog and one digital network) or tri-mode (analog and two digital networks).

Multinode computer *n.* A computer that uses multiple processors to share in the computation of a complex task. See also central processing unit, parallel processing.

Multipart forms *n.* Computer printer paper arranged in sets with carbon paper between the sheets (or with a chemical coating that emulates carbon on the back of each sheet except the last) to produce copies of output from impact printers. Multipart forms are designated by the number of copies in a set, such as two-part, three-part, and so on.

Multipartite virus *n.* A type of virus that combines characteristics and techniques of both boot sector and file viruses. Multipartite viruses first infect either system sectors or files and then spread quickly to infect the entire system. Because of their multiple capabilities, multipartite viruses are difficult to remove from an infected system. Also called: bimodal virus, bipartite virus. See also boot.

Multipass sort *n.* A sorting operation that, usually because of the sorting algorithm being used, requires two or more passes through the data before completion. See also bubble sort, insertion sort, Shell sort, sort algorithm.

Multiple-document interface *n.* See MDI.

Multiple inheritance *n.* A feature of some object-oriented programming languages that allows a new class to be derived from several existing classes. Multiple inheritance both extends and combines existing types. Acronym: MI. See also class, inherit, type.

Multiple instruction, multiple data streams *n.* See MIMD.

Multiple master font *n.* An advanced font creation and management classification developed by Adobe. A multiple master font contains two or more sets of font outlines or master designs that determine the dynamic range of each design axis in a typeface. Multiple master fonts include one or more design axes—weight, width, style, and optical size—that allow the user to create thousands of variations on a single typeface.

Multiple-pass printing *n.* A form of dot-matrix printing in which the print head makes more than one pass across the page for each printed line, printing each line a second time exactly on top of the first pass. Multiple-pass printing can be used with dot-matrix printers to darken the print and smooth out errors in alignment. On better printers, a second pass might occur after the paper is moved up slightly, so that the dots in the characters overlap to create a crisper, darker image.

Multiple recipients *n.* 1. The capability of sending e-mail to more than one user at a time by listing more than one e-mail address on a line. Delimiters such as commas or semicolons are used to separate the e-mail addresses. See also e-mail (definition 1), mailing list. 2. The subscribers on a mailing list. A message sent to the list is addressed to the "multiple recipients of" the list.

Multiple regression *n.* A statistical technique that seeks to describe the behaviour of a so-called "dependent" variable in terms of the observed behaviour of numerous other, "independent" variables thought to affect it. For each independent variable, a regression analysis can determine the correlation coefficient of the independent variable—that is, the degree to which variations in the independent variable cause changes in the dependent variable. See also dependent variable.

Multiple-user system *n.* See multiuser system.

Multiplexer *n.* A device for funneling several different streams of data over a common communications line. Multiplexers are used either to attach many communications lines to a smaller number of communications ports or to attach a large number of communications ports to a smaller number of communications lines. Acronym: MUX.

Multiplexer channel *n.* One of the inputs to a multiplexer. See also multiplexer.

Multiplexing *n.* A technique used in communications and input/output operations for transmitting a number of separate signals simultaneously over a single channel or line. To maintain the integrity of each signal on the channel, multiplexing can separate the signals by time, space, or frequency. The device used to combine the signals is a multiplexer. See also FDM, space-division multiplexing, time-division multiplexing.

Multiplicand *n.* In arithmetic, the number that is multiplied by another number (the multiplier). In mathematics, the multiplicand and the multiplier are interchangeable, depending on how the problem is stated, because the result is the same if the two are reversed—for example, 2 x 3 and 3 x 2. In arithmetic performed by computers, however, the multiplicand is different from the multiplier because computer multiplication is usually performed as addition. Therefore, 2 x 3 means "add 2 three times," whereas 3 x 2 means "add 3 two times." See also factor.

Multiplier *n.* 1. In arithmetic, the number that indicates how many times another number (the multiplicand) is multiplied. See also factor. 2. In computing, an electronic device independent of the central processing unit (CPU) that performs multiplication by adding the multiplicand according to the value of the digits in the multiplier.

Multipoint configuration *n.* A communications link in which multiple stations are connected sequentially to the same communications line. Typically, the communications line is controlled by a primary station, such as a computer, and the stations attached to the line are secondary. See the illustration.

Multiport repeater *n.* See active hub.

Multiprocessing *n.* A mode of operation in which two or more connected and roughly equal processing units each carry out one or more processes (programmes or sets of instructions) in tandem. In multiprocessing, each processing unit works on a different set of instructions or on different parts of the same process. The objective is increased speed or computing power, the same as in parallel processing and in the use of special units called coprocessors.

Multiprogramming *n.* A form of processing in which a computer holds more than one programme in memory and works on them in round-robin fashion—that is, by sharing out the processor's time so that each programme receives some attention some of the time. This way of working is in contrast to using the processor to run one programme at a time.

Multiscan monitor *n.* A computer monitor capable of adapting to different video frequencies to accommodate multiple screen resolutions and to support different video adapters and graphics display methods.

Multistation Access Unit *n.* See MAU.

Multisystem network *n.* A communications network in which two or more host computers can be accessed by network users.

Multitasking *n.* A form of processing supported by most current operating systems in which a computer works on multiple tasks—roughly, separate "pieces" of work—seemingly at the same time by parceling out the processor's time among the different tasks. Multitasking can be either cooperative or preemptive. In the former, the operating system relies on the task to voluntarily cede control to another task; in the latter, the operating system decides which task receives priority. See also background1, context switching, cooperative multitasking, foreground1, time slice.

Multithreaded application *n.* A programme capable of running more than one programme thread simultaneously. See also multithreading (definition 1), thread (definition 1).

Multithreading *n.* 1. The running of several processes in rapid sequence (multitasking) within a single programme. See also thread (definition 1). 2. In data manipulation, a technique in which nodes in a tree data structure contain pointers to higher nodes to make traversal of the structure more efficient. See also thread (definition 2).

Multi-tier *n.* See three-tier.

Multiuser *n.* See multiuser system.

Multiuser dungeon *n.* See MUD.

Multiuser simulation environment *n.* See MUD.

Multiuser system *n.* Any computer system that can be used by more than one person. Although a microcomputer shared by several people can be considered a multiuser system, the term is generally reserved for machines that can be accessed simultaneously by several people through communications facilities or via network terminals.

Multum in parvo mapping *n.* See MIP mapping.

MUMPS *n.* Acronym for Mass(achusetts) Utility Multi Programming System. An advanced, high-level programming language and integrated database developed in 1966 at Massachusetts General Hospital and used widely by health care businesses. A unique feature of MUMPS is its ability to store both data and programme fragments in its database.

Munging *n.* See address munging.

MUSE *n.* See MUD. Short for multiuser simulation environment..

.museum *n.* One of seven new top-level domain names approved in 2000 by the Internet Corporation for Assigned Names and Numbers (ICANN), .museum is meant for use by museum Web sites.

Musical Instrument Digital Interface *n.* See MIDI.

Mutual exclusion *n.* A programming technique that ensures that only one programme or routine at a time can access some resource, such as a memory location, an I/O port, or a file, often through the use of semaphores, which are flags used in programmes to coordinate the activities of more than one programme or routine. See also semaphore.

My Briefcase *n.* A Windows 9x utility, helpful for workers away from the office, that manages the updating of modified files once the remote user's computer is connected back on the office network.

Mylar *n.* A polyester film product created by DuPont, often used as the base for magnetically coated storage media (disks and tape) and for carbon ribbons used with impact printers.

Mylar ribbon *n.* See carbon ribbon.

My two cents *n.* An expression used informally in newsgroup articles and, less frequently, e-mail messages or mailing lists, to indicate that the message is the writer's contribution to an ongoing discussion. Also called: $0.02. See also mailing list, newsgroup.

N

n prefix See nano-.

NACN *n.* See North American Cellular Network.

Nagware *n.* Slang for computer shareware that, on starting or before closing, displays a prominent reminder to pay for the programme. See also shareware.

NAK *n.* Acronym for negative acknowledgement. A control code, ASCII character 21 (hexadecimal 15), transmitted to a sending station or computer by the receiving unit as a signal that transmitted information has arrived incorrectly.

NAK attack *n.* Acronym for negative acknowledgement attack. A hacker attack that uses the negative acknowledgement control code character to enter a seemingly secure system. A NAK attack uses weaknesses in the system handling NAK replies that may leave it temporarily unprotected. See also NAK.

Naked PC *n.* A personal computer sold without an operating system (OS) installed. The purchaser of a naked PC must then choose and install an OS before the computer can be used. Naked PCs are chiefly purchased by users with some degree of expertise with computer equipment who may want to install a version of Linux or an offshoot OS. Computer and software manufacturers have expressed concern over the possibility of software piracy with the sale of naked PCs.

.name *n.* One of seven new top-level domain names approved in 2000 by the Internet Corporation for Assigned Names and Numbers (ICANN), .name is meant for registration by individuals for personal Web sites. The seven new domain names became available for use in the spring of 2001.

Name Binding Protocol *n.* See NBP.

Named anchor *n.* In HTML, a tag within a document that can act as a destination for a hyperlink. Named anchors are useful because they allow a link to a specific location within a document. Also called: named target. See also anchor (definition 2), HTML, hyperlink.

Named entity *n.* See character entity.

Named pipes *n.* In programming, one-way (simplex) or two-way (duplex) connections used to transfer data between processes. Named pipes are portions of memory set aside for temporary data storage. They are created by server processes and can be used simultaneously by more than one client process, each accessing a separate instance with its own buffers and handles. Named pipes can be used to transfer data either locally or on a network.

Named target *n.* See named anchor.

Name server *n.* See CSO name server, DNS server.

Namespace *n.* 1. A grouping of one or more names that represent individual objects within the group in a shared computing environment, such as a network. The names within a namespace are unique, are created according to the same rules, and can be resolved into a particular identifying item of information, such as an IP address or a network device. A namespace can be either flat—a single collection of unique names—or hierarchical, as is the Internet's DNS (Domain Name System), which is based on a treelike structure that is refined through successive levels beginning with the root server and the Internet's top-level domains (.com, .net, .org, and so on). In everyday terms, a namespace is comparable to a telephone book, in which each name is unique and resolves to the phone number and address of a particular individual, business, or other entity. 2. A means of identifying elements and attributes in an XML document by assigning them a two-part name with the first part being the namespace and the second part being the functional name. A namespace identifies a set of names to prevent confusion when multiple objects with identical functional names are taken from different sources and brought together in the same XML document. Namespaces typically reference a Uniform Resource Identifier (URI) because each URI will be unique.

Name-value pair *n.* 1. In the Perl programming language, a data set in which the data is associated with a name. See also Perl. 2. In CGI programming, one of the data items collected from an HTML form by the browser and passed through the server to a CGI script for processing. See also CGI, CGI script, HTML.

Naming container *n.* Any ASP.NET control that implements the INamingContainer interface. This is a marker interface that enables a control to create a new naming scope under itself so that ID attributes assigned to its child controls are unique within the entire ASP.NET page that contains the control.

NAMPS *n.* Acronym for Narrow-band Analog Mobile Phone Service. A standard proposed by Motorola Corporation that combines the current AMPS cellular telephone standard with digital signaling information, resulting in higher performance and increased capabilities. See also AMPS.

NAND *n.* Short for NOT AND. A logical operation that combines the values of two bits (0,1) or two Boolean values (false, true) that returns a value of 1 (or true) if one input value is 0 (or false), and returns a 0 (false) only if both inputs are true.

NAND gate *n.* Short for NOT AND gate. A digital circuit whose output is true (1) if any input is false (0). A NAND gate is an AND circuit (output with the value of 1 when all input values are 1) followed by a NOT circuit (output that is the logical complement of the input). Thus, NAND gate output is high if any of its inputs are low. See also AND gate, gate (definition 1), NOT gate.

Nano- prefix Abbreviated *n.* Metric prefix meaning 10–9 (one billionth).

Nanosecond *n.* One billionth of a second. A nanosecond is a time measure used to represent computing speed, particularly the speed at which electrical signals travel through circuits within the computer. Acronym: ns.

NAP *n.* See Network Access Point.

Napster *n.* An Internet music search application that allows users to search for and swap MP3 files over the Web. In response to a user request for a song or an artist, Napster searches the hard drives of all other Napster users on line. When the requested item is found, the file is downloaded to the computer making the request. Napster also includes a chat room and a library of most popular items. The introduction of Napster in 1999 sparked heated debate over copyright and digital distribution issues. See also MP3.

Narrowband *n.* A bandwidth set aside by the FCC for mobile or portable radio services, such as advanced two-way paging systems, including transmission rates between 50 bps and 64 Kbps. Narrowband formerly referred to the bandwidth from 50 to 150 bps. See also bandwidth, FCC.

Narrowband ISDN *n.* Name used to distinguish current ISDN lines from the developing broadband ISDN technology. See also broadband ISDN, ISDN.

Narrowcast *vb.* To transmit data or programming to a defined or limited area or audience. A cable television company narrowcasts its programmes only to subscribers, whereas network television stations broadcast to everyone with reception equipment in their transmission range. On the Web, content delivered to users via push technology represents a form of narrowcasting. See also unicast.

Narrow SCSI *n.* A SCSI or SCSI-2 interface that can transfer data only 8 bits at a time. See also SCSI, SCSI-2.

NAS *n.* Acronym for Network-Attached Storage. A platform-independent storage appliance connected to a network. NAS uses a storage unit with a built-in server that can communicate with clients over a network. NAS devices are popular for ease of maintenance, manageability, and scalability.

NAT *n.* Acronym for Network Address Translation. The process of converting between IP addresses used within an intranet or other private network and Internet IP addresses. This approach makes it possible to use a large number of addresses within the private network without depleting the limited number of available numeric Internet IP addresses. Variations of NAT displaying similar functions include IP aliasing, IP masquerading, and Port Address Translation.

National attachment point *n.* See Network Access Point.

National Center for Supercomputing Applications *n.* See NCSA (definition 1).

National Committee for Information Technology Standards *n.* A committee formed by the Information Technology Industry Council to develop national standards for use in the information technology industry and to promote those standards for international use. Acronym: NCITS.

National Computer Security Association *n.* See ICSA.

National Information Infrastructure *n.* A U.S. government programme to extend and oversee the development of the Information Superhighway. The National Information Infrastructure is made up of a high-bandwidth, wide area network that can carry data, fax, video, and voice transmissions to users throughout the United States. The network is being developed mostly by private carriers. Many of the services, which are aimed at enabling the efficient creation and dissemination of information, are already available on the Internet itself, including increased accessibility to quality education through distance learning and increased access to government services. Acronym: NII. See also Information Superhighway, Internet2, Next Generation Internet.

National Institute of Standards and Technology *n.* A branch of the U.S. Commerce Department that works to develop and encourage standards for measurement, science, and technology in order to promote commerce and improve productivity in the marketplace. Prior to 1988, the National Institute of Standards and Technology was known as the National Bureau of Standards. Acronym: NIST.

National language support *n.* 1. The practice of creating programmes that can display text in any language necessary. 2. A function in Windows that enables you to specify system and user locale information. Acronym: NLS.

National Science Foundation *n.* A U.S. government agency intended to promote scientific research by funding both research projects and projects that facilitate scientific communication, such as NSFnet, the former backbone of the Internet. Acronym: NSF. See also backbone (definition 1), NSFnet.

Native *adj.* Of, pertaining to, or characteristic of something that is in its original form. For example, many applications are able to work with files in a number of formats; the format the application uses internally is its native file format. Files in other formats must be converted to the application's native format before they can be processed by the application.

Native application *n.* A programme that is designed specifically for a particular type of microprocessor, that is, a programme that is binary compatible with a processor. A native application generally will run much faster than a nonnative application, which must be run with the help of an emulator programme. See also binary compatibility, emulator.

Native code *n.* Code that has been compiled to processor-specific machine code.

Native compiler *n.* A compiler that produces machine code for the computer on which it is running, as opposed to a cross-compiler, which produces code for another type of computer. Most compilers are native compilers. See also compiler (definition 2), cross-compiler.

Native file format *n.* The format an application uses internally to process data. The application must convert files in other formats to the native format before it can work with them. For example, a word processor might recognise text files in ASCII text format, but it will convert them to its own native format before it displays them.

Native language *n.* See host language.

Natural language *n.* A language spoken or written by humans, as opposed to a programming language or a machine language. Understanding natural language and approximating it in a computer environment is one goal of research in artificial intelligence.

Natural-language processing *n.* A field of computer science and linguistics that studies computer systems that can recognise and react to human language, either spoken or written. See also artificial intelligence.

Vatural language query *n.* A query to a database system that is composed in a subset of a natural language, such as English or Japanese. The query must conform to some restrictive syntax rules so that the system can parse it. See also parse, syntax.

Natural-language recognition *n.* See speech recognition.

Natural language support *n.* A voice recognition system that allows the user to use verbal commands in his or her own language to direct a computer's actions. Acronym: NLS.

Natural number *n.* An integer, or whole number, that is equal to or greater than zero. See also integer.

Navigation bar *n.* On a Web page, a grouping of hyperlinks for getting around in that particular Web site. See also hyperlink.

Navigation keys *n.* The keys on a keyboard controlling cursor movement, including the four arrow keys and the Backspace, End, Home, Page Down, and Page Up keys. See also arrow key, Backspace key, End key, Home key, Page Down key, Page Up key.

Navigator *n.* See Netscape Navigator.

NBP *n.* Acronym for Name Binding Protocol. A protocol used on AppleTalk local area networks to translate between node names (known to users) and numeric AppleTalk addresses. NBP operates at the transport level (level 4 of the ISO/OSI reference model). See also AppleTalk, communications protocol, ISO/OSI reference model.

NC *n.* See network computer.

NCC *n.* See network-centric computing.

N-channel MOS *n.* See NMOS.

NCITS *n.* See National Committee for Information Technology Standards.

NCP *n.* See Point-to-Point Protocol.

NCR paper *n.* Short for no carbon required paper. A special paper used for multipart forms. NCR paper is impregnated with a chemical that darkens it when pressure is applied. See also multipart forms.

NCSA *n.* 1. Acronym for National Center for Supercomputing Applications. A research center located at the University of Illinois at Urbana-Champaign. NCSA was founded in 1985 as a part of the National Science Foundation, specialising in scientific visualisation tasks, but is best known as the home of NCSA Mosaic, the first graphical Web browser, and of NCSA Telnet. See also Mosaic, NCSA Telnet. 2. See ICSA.

NCSA Mosaic *n.* See Mosaic.

NCSA server *n.* The HTTP server developed by the National Center for Supercomputing Applications of the University of Illinois. This server and the CERN server were the first HTTP servers developed for the World Wide Web and are available free through downloading. See also HTTP server (definition 1), NCSA (definition 1).

NCSA Telnet *n.* A freeware telnet client programme developed and distributed by the National Center for Supercomputing Applications. See also client (definition 2), NCSA (definition 1).

NDIS *n.* Acronym for Network Driver Interface Specification, a software interface, or set of rules, designed to enable different network protocols to communicate with a variety of network adapters. Providing a standard—a common "language"—for the drivers used by network adapters, NDIS enables a single network adapter to support multiple protocols and, conversely, also enables a single protocol to work with network adapters from different vendors. See also device driver.

NDMP *n.* Acronym for Network Data Management Protocol. An open protocol for network-based backups of file servers that allows platform-independent data storage. See also backup, communications protocol, file server.

NDR *n.* See nondestructive readout.

NDRO *n.* See nondestructive readout.

NDS *n.* Acronym for Novell Directory Services. A feature introduced in Novell Netware 4.0 that provides access to directories that may be located on one or more servers.

Near-letter-quality *adj.* A print mode on high-end dot-matrix printers that produces clearer, darker characters than normal (draft-quality) printing. Near-letter-quality printing, although it is sharper than plain dot-matrix printing, is not as legible as output from a fully-formed-character printer, such as a daisy-wheel printer. Acronym: NLQ. See also print quality.

Negation *n.* The conversion of a two-state (binary) signal or bit pattern to its opposite state—for example, the conversion of 1001 to 0110.

Negative acknowledgement *n.* See NAK.

Negative entry *n.* The act of assigning a negative sign to a number that has been entered into a calculator, thereby transforming the number to a negative number.

Nest *vb.* To embed one construct inside another. For example, a database may contain a nested table (a table within a table), a programme may contain a nested procedure (a procedure declared within a procedure), and a data structure may include a nested record (a record containing a field that is itself a record).

Nested transaction *n.* In programming, an operation or sequence of operations taking place within a larger transaction. A nested transaction can be aborted without requiring abortion of the larger transaction. Also called: subtransaction. See also nest.

.net *n.* In the Internet's Domain Name System, the top-level domain that identifies addresses of network providers. The designation .net appears at the end of the address. See also DNS (definition 1), domain (definition 3).

net.- prefix A prefix used to describe people and institutions on the Internet. For example, a very well respected person might be described as a net.god.

Net *n.* 1. Short for Internet. 2. Short for Usenet.

.NET *n.* The set of Microsoft technologies that provides tools for connecting information, people, systems, and devices. The technologies provide individuals and organisations with the ability to build, host, deploy, and use XML Web service connected solutions.

net address *n.* 1. A World Wide Web address (URL). See also URL. 2. An e-mail address. 3. The DNS name or IP address of a machine. See also DNS (definition 1), IP address. 4. The address, burned into a network adapter, that is used to uniquely identify a node on a network. See also network interface card.

NetBEUI *n.* Short for NETBIOS Extended User Interface. NetBEUI is a network protocol created by IBM and now used by Microsoft, HP, and Compaq. It is usually used in small, department-size local area networks (LANs) of 1 to 200 clients. It can use Token Ring source routing as its only method of routing. It is the extended version of the NetBIOS standard. See also CCP, communications protocol, LAN, NetBIOS.

NetBIOS *n.* An application programming interface (API) that can be used by application programmes on a local area network consisting of IBM and compatible microcomputers running MS-DOS, OS/2, or some version of UNIX. Primarily of interest to programmers, NetBIOS provides application programmes with a uniform set of commands for requesting the lower-level network services required to conduct sessions between nodes on a network and to transmit information back and forth. See also application programming interface.

NetBIOS Extended User Interface *n.* See NetBEUI.

Net boot *n.* See PXE boot.

NetBSD *n.* A free version of the BSD UNIX operating system developed as a result of a volunteer effort. NetBSD is highly interoperable, runs on many hardware platforms, and is nearly POSIX compliant. See also BSD UNIX, POSIX.

Netcaster *n.* See netcasting (definition 2).

Netcasting *n.* 1. Synonym for webcasting. 2. A Netscape technology used in Netscape Netcaster that enabled a user to subscribe to channels that pushed Web content to the user's desktop without actively retrieving the information. Netscape

Netcaster, which was part of previous versions of Netscape Navigator, competed with Microsoft Active Desktop. Unlike Active Desktop, which uses Microsoft's Channel Definition Format (CDF), the Netcaster push client was based on existing open standards (HTML, Java, and JavaScript). See also push (definition 2).

.NET Compact Framework *n.* A hardware-independent environment for running programmes on resource-constrained computing devices. It inherits the full .NET Framework architecture of the common language runtime, supports a subset of the .NET Framework class library, and contains classes designed exclusively for the .NET Compact Framework. Supported devices include personal data assistants (PDAs) (such as the Pocket PC), mobile phones, set-top boxes, automotive computing devices, and custom-designed embedded devices built with the Microsoft Windows CE operating system.

.NET data provider *n.* A component of ADO.NET that provides access to data from a relational database.

Netfilter *n.* The packet-filtering system for Linux introduced in the 2.4 kernel. Netfilter is the first stateful firewall implemented in Linux. See also firewall, iptables.

NetFind *n.* See AOL NetFind.

.NET Framework *n.* A platform for building, deploying, and running XML Web services and applications. It provides a highly productive, standards-based, multilanguage environment for integrating existing investments with next generation applications and services, as well as the agility to solve the challenges of deployment and operation of Internet-scale applications. The .NET Framework consists of three main parts: the common language runtime, a hierarchical set of unified class libraries, and a componentised version of ASP called ASP.NET. See also ASP.NET, common language runtime, .NET Framework class library.

.NET Framework class library *n.* A Common Language Specification (CLS)–compliant library of classes, interfaces, and value types that are included in the Microsoft .NET

Framework SDK. This library provides access to system functionality and is designed to be the foundation on which .NET Framework applications, components, and controls are built.

.NET Framework data provider *n.* A component of ADO.NET that provides access to data from a relational data source. A .NET Framework data provider contains classes to connect to a data source, execute commands at the data source, and return query results from the data source, including the ability to execute commands within transactions. A .NET Framework data provider also contains classes to populate a DataSet with results from a data source and propagate changes in a DataSet back to the data source.

net.god *n.* A highly respected person within the Internet community.

Nethead *n.* 1. A person who uses the Internet as if addicted to it. 2. A Grateful Dead fan who participates in the rec.music.gdead newsgroup or some other forum dedicated to that band.

Netiquette *n.* Short for network etiquette. Principles of courtesy observed in sending electronic messages, such as e-mail and Usenet postings. The consequences of violating netiquette include being flamed and having one's name placed in the bozo filter of one's intended audience. Disapproved behaviour includes gratuitous personal insults; posting of large amounts of irrelevant material; giving away the plot of a movie, television show, or novel without warning; posting offensive material without encrypting it; and excessive cross-posting of a message to multiple groups without regard to whether the group members are likely to find it interesting. See also bozo filter, flame2.

Netizen *n.* A person who participates in online communication through the Internet and other networks, especially conference and chat services, such as Internet news or Fidonet.

NetMeeting *n.* A software application developed by Microsoft Corporation to allow video conferencing among parties using personal computers connected via the Internet. NetMeeting allows participants in different locations to view each other, engage in text chat conversations, send and receive videos, exchange information graphically via an electronic whiteboard, share Windows-based applications, and transfer files.

.NET Messenger Service *n.* A popular instant-messaging service provided by Microsoft as part of the .NET strategy. With .NET Messenger Service, formerly called MSN Messenger Service, users can communicate using the Windows Messenger, included in Windows XP, or MSN Messenger applications. See also instant messaging.

.NET My Services *n.* A suite of XML Web services for managing and protecting personal information and interactions across applications, devices, and services. Formerly code-named HailStorm, .NET My Services is based on the Microsoft .NET Passport user-authentication system. The suite of .NET My Services includes services such as .NET ApplicationSettings, .NET Calendar, .NET Contacts, .NET Devices, .NET Documents, .NET Inbox, .NET Locations, .NET Profile, and .NET Wallet. See also .NET, Passport.

NetPC *n.* Short for Network PC. An industry-defined, Windows-based PC system that is small and meant to act as simply an access point. These PCs generally have very small hard drives, no disk drives, and are built to have a very low cost. Some older NetPCs can boot through remote access to a server and user server-based resources for most computing actions.

net.personality *n.* A slang term for a person who has attained some degree of celebrity on the Internet.

net.police *n.* Persons (usually self-appointed) who try to enforce their understanding of the "rules" that apply to conduct on the Internet. Their activities may be directed toward users who violate the rules of netiquette, spammers who send unsolicited advertising as e-mail or to newsgroups, or even people who post "politically incorrect" comments to newsgroups or mailing lists. See also netiquette, spam.

Netscape Navigator *n.* The widely used family of Web browser programmes, made by Netscape Corporation. Versions of

Netscape Navigator are available for the Windows and Macintosh platforms, and for many varieties of UNIX. Netscape Navigator, which is based on NCSA's Mosaic Web browser, was one of the first commercially available Web browsers. In 1999, Netscape Corporation was purchased by America Online. See also Mosaic, Web browser.

Netscape Netcaster *n.* See netcasting (definition 2).

Netscape Server Application Programming Interface *n.* See NSAPI.

Netspeak *n.* The set of conventions for writing English in e-mail, IRCs, and newsgroups. Netspeak is characterised by acronyms (such as IMHO or ROFL) and clarifying devices such as emotags and emoticons. Use of Netspeak should be governed by netiquette. See also emotag, emoticon, IMHO, IRC, netiquette, ROFL.

Netspionage *n.* Corporate-sponsored hacking of a competitor's digital information for the theft of trade secrets.

Net surfing *n.* The practice of exploring the Internet without a specific goal in mind. The concept of Net surfing is similar to (and probably derived from) "channel surfing" in reference to watching television.

Net TV *n.* See Internet television.

NetWare *n.* A family of LAN (local area network) operating system products developed by Novell, Inc. Designed to run on PCs and Macintoshes, Novell NetWare allows users to share files and system resources such as hard disks and printers. See also network operating system.

Network *n.* A group of computers and associated devices that are connected by communications facilities. A network can involve permanent connections, such as cables, or temporary connections made through telephone or other communication links. A network can be as small as a LAN (local area network) consisting of a few computers, printers, and other devices, or it can consist of many small and large computers distributed over a vast geographic area (WAN, or wide area network). See also ALOHAnet, Ethernet (definition 1), LAN, WAN.

Network Access Point *n.* One of the interchange points for Internet traffic, where various Internet network carriers and major ISPs exchange data. When Internet traffic originates on one network and goes to another network, it almost always passes through at least one Network Access Point, or NAP. In the United States, major NAPs include MAE East, in Vienna, Virginia, and MAE West, in San Jose, California (both operated by MCI WorldCom); the Chicago NAP (operated by Ameritech); the Pacific Bell NAP (with multiple locations in California); the Digital Internet Exchange in Palo Alto, California (operated by Digital/Compaq); and the Sprint NAP in Pennsauken, New Jersey. Additional local and regional exchange points are located in many other locations around the world. Acronym: NAP. Also called: National Attachment Point.

Network adapter *n.* See network interface card.

Network Address Translation *n.* See NAT.

Network administrator *n.* The person in charge of operations on a computer network. The duties of a network administrator can be broad and might include such tasks as installing new workstations and other devices, adding and removing individuals from the list of authorised users, archiving files, overseeing password protection and other security measures, monitoring usage of shared resources, and handling malfunctioning equipment. See also system administrator.

Network architecture *n.* The underlying structure of a computer network, including hardware, functional layers, interfaces, and protocols, used to establish communication and ensure the reliable transfer of information. Network architectures are designed to provide both philosophical and physical standards for the complexities of establishing communications links and transferring information without conflict. Various network architectures exist, including the internationally accepted seven-layer ISO Open Systems Interconnection (OSI) model and IBM's Systems Network Architecture (SNA). See also ISO/OSI reference model, SNA.

Network-Attached Storage *n.* See NAS.

network boot *n.* See PXE boot.

Network card *n.* See network interface card.

Network-centric computing *n.* A computing environment in which a network server or servers represent the hub of activity. Considered the "third wave" in large-system computing after mainframe and desktop developments, network-centric computing establishes servers as the main source of computing power, to give users direct access to network-based applications and information. In network-centric computing systems, applications are not preinstalled or uninstalled locally, that is, on the desktop; they are accessed on an as-needed, "on-the-fly" basis. Thus, individual desktop computers do not have to maintain large amounts of disk storage or load and manage application programmes. See also server.

Network computer *n.* A computer designed for use on a network in which programmes and storage are provided by servers. Network computers, unlike dumb terminals, have their own processing power, but their design does not include local storage and they depend on network servers for applications. Acronym: NC.

Network congestion *n.* See congestion.

Network connection *n.* See Ethernet.

Network control programme *n.* In a communications network that includes a mainframe computer, a programme that usually resides in a communications controller and takes over communications tasks such as routing, error control, line control, and polling (checking terminals for transmissions), leaving the main computer free for other functions. See also communications controller.

Network Control Protocol *n.* See Point-to-Point Protocol.

Network database *n.* 1. A database that runs in a network. 2. A database containing the address of other users in the network. 3. In information management, a type of database in which data records can be related to one another in more than one way. A network database is similar to a hierarchical database in the sense that it contains a progression from one record to another. It differs in being less rigidly structured: any single record can point to more than one other record and, conversely, can be pointed to by one or more records. In effect, a network database allows more than one path between any two records, whereas a hierarchical database allows only one, from parent (higher-level record) to child (lower-level record).

Network Data Management Protocol *n.* See NDMP.

Network device driver *n.* Software that coordinates communication between the network adapter card and the computer's hardware and other software, controlling the physical function of the network adapter card.

Network directory *n.* On a local area network, a directory on a disk that is located on a computer other than the one the user is operating. A network directory differs from a network drive in that the user has access to only that directory. Whether the rest of the disk is accessible to the user depends on whether he or she has been granted access rights by the network administrator. On the Macintosh, a network directory is referred to as a shared folder. Also called: networked directory, shared directory. See also network drive, shared folder.

Network drive *n.* On a local area network, a disk drive whose disk is available to other computers on the network. Access to a network drive might not be allowed to all users of the network; many operating systems contain security provisions that enable a network administrator to grant or deny access to part or all of a network drive. Also called: networked drive. See also network directory.

Network Driver Interface Specification *n.* See NDIS.

Networked directory *n.* See network directory.

Networked drive *n.* See network drive.

Networked home *n.* See smart home.

Network File System *n.* See NFS.

Network information center *n.* See NIC (definition 2).

Network interface card *n.* An expansion card or other device used to provide network access to a computer or other device, such as a printer. Network interface cards mediate between the computer and the physical media, such as cabling, over which transmissions travel. Acronym: NIC. Also called: network adapter, network card.

Network Kernel Extension *n.* See NKE.

Network latency *n.* The time it takes for information to be transferred between computers in a network.

Network layer *n.* The third of the seven layers in the ISO/OSI reference model for standardising computer-to-computer communications. The network layer is one level above the data-link layer and ensures that information arrives at its intended destination. It is the middle of the three layers (data-link, network, and transport) concerned with the actual movement of information from one device to another. See the illustration. See also ISO/OSI reference model.

Network meltdown *n.* See broadcast storm, meltdown.

Network model *n.* A database structure, or layout, similar to a hierarchical model, except that records can have multiple parent records as well as multiple child records. A database management system that supports a network model can be used to simulate a hierarchical model. See also CODASYL, network database (definition 3).

Network modem *n.* A modem that is shared by users of a network for calling an online service provider, an ISP, a service bureau, or other online source. See also ISP, modem, online information service, service bureau (definition 2).

Network news *n.* The newsgroups on the Internet, especially those in the Usenet hierarchy.

Network News Transfer Protocol *n.* See NNTP.

Network operating system *n.* An operating system specifically designed to support networking. A server-based network operating system provides networking support for multiple simultaneous users as well as administrative, security, and management functions. On the desktop, a network-aware operating system provides users with the ability to access network resources. Unlike a single-user operating system, a network operating system must acknowledge and respond to requests from many workstations, managing such details as network access and communications, resource allocation and sharing, data protection, and error control. Acronym: NOS. Also called: network OS.

Network operation center *n.* The office in an enterprise that is responsible for maintaining network integrity and improving network efficiency while reducing system downtime. Acronym: NOC.

Network OS *n.* See network operating system.

Network protocol *n.* A set of rules and parameters that defines and enables communication through a network.

Network Query Language *n.* A scripting language for controlling intelligent agents for Web applications. Acronym: NQL.

Network server *n.* See server.

Network services *n.* 1. In a corporate environment, the division that maintains the network and the computers. 2. In a Windows environment, extensions to the operating system that allow it to perform network functions such as network printing and file sharing.

Network software *n.* Software including a component that facilitates connection to or participation in a network.

Network Solutions, Inc. *n.* See NSI.

Network structure *n.* The record organisation used in a particular network model.

Network Terminator 1 *n.* An ISDN device that acts as an interface between an ISDN telephone line and one or more terminal adapters or terminal devices, such as an ISDN telephone. Acronym: NT-1. See also ISDN, ISDN terminal adapter.

Network Time Protocol *n.* An Internet protocol used to synchronise the clocks in computers connected to the Internet. Acronym: NTP. See also communications protocol.

Network topology *n.* See topology.

Network weaving *n.* See leapfrog attack.

NetWorld+Interop *n.* International conference and exhibition for the networking and information technology industry. NetWorld+Interop draws attendees from a variety of industries, including telecommunications, Internet services, and e-commerce. NetWorld+Interop features product exhibits, educational conferences, tutorials, and workshops.

NeuralCast Technology *n.* Technology developed by Real Networks to improve the transmission of digital media over RealNetworks servers. NeuralCast Technology uses a variety of protocols, introduces new techniques to correct errors in streaming signals, and uses telephone and satellite transmissions to coordinate server networks to optimise digital media transmission.

Neural network *n.* A type of artificial-intelligence system modeled after the neurons (nerve cells) in a biological nervous system and intended to simulate the way a brain processes information, learns, and remembers. A neural network is designed as an interconnected system of processing elements, each with a limited number of inputs and an output. These processing elements are able to "learn" by receiving weighted inputs that, with adjustment, time, and repetition, can be made to produce appropriate outputs. Neural networks are used in areas such as pattern recognition, speech analysis, and speech synthesis. See also artificial intelligence (definition 1), pattern recognition.

Newbie *n.* 1. An inexperienced user on the Internet. 2. In a particularly derogatory sense, an inexperienced Usenet user who asks for information that is readily available in the FAQ. See also FAQ.

Newline character *n.* A control character that causes the cursor on a display or the printing mechanism on a printer to move to the beginning of the next line. It is functionally equivalent to a combination of the carriage return (CR) and linefeed (LF) characters. Acronym: NL. See also carriage return, linefeed.

News *n.* The Internet protocol for retrieving files from an Internet newsgroup. You can create hyperlinks to newsgroups using news://.

News.announce.newusers *n.* A newsgroup that contains general information for new users about using Internet newsgroups.

Newsfeed or news feed *n.* Deliveries, exchanges, or distributions of newsgroup articles to and from news servers. Newsfeeds are accomplished through cooperating news servers, which communicate via NNTP through network connections. Also called: feed. See also newsgroup, news server, NNTP.

Newsgroup *n.* A forum on the Internet for threaded discussions on a specified range of subjects. A newsgroup consists of articles and follow-up posts. An article with all of its follow-up posts—which are (supposed to be) related to the specific subject named in the original article's subject line—constitutes a thread. Each newsgroup has a name that consists of a series of words, separated by periods, indicating the newsgroup's subject in terms of increasingly narrow categories, such as rec.crafts.textiles.needlework. Some newsgroups can be read and posted to only on one site; others, such as those in the seven Usenet hierarchies or those in ClariNet, circulate throughout the Internet. See also article, bit. newsgroups, ClariNet, follow-up, Great Renaming, local newsgroups, mail reflector, threaded discussion, traditional newsgroup hierarchy, Usenet.

Newsmaster *n.* The person in charge of maintaining the Internet news server at a particular host. Sending e-mail to "newsmaster@domain.name" is the standard way to reach a given newsmaster.

News. newsgroups *n.* Usenet newsgroups that are part of the news. hierarchy and begin with "news." These newsgroups cover topics that deal with Usenet itself, such as Usenet policy and the creation of new Usenet newsgroups. See also newsgroup, traditional newsgroup hierarchy, Usenet.

.newsrc *n.* The file extension that identifies a setup file for UNIX-based newsreaders. The setup file typically contains a current list of newsgroups that the user subscribes to and the articles in each newsgroup that the user has already read. See also newsreader, setup (definition 2).

Newsreader *n.* A Usenet client programme that enables a user to subscribe to Usenet newsgroups, read articles, post follow-ups, reply by e-mail, and post articles. Many Web browsers also provide these functions. See also article, e-mail (definition 1), follow-up, newsgroup, Usenet, Web browser.

News server *n.* A computer or programme that exchanges Internet newsgroups with newsreader clients and other servers. See also newsgroup, newsreader.

Newton *n.* A personal digital assistant (PDA) developed by Apple Computer, Inc. See also PDA.

Newton OS *n.* The operating system that controls the Newton MessagePad personal digital assistant (PDA). See also PDA.

NeXT *n.* A computer designed and produced by NeXT Computer, Inc. (later NeXT Software, Inc.), a computer manufacturer and software developer founded in 1985 by Steven Jobs. NeXT was purchased by Apple Computer in 1997.

Next Generation Internet *n.* An initiative funded by the U.S. federal government designed to develop faster, more powerful networking technologies than are available on the current global Internet. The Next Generation Internet, or NGI, was begun in 1997 under the auspices of a number of government agencies, including DARPA (Defense Advanced Research Projects Agency), NASA (National Aeronautics & Space Administration), and the NSF (National Science Foundation). Its objective is to develop advanced networking technologies and to demonstrate them on university and government test networks running 100 to 1000 times faster than the current Internet. The technologies developed are intended for eventual use by schools, businesses, and the general public. Acronym: NGI.

NFS *n.* Acronym for Network File System. A distributed file system that allows users to access remote files and directories on a network as if they were local. NFS is compatible with Microsoft Windows and UNIX-based systems, including Linux and Mac OS X.

NGI *n.* See Next Generation Internet.

Nibble or nybble *n.* Half a byte (4 bits).

NIC *n.* 1. See network interface card. 2. Acronym for network information center. An organisation that provides information about a network and other support to users of the network. The principal NIC for the Internet is InterNIC. Intranets and other private networks may have their own NICs. See also InterNIC.

NiCad battery *n.* See nickel cadmium battery.

NIC handle *n.* See handle.

Nickel cadmium battery *n.* A rechargeable battery that uses an alkaline electrolyte. Nickel cadmium batteries typically have a longer operating life and storage life than similar lead-acid batteries. Also called: NiCad battery.

Nickel metal hydride battery *n.* A rechargeable battery that offers longer life and superior performance compared with similar nickel cadmium or other alkaline batteries. Also called: NiMH battery.

Nickname *n.* A name used in the destination field of an e-mail editor in place of one or more complete network addresses. For example "Fred" might be a nickname for fred@history.washington.edu. If the nickname has been established within the programme, a user need only type "Fred" instead of the entire address, or perhaps "history faculty" instead of all the individual faculty addresses. See also alias (definition 2).

NIDS *n.* Acronym for network-based intrusion-detection System. A type of intrusion detection system (IDS) that analyses the individual packets moving across a network. NIDS can detect packets that a firewall might not catch. See also IDS.

NII *n.* See National Information Infrastructure.

Nil pointer *n.* See null pointer.

Nimda worm *n.* A persistent worm that can slow or freeze mail servers, take control of Web pages, and infect systems through several different means. The Nimda worm spreads as an attached file through e-mail, through an Internet scan for vulnerable Web servers, through a Java-Script on an infected Web page, or through network sharing. The Nimda worm first appeared in 2001, with several variants following the original version.

NiMH battery *n.* See nickel metal hydride battery.

Nine's complement *n.* A number in the base-10 (decimal) system that is the complement of another number. It is derived by subtracting each digit of the number to be complemented from 1 less than the base. For example, the nine's complement of 64 is 35—the number derived by subtracting 6 from 9 and 4 from 9. See also complement.

NIS *n.* Acronym for Network Information Service. See Yellow Pages (definition 1).

NIST *n.* See National Institute of Standards and Technology.

***NIX** *n.* Slang for any UNIX-related operating system, or all UNIX-related operating systems. *NIX typically refers to UNIX and Linux, and may also include Mac OS X.

Nixpub *n.* A list of ISPs (Internet service providers) available in the newsgroups comp.bbs.misc and alt.bbs. See also ISP.

NKE *n.* Acronym for Network Kernel Extension. A modification or extension of the Mac OS X networking infrastructure. NKEs may be loaded or unloaded dynamically, without recompiling the kernel or without the need to reboot the system. NKEs allow the creation and configuration of protocol stacks and modules that may monitor or modify network traffic or add other networking features to the kernel.

NMOS or N-MOS *n.* Acronym for N-channel metal-oxide semiconductor. A semiconductor technology in which the conduction channel in MOSFETs is formed by the movement of electrons rather than holes (electron "vacancies" created as electrons move from atom to atom). Because electrons move faster than holes, NMOS is faster than PMOS, although it is more difficult and more expensive to fabricate. See also MOS, MOSFET, N-type semiconductor.

NNTP *n.* Acronym for Network News Transfer Protocol. A de facto protocol standard on the Internet used to distribute news articles and query news servers.

NOC *n.* See network operation center.

Node *n.* 1. A junction of some type. 2. In networking, a device, such as a client computer, a server, or a shared printer, that is connected to the network and is capable of communicating with other network devices. 3. In tree structures, a location on the tree that can have links to one or more nodes below it. Some authors make a distinction between node and element, with an element being a given data type and a node comprising one or more elements as well as any supporting data structures. See also element (definition 1), graph, pointer (definition 1), queue, stack, tree.

Noise *n.* 1. Any interference that affects the operation of a device. 2. Unwanted electrical signals, produced either naturally or by the circuitry, that distort or degrade the quality or performance of a communications channel. See also distortion.

Nonbreaking space *n.* A character that replaces the standard space character in order to keep two words together on one line rather than allowing a line to break between them.

Noncompetes *n.* An agreement between employer and employee that states that the employee will not accept work with a competing company for a specified length of time after leaving the employer's company. Noncompete agreements are common in high-tech companies and are typically requested to help maintain company secrets and retain valuable employees.

Nonconductor *n.* See insulator.

Noncontiguous data structure *n.* In programming, a data structure whose elements are not stored contiguously in memory. Data structures such as graphs and trees, whose elements are connected by pointers, are noncontiguous data structures.

Nondedicated server *n.* A computer on a network that can function as both a client and a server; typically, a desktop machine on a peer-to-peer network.

Nondestructive readout *n.* A reading operation that does not destroy the data read, either because the storage technology is capable of retaining the data or because the reading operation is accompanied by a data refresh (update) function. Acronym: NDR, NDRO.

Nonexecutable statement *n.* 1. A programme statement that cannot be executed because it lies outside the flow of execution through the programme. For example, a statement immediately following a return() statement but before the end of the block in C is nonexecutable. 2. A type definition, variable declaration, preprocessor command, comment, or other statement in a programme that is not translated into executable machine code.

Nonimpact printer *n.* Any printer that makes marks on the paper without striking it mechanically. The most common types are ink-jet, thermal, and laser printers. See also ink-jet printer, laser printer, thermal printer.

Noninterlaced *adj.* Pertaining to a display method on raster-scan monitors in which the electron beam scans each line of the screen once during each refresh cycle.

Nonmaskable interrupt *n.* A hardware interrupt that bypasses and takes priority over interrupt requests generated by software and by the keyboard and other such devices. A nonmaskable interrupt cannot be overruled (masked) by another service request and is issued to the microprocessor only in disastrous circumstances, such as severe memory errors or impending power failures. Acronym: NMI.

Nonprocedural language *n.* A programming language that does not follow the procedural paradigm of executing statements, subroutine calls, and control structures sequentially but instead describes a set of facts and relationships and then is queried for specific results.

Nonreturn to zero *n.* 1. In data transmission, a method of encoding data in which the signal representing binary digits alternates between positive and negative voltage when there is a change in digits from 1 to 0 or vice versa. In other words, the signal does not return to a zero, or neutral, level after transmission of each bit. Timing is used to distinguish one bit from the next. 2. In the recording of data on a magnetic surface, a method in which one magnetic state represents a 1 and, usually, the opposite state represents a 0. Acronym: NRZ.

Nontrivial *adj.* Being either difficult or particularly meaningful. For example, a complicated programmed procedure to handle a difficult problem would represent a nontrivial solution.

Non-Uniform Memory Access *n.* See NUMA.

Nonuniform memory architecture *n.* A system architecture designed for Sequent's Non-Uniform Access Memory, a type of distributed shared memory using a number of shared memory segments instead of a single centralised physical memory. Acronym: NUMA.

Nonvolatile memory *n.* A storage system that does not lose data when power is removed from it. Intended to refer to core memory, ROM, EPROM, flash memory, bubble memory, or battery-backed CMOS RAM, the term is occasionally used in reference to disk subsystems as well. See also bubble memory, CMOS RAM, core, EPROM, flash memory, ROM.

NO-OP *n.* See no-operation instruction.

No-operation instruction *n.* A machine instruction that has no results other than to cause the processor to use up clock cycles. Such instructions are useful in certain situations, such as padding out timing loops or forcing subsequent instructions to align on certain memory boundaries. Acronym: NO-OP, NOP. See also machine instruction.

NOP *n.* See no-operation instruction.

NOR gate *n.* Short for NOT OR gate. A digital circuit whose output is true (1) only if all inputs are false (0). A NOR gate is an OR circuit (output with the value of 1 if any input value is 1) followed by a NOT circuit (output that is the logical complement of the input). See also gate (definition 1), NOT gate, OR gate.

Normal distribution *n.* In statistics, a type of function that describes the probabilities of the possible values of a random variable. The function, whose graph is the familiar bell-shaped curve, can be used to determine the probability that the value of the variable will fall within a particular interval of values.

Normal form *n.* 1. In a relational database, an approach to structuring (organising) information in order to avoid redundancy and inconsistency and to promote efficient maintenance, storage, and updating. Several "rules" or levels of normalisation are accepted, each a refinement of the preceding one. Of these, three forms are commonly used: first normal (1NF), second normal (2NF), and third normal (3NF). First normal forms, the least structured, are groups of records (such as employee lists) in which each field (column) contains unique and nonrepeating information. Second and third normal forms break down first normal forms, separating them into different tables by defining successively finer interrelationships between fields. Second normal forms do not include fields that are subsets of fields other than the primary (key) field; for example, a second normal form keyed to employee name would not include both job grade and hourly rate if pay were dependent on job grade. Third normal forms do not include fields that provide

Normal hyphen *n.* See hyphen.

Normalise *vb.* 1. In programming, to adjust the fixed-point and exponent portions of a floating-point number to bring the fixed-point portions within a specific range. 2. In database management, to apply a body of techniques to a relational database in order to minimise the inclusion of duplicate information. Normalisation greatly simplifies query and update management, including security and integrity considerations, although it does so at the expense of creating a larger number of tables. See also normal form (definition 1).

North American Cellular Network *n.* Telecommunications network that enables wireless phone users in North America to send and receive calls when roaming outside their service area. Acronym: NACN.

NOS *n.* See network operating system.

NOT *n.* An operator that performs Boolean or logical negation. See also Boolean operator, logical operator.

NOT AND *n.* See NAND.

Notation *n.* In programming, the set of symbols and formats used to describe the elements of programming, mathematics, or a scientific field. A language's syntax is defined in part by notation. See also syntax.

Notebook computer *n.* See portable computer.

NOT gate *n.* One of the three basic logic gates (with AND and OR) from which all digital systems can be built. The NOT circuit, also referred to as an inverter, has output that is the reverse of its input—that is, the output is true (1) if the input is false (0) and false (0) if the input is true (1). See also AND gate, gate (definition 1), OR gate.

Notification *n.* A signal from the operating system that an event has occurred.

Novell Directory Services *n.* See NDS.

Novell NetWare *n.* See NetWare.

NPN transistor *n.* A type of transistor in which a base of P-type material is sandwiched between an emitter and a collector of N-type material. The base, emitter, and collector are the three terminals through which current flows. In an NPN transistor, electrons represent the majority of the charge carriers, and they flow from the emitter to the collector. See the illustration. See also N-type semiconductor, P-type semiconductor.

NPN transistor.

NQL *n.* See Network Query Language.

NRZ *n.* See nonreturn to zero.

ns *n.* See nanosecond.

NSAPI *n.* Acronym for Netscape Server Application Programming Interface. A specification for interfaces between the Netscape HTTP server and other application programmes. NSAPI can be used to provide access to application programmes from a Web browser through a Web server. See also HTTP server (definition 1), Web browser.

NSF *n.* See National Science Foundation.

NSFnet *n.* Short for the National Science Foundation Network. A WAN (wide area network), developed by the National Science Foundation to replace ARPANET for civilian purposes.

NSFnet served as a major backbone for the Internet until mid-1995. Backbone services in the United States for the Internet are now provided by commercial carriers. See also ARPANET, backbone (definition 1).

NSFnet Network Information Center *n.* See InterNIC.

NSI *n.* Acronym for Network Solutions, Inc. The organisation responsible, since 1992, for registering top-level Internet domain names and maintaining the authoritative ("A") database of top-level domains replicated daily on 12 other root servers on the Internet. In 1998, with the privatisation of Internet administration, the functions performed by NSI (under cooperative agreement with the U.S. National Science Foundation) became the responsibility of ICANN, a new, nonprofit organisation. NSI remains active, but its association with the U.S. government entered the "ramping down" phase in 1998/1999. See also IANA, ICANN.

NT *n.* See Windows NT.

NT-1 *n.* See Network Terminator 1.

NT file system *n.* See NTFS.

NTFS *n.* Acronym for NT file system. An advanced file system designed for use specifically with the Windows NT operating system. It supports long filenames, full security access control, file system recovery, extremely large storage media, and various features for the Windows NT POSIX subsystem. It also supports object-oriented applications by treating all files as objects with user-defined and system-defined attributes. See also FAT file system, HPFS, POSIX.

NTLM authentication protocol *n.* A challenge/response authentication protocol. The NTLM authentication protocol was the default for network authentication in Windows NT version 4.0 and earlier and Windows Millennium Edition (Windows Me) and earlier. The protocol continues to be supported in Windows 2000 and Windows XP but no longer is the default. See also Kerberos.

NTP *n.* Acronym for Network Time Protocol. A protocol used for synchronising the system time on a computer to that of a server or other reference source such as a radio, satellite receiver, or modem. NTP provides time accuracy within a millisecond on local area networks and a few tens of milliseconds on wide area networks. NTP configurations may utilise redundant servers, diverse network paths, and cryptographic authentication to achieve high accuracy and reliability.

NTSC *n.* Acronym for National Television System (later changed to Standards) Committee. The standards-setting body for television and video in the United States. It is the sponsor of the NTSC standard for encoding colour, a coding system compatible with black-and-white signals and the system used for colour broadcasting in the United States.

N-type semiconductor *n.* Semiconductor material in which electrical conduction is carried by electrons, in contrast to P-type semiconductors, in which conduction is carried by holes—that is, electron "vacancies." N-type semiconductors are created by adding a dopant with an excess of electrons during the manufacturing process. See also semiconductor.

NuBus *n.* A high-performance expansion bus used in Macintosh computers, offering high bandwidth and multiple bus controllers. Invented at the Massachusetts Institute of Technology (MIT), NuBus was eventually licensed to Texas Instruments and other companies. See also bus.

Nudge *vb.* To move an object one pixel at a time.

Nuke *vb.* 1. To erase a file, directory, or entire hard disk. 2. To stop a process in an operating system, an application, or a programme. Also called: kill.

NUL *n.* 1. A character code with a null value; literally, a character meaning "nothing." Although it is real in the sense of being recognizable, occupying space internally in the computer, and being sent or received as a character, a NUL character displays nothing, takes no space on the screen or on paper, and causes no specific action when sent to a printer. In ASCII, NUL is represented by the character code 0. See also ASCII. 2. A "device," recognised by the operating system, that can be addressed like a physical output device (such as a printer) but that discards any information sent to it.

Null character *n.* See NUL.

Null cycle *n.* The shortest amount of time required for execution of a programme; the time needed to cycle through the programme without requiring it to process new data or loop through sets of instructions.

Null modem *n.* A way of connecting two computers via a cable that enables them to communicate without the use of modems. A null modem cable accomplishes this by crossing the sending and receiving wires so that the wire used for transmitting by one device is used for receiving by the other and vice versa. See the illustration.

Null modem cable *n.* A serial data cable used to connect two personal computers, without a modem or other DCE device in between, through the computers' serial ports. Because both computers use the same pins to send data, a null modem cable connects the output pins in one computer's serial port to the input pins in the other. A null modem cable is used to transfer data between two personal computers in close proximity. See also serial port.

Null pointer *n.* A pointer to nothing—usually a standardised memory address, such as 0. A null pointer usually marks the last of a linear sequence of pointers or indicates that a data search operation has come up empty. Also called: nil pointer. See also pointer (definition 1).

Null string *n.* A string containing no characters; a string whose length is zero. See also string.

Null-terminated string *n.* See ASCIIZ string.

NUMA *n.* Acronym for Non-Uniform Memory Access. A multiprocessing architecture that manages memory according to its distance from the processor. Banks of memory at various distances require different amounts of access time, with local memory accessed faster than remote memory. See also SMP.

Number cruncher *n.* 1. A computer that is able to quickly perform large amounts of mathematical computations. 2. A powerful workstation. 3. A programme whose main task is to perform mathematical computations—for example, a statistical programme. 4. A person who uses a computer to analyse numbers.

Number crunching *vb.* The calculation of large amounts of numeric data. Number crunching can be repetitive, mathematically complex, or both, and it generally involves far more internal processing than input or output functions. Numeric coprocessors greatly enhance the ability of computers to perform these tasks.

Numerical analysis *n.* The branch of mathematics devoted to finding ways to solve abstract mathematical problems and finding concrete or approximate solutions for them.

Numeric coprocessor *n.* See floating-point processor.

Numeric keypad *n.* A calculator-style block of keys, usually at the right side of a keyboard, that can be used to enter numbers. In addition to keys for the digits 0 through 9 and keys for indicating addition, subtraction, multiplication, and division, a numeric keypad often includes an Enter key (usually not the same as the Enter or Return key on the main part of the keyboard). On Apple keyboards, the numeric keypad also includes a Clear key that usually functions like the Backspace key for deleting characters. In addition, many of the keys can serve dual purposes, such as cursor movement, scrolling, or editing tasks, depending on the status of the Num Lock key. See the illustration. See also Num Lock key.

Numeric keypad.

Numeric messaging *n.* Service that enables wireless phones and pagers to receive messages consisting only of numeric information, such as phone numbers.

Numeric paging *n.* See numeric messaging.

Num Lock key *n.* Short for Numeric Lock key. A toggle key that, when turned on, activates the numeric keypad so that its keys can be used for calculator-style data entry. When the Num Lock key is toggled off, most of the numeric keypad keys are used for cursor movement and onscreen scrolling. See also numeric keypad.

NVM *n.* Acronym for Non-Volatile Memory. Memory that persists in its state when the power is removed. Also called: Flash memory.

NVRAM *n.* Acronym for Non-Volatile Random Access Memory. Non-volatile read/write memory or normally volatile memory that has been fitted with a battery backup to retain data. See also NVM.

NWLink *n.* An implementation of the Internetwork Packet Exchange (IPX), Sequenced Packet Exchange (SPX), and NetBIOS protocols used in Novell networks. NWLink is a standard network protocol that supports routing and can support NetWare client-server applications, where NetWare-aware Sockets-based applications communicate with IPX/SPX Sockets-based applications. See also IPX/SPX, NetBIOS, RIPX.

Nybble *n.* See nibble.

O

OAGI *n.* Acronym for Open Applications Group, Inc. A nonprofit consortium of software vendors and businesses created to develop and define XML-based interoperability specifications and standards among enterprise-scale applications. The OAGI was formed in 1995 by a small number of business enterprise software companies and organisations and has grown to more than sixty member companies.

OAGIS *n.* Acronym for Open Applications Group Integration Specification. A set of XML-based specifications and standards designed to promote B2B e-commerce by providing interoperability between enterprise-scale applications and between companies. OAGIS includes business document specifications and definitions, business process scenarios, and templates for business forms such as invoices and requisitions. OAGIS is overseen by the Open Applications Group, Inc., a nonprofit consortium of software vendors and customers. See also OAGI.

OASIS *n.* Acronym for Organisation for the Advancement of Structured Information Standards. A consortium of technology companies formed to develop guidelines for use of XML (Extensible Markup Language) and related information standards.

Oberon *n.* An extensible object-oriented language based on Modula-2, whose later versions support the .NET Framework. Also called: Active Oberon for .NET.

Object *n.* 1. Short for object code (machine-readable code). 2. In object-oriented programming, a variable comprising both routines and data that is treated as a discrete entity. See also abstract data type, module (definition 1), object-oriented programming. 3. In graphics, a distinct entity. For example, a bouncing ball might be an object in a graphics programme. 4. A single, runtime instance of object type that the operating system defines. Objects visible in user mode include event, file, I/O completion port, key, object directory, port, process, section, semaphore, symbolic link, thread, timer, and token objects. Many user-mode objects are implemented through the use of a corresponding kernel-mode object. Kernel-mode-only objects include adapter, APC, controller, device, device queue, DPC, driver, interrupt, mutex, and stream file objects.

Object code *n.* The code, generated by a compiler or an assembler, that was translated from the source code of a programme. The term most commonly refers to machine code that can be directly executed by the system's central processing unit (CPU), but it can also be assembly language source code or a variation of machine code. See also central processing unit.

Object computer *n.* The computer that is the target of a specific communications attempt.

Object database *n.* See object-oriented database.

Object Database Management Group *n.* An organisation that promotes standards for object databases and defines interfaces to object databases. Acronym: ODMG. See also OMG.

Object file *n.* A file containing object code, usually the output of a compiler or an assembler and the input for a linker. See also assembler, compiler (definition 2), linker, object code.

Objective-C *n.* An object-oriented version of the C language developed in 1984 by Brad Cox. It is most widely known for being the standard development language for the NeXT operating system. See also object-oriented programming.

Object linking and embedding *n.* See OLE.

Object Management Architecture *n.* See OMA.

Object Management Group *n.* See OMG.

Object model *n.* 1. The structural foundation for an object-oriented language, such as C++. This foundation includes such principles as abstraction, concurrency, encapsulation, hierarchy, persistence, polymorphism, and typing. See also abstract data type, object (definition 2), object-oriented programming, polymorphism. 2. The structural foundation for an object-oriented design. See also object-oriented design. 3. The structural foundation for an object-oriented application.

Object module *n.* In programming, the object-code (compiled) version of a source-code file that is usually a collection of routines and is ready to be linked with other object modules. See also linker, module (definition 1), object code.

Object-oriented *adj.* Of, pertaining to, or being a system or language that supports the use of objects. See also object (definition 2).

Object-oriented analysis *n.* A procedure that identifies the component objects and system requirements of a system or process that involves computers and describes how they interact to perform specific tasks. The reuse of existing solutions is an objective of this sort of analysis. Object-oriented analysis generally precedes object-oriented design or object-oriented programming when a new object-oriented computer system or new software is developed. See also object (definition 2), object-oriented design, object-oriented programming.

Object-oriented database *n.* A flexible database that supports the use of abstract data types, objects, and classes and that can store a wide range of data, often including sound, video, and graphics, in addition to text and numbers. Some object-oriented databases allow data retrieval procedures and rules for processing data to be stored along with the data or in place of the data. This allows the data to be stored in areas other than in the physical database, which is often desirable when the data files are large, such as those for video files. Acronym: OODB. See also abstract data type, class, object (definition 2).

Object-oriented design *n.* A modular approach to creating a software product or computer system, in which the modules (objects) can be easily and affordably adapted to meet new needs. Object-oriented design generally comes after object-oriented analysis of the product or system and before any actual programming. See also object (definition 2), object-oriented analysis.

Object-oriented graphics *n.* Computer graphics that are based on the use of graphics primitives, such as lines, curves, circles, and squares. Object-oriented graphics, used in applications such as computer-aided design and drawing and illustration programmes, describe an image mathematically as a set of instructions for creating the objects in the image. This approach contrasts with the use of bitmapped graphics, in which a graphic is represented as a group of black-and-white or coloured dots arranged in a certain pattern. Object-oriented graphics enable the user to manipulate objects as units. Because objects are described mathematically, object-oriented graphics can be layered, rotated, and magnified relatively easily. Also called: structured graphics. See also graphics primitive.

Object-oriented interface *n.* A user interface in which elements of the system are represented by visible screen entities, such as icons, that are used to manipulate the system elements. Object-oriented display interfaces do not necessarily imply any relation to object-oriented programming. See also object-oriented graphics.

Object-oriented operating system *n.* An operating system based on objects and designed in a way that facilitates software development by third parties, using an object-oriented design. See also object (definition 2), object-oriented design.

Object-oriented programming *n.* A programming paradigm in which a programme is viewed as a collection of discrete objects that are self-contained collections of data structures and routines that interact with other objects. Acronym: OOP. See also C++, object (definition 2), Objective-C.

Object Pascal *n.* An object-oriented derivative of Pascal. See also Pascal.

Object-relational server *n.* A database server that supports object-oriented management of complex data types in a relational database. See also database server, relational database.

Object request broker *n.* See ORB.

Object wrapper *n.* In object-oriented applications, a means of encapsulating a set of services provided by a non-object-oriented application so that the encapsulated services can be treated as an object. See also object (definition 2).

Oblique *adj.* Describing a style of text created by slanting a roman font to simulate italics when a true italic font isn't available on the computer or printer. See also font, italic, roman.

OC3 *n.* Short for optical carrier 3. One of several optical signal circuits used in the SONET high-speed fiberoptic data transmission system. OC3 carries a signal of 155.52 Mbps, the minimum transmission speed for which SONET and the European standard, SDH, are fully interoperable. See also SONET.

OCR *n.* See optical character recognition.

Octal *n.* The base-8 number system consisting of the digits 0 through 7, from the Latin octo, meaning "eight." The octal system is used in programming as a compact means of representing binary numbers. See also base (definition 2).

Octet *n.* A unit of data that consists of exactly 8 bits, regardless of the number of bits a computer uses to represent a small amount of information such as a character.

OCX *n.* Short for OLE custom control. A software module based on OLE and COM technologies that, when called by an application, produces a control that adds some desired feature to the application. OCX technology is portable across platforms, works on both 16-bit and 32-bit operating systems, and can be used with many applications. It is the successor to VBX (Visual Basic custom control) technology, which supported only Visual Basic applications, and is the basis for ActiveX controls. OCXs have, in fact, been superseded by ActiveX controls, which are much smaller and therefore work much better over the Internet. See also ActiveX control, COM (definition 2), control (definition 2), OLE, VBX, Visual Basic.

ODBC *n.* Acronym for Open Database Connectivity. In the Microsoft WOSA (Windows Open System Architecture) structure, an interface providing a common language for Windows applications to gain access to a database on a network. See also WOSA.

ODBC driver *n.* Short for Open Database Connectivity driver. A programme file used to connect to a particular database. Each database programme, such as Access or dBASE, or database management system, such as SQL Server, requires a different driver.

ODBMG *n.* See Object Database Management Group.

Odd parity *n.* See parity.

ODI *n.* Acronym for Open Data-link Interface. A specification developed by Novell to enable a network interface card (NIC) to support multiple protocols, such as TCP/IP and IPX/SPX. ODI also simplifies development of device drivers by eliminating concern about the particular protocol to be used in transferring information over the network. ODI is comparable in some ways to the Network Driver Interface Specification, or NDIS. See also NDIS, network adapter.

ODMA *n.* Acronym for Open Document Management API. A specification for a standard application programme interface that enables desktop applications, such as Microsoft Word, to interact seamlessly with specialised document management systems (DMS) installed on network servers. The ODMA specification is the property of the Association for Information & Image Management (AIIM). See also API, document management system.

OEM *n.* See original equipment manufacturer.

OFC *n.* See Open Financial Connectivity.

Office *n.* Microsoft's family of individual and business application software suites for the Windows and Macintosh platforms. Office is built around three core products: Word for word processing, Excel for spreadsheets, and Outlook for e-mail and collaboration. Office XP, the most recent version for the Windows platform, is available in several versions: the Office XP Standard or Standard for Students and Teachers version, which includes Word, Excel, Outlook, and PowerPoint; the

Office XP Professional version, which adds Access; Office XP Developer, which includes Word, Excel, Outlook, PowerPoint, Access, FrontPage, Microsoft's new SharePoint Team Services collaboration and team Web solution, and Developer Tools; and finally, Office XP Professional Special Edition, which offers all the programmes in Office XP Professional plus FrontPage, SharePoint Team Services, Publisher, and IntelliMouse Explorer. Office v. X for Mac is the most recent version for the Macintosh and includes Word, Entourage (for e-mail and collaboration), Excel, and PowerPoint. See the table.

Table O.1 Application Specifications

Product	Function	Platform
Word	Word processing	Windows, Macintosh
Excel	Spreadsheets	Windows, Macintosh
Outlook	E-mail, collaboration	Windows
Entourage	E-mail, collaboration	Macintosh
Publisher	Desktop publishing	Windows
Access	Database management	Windows
PowerPoint	Presentation graphics	Windows, Macintosh
FrontPage	Web site creation	Windows
SharePoint Team Services	Team Web solution	Windows

Office automation *n.* The use of electronic and communications devices, such as computers, modems, and fax machines and any associated software, to perform office functions mechanically rather than manually.

Offline *adj.* 1. In reference to a computing device or a programme, unable to communicate with or be controlled by a computer. 2. In reference to one or more computers, being disconnected from a network. 3. Colloquially, a reference to moving a discussion between interested parties to a later, more appropriate, time.

Offline navigator *n.* Software designed to download e-mail, Web pages, or newsgroup articles or postings from other online forums and save them locally to a disk, where they can be browsed without the user paying the cost of idle time while being connected to the Internet or an online information service. Also called: offline reader.

Offline reader *n.* See offline navigator.

Offline storage *n.* A storage resource, such as a disk, that is not currently available to the system.

Offload *vb.* To assume part of the processing demand from another device. For example, some LAN-attached gateways can offload TCP/IP processing from the host machine, thereby freeing up significant processing capacity in the CPU. See also central processing unit, gateway, host, TCP/IP.

Offset *n.* In relative addressing methods, a number that tells how far from a starting point a particular item is located. See also relative address.

Off-the-shelf *adj.* Ready-to-use; packaged. The term can refer to hardware or software.

Ohm *n.* The unit of measure for electrical resistance. A resistance of 1 ohm will pass 1 ampere of current when a voltage of 1 volt is applied.

OLAP *n.* See OLAP database.

OLAP database *n.* Short for online analytical processing database. A relational database system capable of handling queries more complex than those handled by standard relational databases, through multidimensional access to data (viewing the data by several different criteria), intensive calculation capability, and specialised indexing techniques. See also database, query (definition 1), relational database.

OLAP provider *n.* A set of software that provides access to a particular type of OLAP database. This software can include a data source driver and other client software that is necessary to connect to a database. See also OLAP database.

OLE *n.* Acronym for object linking and embedding. A technology for transferring and sharing information among applications. When an object, such as an image file created with a paint programme, is linked to a compound document, such as a spreadsheet or a document created with a word processing programme, the document contains only a reference to the object; any changes made to the contents of a linked object will be seen in the compound document. When an object is embedded in a compound document, the document contains a copy of the object; any changes made to the contents of the original object will not be seen in the compound document unless the embedded object is updated.

OLED *n.* Acronym for Organic Light-Emitting Device. Technology developed for the production of thin, lightweight digital displays. An OLED features a series of thin organic films between two conductors. When current is applied, bright light is emitted. OLED displays are lightweight, durable, and power-efficient.

OLE Database *n.* An application programming interface developed by Microsoft for accessing databases. OLE Database is an open specification that can interface with all types of data files on a computer network. Acronym: OLE DB.

OLTP *n.* Acronym for online transaction processing. A system for processing transactions as soon as the computer receives them and updating master files immediately in a database management system. OLTP is useful in financial record keeping and inventory tracking. See also database management system, transaction processing.

OM-1 *n.* See OpenMPEG Consortium.

OMA *n.* Acronym for Object Management Architecture. A definition developed by the Object Management Group (OMG) for object-oriented distributed processing. OMA includes the Common Object Request Broker Architecture (CORBA). See also CORBA, OMG.

OMG *n.* Acronym for Object Management Group. A nonprofit organisation that provides a framework of standards for object-oriented interfaces. The open and nonproprietary architecture developed and managed by the OMG allows developers to work with a large toolkit of standard components in building applications with a solid common foundation. The OMG was formed in 1989 by a group of software developers and system vendors and now has more than six hundred member companies.

On-board computer *n.* A computer that resides within another device.

On-chip cache *n.* See L1 cache.

On-demand publishing point *n.* A type of publishing point that streams content in such a way that the client can control (start, stop, pause, fast-forward, or rewind) the content. Typically, the on-demand content is a Windows Media file or a directory of files. Content streamed from an on-demand publishing point is always delivered as a unicast stream. Formerly called a station.

One-off *n.* 1. A product that is produced one at a time, instead of being mass produced. 2. A CD-ROM created on a CD-R machine, which can create only one copy of a CD-ROM at a time.

One-pass compiler *n.* A compiler that needs to read through a source file only once to produce the object code. The syntax of some languages makes it impossible to write a one-pass compiler for those languages. See also compiler (definition 2).

One's complement *n.* A number in the binary (base-2) system that is the complement of another number. See also complement.

One-to-many relationship *n.* An association between two tables in which the primary key value of each record in the primary table corresponds to the value in the matching field or fields of many records in the related table.

One-to-many replication *n.* A server configuration allowing replication of data from one or more large servers to a greater number of smaller servers.

One-to-one relationship *n.* An association between two tables in which the primary key value of each record in the primary table corresponds to the value in the matching field or fields of one and only one record in the related table.

One-way trust *n.* A type of trust relationship in which only one of the two domains trusts the other domain. For example, domain A trusts domain B and domain B does not trust domain A. All one-way trusts are nontransitive. See also transitive trust, two-way trust.

Onion routing *n.* An anonymous communication technique first developed by the U.S. Navy, in which a message is wrapped in layers of encryption and passed through several intermediate stations to obscure its point of origin. In onion routing, data packets are sent through a complex network of routers, each of which opens an anonymous connection to the next, until it reaches its destination. When the packet is received by the first onion router, it is encrypted once for each additional router it will pass through. Each subsequent onion router unwraps one layer of encryption until the message reaches its destination as plain text.

Online *adj.* 1. In reference to a computing device or a programme, activated and ready for operation; capable of communicating with or being controlled by a computer. 2. In reference to one or more computers, connected to a network. 3. In reference to a user, currently connected to the Internet, an online service, or a BBS or using a modem to connect to another modem. 4. In reference to a user, being able to connect to the Internet, an online service, or a BBS by virtue of having an account that gives one access.

Online analytical processing *n.* See OLAP database.

Online community *n.* 1. All users of the Internet and World Wide Web collectively. 2. A local community that places political forums on line for the discussion of local government or issues of public concern. 3. Members of a specific newsgroup, mailing list, MUD, BBS, or other online forum or group. See also BBS (definition 1), mailing list, MUD, newsgroup.

Online game *n.* A game that is meant to be played while connected to the Internet, intranet, or other network, with one or more other people simultaneously connected. Online games allow gamers to interact with other players without having their physical presence necessary. See also computer game.

Online help *n.* See help.

Online information service *n.* A business that provides access to databases, file archives, conferences, chat groups, and other forms of information through dial-up, or dedicated communications links, or through the Internet. Most online information services also offer access to the Internet connections along with their own proprietary services. The largest consumer online information services in the U.S. are America Online, CompuServe, and MSN.

Online Privacy Alliance *n.* See OPA.

Online service *n.* See online information service.

Online state *n.* The state of a modem when it is communicating with another modem.

Online transaction processing *n.* See OLTP.

Onscreen keyboard *n.* An interactive keyboard that appears as a graphical image on the display screen of a computing device. A user spells words by tapping the letters on the screen with a stylus. Onscreen keyboards appear primarily on personal digital assistants (PDAs) and other handheld computing devices that are too small to contain a traditional keyboard. on the fly adv. Doing a task or process as needed without suspending or disturbing normal operations. For example, it is often said that an HTML document can be edited on the fly because its content can be revised without the need to completely shut down or re-create the Web site on which it resides. See also HTML document, Web site.

OO *adj.* See object-oriented.

OOP *n.* See object-oriented programming.

OPA *n.* Acronym for Online Privacy Alliance. An organisation of over eighty Internet companies and trade associations created to be the voice of the industry on digital privacy issues. The OPA stresses the need for consumer trust and encourages online businesses to post privacy policies. The OPA created a set of guidelines for privacy policies that have become the industry standard.

Opacity *n.* The quality that defines how much light passes through an object's pixels. If an object is 100 per cent opaque, no light passes through it.

Opcode *n.* See operation code.

Open 1 *adj.* Of, pertaining to, or providing accessibility. For example, an open file is one that can be used because a programme has issued an open file command to the operating system.

Open 2 *vb.* To make an object, such as a file, accessible.

Open Applications Group, Inc. *n.* See OAGI.

Open architecture *n.* 1. Any computer or peripheral design that has published specifications. A published specification lets third parties develop add-on hardware for a computer or device. 2. A design that provides for expansion slots on the motherboard, thereby allowing the addition of boards to enhance or customise a system.

OpenCyc *n.* An open source artificial intelligence platform. OpenCyc forms the foundation of knowledge-dependent applications such as speech understanding, database integration, and e-mail routing and prioritising. OpenCyc development is administered through OpenCyc.org.

Open Data-link Interface *n.* See ODI.

OpenDoc *n.* An object-oriented application programming interface (API) that enables multiple independent programmes (component software) on several platforms to work together on a single document (compound document). Similar to OLE, OpenDoc allows images, sound, video, other documents, and other files to be embedded or linked to the document. OpenDoc is supported by an alliance that includes Apple, IBM, the Object Management Group, and the X Consortium. See also application programming interface, component software.

Open Document Management API *n.* See ODMA.

Open file *n.* A file that can be read from, written to, or both. A programme must first open a file before the file's contents can be used, and it must close the file when done. See also open2.

Open Financial Connectivity *n.* The Microsoft specification for an interface between electronic banking services and Microsoft Money personal finance software. Acronym: OFC.

OpenGL *n.* An industry standard application programming interface (API) for 3D graphics rendering and 3D hardware acceleration. OpenGL is cross-platform and is available for all major operating systems.

Open Group *n.* A consortium of computer hardware and software manufacturers and users from industry, government, and academia that is dedicated to the advancement of multi-vendor information systems. The Open Group was formed in 1996 as a consolidation of the Open Software Foundation and X/Open Company Limited.

OpenMPEG Consortium *n.* An international organisation of hardware and software developers for promoting the use of the MPEG standards. Acronym: OM-1. See also MPEG.

Open Prepress Interface *n.* See OPI.

Open Profiling Standard *n.* An Internet personalisation and privacy specification submitted for consideration to the World Wide Web Consortium by Netscape Communications Corporation, Firefly Network, Inc., and VeriSign, Inc. Open Profiling Standard (OPS) enables users to customise online services while protecting their privacy. To achieve personalisation and privacy concomitantly, OPS is based on the concept of a Personal Profile, which is stored on the individual's computer and contains the user's unique identification, demographic and contact data, and possibly content preferences. This information remains under the user's control and can be released wholly or in part to the requesting site. Acronym: OPS. See also cookie, digital certificate.

Open shop *n.* A computer facility that is open to users and not restricted to programmers or other personnel. An open shop is one in which people can work on or attempt to solve computer problems on their own rather than handing them over to a specialist.

Open Shortest Path First *n.* See OSPF.

Open Software Foundation *n.* See OSF.

Open source *n.* The practice of making the source code (programme instructions) for a software product freely available, at no cost, to interested users and developers, even though they were not involved in creating the original product. The distributors of open source software expect and encourage users and outside programmers to examine the code in order to identify problems, and to modify the code with suggested improvements and enhancements. Widely used open source products include the Linux operating system and the Apache Web server.

Open standard *n.* A publicly available set of specifications describing the characteristics of a hardware device or software programme. Open standards are published to encourage interoperability and thereby help popularise new technologies. See also standard (definition 2).

Open system *n.* 1. In communications, a computer network designed to incorporate all devices—regardless of the manufacturer or model—that can use the same communications facilities and protocols. 2. In reference to computer hardware or software, a system that can accept add-ons produced by third-party suppliers. See also open architecture (definition 1).

Open Systems Interconnection reference model *n.* See ISO/OSI reference model.

OpenType *n.* A collaborative initiative by Microsoft and Adobe to unify support for Microsoft TrueType and Adobe PostScript Type 1 fonts. The OpenType font format enables font creators and users to work with the font type that best suits their needs without having to worry about whether the font is based on TrueType or PostScript technology. Also called: TrueType Open version 2. See also PostScript font, TrueType.

Opera *n.* A Web browser developed by Opera Software S/A. Opera is notable for its strict W3C standards support. Opera is often chosen by Web developers to test Web sites for W3C compliance. See also W3C, Web browser.

Operand *n.* The object of a mathematical operation or a computer instruction.

Operating system *n.* The software that controls the allocation and usage of hardware resources such as memory, central processing unit (CPU) time, disk space, and peripheral devices. The operating system is the foundation software on which applications depend. Popular operating systems include Windows 98, Windows NT, Mac OS, and UNIX. Acronym: OS. Also called: executive.

Operation *n.* 1. A specific action carried out by a computer in the process of executing a programme. 2. In mathematics, an action performed on a set of entities that produces a new entity. Examples of mathematical operations are addition and subtraction.

Operation code *n.* The portion of a machine language or assembly language instruction that specifies the type of instruction and the structure of the data on which it operates. Also called: opcode. See also assembly language, machine code.

Operations research *n.* The use of mathematical and scientific approaches to analyse and improve efficiency in business, management, government, and other areas. Developed around the beginning of World War II, operations research was initially used to improve military operations during the war. The practice later spread to business and industry as a means of breaking down systems and procedures and studying their parts and interactions to improve overall performance. Operations research involves use of the critical path method, statistics, probability, and information theory.

Operator *n.* 1. In mathematics and in programming and computer applications, a symbol or other character indicating an operation that acts on one or more elements. See also binary, unary. 2. A person who controls a machine or system such as a computer or telephone switchboard.

Operator associativity *n.* A characteristic of operators that determines the order of evaluation in an expression when adjacent operators have equal precedence. The two possibilities are left to right and right to left. The associativity for most operators is left to right. See also expression, operator (definition 1), operator precedence.

Operator overloading *n.* The assignment of more than one function to a particular operator, with the implication that the operation performed will vary depending on the data type (operands) involved. Some languages, such as Ada and C++, specifically allow for operator overloading. See also Ada, C++, function overloading, operator (definition 1).

Operator precedence *n.* The priority of the various operators when more than one is used in an expression. In the absence of parentheses, operations with higher precedence are performed first. See also expression, operator (definition 1), operator associativity.

OPI *n.* Acronym for Open Prepress Interface. A format for preparing digital publication text and graphics for printing, introduced by Aldus (now Adobe), creating a low-resolution graphic for layout and a high-resolution graphic for print. Depending on the method used, the OPI process creates a single file that allows for colour layer extraction though a desktop colour separation programme or creates multiple colour-separated files when using DCS (Desktop Colour Separation).

OPS *n.* See Open Profiling Standard.

Optical character recognition *n.* The process in which an electronic device examines printed characters on paper and determines their shapes by detecting patterns of dark and light. Once the scanner or reader has determined the shapes, character recognition methods—pattern matching with stored sets of characters—are used to translate the shapes into computer text. Acronym: OCR. See also character recognition.

Optical communications *n.* The use of light and of light-transmitting technology, such as optical fibers and lasers, in sending and receiving data, images, or sound.

Optical disc *n.* See compact disc.

Optical drive *n.* A disk drive that reads and often can write data on optical (compact) discs. Examples of optical drives include CD-ROM drives and WORM disk drives. See also CD-ROM drive, compact disc, WORM.

Optical fiber *n.* A thin strand of transparent material used to carry optical signals. Optical fibers are constructed from special kinds of glass and plastic, and they are designed so that a beam of light introduced at one end will remain within the fiber, reflecting off the inner surfaces as it travels down the length of the fiber. Optical fibers are inexpensive, compact, and lightweight and are often packaged many hundred to a single cable. See also fiber optics.

Optical mouse *n.* 1. A type of mouse that uses a CMOS digital camera and a digital signal processor to detect motion. The camera photographs the surface over which the mouse moves 1500 times per second, and the digital signal processor uses the photographs to convert the mouse movement into onscreen movements of the cursor. IntelliMouse Explorer and IntelliMouse with IntelliEye, two optical mouse models with no moving parts and requiring no special mouse pad, were introduced by Microsoft in 1999. See also mouse. 2. A type of mouse that uses a pair of light-emitting diodes (LEDs) and a special reflective grid pad to detect motion. The two lights are of different colours, and the special mouse pad has a grid of lines in the same colours, one colour for vertical lines and another for horizontal lines. Light detectors paired with the LEDs sense when a coloured light passes over a line of the same colour, indicating the direction of movement. See also mouse.

Optical reader *n.* A device that reads text from printed paper by detecting the pattern of light and dark on a page and then applying optical character recognition methods to identify the characters. See also optical character recognition.

Optical recognition *n.* See optical character recognition.

Optical scanner *n.* An input device that uses light-sensing equipment to scan paper or another medium, translating the pattern of light and dark or colour into a digital signal that can be manipulated by either optical character recognition software or graphics software. Scanners have different methods for holding the input medium, including flatbed, whereby the medium is held on a piece of glass; sheet-fed, whereby sheets of paper are pulled over a stationary scanning mechanism; handheld, whereby the user moves the device over the document to be scanned; and overhead, whereby the document is placed face up on a stationary bed below a small tower, which moves across the page.

Optical switching *n.* A technology in which transmissions are sent as light from origin to destination. With optical switching, transmissions are switched through banks of adjustable, circular millimeter mirrors at cross connections, meaning signals don't need to be converted from light to electronic and back during transmission. When used with wave-division multiplexing (WDM), all-optical traffic may be 100 times faster than electrical transmission. See also photonics.

Optimisation *n.* 1. In programming, the process of producing more efficient (smaller or faster) programmes through selection and design of data structures, algorithms, and instruction sequences. 2. The process of a compiler or assembler in producing efficient executable code. See also optimising compiler.

Optimise *vb.* 1. In Web design functions, to reduce the file size of a photo or graphic to allow faster loading. Files are typically optimised through a combination of means such as reducing overall image quality and fine-tuning colour information. 2. To fine-tune an application for improved performance. See also optimisation.

Optimizer *n.* A programme or device that improves the performance of a computer, network, or other device or system. For example, a disk optimizer programme reduces file access time.

Optimising compiler *n.* A compiler that analyses its output (assembly language or machine code) to produce more efficient (smaller or faster) instruction sequences.

Opt-in *vb.* To choose to receive certain services or features offered by an e-business. With the opt-in process, a user is not automatically enrolled in services or features. The user must choose to enroll in a service or feature.

Optional hyphen *n.* See hyphen.

Option key *n.* A key on Apple Macintosh keyboards that, when pressed in combination with another key, produces special characters—graphics, such as boxes; international characters, such as currency symbols; and special punctuation marks, such as en dashes and em dashes. The Option key serves a purpose similar to that of the Control key or the Alt key on IBM and compatible keyboards in that it changes the meaning of the key with which it is used.

Options *n.* See Preferences.

Optoelectronics *n.* The branch of electronics in which the properties and behaviour of light are studied. Optoelectronics deals with electronic devices that generate, sense, transmit, and modulate electromagnetic radiation in the infrared, visible, and ultraviolet portions of the electromagnetic spectrum.

Optomechanical mouse *n.* A type of mouse in which motion is translated into directional signals through a combination of optical and mechanical means. The optical portion includes pairs of light-emitting diodes (LEDs) and matching sensors; the mechanical portion consists of rotating wheels with cutout slits. When the mouse is moved, the wheels turn and the light from the LEDs either passes through the slits and strikes a light sensor or is blocked by the solid portions of the wheels. These changes in light contact are detected by the pairs of sensors and interpreted as indications of movement. Because the sensors are slightly out of phase with one another, the direction of movement is determined based on which sensor is the first to regain light contact. Because it uses optical equipment instead of mechanical parts, an optomechanical mouse eliminates the need for many of the wear-related repairs and maintenance necessary with purely mechanical mice, but it does not require the special operating surfaces associated with optical mic

Opt-out *vb.* To choose not to receive certain services or features offered by an e-business. Some e-businesses automatically enroll users in a predetermined range of services, but allow users to opt-out of features in which they do not choose to participate.

OR *n.* A logical operation for combining two bits (0 or 1) or two Boolean values (false or true). If one or both values are 1 (true), it returns the value 1 (true). See the table.

Table O.2 The results of the OR logical operation.

a	b	a OR b
0	0	0
0	1	1
1	0	1
1	1	1

Orange Book *n.* 1. A U.S. Department of Defense standards document entitled "Trusted Computer System Evaluation Criteria, DOD standard 5200.28-STD, December, 1985," which defines a system of ratings from A1 (most secure) to D (least secure), indicating the ability of a computer system to protect sensitive information. 2. A specifications book written by the Sony and Philips Corporations, covering the compact disc write-once formats (CD-R, PhotoCD). See also CD-R, ISO 9660, PhotoCD.

ORB *n.* Acronym for object request broker. In client/server applications, an interface to which the client makes a request for an object. The ORB directs the request to the server containing the object and then returns the resulting values to the client. See also client (definition 1), CORBA.

Order 1 *n.* 1. In computing, the relative significance of a digit or byte. High-order refers to the most significant (usually leftmost) digit or byte; low-order refers to the least significant (usually rightmost) digit or byte. 2. The magnitude of a database in terms of the number of fields it contains. 3. The sequence in which arithmetic operations are performed.

Order 2 *vb.* To arrange in a sequence, such as alphabetic or numeric.

Ordinal number *n.* A number whose form indicates position in an ordered sequence of items, such as first, third, or twentieth.

.org *n.* In the Internet's Domain Name System, the top-level domain that identifies addresses operated by organisations that do not fit any of the other standard domains. For instance, the Public Broadcasting System (PBS) is neither a commercial, for-profit corporation (.com) nor an educational institution with enrolled students (.edu), so it has the Internet address pbs.org. The designation .org appears at the end of the address.

Organic Light-Emitting Device *n.* See OLED.

Organisation for the Advancement of Structured Information Standards *n.* See OASIS.

OR gate *n.* One of the three basic logic gates (with AND and NOT) from which all digital systems can be built. The output of an OR circuit is true (1) if any input is true. See also AND gate, gate (definition 1), NOT gate.

Orientation *n.* See landscape mode, portrait mode.

Original equipment manufacturer *n.* The maker of a piece of equipment. In making computers and related equipment, manufacturers of original equipment typically purchase components from other manufacturers of original equipment, integrate them into their own products, and then sell the products to the public. Acronym: OEM.

Original Macintosh keyboard *n.* The keyboard supplied as standard equipment with the 128-KB Apple Macintosh and the Mac 512K. The original Macintosh keyboard is small and has no numeric keypad or function keys. Also, because the overall design goal was that the Macintosh should feel familiar, the only elements of this 58-key keyboard that differ from a typewriter keyboard are the Option keys at both ends of the bottom row, the Command key to the left of the Spacebar, and the Enter key to the right of the Spacebar.

Orphan *n.* The first line of a paragraph printed alone at the bottom of a page or column of text, or the last line of a paragraph printed alone at the top of a page or column. Orphans are visually unattractive and thus undesirable in printed materials.

Orphan file *n.* A file that remains on a system after it has ceased to be of use. For example, a file may be created to support a particular application but may remain after the application has been removed.

OS *n.* See operating system.

OS/2 *n.* Short for Operating System/2. A protected-mode, virtual-memory, multitasking operating system for personal computers based on the Intel 80286, 80386, i486, and Pentium processors. OS/2 can run most MS-DOS applications and can read all MS-DOS disks. OS/2's Presentation Manager provides a graphical user interface. The latest version, known as OS/2 Warp 4, is a 32-bit operating system that provides networking, Internet, and Java support, as well as speech recognition technology. OS/2 was initially developed as a joint project of Microsoft and IBM but later became an IBM product. See also protected mode, virtual memory.

Oscillation *n.* A periodic change or alternation. In electronics, oscillation refers to a periodic change in an electrical signal.

Oscillator *n.* An electronic circuit that produces a periodically varying output at a controlled frequency. Oscillators, an important type of electronic circuit, can be designed to provide a constant or an adjustable output. Some oscillator circuits use a quartz crystal to generate a stable frequency. Personal computers use an oscillator circuit to provide the clock frequency—typically 1 to 200 megahertz (MHz)—that drives the processor and other circuits.

Oscilloscope *n.* A test and measurement instrument that provides a visual display for an electrical signal. Most commonly, oscilloscopes are used to create a display of voltage over time. Also called: cathode-ray oscilloscope.

OSF *n.* Acronym for Open Software Foundation. A nonprofit consortium of firms (including DEC, Hewlett-Packard, and IBM), formed in 1988, that promotes standards and specifications for programmes operating under UNIX and licenses software (as source code) to its members. OSF's products include the Distributed Computing Environment, the graphical user interface Motif, and the OSF/1 operating system (a variant of UNIX).

OSI *n.* See ISO/OSI reference model.

OSI protocol stack *n.* The set of protocols based on—and corresponding to—the ISO/OSI reference model.

OSI reference model *n.* See ISO/OSI reference model.

OSPF *n.* Acronym for Open Shortest Path First. A routing protocol for IP networks, such as the Internet, that allows a router to calculate the shortest path to each node for sending messages. The router sends information on the nodes it is linked to, called link-state advertisements, to other routers on the network to accumulate link-state information to make its calculations. See also communications protocol, node (definition 2), path (definition 1), router.

OS X *n.* See Mac OS X.

OTOH *n.* Acronym for on the other hand. A shorthand expression often used in e-mail, Internet news, and discussion groups.

Outbox *n.* In many e-mail applications, the default mailbox where the programme stores outgoing messages. See also e-mail(definition 1), mailbox.

Outdent *n.* See hanging indent.

Outer join *n.* In database management, an operator in relational algebra. An outer join performs an extended join operation in which the tuples (rows) in one relation (table) that have no counterpart in the second relation appear in the resulting relation concatenated with all null values.

Outline font *n.* A font (type design) stored in a computer or printer as a set of outlines for drawing each of the alphabetic and other characters in a character set. Outline fonts are templates rather than actual patterns of dots and are scaled up or down to match a particular type size. Such fonts are most often used for printing, as is the case with most PostScript fonts on a PostScript-compatible laser printer and TrueType fonts.

Outlook *n.* Microsoft's messaging and collaboration application software. A member of the Microsoft Office suite, Outlook includes e-mail, an integrated calendar, and contact-management and task-management features, and it also provides support for building customised tools, such as special-purpose forms, for collaborative functions.

Out-of-band signaling *n.* Transmission of some signals, such as control information, on frequencies outside the bandwidth available for voice or data transfer on a communications channel.

Output 1 *n.* The results of processing, whether sent to the screen or printer, stored on disk as a file, or sent to another computer in a network.

Output 2 *vb.* To send out data by a computer or sound by a speaker.

Output area *n.* See output buffer.

Output-bound *n.* See input/output-bound.

Output buffer *n.* A portion of memory set aside for temporary storage of information, leaving main memory for storage, display, printing, or transmission. See also buffer.

Output channel *n.* See channel (definition 1), input/output channel.

Output simulation *n.* A feature of colour management applications in which a computer display is calibrated to help predict the results of printing a graphics file on a specific device. Also called: soft proofing.

Output stream *n.* A flow of information that leaves a computer system and is associated with a particular task or destination. In programming, an output stream can be a series of characters sent from the computer's memory to a display or to a disk file.

Outsourcing *n.* The assignment of tasks to independent contractors, such as individual consultants or service bureaus.

Tasks such as data entry and programming are often performed via outsourcing.

OverDrive *n.* A type of microprocessor from Intel designed to replace a computer's existing i486SX or i486DX microprocessor. The OverDrive is functionally identical to Intel's i486DX2 microprocessor, but it is an end-user product, whereas the i486DX2 is sold only to computer manufacturers who build it into their own systems. Upgrading a system with an OverDrive processor differs from system to system, and some systems might not be able to support an OverDrive processor. See also i486DX, i486SL, i486SX, microprocessor.

Overflow *n.* 1. Generally, the condition that occurs when data resulting from input or processing requires more bits than have been provided in hardware or software to store the data. Examples of overflow include a floating-point operation whose result is too large for the number of bits allowed for the exponent, a string that exceeds the bounds of the array allocated for it, and an integer operation whose result contains too many bits for the register into which it is to be stored. See also overflow error. 2. The part of a data item that cannot be stored because the data exceeds the capacity of the available data structure.

Overflow error *n.* An error that arises when a number, often the result of an arithmetic operation, is too large to be contained in the data structure that a programme provides for it.

Overhead *n.* Work or information that provides support—possibly critical support—for a computing process but is not an intrinsic part of the operation or data. Overhead often adds to processing time but is generally necessary.

Overlaid windows *n.* See cascading windows.

Overlapped communication operation *n.* The performance of two distinct communication operations simultaneously; for example, a simultaneous read/write operation. Windows CE does not support overlapped communication operation, but it does support multiple read/writes pending on a device.

Overlay 1 *n.* 1. A section of a programme designed to reside on a designated storage device, such as a disk, and to be loaded into memory when needed, usually overwriting one or more overlays already in memory. Use of overlays allows large programmes to fit into a limited amount of memory, but at the cost of speed. 2. A printed form positioned over a screen, tablet, or keyboard for identification of particular features. See also keyboard template.

Overlay 2 *vb.* 1. In computer graphics, to superimpose one graphic image over another. 2. In video, to superimpose a graphic image generated on a computer over video signals, either live or recorded.

Overprint *vb.* The process of printing an element of one colour over one of another colour without removing, or knocking out, the material underneath.

Override *vb.* To prevent something from happening in a programme or in an operating system or to initiate another response. For example, a user can often override and thus abort a lengthy sorting procedure in a database programme by pressing the Escape key.

Overrun *n.* In information transfer, an error that occurs when a device receiving data cannot handle or make use of the information as rapidly as it arrives. See also input/output-bound.

Overscan *n.* The part of a video signal sent to a raster display that controls the area outside the rectangle containing visual information. The overscan area is sometimes coloured to form a border around the screen.

Overshoot *n.* The phenomenon in which a system suffers from a time delay in responding to input and continues to change state even after it has reached the desired state. This situation requires that correcting input be made so that the system reaches the desired state. For example, the arm carrying the heads in a hard disk drive might move slightly past the desired track before it stops, requiring another signal to pull it back.

Overstrike *vb.* To type or print one character directly over another so that the two occupy the same space on the page or screen.

Overtype mode *n.* See overwrite mode.

Overwrite mode *n.* A text-entry mode in which newly typed characters replace existing characters under or to the left of the cursor insertion point. Also called: overtype mode, typeover mode.

Overwriting virus *n.* A type of virus that overwrites the host file it has infected, destroying the original data. Also called: overwrite virus.

Oz *n.* A concurrent, object-oriented programming language. communications over the public phone system, including signaling, coding, and circuit characteristics.

P

P2P or P-to-P *n.* An Internet-based networking option in which two or more computers connect directly to each other to communicate and share files without use of a central server. Interest in P2P networking blossomed with the introduction of Napster and Gnutella. See also peer-to-peer architecture, peer-to-peer -communications. Short for Peer-to-Peer.

P3P *n.* Acronym for Platform for Privacy Preferences. An open W3C protocol that allows Internet users to control the type of personal information that is collected by the Web sites they visit. P3P uses User Agents built into browsers and Web applications to allow P3P-enabled Web sites to communicate privacy practices to users before they log on to the Web site. P3P compares the Web site's privacy policies with the user's personal set of privacy preferences, and it reports any disagreements to the user.

P5 *n.* Intel's internal working name for the Pentium microprocessor. Although, it was not intended to be used publicly, the name P5 leaked out to the computer-industry trade press and was commonly used to reference the microprocessor before it was released. See also 586, Pentium.

Pack *vb.* To store information in a more compact form. Packing eliminates unnecessary spaces and other such characters and may use other special methods of compressing data as well. It is used by some programmes to minimise storage requirements.

Package *n.* 1. A computer application consisting of one or more programmes created to perform a particular type of work—for example, an accounting package or a spreadsheet package.

2. In electronics, the housing in which an electronic component is packaged. See also DIP. 3. A group of classes or interfaces and a keyword in the Java programming language. Packages are declared in Java by using the "package" keyword. See also class, declare, interface (definition 1), keyword.

Packaged software *n.* A software programme sold through a retail distributor, as opposed to custom software. See also canned software.

Packed decimal *adj.* A method of encoding decimal numbers in binary form that maximises storage space by using each byte to represent two decimal digits. When signed decimal numbers are stored in packed decimal format, the sign appears in the rightmost four bits of the rightmost (least significant) byte.

Packet *n.* 1. A unit of information transmitted as a whole from one device to another on a network. 2. In packet-switching networks, a transmission unit of fixed maximum size that consists of binary digits representing both data and a header containing an identification number, source and destination addresses, and sometimes error-control data. See also packet switching.

Packet assembler and disassembler *n.* See packet assembler/disassembler.

Packet assembler/disassembler *n.* An interface between non-packet-switching equipment and a packet-switching network. Acronym: PAD.

Packet filtering *n.* The process of controlling network access based on IP addresses. Firewalls will often incorporate filters that allow or deny users the ability to enter or leave a local area network. Packet filtering is also used to accept or reject packets such as e-mail, based on the origin of the packet, to ensure security on a private network. See also firewall, IP address, packet (definition 1).

Packet flooding *n.* A technique employed in a number of DoS (denial of service) attacks in which a flood of packets of data are sent to a target server, overwhelming the computer and rendering it unable to respond to legitimate network requests.

Examples of specific types of packet flooding include smurf attacks and SYN flood attacks. See also DoS, packet, smurf attack, SYN flood.

Packet header *n.* The portion of a data packet that precedes the body (data). The header contains data, such as source and destination addresses and control and timing information, that is needed for successful transmission.

Packet Internet Groper *n.* See ping(definition 1).

Packet sniffer *n.* A hardware and/or software device that examines every packet sent across a network. To work, a packet sniffer must be installed in the same network block as the network it is intended to sniff. Designed as a problem-solving tool to isolate problems degrading network performance, packet sniffers have become security risks on some networks because crackers can use them to capture nonencrypted user IDs, passwords, credit card numbers, e-mail addresses, and other confidential information. See also cracker, packet.

Packet switching *n.* A message-delivery technique in which small units of information (packets) are relayed through stations in a computer network along the best route available between the source and the destination. A packet-switching network handles information in small units, breaking long messages into multiple packets before routing. Although each packet may travel along a different path, and the packets composing a message may arrive at different times or out of sequence, the receiving computer reassembles the original message correctly. Packet-switching networks are considered to be fast and efficient. To manage the tasks of routing traffic and assembling/disassembling packets, such a network requires some intelligence from the computers and software that control delivery. The Internet is an example of a packet-switching network. Standards for packet switching on networks are documented in the International Telecommunication Union (ITU) recommendation X.25.

Packet Switching Exchange *n.* An intermediary switching station in a packet-switching network.

Packet trailer *n.* The portion of a data packet that follows the body (data). The trailer typically contains information related to error checking and correction. See also packet.

Packing density *n.* The number of storage units per length or area of a storage device. Bits per inch is one measure of packing density.

Pack IT *n.* A file format used on the Apple Macintosh to represent collections of Mac files, possibly Huffman compressed. See also Huffman coding, Macintosh.

PAD *n.* See packet assembler/disassembler.

Pad character *n.* In data input and storage, an extra character inserted as filler to use up surplus space in a predefined block of a specified length, such as a fixed-length field.

Padding *n.* In data storage, the addition of one or more bits, usually zeros, to a block of data to fill it, to force the actual data bits into a certain position, or to prevent the data from duplicating a bit pattern that has an established meaning, such as an embedded command.

Paddle *n.* An early type of input device often used with computer games especially for side-to-side or up-and-down movements of an onscreen object. A paddle is less sophisticated than a joystick because it permits the user, by turning a dial, to specify movement along only a single axis. The paddle got its name because its most popular use was to control the onscreen paddles in the simple early video games, such as Pong.

Paddle switch *n.* Any switch that has a wide handle. The large on/off switch on many IBM personal computers is one type of paddle switch.

Page *n.* 1. In word processing, the text and display elements to be printed on one side of a sheet of paper, subject to formatting specifications such as depth, margin size, and number of columns. 2. A fixed-size block of memory. When used in the context of a paging memory system, a page is a block of memory whose physical address can be changed via mapping hardware. See also EMS, memory management unit, virtual memory. 3. In computer graphics, a portion of display memory that contains one complete full-screen image; the internal representation of a screenful of information.

Page banner *n.* A section of a Web page containing a graphic element and text, such as the page title. Page banners are usually displayed at the top of a Web page. Page banners can also be used to link to other Web sites for advertising purposes. Also called: banner.

Page break *n.* The point at which the flow of text in a document moves to the top of a new page. Most word processors automatically place page breaks when the material on the page reaches a specified maximum. By contrast, a "hard" or "manual" page break is a command or a code inserted by the user to force a page break at a specific place in the text. See also form feed.

Paged address *n.* In the 80386, i486, and Pentium paged memory architecture, an address in memory created by combining the processes of segment translation and page translation. In the paged-memory scheme, which requires that the microprocessor's paging feature be enabled, logical addresses are transformed into physical addresses in two steps: segment translation and page translation. The first step, segment translation, converts a logical to a linear address—an address that refers indirectly to a physical address. After the linear address is obtained, the microprocessor's paging hardware converts the linear address to a physical address by specifying a page table (an array of 32-bit page specifiers), a page (a 4-KB unit of contiguous addresses within physical memory) within that table, and an offset within that page. This information collectively refers to a physical address.

Page-description language *n.* A programming language, such as PostScript, that is used to describe output to a printer or a display device, which then uses the instructions from the page-description language to construct text and graphics to create the required page image. Page-description languages are like other computer languages, with logical programme flow allowing for sophisticated manipulation of the output. A page-description language, like a blueprint, sets out specifications (as for fonts and type sizes) but leaves the work of drawing characters and graphics to the output device itself. Because this approach delegates the detail work to the device that produces the output, a page-description language is machine-independent. These abilities come at a price, however. Page-description languages require printers with processing power and memory comparable to, and often exceeding, that of personal computers. Acronym: PDL. See also PostScript.

Paged memory management unit *n.* A hardware unit that performs tasks related to accessing and managing memory used by different applications or by virtual-memory operating systems. Acronym: PMMU.

Page Down key *n.* A standard key (often labeled "PgDn") on most computer keyboards whose specific meaning is different in different programmes. In many cases, it moves the cursor down to the top of the next page or a specific number of lines.

Page fault *n.* The interrupt that occurs when software attempts to read from or write to a virtual memory location that is marked "not present." The mapping hardware of a virtual memory system maintains status information about every page in the virtual address space. A page either is mapped onto a physical address or is not present in physical memory. When a read or write to an unmapped virtual address is detected, the memory management hardware generates the page fault interrupt. The operating system must respond to the page fault by swapping in the data for the page and updating the status information in the memory management unit. See also page (definition 2), swap (definition 2), virtual memory.

Page frame *n.* A physical address to which a page of virtual memory may be mapped. In a system with 4096-byte pages, page frame 0 corresponds to physical addresses 0 through 4095. See also paging, virtual memory.

Page-image buffer *n.* Memory in a page printer used to hold the bit map (image) of a page as the printer's raster image processor builds the page and as the printer produces the page. See also page printer, raster image processor.

Page-image file *n.* A file containing the necessary code for a printer or other display device to create the page or screen image. See also PostScript.

Page-jacking *n.* A deceptive practice that detours Web visitors from legitimate sites generated as search engine results to copycat Web pages, from which they will be redirected to pornographic or other unwanted sites. Page-jacking is accomplished by copying the contents and metatags of a Web page, altering its title and content so that, on search results, it displays before the original, and then submitting the copied page to search engines. When clicking on the link to the copied site, the visitor will instead be redirected to an unwanted and unrelated site. See also metatag.

Page layout *n.* In desktop publishing, the process of arranging text and graphics on the pages of a document. Page-layout programmes excel in text placement and management of special effects applied to text. Although page-layout programmes are generally slower than word-processing programmes, they can perform such advanced tasks as flowing text into complex multicolumn page designs, printing documents in signatures, managing colour separations, and supporting sophisticated kerning and hyphenation.

Page makeup *n.* The assembling of graphics and text on a page in preparation for printing.

Page mode RAM *n.* A specially designed dynamic RAM that supports access to sequential memory locations with a reduced cycle time. This is especially attractive in video RAM, in which each location is accessed in ascending order to create the screen image. Page mode RAM can also improve the execution speed of code because code tends to execute sequentially through memory. See also cycle time, dynamic RAM.

Page orientation *n.* See landscape mode, portrait mode.

Page printer *n.* Any printer, such as a laser printer, that prints an entire page at once. Because page printers must store the entire page in memory before printing, they require relatively large amounts of memory.

Pager *n.* Pocket-sized wireless electronic device that uses radio signals to record incoming phone numbers or short text messages. Some pagers allow users to send messages as well. Also called: beeper.

Page reader *n.* See document reader.

Page setup *n.* A set of choices that affect how a file is printed on the page. Page setup might reflect the size of paper going into the printer, the page margins, the specific pages in the document to be printed, whether the image is to be reduced or enlarged when printed, and whether another file is to be printed immediately after the first file is printed.

Pages per minute *n.* See PPM.

Page Up key *n.* A standard key (often labeled "PgUp") on most computer keyboards whose specific meaning is different in different programmes. In many cases, it moves the cursor up to the top of the previous page or a specific number of lines.

Pagination *n.* 1. The process of dividing a document into pages for printing. 2. The process of adding page numbers, as in a running head.

Paging *n.* A technique for implementing virtual memory. The virtual address space is divided into a number of fixed-size blocks called pages, each of which can be mapped onto any of the physical addresses available on the system. Special memory management hardware (MMU or PMMU) performs the address translation from virtual addresses to physical addresses. See also memory management unit, paged memory management unit, virtual memory.

Paging file *n.* A hidden file on the hard disk that operating systems (such as Windows, Mac OS X, and UNIX) use to hold parts of programmes and data files that do not fit in memory. The paging file and physical memory, or RAM, make up virtual memory. Data is moved from the paging file to memory as needed and moved from memory to the paging file to make room for new data in memory. Also called: swap file. See also virtual memory.

Paint 1 *n.* A colour and pattern used with graphics programmes to fill areas of a drawing, applied with tools such as a paintbrush or a spraycan.

Paint 2 *vb.* To fill a portion of a drawing with paint (colour or a pattern).

Paintbrush *n.* An artist's tool in a paint programme or another graphics application for applying a streak of solid colour to an image. The user can usually select the width of the streak. See also paint programme.

Paint programme *n.* An application programme that creates graphics as bit maps. A paint programme, because it treats a drawing as a group of dots, is particularly appropriate for freehand drawing. Such a programme commonly provides tools for images requiring lines, curves, and geometric shapes but does not treat any shape as an entity that can be moved or modified as a discrete object without losing its identity.

Palette *n.* 1. In paint programmes, a collection of drawing tools, such as patterns, colours, brush shapes, and different line widths, from which the user can choose. 2. A subset of the colour look-up table that establishes the colours that can be displayed on the screen at a particular time. The number of colours in a palette is determined by the number of bits used to represent a pixel. See also colour bits, colour look-up table, pixel.

Palmtop *n.* A portable personal computer whose size enables it to be held in one hand while it is operated with the other hand. A major difference between palmtop computers and laptop computers is that palmtops are usually powered by off-the-shelf batteries such as AA cells. Palmtop computers typically do not have disk drives; rather, their programmes are stored in ROM and are loaded into RAM when they are switched on. More recent palmtop computers are equipped with PCMCIA slots to provide wider flexibility and greater capability. See also handheld PC, PCMCIA slot, portable computer.

PAM *n.* See pulse amplitude modulation.

Panning *n.* In computer graphics, a display method in which a viewing window on the screen scans horizontally or vertically, like a camera, to bring offscreen extensions of the current image smoothly into view.

Pantone Matching System *n.* In graphic arts and printing, a standard system of ink colour specification consisting of a swatch book in which each of about 500 colours is assigned a number. Acronym: PMS. See also colour model.

PAP *n.* 1. Acronym for Password Authentication Protocol. A method for verifying the identity of a user attempting to log on to a Point-to-Point Protocol (PPP) server. PAP is used if a more rigorous method, such as the Challenge Handshake Authentication Protocol (CHAP), is not available or if the user name and password that the user submitted to PAP must be sent to another programme without encryption. 2. Acronym for Printer Access Protocol. The protocol in AppleTalk networks that governs communication between computers and printers.

Paper feed *n.* A mechanism that moves paper through a printer. In laser printers and other page printers, the paper feed is usually a series of rollers that firmly grip and align the paper. In dot-matrix printers, the paper feed is usually a pin feed or tractor feed, in which small pins drag or push paper that has detachable edges punched with sprocket holes. Friction feed is another type of paper feed, in which the paper is gripped between the platen and pressure rollers and pulled by rotation of the platen.

Paperless office *n.* The idealised office in which information is entirely stored, manipulated, and transferred electronically rather than on paper.

Paper-white *adj.* Of, pertaining to, or being a type of monochrome computer monitor whose default operating colours are black text on a white background. Paper-white monitors are popular in desktop publishing and word processing environments because the monitor most closely resembles a white sheet of paper printed with black characters.

Paper-white monitor *n.* A display monitor in which text and graphics characters are displayed in black against a white background to resemble the appearance of a printed page. Some manufacturers use the name to refer to a background that is tinted in a manner corresponding to bonded paper.

Paradigm *n.* An archetypal example or pattern that provides a model for a process or system.

Paragraph *n.* 1. In word processing, any part of a document preceded by one paragraph mark and ending with another. To the programme, a paragraph represents a unit of information that can be selected as a whole or given formatting distinct from the surrounding paragraphs. 2. On IBM and other computers built around the Intel 8088 or 8086 microprocessor, a 16-byte section of memory beginning at a location (address) that can be divided evenly by 16 (hexadecimal 10).

Parallel *adj.* 1. Of or relating to electronic circuits in which the corresponding terminals of two or more components are connected. 2. In geometry and graphics, of, relating to, or being lines that run side by side in the same direction in the same plane without intersecting. 3. In data communications, of, relating to, or being information that is sent in groups of bits over multiple wires, one wire for each bit in a group. See also parallel interface. 4. In data handling, of or relating to handling more than one event at a time, with each event having its own portion of the system's resources. See also parallel processing.

Parallel access *n.* The ability to store or retrieve all of the bits composing a single unit of information, such as a byte or a word (usually two bytes), at the same time. Also called: simultaneous access.

Parallel adder *n.* A logic device that processes the addition of several (typically 4, 8, or 16) binary inputs simultaneously rather than sequentially, as is the case with half adders and full adders. Parallel adders speed processing because they require fewer steps to produce the result.

Parallel algorithm *n.* An algorithm in which more than one portion of the algorithm can be followed at one time. Parallel algorithms are usually used in multiprocessing environments.

Parallel circuit *n.* A circuit in which the corresponding leads of two or more of the circuit components are connected. In a parallel circuit, there are two or more separate pathways between points. The individual components in a parallel circuit all receive the same voltage but share the current load.

Parallel computer *n.* A computer that uses several processors that work concurrently. Software written for parallel computers can increase the amount of work done in a specific amount of time by dividing a computing task among several simultaneously functioning processors. See also parallel processing.

Parallel computing *n.* The use of multiple computers or processors to solve a problem or perform a function. See also array processor, massively parallel processing, pipeline processing, SMP.

Parallel connection *n.* See parallel interface.

Parallel database *n.* A database system involving the concurrent use of two or more processors or operating system processes to service database management requests such as SQL queries and updates, transaction logging, I/O handling, and data buffering. A parallel database is capable of performing a large number of simultaneous tasks across multiple processors and storage devices, providing quick access to databases containing many gigabytes of data.

Parallel Data Structure *n.* See PDS (definition 2).

Parallel execution *n.* See concurrent execution.

Parallel interface *n.* The specification of a data transmission scheme that sends multiple data and control bits simultaneously over wires connected in parallel. The most common parallel interface is the Centronics interface. See also Centronics parallel interface.

Parallel port *n.* An input/output connector that sends and receives data 8 bits at a time, in parallel, between a computer and a peripheral device such as a printer, scanner, CD-ROM, or other storage device. The parallel port, often called a Centronics interface after the original design standard, uses a 25-pin connector called a DB-25 connector that includes three groups of lines: four for control signals, five for status signals, and eight for data. See also Centronics parallel interface, ECP, EPP, IEEE 1284, input/output port.

Parallel printer *n.* A printer that is connected to the computer via a parallel interface. In general, a parallel connection can move data between devices faster than a serial connection can. The parallel interface is preferred in the IBM PC world because its cabling is more standardised than that of the serial interface and because the computer's operating system assumes that the system printer is attached to the parallel port. See also parallel interface.

Parallel processing *n.* A method of processing that can run only on a computer that contains two or more processors running simultaneously. Parallel processing differs from multiprocessing in the way a task is distributed over the available processors. In multiprocessing, a process might be divided up into sequential blocks, with one processor managing access to a database, another analysing the data, and a third handling graphical output to the screen. Programmers working with systems that perform parallel processing must find ways to divide a task so that it is more or less evenly distributed among the processors available.

Parallel server *n.* A computer system that implements some form of parallel processing to improve its performance as a server. See also SMP server.

Parallel transmission *n.* The simultaneous transmission of a group of bits over separate wires. With microcomputers, parallel transmission refers to the transmission of 1 byte (8 bits). The standard connection for parallel transmission is known as the Centronics interface. See also Centronics parallel interface.

Parameter *n.* In programming, a value that is given to a variable, either at the beginning of an operation or before an expression is evaluated by a programme. Until the operation is completed, a parameter is effectively treated as a constant value by the programme. A parameter can be text, a number, or an argument name assigned to a value that is passed from one routine to another. Parameters are used as a means of customising programme operation. See also argument, pass by address, pass by value, routine.

Parameter-driven *adj.* Of, pertaining to, or being a programme or an operation whose character or outcome is determined by the values of the parameters that are assigned to it.

Parameter passing *n.* In programming, the substitution of an actual parameter value for a formal parameter when a procedure or function call is processed.

Parameter RAM *n.* A few bytes of battery-backed CMOS RAM on the motherboards of Apple Macintosh computers. Information about the configuration of the system is stored in parameter RAM. Acronym: PRAM. See also CMOS RAM.

PARC *n.* See Xerox PARC.

Parent/child *adj.* 1. Pertaining to or constituting a relationship between processes in a multitasking environment in which the parent process calls the child process and most often suspends its own operation until the child process aborts or is completed. 2. Pertaining to or constituting a relationship between nodes in a tree data structure in which the parent is one step closer to the root (that is, one level higher) than the child.

Parity *n.* The quality of sameness or equivalence, in the case of computers usually referring to an error-checking procedure in which the number of 1s must always be the same—either even or odd—for each group of bits transmitted without error. If parity is checked on a per-character basis, the method is called vertical redundancy checking, or VRC; if checked on a block-by-block basis, the method is called longitudinal redundancy checking, or LRC. In typical modem-to-modem communications, parity is one of the parameters that must be agreed upon by sending and receiving parties before transmission can take place. See the table. See also parity bit, parity check, parity error.

Table P.1 Types of Parity.

Type	Description
Even parity	The number of 1s in each successfully transmitted set of bits must be an even number.
Odd parity	The number of 1s in each successfully transmitted set of bits must be an odd number.
No parity	No parity bit is used.
Space parity	A parity bit is used and is always set to 0.
Mark parity	A parity bit is used and is always set to 1.

Parity bit *n.* An extra bit used in checking for errors in groups of data bits transferred within or between computer systems. With PCs, the term is frequently encountered in modem-to-modem communications, in which a parity bit is often used to check the accuracy with which each character is transmitted, and in RAM, where a parity bit is often used to check the accuracy with which each byte is stored.

Parity check *n.* The use of parity to check the accuracy of transmitted data. See also parity, parity bit.

Parity error *n.* An error in parity that indicates an error in transmitted data or in data stored in memory. If a parity error occurs in communications, all or part of a message must be retransmitted; if a parity error occurs in RAM, the computer usually halts. See also parity, parity bit.

Park *vb.* To position the read/write head over a portion of a disk that stores no data (and therefore can never be damaged) or beyond the surface of the disk, prior to shutting down the drive, especially in preparation for moving it. Parking can be performed manually, automatically, or by a disk utility programme.

Parrallaxing *n.* A 3-D animation technique, often used by computer game developers, where backgrounds are displayed using different levels of speed to achieve realism. For example, distant levels move at a slower speed than closer levels, thereby giving the illusion of depth. See also animation.

Parse *vb.* To break input into smaller chunks so that a programme can act upon the information.

Parser *n.* An application or device that breaks data into smaller chunks so that an application can act on the information. See also parse.

Partition *n.* 1. A logically distinct portion of memory or a storage device that functions as though it were a physically separate unit. 2. In database programming, a subset of a database table or file.

Partition Boot Sector *n.* The first sector in the system (startup) partition of a computer's bootable hard disk, or the first sector of a bootable floppy disk. On an x86-based computer, the Partition Boot Sector is read into memory at startup by the Master Boot Record. It is the Partition Boot Sector that contains the instructions required to begin the process of loading and starting the computer's operating system. See also Master Boot Record, partition table.

Partition table *n.* A table of information in the first sector of a computer's hard disk that tells where each partition (discrete portion of storage) on the disk begins and ends. The physical locations are given as the beginning and ending head, sector, and cylinder numbers. In addition to these "addresses," the partition table identifies the type of file system used for each partition and identifies whether the partition is bootable—whether it can be used to start the computer. Although it is a small data structure, the partition table is a critical element on the hard disk.

Partnership *n.* The settings on a desktop computer and Windows CE device that allow information to be synchronised, as well as copied or moved between the computer and device. The mobile device can have partnerships with up to two desktop computers. See also synchronisation (definition 6).

Pascal *n.* A concise procedural language designed between 1967 and 1971 by Niklaus Wirth. Pascal, a compiled, structured language built upon ALGOL, simplifies syntax while adding data types and structures such as subranges, enumerated data types, files, records, and sets. See also ALGOL, compiled language.

pASP *n.* See pocket Active Server Pages.

Pass 1 *n.* In programming, the carrying out of one complete sequence of events.

Pass 2 *vb.* To forward a piece of data from one part of a programme to another. See also pass by address, pass by value.

Pass by address *n.* A means of passing an argument or parameter to a subroutine. The calling routine passes the address (memory location) of the parameter to the called routine, which can then use the address to retrieve or modify the value of the parameter. Also called: pass by reference. See also argument, call.

Pass by reference *n.* See pass by address.

Pass by value *n.* A means of passing an argument or a parameter to a subroutine. A copy of the value of the argument is created and passed to the called routine. When this method is used, the called routine can modify the copy of the argument, but it cannot modify the original argument. See also argument, call.

Passivation *n.* In Sun Microsystems's J2EE network platform, the process of "turning off" an enterprise java bean (EJB) by caching it from memory to secondary storage. See also Enterprise JavaBeans, J2EE.

Passive hub *n.* A type of hub used on ARCnet networks that passes signals along but has no additional capability. See also ARCnet.

Passive-matrix display *n.* An inexpensive, low-resolution liquid crystal display (LCD) made from a large array of liquid crystal cells that are controlled by transistors outside of the display screen. One transistor controls an entire row or column of pixels. Passive-matrix displays are commonly used in portable computers, such as laptops and notebooks, because of their thin width. While these displays have good contrast for monochrome screens, the resolution is weaker for colour screens. These displays are also difficult to view from any angle other than straight on, unlike active-matrix displays.

However, computers with passive-matrix displays are considerably cheaper than those with active-matrix screens. Also called: dual-scan display. See also liquid crystal display, supertwist display, transistor, twisted nematic display.

Passive node *n.* A network node that "listens" for transmissions but is not actively involved in passing them along the network; typical of a node on a bus network. See also bus network, node (definition 2).

Passport *n.* A suite of personal identification services from Microsoft that consolidates user names, passwords, and other information. With the Passport single sign-in service, a user enters one name and password at any Passport site on the Internet; after signing in to one Passport site, a user can sign in to others without reentering the information. Passport also provides a server-based wallet service that stores credit card and billing information, a Kids Passport service, and a public-profile service. Passport is one of the foundation services of the Microsoft .NET initiative. See also .NET, .NET My Services, single sign-on, wallet.

Pass-through *adj.* 1. In general, a reference to something that acts as an intermediary between other entities. For example, a pass-through proxy server allows external access to an internal (protected) server by passing requests from the requesting client to the server without allowing direct access. 2. Pertaining to a device or connector that moves a signal or set of signals from the input to the output without making any changes. For example, a peripheral device such as a SCSI adapter might have a pass-through parallel I/O port for connecting a printer through the same connector.

Password *n.* The string of characters entered by a user to verify his or her identity to the network. The system compares the code against a stored list of authorised passwords and users. If the code is legitimate, the system allows the user access at whatever security level has been approved for the owner of the password. Ideally a password is a combination of text, numbers, and punctuation or other characters that cannot be guessed at or easily cracked by intruders.

Password attack *n.* An attack on a computer or network in which a password is stolen and decrypted or is revealed by a password dictionary programme. The compromised password opens the network to the hacker and may also be used to reveal additional network passwords. See also password sniffing.

Password Authentication Protocol *n.* See PAP (definition 1).

Password protection *n.* The use of passwords as a means of allowing only authorised users access to a computer system or its files.

Password shadowing *n.* A security system in which an encrypted password is stored in a separate "shadow" file, and its place is taken by a token representing the password. Password shadowing is used as protection from password attacks. See also password attack, password sniffing.

Password sniffing *n.* A technique employed by hackers to capture passwords by intercepting data packets and searching them for passwords. Also called: packet sniffing.

Paste *vb.* To insert text or a graphic that has been cut or copied from one document into a different location in the same or a different document. See also cut, cut and paste.

Patch 1 *n.* A piece of object code that is inserted in an executable programme as a temporary fix for a bug.

Patch 2 *vb.* In programming, to repair a deficiency in the functionality of an existing routine or programme, generally in response to an unforeseen need or set of operating circumstances. Patching is a common means of adding a feature or a function to a programme until the next version of the software is released.

Path *n.* 1. In communications, a link between two nodes in a network. 2. A route through a structured collection of information, as in a database, a programme, or files stored on disk. 3. In programming, the sequence of instructions a computer carries out in executing a routine. 4. In information processing, such as the theory underlying expert (deductive) systems, a logical course through the branches of a tree of inferences leading to a conclusion. 5. In file storage, the route followed by the operating system through the directories in finding, sorting, and retrieving files on a disk. 6. In graphics, an accumulation of line segments or curves to be filled or drawn.

Path menu *n.* In windowed environments, the menu or drop box used to enter the universal naming convention path to a shared network resource.

Pathname *n.* In a hierarchical filing system, a listing of the directories or folders that lead from the current directory to a file. Also called: directory path.

Pattern recognition *n.* 1. A broad technology describing the ability of a computer to identify patterns. The term usually refers to computer recognition of visual images or sound patterns that have been converted to arrays of numbers. 2. The recognition of purely mathematical or textual patterns.

Pause key *n.* 1. A key on a keyboard that temporarily stops the operation of a programme or a command. The Pause key is used, for example, to halt scrolling so that a multiscreen listing or document can be read. 2. Any key that creates a pause in an operation. For example, many game programmes have a Pause key, often simply the P key, that temporarily suspends the game.

Payload *n.* The effects caused by a virus or other malicious code. The payload of a virus may include moving, altering, overwriting, and deleting files, or other destructive activity. A virus or worm may contain more than one payload, each with a separate trigger.

PB *n.* See petabyte.

PB SRAM *n.* See pipeline burst static RAM.

PBX *n.* Acronym for Private Branch Exchange. An automatic telephone switching system that enables users within an organisation to place calls to each other without going through the public telephone network. Users can also place calls to outside numbers.

PC *n.* 1. A microcomputer that conforms to the standard developed by IBM for personal computers, which uses a microprocessor in the Intel 80x86 family (or compatible) and can execute the BIOS. See also 8086, BIOS, clone, IBM PC. 2. A computer in IBM's Personal Computer line. Also called: IBM PC. See also PC-compatible (definition 1), personal computer.

PC Card *n.* An add-in card that conforms to the PCMCIA specification. A PC Card is a removable device, approximately the same size as a credit card, that is designed to plug into a PCMCIA slot. Release 1 of the PCMCIA specification, introduced in June 1990, specified a Type I card that is 3.3 millimeters thick and is intended to be used primarily as a memory-related peripheral. Release 2 of the PCMCIA specification, introduced in September 1991, specifies both a 5-millimeter-thick Type II card and a 10.5-millimeter-thick Type III card. Type II cards accommodate devices such as modem, fax, and network cards. Type III cards accommodate devices that require more space, such as wireless communications devices and rotating storage media (such as hard disks). See also PCMCIA, PCMCIA slot.

PC Card slot *n.* See PCMCIA slot.

PC-compatible *adj.* Conforming to IBM PC/XT and PC/AT hardware and software specifications, which have been the de facto standard in the computing industry for personal computers that use the Intel 80x86 family or compatible chips. Most PC-compatible computers today are developed outside of IBM; they are still sometimes referred to as clones. Also called: IBM PC. See also 8086, clone, de facto standard, IBM AT, Wintel.

PC-DOS *n.* Acronym for Personal Computer Disk Operating System. The version of MS-DOS sold by IBM. MS-DOS and PC-DOS are virtually identical, although file-names of utility programmes sometimes differ in the two versions. See also MS-DOS.

PC Expo *n.* Annual exposition centering on issues relating to the personal computer industry. PC Expo encompasses product exhibitions and educational events covering a wide range of topics affecting personal computing.

P-channel MOS *n.* See PMOS.

PCI *n.* See PCI local bus.

PCI card *n.* Abbreviation for Peripheral Component Interconnect card. A card that fits into a PCI local bus to add functionality to a PC. Examples of the types of PCI cards available include TV tuner cards, video adapters, and network interface cards. See also card, PCI local bus.

PCI expansion slot *n.* A connection socket for a peripheral designed for the Peripheral Component Interconnect (PCI) local bus on a computer motherboard.

PCI Industrial Computer Manufacturers Group *n.* See PICMG.

PCI local bus *n.* Short for Peripheral Component Interconnect local bus. A specification introduced by Intel Corporation that defines a local bus system that allows up to 10 PCI-compliant expansion cards to be installed in the computer. A PCI local bus system requires the presence of a PCI controller card, which must be installed in one of the PCI-compliant slots. Optionally, an expansion bus controller for the system's ISA, EISA, or Micro Channel Architecture slots can be installed as well, providing increased synchronisation over all the system's bus-installed resources. The PCI controller can exchange data with the system's CPU either 32 bits or 64 bits at a time, depending on the implementation, and it allows intelligent, PCI-compliant adapters to perform tasks concurrently with the CPU using a technique called bus mastering. The PCI specification allows for multiplexing, a technique that permits more than one electrical signal to be present on the bus at one time. See also local bus.

PCIX *n.* 1. Acronym for Peripheral Component Interconnect Extended. A computer bus technology developed by IBM, Compaq, and Hewlett-Packard that allows data to be transferred at greater speeds. PCIX increases the speed of data from 66 MHz to 133 MHz, but it will not run faster than the connected peripherals or computer processor will allow. PCI and PCIX peripherals are compatible with one another. Also called: PCI-X. 2. Acronym for Permission-based Customer

Information Exchange. A framework for the organisation and exchange of information between customer and vendor. PCIX allows different companies to map information into a customer-friendly, permission-based format without changing internal database structures.

PCL *n.* See Printer Control Language.

PCM *n.* See pulse code modulation.

PCMCIA *n.* Acronym for Personal Computer Memory Card International Association. A group of manufacturers and vendors formed to promote a common standard for PC Card–based peripherals and the slot designed to hold them, primarily on laptop, palmtop, and other portable computers, as well as for intelligent electronic devices. PCMCIA is also the name of the standard for PC Cards, first introduced in 1990 as release 1. See also PC Card, PCMCIA slot.

PCMCIA card *n.* See PC Card.

PCMCIA connector *n.* The 68-pin female connector inside a PCMCIA slot designed to hold the 68-pin male connector on a PC Card. See also PC Card, PCMCIA slot.

PCMCIA slot *n.* An opening in the housing of a computer, peripheral, or other intelligent electronic device designed to hold a PC Card. Also called: PC Card slot. See also PC Card, PCMCIA connector.

PC memory card *n.* 1. An add-in circuit card that increases the amount of RAM in a system. See also memory card. 2. A Type I PC Card as specified by PCMCIA. In this context, such a card consists of conventional static RAM chips powered by a small battery and is designed to provide additional RAM to the system. See also PC Card.

PCMIA device *n.* See PC Card.

P-code *n.* See pseudocode.

PCS *n.* See Personal Communications Services.

PCT *n.* 1. Acronym for programme comprehension tool. A software engineering tool that facilitates the process of understanding the structure and/or functionality of computer programmes. 2. Acronym for Private Communications Technology, a protocol standard drafted by Microsoft and submitted to the IETF for consideration. PCT, like the Netscape-designed SSL (Secure Sockets Layer), supports authentication and encryption for securing privacy in Internet communications. 3. Acronym for Personal Communications Technology. An enhanced version of Secure Sockets Layer (SSL).

.pcx *n.* The file extension that identifies bitmapped images in the PC Paintbrush file format.

PC/XT *n.* The second-generation of the original IBM Personal Computer. The IBM PC/XT was introduced in 1983 and was the first of the PC computers to support hard disks. See also IBM PC.

PC/XT keyboard *n.* The keyboard for the PC/XT. Strong, reliable, and equipped with 83 keys, the PC/XT keyboard offers a typist an audible click. See also IBM PC, PC/XT.

PDA *n.* Acronym for Personal Digital Assistant. A lightweight palmtop computer designed to provide specific functions like personal organisation (calendar, note taking, database, calculator, and so on) as well as communications. More advanced models also offer multimedia features. Many PDA devices rely on a pen or other pointing device for input instead of a keyboard or mouse, although some offer a keyboard too small for touch typing to use in conjunction with a pen or pointing device. For data storage, a PDA relies on flash memory instead of power-hungry disk drives. See also firmware, flash memory, handheld PC, PC Card, pen computer.

PDC *n.* See Primary Domain Controller.

PD-CD drive *n.* Short for phase change rewritable disc-compact disc drive. A storage device that combines a CD-ROM drive and a phase change rewritable disc (PD) drive, which can store up to 650 megabytes of data on cartridges of rewritable optical discs. See also phase-change recording.

PDD *n.* Acronym for Portable Digital Document. A graphics file created from a document by QuickDraw GX under Mac OS.

PDDs are stored in a form that is independent of printer resolution; they print at the highest resolution available on the printer used; and they can contain the original fonts used in the document. Therefore, a PDD can be printed by a computer other than the one on which it was created.

.pdf *n.* The file extension that identifies documents encoded in the Portable Document Format developed by Adobe Systems. To display or print a .pdf file, the user should obtain the freeware Adobe Acrobat Reader. See also Acrobat, Portable Document Format.

PDS *n.* 1. Acronym for Processor Direct Slot. An expansion slot in Macintosh computers that is connected directly to the CPU signals. There are several kinds of PDS slots with different numbers of pins and different sets of signals, depending on which CPU is used in a particular computer. 2. Acronym for Parallel Data Structure. A hidden file, located in the root directory of a disk that is shared under AppleShare, that contains access privilege information for folders.

Peachy virus *n.* A virus, first detected in 2001, that was the first to attempt to spread itself through PDF files. The Peachy virus takes advantage of an Adobe Acrobat feature that enables users to embed files in PDF documents. The embedded Peachy virus file infects the computer of a user who downloads the PDF file and then opens the file in Adobe Acrobat.

Peek *vb.* 1. To read a byte from an absolute memory location. Peek commands are often found in programming languages such as Basic that do not normally allow access to specific memory locations. 2. To look at the next character in a buffer associated with an input device without actually removing the character from the buffer.

Peer *n.* Any of the devices on a layered communications network that operate on the same protocol level. See also network architecture.

Peer-to-peer architecture *n.* A network of two or more computers that use the same programme or type of programme to communicate and share data. Each computer, or peer, is considered equal in terms of responsibilities and each acts as a server to the others in the network. Unlike a client/server architecture, a dedicated file server is not required. However, network performance is generally not as good as under client/server, especially under heavy loads. Also called: peer-to-peer network. See also peer, peer-to-peer communications, server.

Peer-to-peer communications *n.* Interaction between devices that operate on the same communications level on a network based on a layered architecture. See also network architecture.

Peer-to-peer network *n.* See peer-to-peer architecture.

Pen-based computing *n.* The process of entering handwritten symbols into a computer via a stylus and pressure-sensitive pad. See also pen computer.

Pen computer *n.* Any of a class of computers whose primary input device is a pen (stylus) instead of a keyboard. A pen computer is usually a smaller, handheld device and has a flat semiconductor-based display such as an LCD display. It requires either a special operating system designed to work with the pen input device or a proprietary operating system designed to work with a specific-purpose device. The pen computer is the primary model for an emerging class of computers known as personal digital assistants (PDAs). See also clipboard computer, PC Card, PDA.

Penguin *n.* Slang for the Linux operating system or a Linux user. The name comes from the penguin character used as the Linux mascot. See also Tux.

Pen plotter *n.* A traditional graphics plotter that uses pens to draw on paper. Pen plotters use one or more coloured pens, either fiber-tipped pens or, for highest-quality output, drafting pens. See also plotter.

Pentium *n.* A family of 32-bit microprocessors introduced by Intel in March 1993 as the successor to the i486. The Pentium family is composed of superscalar, CISC-based microprocessors containing between 3 million (earlier models) and 28 million transistors. They have a 32-bit address bus, a 64-bit data bus, a built-in floating-point unit and memory management unit, built-in caches, and a System Management

Mode (SMM), which provides the microprocessor with the ability to slow or halt some system components when the system is idle or performing non-CPU-intensive tasks, thereby lessening power consumption. The Pentium also employs branch prediction, resulting in faster system performance. In addition, the Pentium has built-in features to ensure data integrity, and it supports functional redundancy checking (FRC). The Pentium II introduced MMX media enhancement support. See also branch prediction, CISC, functional redundancy checking, i486DX, L1 cache, L2 cache, microprocessor, MMX, P5, SIMD, superscalar.

Pentium upgradable *n.* 1. An i486 motherboard capable of being adapted to run a Pentium-class processor. See also i486DX, microprocessor, motherboard, Pentium. 2. A 486 PC that can be upgraded to Pentium class by adding a Pentium processor. See also i486DX.

Perfboard *n.* See breadboard. Short for perforated fiber board.

Performance monitor *n.* A process or programme that appraises and records status information about various system devices and other processes.

Period *n.* The length of time required for an oscillation to complete one full cycle. For an oscillating electrical signal, the period is the time between waveform repetitions. If f is the frequency of oscillation in hertz, and t is the period in seconds, then t = 1/f.

Peripheral *n.* In computing, a device, such as a disk drive, printer, modem, or joystick, that is connected to a computer and is controlled by the computer's microprocessor. Also called: peripheral device. See also console.

Peripheral Component Interconnect *n.* See PCI local bus.

Peripheral power supply *n.* An auxiliary source of electricity used by a computer or a device as a backup in case of a power failure. Acronym: PPS.

Perl *n.* Acronym for Practical Extraction and Report Language. An interpreted language, based on C and several UNIX utilities. Perl has powerful string-handling features for extracting information from text files. Perl can assemble a string and send it to the shell as a command; hence, it is often used for system administration tasks. A programme in Perl is known as a script. Perl was devised by Larry Wall at NASA's Jet Propulsion Laboratory.

Permanent storage *n.* A recording medium that retains the data recorded on it for long periods of time without power. Ink on paper is by far the most widely used permanent storage, but data can be transferred from paper to a computer only with difficulty. Typically, some form of magnetic medium, such as floppy disk or tape, is preferable. Magnetic media are generally accepted as permanent, even though the magnetic fields that encode data in the media tend to fade eventually (in five years or more). See also nonvolatile memory.

Permanent swap file *n.* In Windows, a file composed of contiguous disk sectors used for virtual memory operations. See also swap file, virtual memory.

Permanent virtual circuit *n.* See PVC.

Permission *n.* In a networked or multiuser computer environment, the ability of a particular user to access a particular resource by means of his or her user account. Permissions are granted by the system administrator or other authorised person. Several levels of access can be given: read only, read and write (view and change), or read, write, and delete. Also called: Access permission.

Permission class *n.* A class that defines access to a resource or defines an identity by supporting authorisation checks.

Permission object *n.* An instance of a permission class that represents access rights to resources or identity. A permission object can be used to specify a request, a demand, or a grant of permission.

Permissions log *n.* A file on a network or multiuser computer environment where permissions for users are stored. When a user attempts to access a resource on the system, the permissions log is checked to see whether the user has permission to use it.

Perpendicular recording *n.* A method of increasing storage capacity on magnetic media by aligning the magnetic dipoles, whose orientation determines bit values, in a direction that is perpendicular to the recording surface. Also called: vertical recording.

Per-pixel lighting *n.* A lighting scheme used in 3D computer game rendering and other digital animation applications that calculates proper lighting for every pixel displayed. Per-pixel lighting allows highly realistic lighting effects but requires significant video card capabilities to display properly. Also called: Phong shading.

Per Seat Licensing *n.* A licensing mode that requires a separate Client Access License for each client computer, regardless of whether all the clients access the server at the same time. See also client.

Per Server Licensing *n.* A licensing mode that requires a separate Client Access License for each concurrent connection to the server, regardless of whether there are other client computers on the network that do not happen to connect concurrently.

Persistence *n.* A characteristic of some light-emitting materials, such as the phosphors used in CRTs, that causes an image to be retained for a short while after being irradiated, as by an electron beam in a CRT. The decay in persistence is sometimes called luminance decay.

Persistent client connection *n.* See persistent connection.

Persistent connection *n.* A connection to a client that remains open after a server sends a response. Included in HTTP 1.1 and similar to the Netscape HTTP 1.0 Keep-Alive extension, persistent connections are used to improve Internet efficiency and performance by eliminating the overhead associated with multiple connections. Also called: persistent client connection. See also pipelining (definition 1).

Persistent data *n.* Data that is stored in a database or on tape so that it is retained by the computer between sessions.

Persistent link *n.* See hot link (definition 1).

Persistent storage *n.* Memory that remains intact when the power to a device is turned off, such as ROM. See also memory.

Personal Communications Services *n.* Term used by the United States Federal Communications Commission (FCC) to cover a range of wireless, all-digital communications technologies and services, including cordless phones, voice mail, paging, faxing, and personal digital assistants (PDAs). Personal Communications Services, or PCS, is divided into narrowband and broadband categories. Narrowband, which operates in the 900 MHz band of frequencies, provides paging, data messaging, faxing, and one- and two-way electronic messaging capabilities. Broadband, which operates in the 1850 MHz to 1990 MHz range and is considered the next-generation PCS, enables two-way voice, data, and video communications. The cellular phone technologies known as GSM (Global System for Mobile Communications), CDMA (Code Division Multiple Access), and TDMA (Time Division Multiple Access) are included in the PCS category. Acronym: PCS.

Personal computer *n.* A computer designed for use by one person at a time. Personal computers do not need to share the processing, disk, and printer resources of another computer. IBM PC–compatible computers and Apple Macintoshes are both examples of personal computers. Acronym: PC.

Personal Computer *n.* See IBM PC.

Personal Computer Memory Card International Association *n.* See PCMCIA.

Personal digital assistant *n.* See PDA.

Personal finance manager *n.* A software application designed to assist the user in performing simple financial accounting tasks, such as balancing checkbooks and paying bills.

Personal Handyphone System *n.* A device developed in Japan to act as a cellular phone that can handle phone, FAX, and voice. Acronym: PHS.

Personal identification number *n.* See PIN.

Personal information manager *n.* See PIM.

Personalisation technology *n.* An e-commerce marketing technique in which Web sites and services analyse the interests of individual customers. The e-business then uses this information to deliver services, product offerings, and advertising that match each customer's personal interests.

Personal Web Server *n.* Microsoft applications that allow a computer running the Windows family of operating systems to function as a Web server for publishing personal Web pages and intranet sites. Personal Web Server is available as part of Microsoft Windows NT 4.0 Option Pack (NTOP), Windows 98, and Windows 95 OEM Service Release 2. FrontPage Personal Web Server is available as part of FrontPage 1.1, FrontPage 97, FrontPage 98, and FrontPage 2000.

Perspective view *n.* In computer graphics, a display method that shows objects in three dimensions (height, width, and depth), with the depth aspect rendered according to the desired perspective. An advantage of perspective view is that it presents a more accurate representation of what the human eye perceives.

peta- prefix Denotes 1 quadrillion (1015). In computing, which is based on the binary (base 2) numbering system, peta- has a literal value of 1,125,899,906,842,624, which is the power of 2 (250) closest to 1 quadrillion. Abbreviation: P.

Petabyte *n.* Either 1 quadrillion bytes or 1,125,899,906,842,624 bytes.Abbreviation: PB.

PGA *n.* See pin grid array, Professional Graphics Adapter.

PgDn key *n.* See Page Down key.

PGP *n.* Acronym for Pretty Good Privacy. A programme for public key encryption, using the RSA algorithm, developed by Philip Zimmermann. PGP software is available in unsupported free versions and supported commercial versions. See also privacy, public key encryption, RSA encryption.

PgUp key *n.* See Page Up key.

Phage virus *n.* A destructive virus that affects the Palm operating system (OS). Phage copies itself, overwriting application files and destroying them. Once the first host file is infected, Phage will spread to all available files. Phage may be spread from one Palm device to another by beaming or connection with a docking station. Phage was one of the first viruses created specifically to affect handheld wireless devices and the first to impact the Palm OS.

Phase *n.* A relative measurement that describes the temporal relationship between two signals that have the same frequency. Phase is measured in degrees, with one full oscillation cycle having 360 degrees. The phase of one signal can lead or follow the other by 0 through 180 degrees.

Phase-change recording *n.* In optical media, a recording technique that uses a laser beam focused on a microscopic portion of metallic crystal to alter the reflectiveness of its structure in such a way that the change can be read as a 0 bit or 1 bit, depending on whether the resulting structure reflects or absorbs the laser light. See also PD-CD drive.

Phase encoding *n.* 1. The process of placing digital information on an analog carrier wave while periodically changing the phase of the carrier to increase the bit density of the transmission. See also Manchester coding, phase. 2. A recording technique used with magnetic storage devices in which each data-holding unit is divided into two parts, each of which is magnetised so that it is opposite in polarity to the other.

Phase-locked *adj.* Of, pertaining to, or characteristic of the relationship between two signals whose phases relative to each other are kept constant by a controlling mechanism, such as an electronic device.

Phase modulation *n.* A method of imposing information onto a waveform signal by shifting the phase of the wave to represent information, such as the binary digits 0 and 1. See also phase-shift keying.

Phase-shift keying *n.* A communications method used by modems to encode data that relies on phase shifts in a carrier wave to represent digital information. In its simplest form, phase-shift keying allows the phase of the carrier wave to be in either of two states: shifted 0 degrees or shifted 180 degrees, effectively reversing the phase of the wave. This straightforward phase-shift keying, however, is useful only when each phase can be measured against an unchanging reference value, so a more sophisticated technique called differential phase-shift keying, or DPSK, is used in many modems. In differential phase-shift keying, the phase of the carrier wave is shifted to represent more than two possible states, and each state is interpreted as a relative change from the state preceding it. No reference values or timing considerations are required and because more than two states are possible, more than one binary digit can represent each state. Acronym: PSK. See also phase modulation.

Phoenix BIOS *n.* An IBM-compatible ROM BIOS manufactured by Phoenix Technologies, Ltd. A popular ROM BIOS in many so-called PC clone computers, the Phoenix BIOS was an early leader among the IBM-compatible computers shortly after they began to appear in the marketplace. See also BIOS, ROM BIOS.

Phone connector *n.* An attachment, usually an RJ-11 connector, used to join a telephone line to a device such as a modem.

Phoneline networking *n.* The use of telephone wiring for connecting computers and other devices in a small network, such as a home network. See also HomePNA.

Phoneme *n.* In linguistics, the smallest unit of speech that distinguishes one word sound from another. Phonemes are the elements on which computer speech is based.

Phono connector *n.* An attachment used to connect a device, such as a microphone or a pair of headphones, to a piece of audio equipment or to a computer peripheral or adapter with audio capability.

Phosphor *n.* Any substance capable of emitting light when struck by radiation. The inside surface of a CRT screen is coated with a phosphor that, when excited by an electron beam, displays an image on the screen. See also persistence.

PhotoCD *n.* A digitizing system from Kodak that allows 35mm film pictures, negatives, slides, and scanned images to be stored on a compact disc. Images are stored in a file format called Kodak PhotoCD IMAGE PAC File Format, or PCD. Many photography or film development businesses offer this service. Images stored on a PhotoCD can usually be viewed by any computer with CD-ROM capabilities and the software required to read PCD. Such images can also be viewed using one of a variety of players designed to display images stored on CDs.

Photo cell *n.* See photoelectric device.

Photocomposition *n.* In traditional typesetting, the use of photographic and electronic equipment in laying out and producing a printed page. In desktop publishing, phototypesetters are used to accomplish the same ends. See also phototypesetter.

Photoconductor *n.* A material that exhibits increased conductivity when it is exposed to a source of light. Photoconductors are used in photodetectors, which are used in fiber optics to register light and convert it into electrical pulses. See also fiber optics.

Photo editor *n.* A graphics application used to manipulate an image, such as a scanned photograph, digitally.

Photoelectric device *n.* A device that uses light to create or modulate an electric signal. A photoelectric device uses semiconductor material and falls in one of two categories. In one type (photocell), light falling on the semiconductor generates an electrical current. In another type of device (photosensor), light changes the resistance of the semiconductor material, modulating an applied voltage.

Photolithography *n.* A technique used in the fabrication of integrated circuits. The circuit pattern is drawn, photographed, and reduced to a negative having the desired final size. This negative is called the photomask. Light is passed through the photomask onto a wafer made of semiconductor material that has been coated with a photoresistive material. Where light strikes the photoresistive material, its composition is changed. In the next step, the photoresistive material not affected by light is washed off. Finally, the semiconductor material is exposed to an etching solution that eats away the surface not protected by the photoresistive material, creating the desired circuit pattern on the surface of the wafer. See also photomask, photoresist.

Photomask *n.* A photographic negative image of a circuit pattern used in fabrication of integrated circuits. See also photolithography.

Photonics *n.* Optoelectronic systems that transmit visible light or infrared energy. Photonic systems are used with fiber optic networks and optical circuits. Photonic networks offer dramatic increases in speed and bandwidth, allowing significantly greater amounts of information to be encoded and transmitted than with traditional cabling solutions.

Photorealism *n.* The process of creating images that are as close to photographic or "real-life" quality as possible. In computer graphics, photorealism requires powerful computers and highly sophisticated software and is heavily mathematical. See also ray tracing.

Photoresist *n.* A compound that is used in photolithographic fabrication of integrated circuits and printed circuit boards. When exposed to ultraviolet light through a photomask, the photoresistive material exposed to the light polymerises (hardens); the areas not exposed can be washed away, leaving the pattern of traces on the substrate. Subsequent etching removes areas not protected by the polymerised photoresist.

Photosensor *n.* See photoelectric device.

Photoshop *n.* Adobe software product for digital image editing and enhancement, photo retouching, and colour management of graphic images. Photoshop includes such features as multiple undo, text editing with formatting control, and enhanced colour management and controls. The programme supports numerous Web and graphics file formats and runs on both the Windows and Power Macintosh platforms.

Phototypesetter *n.* A printer similar to a laser printer but capable of resolutions over 2,000 dots per inch. Phototypesetters apply light directly to a photographic film or photosensitive paper. See also photocomposition.

Photovoltaic cell *n.* See solar cell.

PHP *n.* Acronym for PHP: Hypertext Preprocessor. An open source scripting language used with HTML documents to execute server-side interactive functions. PHP runs on all major operating systems and is primarily used with Linux and UNIX Web servers or on Windows servers with add-on software. PHP may be embedded in a Web page and used to access and present database information. An HTML document that contains a PHP script usually has a .php filename extension. Originally PHP stood for "Personal Home Page," with later versions standing for "PHP Hypertext Preprocessor" or simply PHP. The syntax of PHP is fairly simple and very similar to that of Perl, with some aspects of Bourne shell, JavaScript, and C. It can also be regarded as a technology (server-side environment for ported script engines, like ASP).

Phreak 1 *n.* A person who breaks into, or cracks, telephone networks or other secured systems. In the 1970s, the telephone system used audible tones as switching signals, and phone phreaks used homebrew hardware to match the tones and steal long-distance service. See also homebrew.

Phreak 2 *vb.* To break into, or crack, phone networks or computer systems. See also homebrew.

PHS *n.* See Personal Handyphone System.

Physical *adj.* In computing, of, pertaining to, or characteristic of a real, as opposed to a conceptual, piece of equipment or frame of reference.

Physical address *n.* An address that corresponds to a hardware memory location. In simple processors such as the 8088 and the 68000, every address is a physical address. In processors supporting virtual memory, programmes reference virtual addresses, which are then mapped by memory management hardware onto physical addresses. Also called: hardware address. See also memory management unit, paging, virtual memory.

Physical-image file *n.* A hard disk copy of the material to be recorded onto a CD-ROM. Creating a complete copy precludes problems in writing the CD-ROM because of delays in assembling the material from a scattered group of files. See also CD-ROM.

Physical layer *n.* The first, or lowest, of the seven layers in the ISO/OSI reference model for standardising computer-to-computer communications. The physical layer is totally hardware-oriented and deals with all aspects of establishing and maintaining a physical link between communicating computers. Among specifications covered on the physical layer are cabling, electrical signals, and mechanical connections.

Physical memory *n.* Memory actually present in the system, as opposed to virtual memory. A computer might have 64 megabytes of physical RAM but support a virtual memory capacity of 1 gigabyte or more.

Physical network *n.* One of two ways of describing the topology, or layout, of a computer network; the other is logical network. A physical network refers to the actual configuration of the hardware forming a network—that is, to the computers, connecting hardware, and especially the cabling patterns that give the network its shape. Basic physical layouts include the bus, ring, and star topologies. See also bus network, logical network, ring network, star network.

Physical storage *n.* See real storage.

pi *n.* A mathematical constant equal to approximately 3.1415926535897932, describing the ratio of the circumference of a circle to its diameter.

PIC *n.* See programmable interrupt controller.

Pica *n.* 1. With reference to typewriters, a fixed-width type font that fits 10 characters to the linear inch. See also pitch. 2. As used by typographers, a unit of measure equal to 12 points or approximately 1/6 inch. See also point1 (definition 1).

PICMG *n.* Acronym for the PCI Industrial Computer Manufacturers Group. A consortium of more than 350 computer product vendors, this non-profit organisation develops specifications for PCI-based devices, such as the CompactPCI specification. See also CompactPCI.

Pico- prefix Denotes one trillionth (10–12), or, in the British numbering system, one million millionth. Abbreviation: p.

PicoJava *n.* A microprocessor developed by Sun Microsystems, Inc., that executes Java code. See also Java.

Picosecond *n.* One trillionth of a second. Abbreviation: psec.

PICS *n.* See Platform for Internet Content Selection.

.pict *n.* The file extension that identifies graphic images in the Macintosh PICT format. See also PICT.

PICT *n.* A file-format standard for encoding graphical images, both object-oriented and bitmapped. The PICT file format was first used in Macintosh applications, but many PC applications can read the format too. See also bitmapped graphics, object-oriented graphics.

Picture element *n.* See pixel.

Pie chart *n.* A type of graph that presents values as percentages (slices) of a whole (a pie).

Piezoelectric *adj.* Of, pertaining to, or characteristic of crystals that can convert between mechanical and electrical energy. An electric potential applied to a piezoelectric crystal causes a small change in the shape of the crystal. Likewise, physical pressure applied to the crystal creates an electrical potential difference between the surfaces of the crystal.

Piggyback board *n.* A printed circuit board that plugs into another circuit board to enhance its capabilities. A piggyback board is sometimes used to replace a single chip, in which case the chip is removed and the piggyback board is inserted into the empty socket. See also daughterboard.

Pilot *n.* A series of popular handheld personal digital assistants (PDAs) designed by Palm and based on the Palm OS operating system. Palm introduced its first Pilot model in 1996, followed in 1997 by the PalmPilot, and thereafter by a series of other Palm handheld models.

PILOT *n.* Acronym for Programmed Inquiry, Learning or Teaching. A programming language developed in 1976 by John A. Starkweather and designed primarily for creating applications for computer-aided instruction.

PIM *n.* Acronym for personal information manager. An application that usually includes an address book and organises unrelated information, such as notes, appointments, and names, in a useful way.

Pin *n.* A slender prong. Pins are commonly encountered as the contacts protruding from a male connector. Connectors are often identified by the number of pins they have. Other types of pins are the spidery, leglike metal appendages that connect computer chips to sockets on a circuit board or directly to the circuit board.

PIN *n.* Acronym for personal identification number. A unique code number used to gain access to personal information or assets via an electronic device. PINs are used by a variety of electronic services such as automated bank tellers, Internet sites, and wireless phone services.

Pinch roller *n.* A small cylindrical pulley that presses magnetic tape against the drive's capstan to move the tape over the tape machine's heads. See also capstan.

Pinch-roller plotter *n.* A type of plotter, intermediate between drum and flatbed types, that uses hard rubber or metal wheels to hold the paper against the main roller. See also plotter.

Pin-compatible *adj.* Having pins that are equivalent to the pins on another chip or device. A chip, for example, might have different internal circuitry from that used in another chip, but if the two chips use the same pins for input and output of identical signals, they are pin-compatible.

Pine *n.* Acronym for pine is not elm, or for Programme for Internet News and E-mail. One of the most commonly encountered programmes for reading and composing e-mail on character-based UNIX systems. The pine programme was developed as an improved version of elm at the University of Washington.

Pin feed *n.* A method of feeding paper through a printer in which small pins, mounted on rollers on the ends of the platen, engage holes near the edges of continuous-form paper. See also continuous-form paper, paper feed.

Ping1 *n.* 1. Acronym for Packet Internet Groper. A protocol for testing whether a particular computer is connected to the Internet by sending a packet to its IP address and waiting for a response. The name actually comes from submarine active sonar, where a sound signal—called a "ping"—is broadcast, and surrounding objects are revealed by their reflections of the sound. 2. A UNIX utility that implements the ping protocol.

Ping2 *vb.* 1. To test whether a computer is connected to the Internet using the ping utility. 2. To test which users on a mailing list are current by sending e-mail to the list asking for a response.

Ping of Death *n.* A form of Internet vandalism that entails sending a packet that is substantially larger than the usual 64 bytes over the Internet via the ping protocol to a remote computer. The size of the packet causes the computer to crash or reboot. See also packet (definition 2), ping1 (definition 1).

Ping packet *n.* An "are you there" message transmitted by a Packet Internet Groper programme. A ping packet is sent from one node to the IP (Internet Protocol) address of a network computer to determine whether that node is able to send and receive transmissions. Many shareware and freeware ping utilities for PCs are available for download from the Internet. See also ping1 (definition 1), packet1 (definition 1).

Ping pong *n.* 1. In communications, a technique that changes the direction of transmission so that the sender becomes the receiver and vice versa. 2. In information processing and transfer, the technique of using two temporary storage areas (buffers) rather than one to hold both input and output.

Ping-pong buffer *n.* A double buffer in which each part is alternately filled and flushed, resulting in a more or less continuous stream of input and output data. See also ping pong (definition 2).

Pin grid array *n.* A method of mounting chips on boards, preferred for chips with a very large number of pins. Pin grid array packages have pins protruding from the bottom surface of the chip, as opposed to dual in-line packages and leaderless chip carrier packages, which have pins protruding from the edges. Acronym: PGA.

Pink contract *n.* A non-standard addendum to a contract with an Internet service provider (ISP), specifically offering the client the opportunity to send unsolicited commercial e-mail and put up spam-related Web sites. See also spam.

Pinout *n.* A description or diagram of the pins of a chip or connector. See also pin.

PIO *n.* Acronym for Programmed Input/Output (or, less frequently, Processor Input/Output). One of two transfer methods used in moving data between a disk drive and memory. With PIO, the disk controller moves a block of data into the CPU's registers, and the CPU then moves the data to its intended destination. PIO is characteristic of IDE drives. The alternative data-transfer method, direct memory access (DMA), bypasses the CPU and moves data directly between disk and memory. See also Bus, bus mastering, controller.

Pipe *n.* 1. A portion of memory that can be used by one process to pass information along to another. Essentially, a pipe works like its namesake: it connects two processes so that the output of one can be used as the input to the other. See also input stream, output stream. 2. The vertical line character (%) that appears on a PC keyboard as the shift character on the backslash (\) key. 3. In MS-DOS and UNIX, a command function that transfers the output of one command to the input of a second command.

Pipeline burst static RAM *n.* A type of static RAM that uses burst and pipelining technologies to increase the speed at which information can be provided to a computer's CPU. By pipelining requests so that one is being acted upon at the same time the next is getting underway, pipeline burst static RAM, or PB SRAM, can provide information to the CPU at high speed. PB SRAM is used in L2 caches (rapid-response memory dedicated to storing frequently requested data) on computers running at bus speeds of 75 MHz or higher. Acronym: PB SRAM. See also burst (definition 2), L2 cache, pipelining, static RAM.

Pipeline processing *n.* A method of processing on a computer that allows fast parallel processing of data. This is accomplished by overlapping operations using a pipe, or a portion of memory that passes information from one process to another. See also parallel processing, pipe (definition 1), pipelining (definition 3).

Pipelining *n.* 1. A method of fetching and decoding instructions (preprocessing) in which, at any given time, several programme instructions are in various stages of being fetched or decoded. Ideally, pipelining speeds execution time by ensuring that the microprocessor does not have to wait for instructions; when it completes execution of one instruction, the next is ready and waiting. See also superpipelining. 2. In parallel processing, a method in which instructions are passed from one processing unit to another, as on an assembly line, and each unit is specialised for performing a particular type of operation. 3. The use of pipes in passing the output of one task as input to another until a desired sequence of tasks has been carried out. See also pipe (definition 1), pour.

Piracy *n.* 1. The theft of a computer design or programme. 2. Unauthorised distribution and use of a computer programme.

.pit *n.* A file extension for an archive file compressed with PackIT. See also PackIT.

Pitch *n.* A measure, generally used with monospace fonts, that describes the number of characters that fit in a horizontal inch. See also characters per inch, screen pitch.

PivotChart *adj.* A graphical tool in Microsoft Excel or Access that can be used to display data from a list or database in chart form. Based on user-selected information incorporated in an Excel PivotTable report or list, a PivotChart report provides the ability to chart the data interactively—for example, to "pivot" the chart's point of view from product sales by category to product sales by region or by salesperson. See also PivotTable.

PivotTable *adj.* An interactive table in Microsoft Excel or Access that can show the same data from a list or a database in more than one arrangement. A user can manipulate the rows and columns in a PivotTable to view or summarise the information in different ways for purposes of analysis. In Excel, a PivotTable report is the basis for creating a PivotChart report that displays the same data in chart form. See also PivotChart.

Pivot year *n.* In Year 2000 windowing, a date in a 100-year period that serves as the point from which correct dates can be calculated in systems or software that can store only 2-digit years. For example, a pivot year of 1970 means that the numbers 70 through 99 are interpreted as the years 1970 to 1999, and the numbers 00 through 69 as the years 2000 through 2069. See also windowing.

Pixel *n.* Short for picture (pix) element. One spot in a rectilinear grid of thousands of such spots that are individually "painted" to form an image produced on the screen by a computer or on paper by a printer. A pixel is the smallest element that display or print hardware and software can manipulate in creating letters, numbers, or graphics.

Pixel image *n.* The representation of a colour graphic in a computer's memory. A pixel image is similar to a bit image, which also describes a screen graphic, but a pixel image has an added dimension, sometimes called depth, that describes the number of bits in memory assigned to each onscreen pixel.

Pixel map *n.* A data structure that describes the pixel image of a graphic, including such features as colour, image, resolution, dimensions, storage format, and number of bits used to describe each pixel. See also pixel, pixel image.

PJL *n.* See Printer Job Language.

PJ/NF *n.* Acronym for projection-join normal form. See normal form (definition 1).

PKUNZIP *n.* A shareware utility programme that uncompresses files compressed by the PKZIP shareware utility programme. PKUNZIP is generally made available with PKZIP; distribution of PKUNZIP for commercial purposes is not permitted without obtaining permission from its publisher, PKware, Inc. See also PKZIP.

PKZIP *n.* A widely used shareware utility programme for compressing files. Developed by PKware, Inc., in 1989 and available from a wide variety of sources, PKZIP can combine one or more files into a compressed output file having the extension .zip. A companion utility programme, PKUNZIP, is required to uncompress the compressed files. See also PKUNZIP, shareware, utility programme.

PLA *n.* Acronym for programmable logic array. See field-programmable logic array.

Placeholder *n.* 1. A character that masks or hides another character for security reasons. For example, when a user types a password, an asterisk is displayed on the screen to take the place of each character typed. 2. Text or some other element used in an application as an indicator that the user should enter in his or her own text.

Plain Old Telephone Service *n.* See POTS.

Plaintext *n.* 1. Nonencrypted or decrypted text. See also decryption, encryption. 2. A file that is stored as plain ASCII data.

Plain vanilla *adj.* Ordinary; the standard version of hardware or software without any enhancements. For example, a plain vanilla modem might have data transfer capability but no fax or voice features.

.plan *n.* A file in a UNIX user's home directory that is displayed when other users finger that account. Users can enter information into .plan files at their discretion to provide information in addition to that normally displayed by the finger command. See also finger.

Planar *adj.* 1. In computer graphics, lying within a plane. 2. In the fabrication of semiconductor materials, maintaining the original flat surface of the silicon wafer throughout processing, while the chemicals that make up the elements that control the flow of current are diffused into (and beneath) the surface.

Planar transistor *n.* A special form of transistor that is fabricated with all three elements (collector, emitter, and base) on a single layer of semiconductor material. The structure of a planar transistor permits it to dissipate relatively large amounts of heat, making this design suitable for power transistors.

Plasma display *n.* See gas-discharge display.

Plastic leadless chip carrier *n.* See PLCC.

Plastic transistor *n.* A transistor produced entirely from plastic rather than the traditional silicon. A plastic transistor is flexible enough to be embedded in curved surfaces or folded. Production of plastic transistors begins with a thin piece of clear plastic, onto which layers of plastic are printed or sprayed through a mesh. The result is a lightweight, flexible and transparent transistor that can be manufactured in high volumes for a fraction of the cost of silicon transistors. The flexibility and low-cost of plastic transistors make them useful in applications from transparent foldable displays to one-use product containers. See also electronic paper.

Platen *n.* The cylinder in most impact printers and typewriters, around which the paper wraps and against which the print mechanism strikes the paper. The paper bail, a spring-loaded bar with small rollers, holds the paper smoothly against the platen just above the print mechanism.

Platform *n.* 1. The foundation technology of a computer system. Because computers are layered devices composed of a chip-level hardware layer, a firmware and operating-system layer, and an applications programme layer, the bottommost layer of a machine is often called a platform. 2. In everyday usage, the type of computer or operating system being used.

Platform for Internet Content Selection *n.* A specification for rating and labeling Internet content. Originally developed by the World Wide Web Consortium to enable parents, teachers, administrators, and other caretakers to control the material to which children have online access, its use has expanded to include the protection of privacy and intellectual property. PICS is not itself a system for rating Internet content. Rather, it specifies the format conventions to be used by rating systems in devising labels that can be read by PICS-compatible software. Acronym: PICS.

Platform for Privacy Preference Project *n.* See P3P.

Platform for Privacy Preferences *n.* See P3P.

Platform invoke *n.* The functionality provided by the run time to enable managed code to call unmanaged native DLL entry points.

Platter *n.* One of the individual metal data storage disks within a hard disk drive. Most hard disks have from two to eight platters. See also hard disk.

Player *n.* In relation to digital audio, a programme that plays music and other audio files that have been ripped (transferred from a compact disc to a hard disk) and then encoded in a playable format, such as MP3. See also encoder, MP3, ripper.

PlayStation *n.* Sony Corporation's console computer entertainment gaming system. PlayStation 2, the latest version, is a 128-bit system that features a 300-Mhz processor, 32 MB of Direct RDRAM main memory, and a floating-point performance of 6.2 GFLOPS. PlayStation 2 also offers the capability to play CDs and DVDs. See also computer game, console game.

PL/C *n.* A version of the PL/I programming language developed at Cornell University and used on mainframe computers. See also PL/I.

PLCC *n.* Acronym for plastic leadless chip carrier. An inexpensive variation of the leadless chip carrier (LCC) method of mounting chips on boards. Although the two carriers are similar in appearance, PLCCs are physically incompatible with leadless chip carriers, which are made from a ceramic material. See also leadless chip carrier.

PLD *n.* See programmable logic device.

PL/I *n.* Acronym for Programming Language I (One). A programming language developed by IBM (1964–1969), designed to bring together the key features of FORTRAN, COBOL, and ALGOL while introducing such new concepts as condition-based error handling and multitasking. The result of this effort was a compiled, structured language that was so complex that it never gained widespread acceptance. Nevertheless, PL/I is still used in some academic and research environments. See also ALGOL, COBOL, compiled language, FORTRAN.

PL/M *n.* Acronym for Programming Language for Microcomputers. A programming language derived from PL/I and developed in the early 1970s by Intel Corporation for microprocessors. PL/M was used primarily for the creation of operating systems. See also PL/I.

Plot *vb.* To create a graphic or a diagram by connecting points representing variables (values) that are defined by their positions in relation to a horizontal (x) axis and a vertical (y) axis (and sometimes a depth, or z, axis).

Plotter *n.* Any device used to draw charts, diagrams, and other line-based graphics. Plotters use either pens or electrostatic charges and toner. Pen plotters draw on paper or transparencies with one or more coloured pens. Electrostatic plotters "draw" a pattern of electrostatically charged dots on the paper and then apply toner and fuse it in place. Plotters use three basic types of paper handling: flatbed, drum, and pinch roller. Flatbed plotters hold the paper still and move the pen along both x and y axes. Drum plotters roll the paper over a cylinder. The pen moves along one axis while the drum, with the paper attached, moves along the other. Pinch-roller plotters are a hybrid of the two, in which the pen moves only along one axis while the paper is moved back and forth by small rollers.

PL/SQL *n.* Short for Procedural Language Extension to SQL. Oracle's data manipulation language that allows sequenced or grouped execution of SQL statements and is commonly used to manipulate data in an Oracle database. The syntax is similar to the Ada programming language.

Plug *n.* A connector, especially a male connector, one that fits into a socket. See also male connector.

Plug and play *n.* 1. Generally, a reference to the ability of a computer system to automatically configure a device added to it. Plug and play capability exists in Macintoshes based on the NuBus and, since Windows 95, on PC-compatible computers. 2. When capitalised and, especially, when abbreviated PnP, a set of specifications developed by Intel and Microsoft that allows a PC to configure itself automatically to work with peripherals such as monitors, modems, and printers. A user can plug in a peripheral and "play" it without manually configuring the system. A Plug and Play PC requires both a BIOS that supports Plug and Play and a Plug and Play expansion card. Abbreviation: PnP. See also BIOS, expansion board, peripheral.

Plugboard *n.* A board that permits users to control the operation of a device by plugging cables into sockets.

Plug-compatible *adj.* Equipped with connectors that are equivalent both in structure and in usage. For example, most modems having DB-25 connectors on their rear panels are plug-compatible—that is, one can be replaced by another without the cable having to be rewired.

Plug-in *n.* 1. A small software programme that plugs into a larger application to provide added functionality. 2. A software component that plugs into the Netscape Navigator. Plug-ins permit the Web browser to access and execute files embedded in HTML documents that are in formats the browser normally would not recognize, such as many animation, video, and audio files. Most plug-ins are developed by software companies who have proprietary software in which the embedded files are created.

P-machine *n.* See pseudomachine.

PMML *n.* Acronym for Predictive Model Markup Language. An XML-based language that enables sharing of defined predictive models between compliant vendor applications.

PMMU *n.* See paged memory management unit.

PMOS *n.* Acronym for P-channel metal-oxide semiconductor. A MOSFET semiconductor technology in which the conduction channel is formed by the movement of holes (electron "vacancies" created as electrons move from atom to atom) rather than electrons. Because holes move more slowly than electrons do, PMOS is slower than NMOS, but it is also easier and less expensive to fabricate. See also MOS, MOSFET, P-type semiconductor.

PMS *n.* See PANTONE MATCHING SYSTEM.

PNG *n.* Acronym for Portable Network Graphics. A file format for bitmapped graphic images, designed to be a replacement for the GIF format, without the legal restrictions associated with GIF. See also GIF.

PNNI *n.* Short for Private Network-to-Network Interface. A routing protocol used in ATM networks that provides switches with the ability to communicate changes in the network. Through PNNI, switches can be informed of changes to the network as they occur and can then use the information to make appropriate routing decisions. See also ATM.

PnP *n.* See plug and play (definition 2).

PNP *n.* See PNP transistor.

PNP transistor *n.* A type of bipolar transistor in which a base of N-type material is sandwiched between an emitter and a collector of P-type material. The base, emitter, and collector are the three terminals of the transistor through which current flows. In a PNP transistor, holes (electron "vacancies") are the majority of the charge carriers, and they flow from the emitter to the collector. See also N-type semiconductor, P-type semiconductor.

Pocket Active Server Pages *n.* A scaled-down version of the Active Server Pages optimised for server-side Mobile Channels scripting. Acronym: pASP.

Pocket Excel *n.* A scaled-down version of Microsoft Excel for the Pocket PC. See also Microsoft Excel.

Pocket PC *n.* A personal handheld computing device based on specifications designed by Microsoft and running the Microsoft Windows for Pocket PC operating system. Pocket PCs maintain the look of a Windows operating system display screen and offer compact versions of many of the applications that run on Windows-powered personal computers. A number of manufacturers produce Pocket PCs, including Hewlett-Packard, Compaq, and Casio.

Pocket Word *n.* A scaled-down version of Microsoft Word for the Pocket PC. See also Microsoft Word.

Point 1 *n.* 1. A unit of measure used in printing, equal to approximately 1/72 of an inch. Character height and the amount of space (leading) between lines of text are usually specified in points. 2. A single pixel on the screen, identified by its row and column numbers. 3. A location in a geometric form, represented by two or more numbers that constitute its coordinates.

Point 2 *vb.* To move an arrow or other such indicator to a particular item or position on the screen by using direction keys or by maneuvering a pointing device such as a mouse.

Point-and-click *adj.* Enabling a user to select data and activate programmes by using a mouse or other pointing device to move a cursor to a desired location ("point") and pressing a button on the mouse or other pointing device ("click").

PointCast *n.* An Internet service that delivers and displays a personalised set of news articles to individual users. Unlike the World Wide Web and other Internet applications, PointCast is a push technology, where the server automatically uploads data without a specific command from the client. See also server (definition 2).

Point chart *n.* See scatter diagram.

Point diagram *n.* See scatter diagram.

Pointer *n.* In programming and information processing, a variable that contains the memory location (address) of some data rather than the data itself. See also address1 (definition 1), handle (definition 1), mouse pointer, reference1.

Pointing device *n.* An input device used to control an onscreen cursor for such actions as "pressing" onscreen buttons in dialog boxes, choosing menu items, and selecting ranges of cells in spreadsheets or groups of words in a document. A pointing device is often used to create drawings or graphical shapes. The most common pointing device is the mouse, which was popularised by its use with the Apple Macintosh. Other pointing devices include graphics tablets, styluses, light pens, joysticks, pucks, and trackballs. See also graphics tablet, joystick, light pen, mouse, puck, stylus, trackball.

Point listing *n.* A database of popular Web sites categorised by topics of interest and often rated by design and content.

Point of presence *n.* 1. A point in a wide area network to which a user can connect with a local telephone call. 2. A point at which a long distance telephone carrier connects to a local telephone exchange or to an individual user. Acronym: POP.

Point of sale *n.* See POS.

Point-to-point configuration *n.* A communications link in which dedicated links exist between individual origins and destinations, as opposed to a point-to-multipoint configuration, in which the same signal goes to many destinations (such as a cable TV system), or a switched configuration, in which the signal moves from the origin to a switch that routes the signal to one of several possible destinations. Also called: point-to-point connection.

Point-to-point connection *n.* See point-to-point configuration.

Point-to-point message system *n.* In Sun Microsystems's J2EE network platform, a messaging system that uses message queues to store asynchronous, formatted data for coordinating enterprise applications. Each message is addressed to a specific queue, and client applications retrieve messages from the queues. See also asynchronous, J2EE.

Point-to-Point Protocol *n.* See PPP.

Point-to-point tunneling *n.* A means of setting up secure communications over an open, public network such as the Internet. See also PPTP.

Point-to-Point Tunneling Protocol *n.* See PPTP.

Poisson distribution *n.* A mathematical curve often used in statistics and simulation to represent the likelihood of some event occurring, such as the arrival of a customer in a queue, when the average likelihood is known. This distribution, named after the French mathematician S. D. Poisson, is simpler to calculate than the normal and binomial distributions. See also binomial distribution, normal distribution.

Poke *vb.* To store a byte into an absolute memory location. PEEK (read a byte from memory) and POKE commands are often found in programming languages, such as Basic, that do not normally allow access to specific memory locations.

Polar coordinates *n.* Coordinates of the form (r, q) used to locate a point in two dimensions (on a plane). The polar coordinate r is the length of the line that starts at the origin and ends at the point, and q (Greek theta) is the angle between that line and the positive x-axis.

Polarity *n.* The sign of the potential (voltage) difference between two points in a circuit. When a potential difference exists between two points, one point has a positive polarity and the other a negative polarity. Electrons flow from negative to positive; by convention, however, current is considered to flow from positive to negative.

Polarised component *n.* A circuit component that must be installed with its leads in a particular orientation with respect to the polarity of the circuit. Diodes, rectifiers, and some capacitors are examples of polarised components.

Polarising filter *n.* A transparent piece of glass or plastic that polarises the light passing through it; that is, it allows only waves vibrating in a certain direction to pass through. Polarising filters are often used to reduce glare on monitor screens. See also glare filter.

Polish notation *n.* See prefix notation.

Polling *n.* See autopolling.

Polling cycle *n.* The time and sequence required for a programme to poll each of its devices or network nodes. See also autopolling.

Polygon *n.* Any two-dimensional closed shape composed of three or more line segments, such as a hexagon, an octagon, or a triangle. Computer users encounter polygons in graphics programmes.

Polyline *n.* An open shape consisting of multiple connected segments. Polylines are used in CAD and other graphics programmes. See also CAD.

Polymorphism *n.* In an object-oriented programming language, the ability to redefine a routine in a derived class (a class that inherited its data structures and routines from another class). Polymorphism allows the programmer to define a base class that includes routines that perform standard operations on groups of related objects, without regard to the exact type of each object. The programmer then redefines the routines in the derived class for each type, taking into account the characteristics of the object. See also class, derived class, object (definition 2), object-oriented programming.

Pong *n.* The first commercial video game, a table tennis simulation, created by Nolan Bushnell of Atari in 1972.

Pop *vb.* To fetch the top (most recently added) element of a stack, removing that element from the stack in the process.

POP *n.* See point of presence, Post Office Protocol.

POP3 *n.* Acronym for Post Office Protocol 3. This is the current version of the Post Office Protocol standard in common use on TCP/IP networks. See also Post Office Protocol, TCP/IP.

Populate *vb.* 1. To put chips in the sockets of a circuit board. 2. To import prepared data into a database from a file using a software procedure rather than by having a human operator enter individual records.

Pop-under ad *n.* An advertisement on the Internet that appears in a new window in the background, behind the Web site content. Users may be unaware of the presence of pop-under ads until they close foreground windows at the end of a Web session. Pop-under ads may appear in response to a mouse click, a rollover, or after a user has spent a predetermined amount of time at a Web site. See also pop-up ad.

Pop-up ad *n.* An advertisement on the Internet that appears in a new window in the foreground, often whenever a new page is opened within a site. Pop-up ads may appear in response to a mouse click, a rollover, or after a user has spent a predetermined amount of time at a Web site. See also pop-under ad.

Pop-up Help *n.* An online help system whose messages appear as pop-up windows when the user clicks on a topic or area of the screen about which help is desired. Typically, a special form of click, such as clicking the right mouse button or Option-clicking, will activate pop-up Help, if it is available. See also Balloon Help.

Pop-up menu or popup menu *n.* In a graphical user interface, a menu that appears onscreen when a user selects a certain item. Pop-up menus can appear anywhere on the screen and generally disappear when the user selects an item in the menu. Also called: popup.

Pop-up messages *n.* The messages that appear when pop-up Help is used.

Pop-up window *n.* A window that appears when an option is selected. Typically, the window remains visible until the mouse button is released.

Port 1 *n.* 1. An interface through which data is transferred between a computer and other devices (such as a printer, mouse, keyboard, or monitor), a network, or a direct connection to another computer. The port appears to the CPU as one or more memory addresses that it can use to send or receive data. Specialised hardware, such as in an add-on circuit board, places data from the device in the memory addresses and sends data from the memory addresses to the device. Ports may also be dedicated solely to input or to output. Ports typically accept a particular type of plug used for a specific purpose. For example, a serial data port, a keyboard, and a high-speed network port all use different connectors, so it's not possible to plug a cable into the wrong port. Also called: input/output port. 2. port number.

Port 2 *vb.* 1. To change a programme in order to be able to run it on a different computer. 2. To move documents, graphics, and other files from one computer to another.

Port 25 blocking *n.* An anti-spam technique adopted by many ISPs to prevent bulk mailings of unsolicited commercial e-mail. Spammers may try to use SMTP servers to relay a single commercial e-mail to multiple recipients. Port 25 blocking filters prevent this spam distribution method. Although it is a popular remedy for some spam problems, port 25 blocking may cause problems for legitimate users of non-compatible e-mail programmes.

Portable *adj.* 1. Capable of running on more than one computer system or under more than one operating system. Highly portable software can be moved to other systems with little effort, moderately portable software can be moved only with substantial effort, and nonportable software can be moved only with effort similar to or greater than the effort of writing the original programme. 2. Light enough, rugged enough, and free enough of encumbering external connections to be carried by a user.

Portable computer *n.* Any computer designed to be moved easily. Portable computers can be characterised by size and weight. See the table.

Table P.2 Portable Computers.

Type	Approximate weight	Power source	Comments
Trans-portable	15–30 lb.	House current	Sometimes called luggable; usually has floppy and harddrives; standard CRT screen.
Laptop	8–15 lb.	House current or batteries	Can be held on the lap; usually has a floppy drive;uses flat LCD or plasma screen.
Ultralight	2–8 lb.	Batteries or transformer pack	Easy to carry in a briefcase; sometimes uses RAM drive or EPROM instead of floppy or hard drive; thinner models are known as notebook computers.
Handheld	Less than 2 lb.	Batteries or transformer pack	Also called palmtop or palm-sized; can be held in one hand.

Portable Digital Document *n.* See PDD.

Portable Distributed Objects *n.* Software from NeXT, running under UNIX, that supports an object model in which objects to be stored at various locations on a network can be accessed as though they were at a single location. Acronym: PDO.

Portable Document Format *n.* The Adobe specification for electronic documents that use the Adobe Acrobat family of servers and readers. Acronym: PDF. See also Acrobat, .pdf.

Portable executable file *n.* The file format used for executable programmes as well as for files that are linked together to form executable programmes.

Portable keyboard *n.* A portable keyboard for use with personal digital assistants (PDAs), wireless phones with advanced digital features, and other handheld mobile devices. Light, compact, and easy to carry, most portable keyboards fold for convenient storage and connect to the handheld device via a built-in cradle.

Portable language *n.* A language that runs in the same way on different systems and therefore can be used for developing software for all of them. C, FORTRAN, and Ada are portable languages because their implementations on different systems are highly uniform; assembly language is extremely nonportable.

Portable Network Graphics *n.* See PNG.

Portal *n.* A Web site that serves as a gateway to the Internet. A portal is a collection of links, content, and services designed to guide users to information they are likely to find interesting—news, weather, entertainment, commerce sites, chat rooms, and so on. Yahoo!, Excite, MSN.com, and Netscape NetCenter are examples of portals. See also home page (definition 1), Web site.

Port enumerator *n.* In Windows, part of the Plug and Play system that detects I/O ports and reports them to the configuration manager. See also plug and play (definition 2).

Port expander *n.* A hardware mechanism used for connecting several devices to a single port. Although several devices might be connected, only one can use the port at any given moment.

Portmapper *n.* A service used by Remote Procedure Call (RPC) to assign port numbers. RPC doesn't follow the Well-Known Ports port designations, and only Portmapper is assigned a permanent port number. Because hackers may gain access to portmapper communication, various portmapper security tools are often used to prevent theft of information. See also remote procedure call.

Port number *n.* A number that enables IP packets to be sent to a particular process on a computer connected to the Internet. Some port numbers, called "well-known" port numbers, are permanently assigned; for example, e-mail data under SMTP goes to port number 25. A process such as a telnet session receives an "ephemeral" port number when it starts; data for that session goes to that port number, and the port number goes out of use when the session ends. A total of 65,535 port numbers are available for use with TCP, and the same number are available for UDP. See also IP, Simple Mail Transfer Protocol, socket (definition 1), TCP, UDP.

Portrait mode *n.* A vertical print orientation in which a document is printed across the narrower dimension of a rectangular sheet of paper. This is the print mode typical of most letters, reports, and other such documents.

Portrait monitor *n.* A monitor with a screen shape higher than it is wide. The proportions (but not necessarily the size) of the screen are usually the same as for a sheet of 81/2-by-11-inch paper.

Port replicator *n.* A device that enables easy connection of portable computers to less portable devices, such as printers, monitors, and full-sized keyboards. Instead of having to connect each such device individually to a portable computer, a user can plug it permanently into a port replicator and use it simply by plugging the computer into a single socket, also on the port replicator. Port replicators are comparable to docking stations, but without the same capability for expansion and storage. Also called: convenience adapter. See also docking station, port.

POS *n.* Acronym for point of sale. The place in a store at which goods are paid for. Computerised transaction systems, such as those in use at automated supermarkets, use scanners for reading tags and bar codes, electronic cash registers, and other special devices to record purchases at this point.

POSIT *n.* Acronym for Profiles for Open Systems Internetworking Technology. A set of nonmandatory standards for U.S. government network equipment. POSIT, which recognises the prevalence of TCP/IP, is the successor to GOSIP. See also GOSIP, TCP/IP.

Positional notation *n.* In mathematics, a form of notation whose meaning relies in part on the relative location of the elements involved. For example, common numeric notation is positional notation. In the decimal number 34, the position of the numeral 3 signifies three 10s and the position of the numeral 4 signifies four 1s.

POSIX *n.* Acronym for Portable Operating System Interface for UNIX. An Institute of Electrical and Electronics Engineers (IEEE) standard that defines a set of operating-system services. Programmes that adhere to the POSIX standard can be easily ported from one system to another. POSIX was based on UNIX system services, but it was created in a way that allows it to be implemented by other operating systems. See also service (definition 2).

Post 1 *n.* See article.

Post 2 *vb.* 1. To submit an article in a newsgroup or other online conference or forum. The term is derived from the "posting" of a notice on a physical bulletin board. See also newsgroup. 2. To place a file on a server on a network or on a Web site.

POST *n.* See power-on self test.

Posterisation *n.* See contouring.

Postfix notation *n.* A form of algebraic notation in which the operators appear after the operands. Also called: reverse Polish notation.

Postmaster *n.* The logon name (and therefore the e-mail address) of an account that is responsible for maintaining e-mail services on a mail server. When an account holder is having trouble with e-mail, a message to postmaster or "postmaster@machine.org.domain.name" will usually reach a human who can solve the problem.

Post office *n.* The server and associated storage and mail handling services that provide the centralised location for collection and distribution of e-mail over a network.

Post Office Protocol *n.* A protocol for servers on the Internet that receive, store, and transmit e-mail and for clients on computers that connect to the servers to download and upload e-mail. Acronym: POP.

Postprocessor *n.* A device or a software routine, such as a linker, that operates on data manipulated first by another processor. See also back-end processor (definition 2).

PostScript *n.* A page-description language from Adobe Systems that offers flexible font capability and high-quality graphics. The most well-known page-description language, PostScript uses English-like commands to control page layout and to load and scale outline fonts. Adobe Systems is also responsible for Display PostScript, a graphics language for computer displays that gives users of both PostScript and Display PostScript absolute WYSIWYG (what-you-see-is-what-you-get), which is difficult when different methods are used for displaying and printing. See also outline font, page-description language.

PostScript font *n.* A font defined in terms of the PostScript page-description language rules and intended to be printed on a PostScript-compatible printer. PostScript fonts are distinguished from bitmapped fonts by their smoothness, detail, and faithfulness to standards of quality established in the typographic industry. See also PostScript.

Pot *n.* See potentiometer.

Potential *n.* See electromotive force.

Potentiometer *n.* A circuit element that can be adjusted to provide varying amounts of resistance. The twist-knob and slider-type volume controls on many radios and television sets are potentiometers. Also called: pot.

POTS *n.* Acronym for Plain Old Telephone Service. Basic dialup telephone connections to the public switched network without any added features or functions. A POTS line is nothing but a phone line connected to a simple, single-line telephone instrument.

Pour *vb.* To send a file or the output from a programme to another file or to a device using a pipe. See also pipe (definition 1).

Power *n.* 1. In mathematics, the number of times a value is multiplied by itself—for example, 10 to the third power means 10 times 10 times 10. 2. In computing, the electricity used to run a computer. 3. The speed at which a computer performs and the availability of various features. See also computer power.

PowerBook *n.* Any of several computers in the family of portable Macintosh computers made by Apple.

Power conditioning *n.* A feature of uninterruptible power supply (UPS) that removes spikes, surges, sags, and noise from the power supply. Also called: line conditioning.

Power down *vb.* To shut down (a computer); to turn off the power.

Power failure *n.* Loss of electricity, which causes a loss of unsaved data in a computer's random access memory (RAM) if no backup power supply is connected to the machine.

Power Mac *n.* See Power Macintosh.

Power Macintosh *n.* A Macintosh computer based on the PowerPC processor. The first Power Macintoshes, 6100/60, 7100/66, and 8100/80, were unveiled in 1994. Several upgraded versions followed, and in early 1999 the G3, a PowerPC 750, was released. This was followed later in the year with the unveiling of the Power Macintosh G4. The Power Mac G4 uses the PowerPC 7400 processor and features significant boosts in processing speed. The Power Mac G4 uses Apple's Velocity Engine to process information in 128-bit chunks, allowing sustained performance in excess of one gigaflop. Also called: Power Mac. See also PowerPC.

Power management *n.* The regulation of power consumption on a computer, especially a portable battery-operated device such as a laptop. Power management reduces power to certain components, such as the screen and CPU, to use power efficiently and extend battery life. See also ACPI, Advanced Power Management.

Power-on key *n.* A special key on the Apple ADB and Extended keyboards used for turning on a Macintosh II. The Power-on key is marked with a left-pointing triangle and is used in lieu of the on/off switch. There is no Power-off key; the system is shut down by choosing the Shut Down command from the Special menu.

Power-on self test *n.* A set of routines stored in a computer's read-only memory (ROM) that tests various system components such as RAM, the disk drives, and the keyboard to see whether they are properly connected and operating. If problems are found, these routines alert the user by sounding a series of beeps or displaying a message, often accompanied by a diagnostic numeric value, to the standard output or standard error device (usually the screen). If the power-on self test is successful, it passes control to the system's bootstrap loader. Acronym: POST. See also bootstrap loader.

PowerPC *n.* A microprocessor architecture developed in 1992 by Motorola and IBM, with some participation by Apple. A PowerPC microprocessor is RISC-based and superscalar, with a 64-bit data bus and 32-bit address bus. It also has separate data and instruction caches, although the size of each varies by implementation. All PowerPC microprocessors have multiple integer and floating-point units. The voltage and operating speed varies with the implementation. Starting with the PowerPC 740, the microprocessors were manufactured with copper, instead of aluminum, for better performance and reliability. See also L1 cache, L2 cache, microprocessor, RISC, superscalar.

PowerPC Platform *n.* A platform developed by IBM, Apple, and Motorola based on the 601 and later chips. This platform supports the use of multiple operating systems such as Mac OS, Windows NT, and AIX as well as software designed for those individual operating systems. Acronym: PPCP.

PowerPC Reference Platform *n.* An open system standard developed by IBM. IBM's goal in designing the PowerPC Reference Platform was to ensure compatibility among PowerPC systems built by different companies. Apple's PowerPC Macintoshes are not yet compliant with the PowerPC Reference Platform, but future versions are expected to be.

Acronym: PReP. See also Common Hardware Reference Platform, open system, PowerPC.

PowerPoint *n.* Microsoft's presentation software. PowerPoint includes text-editing and graphics tools that can create slides for public presentations. The presentations can be printed, projected, displayed on a monitor, or, in the version included with Office 2000, saved and published as Web pages.

Power supply *n.* An electrical device that transforms standard wall outlet electricity (115–120 VAC in the United States) into the lower voltages (typically 5 to 12 volts DC) required by computer systems. Personal computer power supplies are rated by wattage; they usually range from about 90 watts at the low end to 250 watts at the high end.

Power surge *n.* See surge.

Power up *vb.* To start up a computer; to begin a cold boot procedure; to turn on the power.

Power user *n.* A person adept with computers, particularly on an applications-oriented level rather than on a programming level. A power user is someone who knows a considerable amount about computers and is comfortable enough with applications to be able to work with their most sophisticated features.

PPCP *n.* See PowerPC Platform.

PPM or ppm *n.* 1. Acronym for pages per minute. A rating of a printer's output capacity—that is, the number of printed pages the printer can produce in one minute. A printer's PPM rating is usually provided by the manufacturer and is based on a "normal" page. Pages with excessive graphics or fonts may reduce a printer's PPM rate dramatically. 2. See pulse position modulation.

PPP *n.* Acronym for Point-to-Point Protocol. A widely used data link protocol for transmitting TCP/IP packets over dial-up telephone connections, such as between a computer and the Internet. PPP, which supports dynamic allocation of IP addresses, provides greater protection for data integrity and security and is easier to use than SLIP, at a cost of greater overhead. PPP itself is based on a Link Control Protocol (LCP) responsible for setting up a computer-to-computer link over telephone lines and a Network Control Protocol (NCP) responsible for negotiating network-layer details related to the transmission. It was developed by the Internet Engineering Task Force in 1991.

PPPoE *n.* Acronym for Point-to-Point Protocol over Ethernet. A specification for connecting users on an Ethernet network to the Internet through a broadband connection, such as a single DSL line, wireless device, or cable modem. Using PPPoE and a broadband modem, LAN users can gain individual authenticated access to high-speed data networks. By combining Ethernet and Point-to-Point Protocol (PPP), PPPoE provides Internet Service Providers (ISPs) with the ability to manipulate a limited number of IP addresses by assigning an address only when the user is connected to the Internet. PPPoE is an efficient way to create a separate connection for each user to a remote server. When the Internet connection is broken, the IP address becomes available to be assigned to another user.

PPS *n.* See peripheral power supply.

PPTP *n.* Acronym for Point-to-Point Tunneling Protocol. An extension of the Point-to-Point Protocol used for communications on the Internet. PPTP was developed by Microsoft to support virtual private networks (VPNs), which allow individuals and organisations to use the Internet as a secure means of communication. PPTP supports encapsulation of encrypted packets in secure wrappers that can be transmitted over a TCP/IP connection. See also virtual network.

PRAM *n.* Short for parameter RAM. A portion of RAM in Macintosh computers that contains configuration information such as the date and time, desktop pattern, and other control panel settings. See also RAM.

P-rating *n.* Short for performance rating. A microprocessor rating system by IBM, Cyrix, and others, based on throughput in realistic applications. Formerly, microprocessor clock speed was widely used as a method of rating, but it does not account for differing chip architectures or different types of work people do with computers. See also central processing unit, clock (definition 1), microprocessor.

Precedence *n.* In applications, the order in which values in a mathematical expression are calculated. In general, application programmes perform multiplication and division first, followed by addition and subtraction. Sets of parentheses can be placed around expressions to control the order in which they are calculated. See also operator associativity, operator precedence.

Precision *n.* 1. The extent of detail used in expressing a number. For example, 3.14159265 gives more precision—more detail—about the value of pi than does 3.14. Precision is related to, but different from, accuracy. Precision indicates degree of detail; accuracy indicates correctness. The number 2.83845 is also more precise than 3.14, but it is less accurate for pi. 2. In programming, numeric values are often referred to as single-precision or double-precision values. The difference between the two is in the amount of storage space allotted to the value. See also double-precision, single-precision.

Precompiler *n.* A programme that reads in a source file and makes certain changes to prepare the source file for compilation. Also called: preprocessor. See also compiler (definition 2).

Preemptive multitasking *n.* A form of multitasking in which the operating system periodically interrupts the execution of a programme and passes control of the system to another waiting programme. Preemptive multitasking prevents any one programme from monopolising the system. Also called: time-slice multitasking. See also multitasking.

Preferences *n.* A menu choice in many graphical user interface applications that allows the user to specify how the application will act each time it is used. For example, in a word processing application the user may be allowed to specify whether the ruler will appear, whether the document will appear in the same way as it will print (including margins), and other choices. Also called: Options, Prefs.

Prefetch *vb.* Preloading buffering data for a streaming video clip before the clip begins playing. When prefetched data is stored on a computer, the video clip can be played without waiting for the initial buffering that usually occurs with streaming media. See also preroll.

Prefix notation *n.* A form of algebraic notation, developed in 1929 by Jan Lukasiewicz, a Polish logician, in which the operators appear before the operands. For example, the expression (a + b) x (c – d) would be written in prefix notation as x + a b – c d. Also called: Polish notation. See also infix notation, postfix notation.

Premiere *n.* Digital video editing software developed by Adobe Systems. The Premiere user interface uses command menus, windows, and floating pallets to make modifications to video clips. A timeline feature presents a graphic presentation of the length of the individual scenes and the order in which they appear. The editor can modify the edits and preview the results before exporting the file into one of several video formats.

PReP *n.* See PowerPC Reference Platform.

Preprocessor *n.* A device or routine that performs preliminary operations on input before passing it on for further processing. See also front-end processor (definition 1).

Preroll *vb.* Data buffering that occurs before a streaming media clip plays. Preroll time varies depending on available bandwidth and the size of the file being buffered.

Presence technology *n.* An application, such as instant messaging, which finds specific users when they are connected to the network and which may alert interested users to each other's presence. Third-generation wireless networks will integrate presence technology with digital cell phones, PDAs, pagers, and other communications and entertainment devices.

Presentation broadcast *n.* A PowerPoint feature that allows you to run a presentation over the Web. The presentation is saved in HTML format and can contain audio and video. It can also be recorded and saved to be viewed later.

Presentation graphics *n.* The representation of business information, such as sales figures and stock prices, in chart form rather than as lists of numbers. Presentation graphics are used to give viewers an immediate grasp of business statistics and their significance. Common examples are area charts, bar charts, line charts, and pie charts. Also called: business graphics.

Presentation layer *n.* The sixth of the seven layers in the ISO/OSI reference model for standardising computer-to-computer communications. The presentation layer is responsible for formatting information so that it can be displayed or printed. This task generally includes interpreting codes (such as tabs) related to presentation, but it can also include converting encryption and other codes and translating different character sets. See the illustration. See also ISO/OSI reference model.

Presentation Manager *n.* The graphical user interface provided with OS/2 versions 1.1 and later. The Presentation Manager derives from the MS-DOS–based Windows environment and provides similar capabilities. The user sees a graphical, window-oriented interface, and the programmer uses a standard set of routines for handling screen, keyboard, mouse, and printer input and output, no matter what hardware is attached to the system. See also OS/2, Windows.

Pressure-sensitive *adj.* Of or pertaining to a device in which pressing on a thin surface produces an electrical connection and causes an event to be registered by the computer. Pressure-sensitive devices include touch-sensitive drawing pens, membrane keyboards, and some touch screens. See also touch screen.

Pretty Good Privacy *n.* See PGP.

Pretty print *n.* A feature of some editors used in programming that formats code so that it is easier to read and understand when printed. For example, a pretty-print feature might insert blank lines to set off modules or indent nested routines to make them easier to spot. See also code(definition 1), editor, module (definition 1), routine.

Preventive maintenance *n.* Routine servicing of hardware intended to keep equipment in good operating condition and to find and correct problems before they develop into severe malfunctions.

Preview *n.* In word processors and other applications, the feature that formats a document for printing but displays it on the video monitor rather than sending it directly to the printer.

PRI *n.* Acronym for Primary Rate Interface. One of two ISDN transmission rate services (the other is the basic rate interface, BRI). PRI has two variations. The first, which operates at 1.536 Mbps, transmits data over 23 B channels and sends signaling information at 64 Kbps over one D channel in the United States, Canada, and Japan. The second, which operates at 1.984 Mbps, transmits data over 30 B channels and sends signaling information at 64 Kbps over one D channel in Europe and Australia. See also BRI, ISDN.

Primary channel *n.* The data-transmission channel in a communications device, such as a modem.

Primary Domain Controller *n.* 1. In Windows NT, a database providing a centralised administration site for resources and user accounts. The database allows users to log onto the domain, rather than onto a specific host machine. A separate account database keeps track of the machines in the domain and allocates the domain's resources to users. 2. In any local area network, the server that maintains the master copy of the domain's user accounts database and that validates logon requests. Acronym: PDC.

Primary key *n.* In databases, the key field that serves as the unique identifier of a specific tuple (row) in a relation (database table). Also called: major key. See also alternate key (definition 1), candidate key.

Primary Rate Interface *n.* See PRI.

Primary storage *n.* Random access memory (RAM); the main general-purpose storage region to which the microprocessor has direct access. A computer's other storage options, such as disks and tape, are called secondary storage or (sometimes) backing storage.

Primitive *n.* 1. In computer graphics, a shape, such as a line, circle, curve, or polygon, that can be drawn, stored, and manipulated as a discrete entity by a graphics programme. A primitive is one of the elements from which a large graphic design is created. 2. In programming, a fundamental element in a language that can be used to create larger procedures that do the work a programmer wants to do.

Print *vb.* In computing, to send information to a printer. The word is also sometimes used in the sense of "show me" or "copy this." For example, the PRINT statement in Basic causes output to be displayed (printed) on the screen. Similarly, an application programme that can be told to print a file to disk interprets the command as an instruction to route output to a disk file instead of to a printer.

Print buffer *n.* A section of memory to which print output can be sent for temporary storage until the printer is ready to handle it. A print buffer can exist in a computer's random access memory (RAM), in the printer, in a separate unit between the computer and the printer, or on disk. Regardless of its location, the function of a print buffer is to free the computer for other tasks by taking print output at high speed from the computer and passing it along at the much slower rate required by the printer. Print buffers vary in sophistication: some simply hold the next few characters to be printed, and others can queue, reprint, or delete documents sent for printing.

Printed circuit board *n.* A flat board made of nonconducting material, such as plastic or fiberglass, on which chips and other electronic components are mounted, usually in predrilled holes designed to hold them. The component holes are connected electrically by predefined conductive metal pathways that are printed on the surface of the board. The metal leads protruding from the electronic components are soldered to the conductive metal pathways to form a connection. A printed circuit board should be held by the edges and protected from dirt and static electricity to avoid damage.

Printer *n.* A computer peripheral that puts text or a computer-generated image on paper or on another medium, such as a transparency film. Printers can be categorised in any of several ways: impact versus nonimpact; print technology; character formation; method of transmission; method of printing; print capability; and print quality.

- Impact versus nonimpact The most common distinction is impact versus nonimpact. Impact printers physically strike the paper and are exemplified by pin dot-matrix printers and daisy-wheel printers; nonimpact printers include every other type of print mechanism, including laser, ink-jet, and thermal printers.
- Print technology Chief among types of print technology are pin dot-matrix, ink-jet, laser, thermal, and (although somewhat outdated) daisy-wheel or thimble printers. Pin dot-matrix printers can be further classified by the number of pins in the print head: 9, 18, 24, and so on.
- Character formation Fully formed characters made of continuous lines (such as those produced by a daisy-wheel printer) versus dot-matrix characters composed of patterns of dots (such as those produced by standard dot-matrix, ink-jet, and thermal printers). Laser printers, while technically dot-matrix are generally considered to produce fully formed characters because their output is very clear and the dots are extremely small and closely spaced.
- Method of transmission Parallel (byte-by-byte transmission) versus serial (bit-by-bit transmission). These categories refer to the means by which output is sent to the printer rather than to any mechanical distinctions. Many printers are available in either parallel or serial versions, and still other printers offer both choices, yielding greater flexibility in installation options.
- Method of printing Character by character, line by line, or page by page. Character printers include standard dot-matrix, ink-jet, thermal, and daisy-wheel printers. Line printers include the band, chain, and drum printers that are commonly associated with large computer installations or networks. Page printers include the electrophotographic printers, such as laser printers.

- Print capability Text-only versus text-and-graphics. Text-only printers, including most daisy-wheel and thimble printers, and some dot-matrix and laser printers, can reproduce only characters for which they have matching patterns, such as embossed type or internal character maps. Text-and-graphics printers—dot matrix, ink-jet, laser, and others— can reproduce all manner of images by "drawing" each as a pattern of dots.
- Print quality Draft versus near-letter quality versus letter quality.

Printer Access Protocol *n.* See PAP (definition 2).

Printer Control Language *n.* A printer control language from Hewlett-Packard, used in its LaserJet, DeskJet, and RuggedWriter printer lines. Because of the LaserJet's dominance in the laser printer market, Printer Control Language has become a de facto standard. Acronym: PCL. Also called: Hewlett-Packard Printer Control Language.

Printer controller *n.* The processing hardware in a printer, especially in a page printer. It includes the raster image processor, the memory, and any general-purpose microprocessors. A printer controller can also reside in a personal computer, attached via a high-speed cable to a printer that simply carries out its instructions.

Printer driver *n.* A software programme designed to enable other programmes to work with a particular printer without concerning themselves with the specifics of the printer's hardware and internal language. Application programmes can communicate properly with a variety of printers by using printer drivers, which handle all of the subtleties of each printer so that the application programme doesn't have to. Today graphical user interfaces offer their own printer drivers, eliminating the need for an application that runs under the interface to have its own printer driver.

Printer engine *n.* The part of a page printer, such as a laser printer, that actually performs the printing. Most printer engines are self-contained, replaceable cartridges. The engine is distinct from the printer controller, which includes all the processing hardware in the printer. The most widely used printer engines are manufactured by Canon.

Printer file *n.* Output that would normally be destined for the printer but has been diverted to a computer file instead. A printer file is created for any of several reasons. For example, it allows output to be transferred to another programme or to another computer. It also allows additional copies to be made at any time by simply copying the print image to the printer. Occasionally, the term printer file is used, incorrectly, to refer to the printer driver.

Printer font *n.* A font residing in or intended for a printer. A printer font can be internal, downloaded, or on a font cartridge.

Printer Job Language *n.* The printer command language developed by Hewlett-Packard that provides printer control at the print-job level. Using PJL commands, you can change default printer settings such as the number of copies to print. PJL commands also permit switching printer languages between print jobs without action by the user. If bi-directional communication is supported, a PJL-compatible printer can send information such as printer model and job status to the print server. Also called: Hewlett-Packard Printer Job Language. Acronym: PJL. See also page-description language, PostScript, Printer Control Language.

Printer port *n.* A port through which a printer can be connected to a personal computer. On PC-compatible machines, printer ports are usually parallel ports and are identified in the operating system by the logical device name LPT. On many newer PCs, the parallel port on the case of the CPU has a printer icon beside it to identify it as a printer port. Serial ports can also be used for some printers (logical device name COM), although configuration is generally required. On Macintoshes, printer ports are usually serial ports and are also used to connect Macs to an AppleTalk network. See also AppleTalk, central processing unit, logical device, parallel port, serial port.

Printer server *n.* See print server.

Print head or printhead *n.* A component of an impact printer that contains the pins or other components that force ink from a ribbon onto paper.

Printing pool *n.* Two or more identical printers that are connected to one print server and act as a single printer. In this case, when you print a document, the print job will be sent to the first available printer in the pool. See also print job, printer.

Print job *n.* A single batch of characters printed as a unit. A print job usually consists of a single document, which can be one page or hundreds of pages long. To avoid having to print individual documents separately, some software can group multiple documents into a single print job. See also print spooler.

Print mode *n.* A general term for the format of print output by a printer. Print modes range from portrait or landscape orientation of the paper to letter quality and size of the print. Dot-matrix printers support two print modes: draft and letter quality (LQ) or near-letter-quality (NLQ). Some printers can interpret both plain text (ASCII) and a page definition language such as PostScript. See also PostScript, printer.

Printout *n.* See hard copy.

Print quality *n.* The quality and clarity of characters produced by a printer. Print quality varies with the type of printer; in general, dot-matrix printers produce lower-quality output than laser printers. The printer mode can also affect quality. See also resolution (definition 1).

Print queue *n.* A buffer for documents and images waiting to be printed. When an application places a document in a print queue, it is held in a special part of the computer's memory, where it waits until the printer is ready to receive it.

Print Screen key *n.* A key on IBM PC and compatible keyboards that normally causes the computer to send a character-based "picture" of the screen contents to the printer. The print screen feature works only when the display is in text mode or CGA graphics mode (the lowest-resolution colour and graphics mode available on IBM compatibles). It will not work properly in other graphics modes. Some programmes use the Print Screen key to capture a screen image and record it as a file on disk. These programmes can typically work in any graphics mode and record the file as a graphics image. When the user is working directly with the MS-DOS operating system, and with some programmes, the combination Control-Print Screen toggles the printer on or off. With printing turned on, the system sends every character to the printer as well as to the screen. The Print Screen key on the Apple Extended Keyboard is included for compatibility with operating systems such as MS-DOS. Also called: PrtSc key.

Print server *n.* A workstation that is dedicated to managing printers on a network. The print server can be any station on the network. Also called: printer server.

Print Server for Macintosh *n.* An AppleTalk network integration service that enables computers running the Macintosh and Windows operating systems to share printers. Also called: MacPrint.

Print spooler *n.* Computer software that intercepts a print job on its way to the printer and sends it to disk or memory instead, where the print job is held until the printer is ready for it. The term spooler is an acronym created from "simultaneous peripheral operations on line."

Print to file *n.* A command in many applications that instructs the programme to format a document for printing and store the formatted document as a file rather than sending it to a printer.

Print wheel *n.* See daisy wheel.

Priority *n.* Precedence in receiving the attention of the microprocessor and the use of system resources. Within a computer, unseen and unnoticed levels of priority are the means by which many different types of potential clashes and disruptions are avoided. Similarly, tasks running on a computer can be assigned priorities that determine when and for how long they receive time from the microprocessor. On networks, stations can be assigned priorities that determine when and how often they can control the communications line, and messages can be assigned priorities that indicate how soon they must be transmitted. See also interrupt.

Priority Frame *n.* A telecommunications protocol developed by Infonet and Northern Telecom, Inc., designed to carry data, facsimile, and voice information.

Privacy *n.* The concept that a user's data, such as stored files and e-mail, is not to be examined by anyone else without that user's permission. A right to privacy is not generally recognised on the Internet. Federal law protects only e-mail in transit or in temporary storage, and only against access by Federal agencies. Employers often claim a right to inspect any data on their systems. To obtain privacy, the user must take active measures such as encryption. See also encryption, PGP, Privacy Enhanced Mail.

Privacy Enhanced Mail *n.* An Internet standard for e mail systems that use encryption techniques to ensure the privacy and security of messages. Acronym: PEM. See also encryption, standard.

Privacy policy *n.* Public statement delineating how a Web site uses the information it gathers from visitors to the site. Some Web sites sell this information to third parties or use the information for marketing purposes. Other sites have strict policies limiting how that information may be used.

Private *adj.* A keyword used in some programming languages to signify that methods or variables can be accessed only by elements residing in the same class or module. See also class, keyword (definition 2), local variable, reserved word, scope.

Private assembly *n.* An assembly that is used by only one application. A private assembly is deployed into the directory structure of the application that uses it. Also called: private side-by-side assembly. See also shared assembly.

Private Branch Exchange *n.* See PBX.

Private channel *n.* In Internet relay chat (IRC), a channel reserved for the use of a certain group of people. Private channel names are hidden from view by the public at large. Also called: secret channel. See also IRC.

Private Communications Technology *n.* See PCT (definition 2).

Private folders *n.* In a shared network environment, those folders on a user's computer that are not accessible by other users on the network.

Private key *n.* One of two keys in public key encryption. The user keeps the private key secret and uses it to encrypt digital signatures and to decrypt received messages. See also public key encryption.

Private line *n.* See dedicated line (definition 1).

Private Network-to-Network Interface *n.* See PNNI.

Privatisation *n.* Generally, the process of turning something over from government to commercial industry control. In the context of computer science and the Internet, the term refers to the government's turning over of various Internet backbones to private industry—for example, control of NSFnet was passed from the government to private business in 1992—and to the government's more recent (1998) privatisation of responsibility for domain names and addresses, which was shifted from IANA and NSI/InterNIC to a new organisation known as ICANN. See also IANA, ICANN, InterNIC.

Privileged instruction *n.* An instruction (usually a machine instruction) that can be executed only by the operating system. Privileged instructions exist because the operating system needs to perform certain operations that applications should not be allowed to perform; therefore, only the operating-system routines have the necessary privilege to execute these particular instructions.

Privileged mode *n.* A mode of execution, supported by the protected mode of the Intel 80286 and higher microprocessors, in which software can carry out restricted operations that manipulate critical components of the system, such as memory and input/output ports (channels). Application programmes cannot be executed in privileged mode; the heart (kernel) of the OS/2 operating system can be, as can the programmes (device drivers) that control devices attached to the system.

Privileges *n.* See access privileges.

PRN *n.* The logical device name for printer. A name reserved by the MS-DOS operating system for the standard print device. PRN usually refers to a system's first parallel port, also known as LPT1.

.pro *n.* One of seven new top-level domain names approved in 2000 by the Internet Corporation for Assigned Names and Numbers (ICANN), .pro is meant for use in Web sites relating to professions such as physicians, accountants, and lawyers. Six of the new domains became available for use in the spring of 2001; negotiations are still underway for the final registry agreement for the .pro domain.

Probability *n.* The likelihood that an event will happen, which can often be estimated mathematically. In mathematics, statistics and probability theory are related fields. In computing, probability is used to determine the likelihood of failure or error in a system or device.

Problem solving *n.* 1. The process of devising and implementing a strategy for finding a solution or for transforming a less desirable condition into a more desirable one. 2. An aspect of artificial intelligence wherein the task of problem solving is performed solely by a programme. See also artificial intelligence.

Procedural language *n.* A programming language in which the basic programming element is the procedure (a named sequence of statements, such as a routine, subroutine, or function). The most widely used high-level languages (C, Pascal, Basic, FORTRAN, COBOL, Ada) are all procedural languages. See also procedure.

Procedural rendering *n.* The rendering of a two-dimensional image from three-dimensional coordinates with texturing according to user-specified conditions, such as direction and degree of lighting.

Procedure *n.* In a programme, a named sequence of statements, often with associated constants, data types, and variables, that usually performs a single task. A procedure can usually be called (executed) by other procedures, as well as by the main body of the programme. Some languages distinguish between a procedure and a function, with the latter (the function) returning a value. See also function, parameter, procedural language, routine, subroutine.

Procedure call *n.* In programming, an instruction that causes a procedure to be executed. A procedure call can be located in another procedure or in the main body of the programme. See also procedure.

Process 1 *n.* A programme or part of a programme; a coherent sequence of steps undertaken by a programme.

Process 2 *vb.* To manipulate data with a programme.

Process-bound *adj.* Limited in performance by processing requirements. See also computation-bound.

Process colour *n.* A method of handling colour in a document in which each block of colour is separated into its subtractive primary colour components for printing: cyan, magenta, and yellow (as well as black). All other colours are created by blending layers of various sizes of halftone spots printed in cyan, magenta, and yellow to create the image. See also colour model, colour separation (definition 1).

Processing *n.* The manipulation of data within a computer system. Processing is the vital step between receiving data (input) and producing results (output)—the task for which computers are designed.

Procmail *n.* An open-source e-mail-processing utility for Linux and other UNIX-based computers and networks. Procmail can be used to create mail servers and mailing lists, filter mail, sort incoming mail, preprocess mail, and perform other mail-related functions.

Prodigy *n.* An Internet service provider (ISP) that offers Internet access and a wide range of related services. Prodigy was founded by IBM and Sears as a proprietary online service, was acquired by International Wireless in 1996, and in 1999 entered into a partnership with SBC Communications. The addition of SBC's Internet customer base made Prodigy the third largest ISP in the United States.

Prodigy Information Service *n.* An online information service founded by IBM and Sears. Like its competitors America Online and CompuServe, Prodigy offers access to databases and file libraries, online chat, special interest groups, e-mail, and Internet connectivity. Also called: Prodigy.

Product *n.* 1. An operator in the relational algebra used in database management that, when applied to two existing relations (tables), results in the creation of a new table containing all possible ordered concatenations (combinations) of tuples (rows) from the first relation with tuples from the second. The number of rows in the resulting relation is the product of the number of rows in the two source relations. Also called: Cartesian product. 2. In mathematics, the result of multiplying two or more numbers. 3. In the most general sense, an entity conceived and developed for the purpose of competing in a commercial market. Although computers are products, the term is more commonly applied to software, peripherals, and accessories in the computing arena.

Production system *n.* In expert systems, an approach to problem solving based on an "IF this, THEN that" approach that uses a set of rules, a database of information, and a "rule interpreter" to match premises with facts and form a conclusion. Production systems are also known as rule-based systems or inference systems. See also expert system.

Professional Graphics Adapter *n.* A video adapter introduced by IBM, primarily for CAD applications. The Professional Graphics Adapter is capable of displaying 256 colours, with a horizontal resolution of 640 pixels and a vertical resolution of 480 pixels. Acronym: PGA.

Professional Graphics Display *n.* An analog display introduced by IBM, intended for use with their Professional Graphics Adapter. See also Professional Graphics Adapter.

Profile 1 *n.* See user profile.

Profile 2 *vb.* To analyse a programme to determine how much time is spent in different parts of the programme during execution.

Profiler *n.* A diagnostic tool for analysing the run-time behaviour of programmes.

Profiles for Open Systems Internetworking Technology *n.* See POSIT.

Program1 *n.* A sequence of instructions that can be executed by a computer. The term can refer to the original source code or to the executable (machine language) version. Also called: software. See also programme creation, routine, statement.

Program2 *vb.* To create a computer programme, a set of instructions that a computer or other device executes to perform a series of actions or a particular type of work.

Programme button *n.* On a handheld device, a navigation control that is pressed to launch an application. Also called: application button.

Programme card *n.* See PC Card, ROM card.

Programme cartridge *n.* See ROM cartridge.

Programme comprehension tool *n.* A software engineering tool that facilitates the process of understanding the structure and/or functionality of computer applications. Acronym: PCT. Also called: software exploration tool.

Programme counter *n.* A register (small, high-speed memory circuit within a microprocessor) that contains the address (location) of the instruction to be executed next in the programme sequence.

Programme creation *n.* The process of producing an executable file. Traditionally, programme creation comprises three steps: (1) compiling the high-level source code into assembly language source code; (2) assembling the assembly language source code into machine-code object files; and (3) linking the machine-code object files with various data files, run-time files, and library files into an executable file. Some compilers go directly from high-level source to machine-code object, and some integrated development environments compress all three steps into a single command. See also assembler, compiler (definition 2), linker, programme.

Programme encapsulation *n.* A method of dealing with programmes with Year 2000 problems that entailed modifying the data with which a programme worked. The input data is modified to reflect a parallel date in the past that the programme can handle. When output is generated, that data is changed again, to reflect the correct date. The programme itself remains unchanged.

Programme file *n.* A disk file that contains the executable portions of a computer programme. Depending on its size and complexity, an application or other programme, such as an operating system, can be stored in several different files, each containing the instructions necessary for some part of the program's overall functioning.

Programme generator *n.* A programme that creates other programmes (usually in source code) based on a set of specifications and relationships given by the user. Programme generators are often used to simplify the task of creating an application. See also 4GL, application generator.

Programme listing *n.* A copy, usually on paper, of the source code of a programme. Some compilers can generate programme listings with line numbers, cross-references, and so on.

Programme logic *n.* The logic behind the design and construction of a programme—that is, the reasons it works the way it does. See also logic error.

Programmable *adj.* Capable of accepting instructions for performing a task or an operation. Being programmable is a characteristic of computers.

Programmable function key *n.* Any of several, sometimes unlabeled, keys on some third-party keyboards that allow the user to "play back" previously stored key combinations or sequences of keystrokes called macros. The same effect can be achieved with a standard keyboard and a keyboard enhancer, the latter of which intercepts the keyboard codes and substitutes modified values; but programmable function keys accomplish this without requiring RAM-resident software.

Programmable interrupt controller *n.* An Intel chip that handles interrupt requests (IRQs). IBM AT machines use two programmable interrupt controllers to accommodate a maximum of 15 IRQs. The programmable interrupt controller has been replaced by the advanced programmable interrupt controller (APIC), which supports multiprocessing. Acronym: PIC. See also IBM AT, IRQ.

Programmable logic array *n.* See field-programmable logic array.

Programmable logic device *n.* A logic chip that is programmed by the customer rather than by the manufacturer. Like a gate array, a programmable logic device consists of a collection of logic gates; unlike a gate array, a programmable logic device need not have its programming completed as part of the manufacturing process. Acronym: PLD. See also logic chip.

Programmable read-only memory *n.* See PROM.

Programme maintenance *n.* The process of supporting, debugging, and upgrading a programme in response to feedback from individual or corporate users or the marketplace in general.

Programmatic interface *n.* 1. A user interface dependent on user commands or on a special programming language, as contrasted with a graphical user interface. UNIX and MS-DOS have programmatic interfaces; the Apple Macintosh and Microsoft Windows have graphical user interfaces. See also command-line interface, graphical user interface, iconic interface. 2. The set of functions any operating system makes available to a programmer developing an application. See also application programming interface.

Programmed Input/Output *n.* See PIO.

Programmed Inquiry, Learning or Teaching *n.* See PILOT.

Programmer *n.* 1. An individual who writes and debugs computer programmes. Depending on the size of the project and the work environment, a programmer might work alone or as part of a team, be involved in part or all of the process from design through completion, or write all or a portion of the programme. See also programme. 2. In hardware, a device used to programme read-only memory chips. See also PROM, ROM (definition 2).

Programmer's switch *n.* A pair of buttons on Macintosh computers that enable the user to reboot the system or to enter a command-line interface at a low level of the operating system. Originally, only programmers testing software were expected to need those functions, so early models of the Macintosh hid the buttons inside the cabinet and supplied a plastic clip that could be attached so that the programmer could push them. In many later models the buttons are built into the cabinet; the button to reboot the system is marked with a triangle pointing leftward, and the other button is marked with a circle.

Programming *n.* The art and science of creating computer programmes. Programming begins with knowledge of one or more programming languages, such as Basic, C, Pascal, or assembly language. Knowledge of a language alone does not make a good programme. Much more can be involved, such as expertise in the theory of algorithms, user interface design, and characteristics of hardware devices. Computers are rigorously logical machines, and programming requires a similarly logical approach to designing, writing (coding), testing, and debugging a programme. Low-level languages, such as assembly language, also require familiarity with the capabilities of a microprocessor and the basic instructions built into it. In the modular approach advocated by many programmers, a project is broken into smaller, more manageable modules—stand-alone functional units that can be designed, written, tested, and debugged separately before being incorporated into the larger programme. See also algorithm, kludge (definition 2), modular design, object-oriented p

Programming language *n.* Any artificial language that can be used to define a sequence of instructions that can ultimately be processed and executed by the computer. Defining what is or is not a programming language can be tricky, but general usage implies that the translation process—from the source code expressed using the programming language to the machine code that the computer needs to work with—be automated by means of another programme, such as a compiler. Thus, English and other natural languages are ruled out, although some subsets of English are used and understood by some fourth-generation languages. See also 4GL, compiler (definition 2), natural language, programme.

Programming Language I *n.* See PL/I.

Programme specification *n.* In software development, a statement of the goals and requirements of a project, as well as the relation of the project to other projects.

Programme state *n.* The condition of a programme (stack contents, memory contents, instruction being executed) at a given moment.

Programme statement *n.* The statement defining the name, briefly describing the operation, and possibly giving other information about a programme. Some languages, such as Pascal, have an explicit programme statement; others do not, or they use other forms (such as the main( ) function in C).

Progressive JPEG *n.* An enhancement to the JPEG graphics file format that gradually displays a photo-realistic picture in a Web browser, showing increasingly detailed versions of the picture until the entire file has finished downloading.

Progressive scanning *n.* 1. A display technique used on computer monitors in which the image is created, line by line, in a single top-to-bottom sweep of the electron gun. The resulting image is of higher quality than is possible with the interlace scanning used for television sets. Progressive scanning might be used on next-generation digital television equipment. It does, however, require twice the signal bandwidth of interlace scanning. 2. A line-by-line (rather than every-other-line) technique used with some video cameras to capture images of moving objects. Such cameras are used primarily for tasks such as monitoring assembly lines and traffic flow.

Project *n.* An operator in the relational algebra used in database management. Given relation (table) A, the project operator builds a new relation containing only a specified set of attributes (columns) of A.

Project 802 *n.* The IEEE project to define networking standards that resulted in the 802.x specifications. See also IEEE, IEEE 802.x.

Project Gutenberg *n.* A project that makes the texts of books that are in the public domain available over the Internet. The files for the books are in plain ASCII, to make them accessible to as many people as possible. Project Gutenberg, based at the University of Illinois at Urbana-Champaign, can be reached at mrcnext.cso.uiuc.edu via FTP or through the Web page http://www.promo.net/pg/. See also ASCII.

Projection-join normal form *n.* See normal form (definition 1).

Project life cycle *n.* A sequence of preplanned stages for taking a project from beginning to end.

Project management *n.* The process of planning, monitoring, and controlling the course and development of a particular undertaking.

Prolog *n.* Short for Programming in Logic. A language designed for logic programming. Prolog evolved during the 1970s in Europe (primarily France and Scotland), and the first Prolog compiler was developed in 1972 by Philippe Roussel, at the University of Marseilles. The language has subsequently attained wide use in the field of artificial intelligence. Prolog is a compiled language that works with the logical relationship between pieces of data rather than mathematical relationships. See also artificial intelligence.

PROM *n.* Acronym for programmable read-only memory. A type of read-only memory (ROM) that allows data to be written into the device with hardware called a PROM programmer. After a PROM has been programmed, it is dedicated to that data, and it cannot be reprogrammed. See also EEPROM, EPROM, ROM (definition 2).

Promiscuous-mode transfer *n.* In network communications, a transfer of data in which a node accepts all packets regardless of their destination address.

PROM programmer *n.* A hardware device that records instructions or data on a PROM (programmable read-only memory) chip or an EPROM (erasable programmable read-only memory) chip. Also called: PROM blaster, PROM blower. See also EPROM, PROM.

Prompt *n.* 1. In command-driven systems, one or more symbols that indicate where users are to enter commands. For instance, in MS-DOS, the prompt is generally a drive letter followed by a greater than symbol (C>). In UNIX, it is usually %. See also command-driven system, DOS prompt. 2. Displayed text indicating that a computer programme is waiting for input from the user.

Propagated error *n.* An error used as input to another operation, thus producing another error.

Propagation *n.* Travel of a signal, such as an Internet packet, from its source to one or more destinations. Propagation of messages over different paths with different lengths can cause messages to appear at a user's computer with varying delivery times. See also propagation delay.

Propagation delay *n.* The time needed by a communications signal to travel between two points; in satellite links, a noticeable delay of between one-quarter second and one-half second, caused by the signal traveling through space.

Propeller head *n.* Slang for a person who is obsessed with computers or other technology; a geek. The name refers to a child's beanie cap topped by a spinning propeller.

Property *n.* In Windows 9x, a characteristic or parameter of an object or device. Properties of a file, for example, include type, size, and creation date and can be identified by accessing the file's property sheet. See also property sheet.

Property sheet *n.* A type of dialog box in Windows 9x, accessed by choosing Properties in the File menu or by right-clicking on an object and selecting Properties, that lists the attributes or settings of an object such as a file, application, or hardware device. A property sheet presents the user with a tabbed, index-card-like selection of property pages, each of which features standard dialog-style controls for customising parameters.

Proportional font *n.* A set of characters in a particular style and size in which a variable amount of horizontal space is allotted to each letter or number. In a proportional font, the letter i, for example, is allowed less space than the letter m.

Proportional spacing *n.* A form of character spacing in which the horizontal space each character occupies is proportional to the width of the character. The letter w, for example, takes up more space than the letter i.

Proprietary *adj.* Of, pertaining to, or characteristic of something that is privately-owned. Generally, the term refers to technology that has been developed by a particular corporation or entity, with specifications that are considered by the owner to be trade secrets. Proprietary technology may be legally used only by a person or entity purchasing an explicit license. Also, other companies are unable to duplicate the technology, both legally and because its specifications have not been divulged by the owner.

Proprietary software *n.* A programme owned or copyrighted by an individual or a business and available for use only through purchase or by permission of the owner.

Protected *n.* A keyword in a programming language (such as Java or C++) used in a method or variable declaration. It signifies that the method or variable can be accessed only by elements residing in its class, subclasses, or classes in the same package. See also class, declaration, method, package, variable.

Protected mode *n.* An operating mode of the Intel 80286 and higher microprocessors that supports larger address spaces and more advanced features than real mode. When started in protected mode, these CPUs provide hardware support for multitasking, data security, and virtual memory. The Windows (version 3.0 and later) and OS/2 operating systems run in protected mode, as do most versions of UNIX for these microprocessors.

Protocol *n.* See communications protocol.

Protocol analyzer *n.* A management tool designed to identify and diagnose computer network problems. A protocol analyzer looks at LAN (local area network) or WAN (wide area network) traffic and finds protocol errors, connection delays, and other network faults. The protocol analyzer can filter and decode traffic, suggest solutions to problems, provide graphical reports, and show traffic by protocol and per cent utilisation. See also communications protocol.

Protocol layer *n.* See layer.

Protocol stack *n.* The set of protocols that work together on different levels to enable communication on a network. For example, TCP/IP, the protocol stack on the Internet, incorporates more than 100 standards including FTP, IP, SMTP, TCP, and Telnet. See also ISO/OSI reference model.

Protocol suite *n.* A set of protocols designed, usually by one vendor, as complementary parts of a protocol stack.

Prototyping *n.* The creation of a working model of a new computer system or programme for testing and refinement. Prototyping is used in the development of both new hardware and software systems and new systems of information management. Tools used in the former include both hardware and support software; tools used in the latter can include databases, screen mockups, and simulations that, in some cases, can be developed into a final product.

Proxy *n.* A computer (or the software that runs on it) that acts as a barrier between a network and the Internet by presenting only a single network address to external sites. By acting as a go-between representing all internal computers, the proxy protects network identities while still providing access to the Internet. See also proxy server.

Proxy server *n.* A firewall component that manages Internet traffic to and from a local area network (LAN) and can provide other features, such as document caching and access control. A proxy server can improve performance by supplying frequently requested data, such as a popular Web page, and can filter and discard requests that the owner does not consider appropriate, such as requests for unauthorised access to proprietary files. See also firewall.

PrtSc key *n.* See Print Screen key.

.ps *n.* The file extension that identifies PostScript printer files. See also PostScript.

PS/2 bus *n.* See Micro Channel Architecture.

PSD *n.* A graphics file format used to create, modify, and display still images in Photoshop, a software application designed by Adobe Systems. PSD files have a file extension of .psd.

PSE *n.* See Packet Switching Exchange.

psec *n.* See picosecond.

Pseudocode *n.* 1. A machine language for a nonexistent processor (a pseudomachine). Such code is executed by a software interpreter. The major advantage of p-code is that it is portable to all computers for which a p-code interpreter exists. The p-code approach has been tried several times in the microcomputer industry, with mixed success. The best known attempt was the UCSD p-System. Abbreviation: p-code. See also pseudomachine, UCSD p-System. 2. Any informal, transparent notation in which a programme or algorithm description is written. Many programmers write their programmes first in a pseudocode that looks much like a mixture of English and their favourite programming language, such as C or Pascal, and then translate it line by line into the actual language being used.

Pseudo compiler *n.* A compiler that generates a pseudolanguage. See also pseudolanguage.

Pseudocomputer *n.* See pseudomachine.

Pseudolanguage *n.* A nonexistent programming language—that is, one for which no implementation exists. The term can refer either to the machine language for a nonexistent processor or to a high-level language for which no compiler exists. See also pseudocode.

Pseudomachine *n.* A processor that doesn't actually exist in hardware but that is emulated in software. A programme written for the pseudomachine can run on several platforms without having to be recompiled. Abbreviation: p-machine. See also pseudocode, UCSD p-System.

Pseudo-op *n.* See pseudo-operation.

Pseudo-operation *n.* In programming, a programme instruction that conveys information to an assembler or compiler but is not translated into a machine language instruction—for example, an instruction that establishes the value of a constant or the manner in which Boolean (logical) expressions are to be evaluated.Abbreviation: pseudo-op.

Pseudo-streaming *n.* A method used for real-time display of audio and video over the Web. Unlike sound or video files that are downloaded to a computer in their entirety before they can be played back, pseudo-streaming enables playback after only a portion of the file—enough to fill a buffer on the receiving computer—has been downloaded. Pseudo-streaming, unlike "true," or Web, streaming, does not depend on server software to dynamically monitor the transmission. It can, however, play back only from the beginning of the file, rather than from any point, as can be the case with true streaming. See also stream.

PSK *n.* See phase-shift keying.

PSN *n.* Acronym for packet-switching network. See packet switching.

PSTN *n.* See Public Switched Telephone Network.

p-system *n.* An operating system based on a pseudomachine implemented in software. A programme written for the p-system is more portable than one written for a machine-dependent operating system. See also UCSD p-System.

P-type semiconductor *n.* Semiconductor material in which electrical conduction is carried by holes ("vacancies" left by electrons). Whether a semiconductor is N-type or P-type depends on the kind of dopant added during manufacture. A dopant with a shortage of electrons results in a P-type semiconductor.

Pub *n.* See /pub.

/pub *n.* Short for public. A directory in an anonymous FTP archive that is accessible by the public and that generally contains files available for free download. See also anonymous FTP.

Public *adj.* A keyword in some programming languages to signify that methods or variables can be accessed by elements residing in other classes or modules. See also class, keyword (definition 2), global variable, reserved word, scope.

Public directory *n.* A directory on an FTP server that is accessible by anonymous users for the purpose of retrieving or storing files. Often the directory is called /pub. See also anonymous FTP, FTP (definition 1), FTP server /pub.

Public domain *n.* The set of all creative works, such as books, music, or software, that are not covered by copyright or other property protection. Works in the public domain can be freely copied, modified, and otherwise used in any manner for any purpose. Much of the information, texts, and software on the Internet is in the public domain, but putting a copyrighted work on the Internet does not put it in the public domain.

Public-domain software *n.* A programme donated for public use by its owner or developer and freely available for copying and distribution.

Public files *n.* Files with no access restrictions.

Public folders *n.* The folders that are made accessible on a particular machine or by a particular user in a shared networking environment.

Public key *n.* One of two keys in public key encryption. The user releases this key to the public, who can use it for encrypting messages to be sent to the user and for decrypting the user's digital signature. See also public key encryption.

Public key cryptography *n.* See public key encryption.

Public key encryption *n.* An asymmetric scheme that uses a pair of keys for encryption: the public key encrypts data, and a corresponding secret key decrypts it. For digital signatures, the process is reversed: the sender uses the secret key to create a unique electronic number that can be read by anyone possessing the corresponding public key, which verifies that the message is truly from the sender. See also private key, public key.

Public rights *n.* In the context of the Internet, the extent to which members of the public are permitted to use (and to place) information on the Internet under intellectual property law. See also fair use, public domain, public-domain software.

Public Switched Telephone Network *n.* The public telephone system.

Publisher *n.* A software application developed by Microsoft Corporation to help businesses create high-quality marketing and business material. A part of the Office product family, Publisher provides business users with design options for a variety of publications, such as newsletters, flyers, brochures, and Web pages.

Publishing point *n.* A publishing point is a virtual directory used for storing content or delivering a live stream. End users reach a publishing point through its URL. There are two types of unicast publishing points: on-demand for stored content and broadcast for live streams. See also on-demand publishing point, broadcast publishing point.

Puck *n.* A pointing device used with a graphics tablet. A puck, which is often used in engineering applications, is a mouselike device with buttons for selecting items or choosing commands and a clear plastic section extending from one end with cross hairs printed on it. The intersection of the cross hairs on the puck points to a location on the graphics tablet, which in turn is mapped to a specific location on the screen. Because the puck's cross hairs are on a transparent surface, a user can easily trace a drawing by placing it between the graphics tablet and the puck and moving the cross hairs over the lines of the drawing. See also graphics tablet, stylus.

Puff and sip device *n.* An assistive computer technology for people with mobility impairments. A puff and sip device is a head-mounted alternative to using a mouse or keyboard. For mouse functionality, the device allows a user to move the mouse pointer without using his or her hands by puffing air into a tube.

Pull *vb.* The process of retrieving data from a network server. See pop.

Pull-down menu *n.* A menu that is pulled down from the menu bar and that remains available as long as the user holds it open.

Pulse *n.* A transient signal, usually brief and with a discrete onset and offset.

Pulse amplitude modulation *n.* A method of encoding information in a signal by varying the amplitude of pulses. The unmodulated signal consists of a continuous train of pulses of constant frequency, duration, and amplitude. During modulation the pulse amplitudes are changed to reflect the information being encoded. See the illustration. Acronym: PAM.

Pulse code modulation *n.* A method of encoding information in a signal by varying the amplitude of pulses. Unlike pulse amplitude modulation (PAM), in which pulse amplitude can vary continuously, pulse code modulation limits pulse amplitudes to several predefined values. Because the signal is discrete, or digital, rather than analog, pulse code modulation is more immune to noise than PAM. Acronym: PCM.

Pulse dialing *n.* See rotary dialing.

Pulse duration modulation *n.* A method of encoding information in a signal by varying the duration of pulses. The unmodulated signal consists of a continuous train of pulses of constant frequency, duration, and amplitude. During modulation, the pulse durations are changed to reflect the information being encoded. See the illustration. Acronym: PDM. Also called: pulse length modulation, pulse width modulation.

Pulse length modulation *n.* See pulse duration modulation.

Pulse position modulation *n.* A method of encoding information in a signal by varying the position of pulses. The unmodulated signal consists of a continuous train of pulses of constant frequency, duration, and amplitude. During modulation, the pulse positions are changed to reflect the information being encoded. See the illustration. Acronym: PPM.

Pulse width modulation *n.* See pulse duration modulation.

Punched card *n.* An outdated computer-input medium made of stiff paper that stores data bits in columns containing patterns of punched holes. The method for creating the patterns used for different byte values is called Hollerith coding. See also Hollerith tabulating/recording machine.

Punched-card reader *n.* See card reader.

Pure procedure *n.* Any procedure that modifies only data that is dynamically allocated (usually on the stack). A pure procedure cannot modify either global data or its own code. This restriction allows a pure procedure to be called simultaneously by separate tasks. See also reentrant code.

Purge *vb.* To eliminate old or unneeded information systematically; to clean up, as files.

Push1 *n.* A technology developed in relation to the World Wide Web, designed to provide end users with personalised Web access by having a site actively "push" requested information to the user's desktop, either automatically or at specified intervals. Push was developed as a means of relieving users from having to actively retrieve ("pull") information from the Web. It is not, as yet, especially popular.

Push2 *vb.* 1. To add a new element to a stack, a data structure generally used to temporarily hold pieces of data being transferred or the partial result of an arithmetic operation. See also stack. 2. In networks and the Internet, to send data or a programme from a server to a client at the instigation of the server. See also push2.

Put *vb.* In programming, to write data, typically to a file; in particular, to write a very small unit of data, such as a character.

PVC *n.* Acronym for permanent virtual circuit. A permanent logical connection between two nodes on a packet-switching network. The PVC appears as a dedicated line to the nodes, but the data can be transmitted on a common carrier. See also common carrier, node (definition 2), packet switching, virtual private network.

PWD *n.* Acronym for print working directory. The UNIX command for displaying the current directory.

PWM *n.* Acronym for pulse width modulation. See pulse duration modulation.

PXE boot *n.* Acronym for Preboot Execution Environment boot. A BIOS-supported technology used to boot a PC remotely. To power on a PC and boot it from the network, PXE must be enabled in the BIOS, and the NIC in the PC must be PXE compliant. PXE boot is specified in the Intel Wired for Management (WfM) standard. Also called: network boot.

Pyramid diagram *n.* A diagram that is used to show foundation-based relationships.

Python *n.* A portable, interpreted, object-oriented programming language developed and freely distributed by its developer. Python runs on many platforms, including UNIX, Windows, OS/2, and Macintosh, and is used for writing TCP/IP applications.

Q

QBasic *n.* An interpreted language. QBasic is a dialect of Basic created by Microsoft for the MS-DOS platform. This language is no longer supported.

QIC *n.* 1. Acronym for quarter-inch cartridge. A storage technology used with tape backup drives and cartridges. A means of backing up data on computer systems, QIC represents a set of standards devised to enable tapes to be used with drives from different manufacturers. The QIC standards specify the length of tape, the number of recording tracks, and the magnetic strength of the tape coating, all of which determine the amount of information that can be written to the tape. Older QIC-80 drives can hold up to 340 MB of compressed data. Newer versions can hold more than 1 GB of information. 2. A consortium of quarter-inch tape manufacturers. Quarter-Inch Cartridge Drive Standards Inc. (QIC) establishes standards for the production of quarter-inch tapes. For example, QIC-40 and QIC-80, designed to use a PC's floppy disk drive controller, are called the "floppy tape standards."

QOS or QoS *n.* See quality of service.

Quadbit *n.* A set of 4 bits representing one of 16 possible combinations. In communications, quadbits are a means of increasing transmission rates by encoding 4 bits at a time, instead of 1 or 2. The 16 quadbits are 0000, 0001, 0010, 0011, 0100, 0101, 0110, 0111, 1000, 1001, 1010, 1011, 1100, 1101, 1110, and 1111.

Quadrature amplitude modulation *n.* In communications, an encoding method that combines amplitude modulation and phase modulation to create a constellation of signal points, each representing one unique combination of bits that can be identified with one possible state that the carrier wave can be in. Acronym: QAM. See also amplitude modulation, constellation, phase-shift keying, trellis-coded modulation.

Quadrature encoding *n.* The most common method used to determine in which direction a mouse is moving. In mechanical mice, movement of the mouse ball is translated into horizontal or vertical movement by a pair of turning disks, one disk for horizontal movement and one disk for vertical movement, each of which makes and breaks contact with two sensors located on it. The two sensors are placed out of phase with each other, and the mouse notes which sensor receives contact first. The phrase quadrature encoding comes from the fact that each sensor sends a square-wave signal 90 degrees out of phase with the other. If the first signal occurs before the second, the mouse is assumed to have been moved in one direction; if the second signal occurs before the first, the mouse is assumed to have been moved in the opposite direction. See also mechanical mouse, mouse, optomechanical mouse.

Quality assurance *n.* A system of procedures carried out to ensure that a product or a system adheres or conforms to established standards. Also called: quality control.

Quality of service *n.* 1. Generally, the handling capacity of a system or service; the time interval between request and delivery of a product or service to the client or customer. 2. In computer technology, the guaranteed throughput (data transfer rate) level.

Quantity *n.* A number—positive or negative, whole or fractional—that is used to indicate a value.

Quantise *vb.* To divide an element into separate, distinct units (quanta) and to assign a value to each resulting unit, especially in the domain of time.

Quantum *n.* 1. In communications, the unit resulting from division of a signal by quantisation. 2. A portion of time allotted on a time-sharing system. 3. An amount of something; for example, in physics, a unit of radiant energy.

Quantum bit *n.* See qubit.

Quantum computing *n.* A theoretical design for computers based on quantum mechanics. Unlike classic (current) digital computers, which calculate sets of values sequentially because a single bit can represent only 1 or 0 at any given time, a quantum computer is based on the ability of each bit to represent more than one value at the same time. Because each quantum bit—called a qubit—represents multiple values, a quantum computer can be in multiple states simultaneously and can thus work on numerous problems at the same time to offer far more computing power than is currently available. Quantum computing is under investigation by the United States Defense Advanced Research Projects Agency (DARPA) and other groups. Although atoms of hydrogen and carbon have been used to create the rudiments of a quantum computer, the technology is still in its infancy.

Quarter-inch cartridge *n.* See QIC (definition 1).

Quartz *n.* The 2-D drawing engine that forms the imaging foundation of the Mac OS X Aqua interface. The Quartz graphics application programming interface (API) is based on Adobe's Portable Document Format (PDF) standard.

Quartz crystal *n.* A precisely shaped and precisely sized piece of the mineral quartz, used for its piezoelectric properties. When a voltage is applied to a quartz crystal, it vibrates at a frequency determined by its size and shape. Quartz crystals are commonly used to control the frequency of oscillator circuits such as the clocks in microcomputers. See also piezoelectric.

Quasi-language *n.* A derogatory term for any programming language that, because of deficiencies, is not suitable for any serious work.

Qubit *n.* Short for quantum bit. The bits (currently, atomic particles) that make up the theoretical machines known as quantum computers. Qubits are unlike bits in current computers in that they exist in more than one state at the same time. They can, therefore, represent both 0 and 1 simultaneously. Qubits, like quantum computers, are based on the science of quantum mechanics.

Query 1 *n.* A specific set of instructions for extracting particular data.

Query 2 *vb.* To extract data from a database and present it for use.

Query by example *n.* A simple-to-use query language implemented on several relational database management systems. Using query by example, the user specifies fields to be displayed, intertable linkages, and retrieval criteria directly onto forms displayed on the screen. These forms are a direct pictorial representation of the table and row structures that make up the database. Thus, the construction of a query becomes a simple "checkoff" procedure from the viewpoint of the user. Acronym: QBE.

Query language *n.* A subset of the data manipulation language; specifically, that portion relating to the retrieval and display of data from a database. It is sometimes used loosely to refer to the entire data manipulation language. See also data manipulation language.

Queue 1 *n.* A multi-element data structure from which (by strict definition) elements can be removed only in the same order in which they were inserted; that is, it follows a first in, first out (FIFO) constraint. There are also several types of queues in which removal is based on factors other than order of insertion—for example, some priority value assigned to each element. See also deque, element (definition 1).

Queue 2 *vb.* To place (an item) in a queue.

Queued access method *n.* A programming technique that minimises input/output delays by synchronising the transfer of information between the programme and the computer's input and output devices. Acronym: QAM.

Queuing *n.* In networking, the process of buffering data in preparation for transmission. See also fair queuing, first in, first out, last in, first out, weighted fair queuing.

QuickDraw *n.* On the Apple Macintosh, the built-in group of routines within the operating system that controls the display of graphics and text. Application programmes call QuickDraw for onscreen displays. See also Toolbox.

QuickDraw 3-D *n.* A version of the Macintosh QuickDraw library that includes routines for doing 3-D graphics calculations. See also QuickDraw.

Quicken *n.* Financial-management software from Intuit, Inc. The personal-finance version, introduced by Intuit in 1984, includes tools for balancing and tracking bank accounts and investments, budgeting, paying bills, planning and preparing tax returns, financial planning, and estate planning. A small-business version, Quicken Home & Business, adds tools for business-related matters, such as invoicing and accounts receivable and payable.

Quicksort *n.* An efficient sort algorithm, described by C.A.R. Hoare in 1962, in which the essential strategy is to "divide and conquer." A quicksort begins by scanning the list to be sorted for a median value. This value, called the pivot, is then moved to its final position in the list. Next, all items in the list whose values are less than the pivot value are moved to one side of the list, and the items with values greater than the pivot value are moved to the other side. Each resulting side is sorted the same way, until a fully sorted list results. See also sort algorithm.

QuickTime *n.* Software components developed by Apple for creating, editing, publishing, and viewing multimedia content. QuickTime, which supports video, animation, graphics, 3-D, VR (virtual reality), MIDI, music, sound, and text, has been part of the Mac OS since version 7 of the operating system and is used in many Macintosh applications. Windows applications can also run QuickTime files but require the installation of special player software. QuickTime is often used on the Web to provide Web pages with video and animation. Most Web browsers support plug-ins for running these types of files. QuickTime is also part of the new MPEG-4 specification. See also MPEG-4.

Quick View *n.* A feature, optionally installed as part of Windows 9x, that provides a set of file viewers for previewing the contents of files without having to start the application(s) that created them. The feature is accessed through the Quick View command, available either from the File menu or by right-clicking a filename. If the feature has been installed but the file type is not supported by a viewer, the Quick View command does not appear.

Quiet answer *n.* A telephone-answering protocol in which incoming calls are answered with silence instead of a tone signal. Some telephone-switching systems use quiet answering. These switching systems expect the caller to provide another phone number, code, or extension after the quiet answer.

Quit 1 *n.* 1. An FTP command that instructs the server to drop the current connection with the client from which it received the command. 2. A command in many applications for exiting the programme.

Quit 2 *vb.* 1. To stop in an orderly manner. 2. To execute the normal shutdown of a programme and return control to the operating system.

QWERTY keyboard *n.* A keyboard layout named for the six leftmost characters in the top row of alphabetic characters on most keyboards—the standard layout of most typewriters and computer keyboards.